Cooking the
Fat-Free, Salt-Free, Sugar-Free
Flavor-Full Way

Cooking the Fat-Free, Salt-Free, Sugar-Free Flavor-Full Way

Marcia Sabaté Williams

THE CROSSING PRESS
FREEDOM, CALIFORNIA

For information on bulk purchases or group discounts for this and other Crossing
Press titles, please contact our Special Sales Manager at 800-777-1048.

Visit our Website on the Internet at: www.crossingpress.com

Library of Congress Cataloging-in-Publication Data

Williams, Marcia Sabaté.
    Cooking the fat-free, salt-free, sugar-free, flavor-full way /
Marcia Sabaté Williams.
        p.   cm.
    ISBN 0-89594-858-3 (paper)
    1. Low-fat diet—Recipes. 2. Salt-free diet—Recipes. 3. Sugar-free diet—
Recipes. I. Title.
RM237.7.W555 1997
641.5'63—dc21   97-24527
                                                                 CIP

This book is dedicated to everyone who learned, with the help of my first two cookbooks, that they could eat a good, sizable meal without anxiety three times a day, plus snacks. And to you, a new cooking friend. It is also dedicated to my dear husband, Ray, whom I believe is still alive mainly due to good-tasting, salt-free, sugar-free, fat-free cooking (he eats every bit); to my boys R. B., Guillaume, and Alex who always encourage me; to my late dear mother, Miriam, who taught me how to cook; and to Ilene Pritikin and the late Nathan Pritikin, who taught me the concepts and benefits of healthy cooking.

Acknowledgments

Many thanks go to Ilene Pritikin of Santa Barbara, California, who took so much time reading and helping me with recipes; Barbara Wellsteed, M.S., Registered Dietitian at Delaronde Hospital in Chalmette, Louisiana; Slidell Feed and Seed Store for help with terminology; my cousin Muriel Hubert, for help with the French expressions and phrases; Pamela Arceneaux of the Historic New Orleans Collection for painstaking research; Charlyn Schmidt, Shirley Mundy, and Wilma Dickey for inspiration and advice; and Andrea Chesman of Vermont, the first editor of this book, for having been so kind and helpful throughout. Thanks also go to the staff of the Federal Drug Administration, Washington, D.C., for their expertise; to Joyce Dakin at the Nutritional Food Store, and Ruby Bouchard at Ruby's Health Food store for looking up many things for me; and to William de Marigny Hyland, attorney, historian, and linguist for his help with both historic and linguistic research. Thanks to May Devitt, Rebecca Taylor, Marilyn Bennkers, Josie Athey, Diane Barringer, Judy Crawford, Kathleen Ezell, Bee Galadas, Jeanne Hays, Eda Parker, and Fran Thomas at the Slidell Library who saved me many trips by looking up things for me on the phone; to the staff of Licatas Seafood and the folks at Boga River Nurseries for expert information; to Jeannette Sapdone at the K & B Drugstore for looking up information; to Ron Yager at Channel 6 TV; to my television producer, Lyn Adams, who believes in me; and to my friend, Pam Lykes for her encouragement. Thanks also to my publishers at The Crossing Press, Elaine and the late John Gill, for making me feel like part of the family, and to Jane Lazear and Cyndi Barnes at The Crossing Press for their concern and help. And last but not least, thanks to my sons R. B., Guillaume, and Alex, and my husband Ray who were willing and expert testers. They complimented me when something was good and were truthful when something wasn't. Thanks to them, only the best recipes got into this book.

TABLE OF CONTENTS

Foreword

Having been in the health care arena all my life I can say quite frankly that Marcia Sabaté Williams' *Cooking the Fat-Free, Salt-Free, Sugar-Free Flavor-Full Way* is an outstanding array of low-cholesterol, low-fat and high-fiber program menus. Today 80 percent of all American school children will not pass the President's Council on Fitness test done each year in our public school system—this points to the significant problem we have in health care. This book offers the solution to the problem that people need a good, strong knowledge base for proper nutrition.

The American public is sadly lacking in good-quality nutritional coaching materials such as Ms. Williams has developed. The variety and depth of work is quite evident in the preparation of this manuscript. Few available materials can offer the quality and scope offered here, paralleling the old adage "you are what you eat." Americans are among the fattest people of any country in the world and this is reflected in a staggering health care bill. By employing Ms. Williams' outstanding recipes along with fitness and good medical supervision, even the novice can attain the highest fitness level possible.

Thank you for asking me to address such an important problem, and it is a great honor to endorse this book.

—Larry Thurstrup, M.D., M. Ed.

INTRODUCTION

Most people, though they may still be resistant to the idea, are aware that there is a fat-free revolution going on. And it is wonderful! It seems that almost everything is available in a low-fat or fat-free version. Oh, yes, I know, sugar is often added to make up for the lack of fat. Fat-free or low-fat products are not necessarily low-calorie just because they have left the fat out. But many fat-free products that are also very low-calorie are coming on the market such as fat-free cream cheese or fat-free yogurt or fat-free mozzarella and cheddar cheeses. There's even fat-free mayonnaise—you can actually make a real cheese sandwich and enjoy real pizza. There are the fat-free, butter-flavored and olive oil-flavored nonstick cooking sprays which help tremendously in baking and sautéing. Flour tortillas, which used to contain lard, are now available completely fat-free. There are even fat-free hot dogs, and fat-free and low-sodium canned soups. It's almost a fat-free paradise out there. There is still too much sodium in many products, but even this is beginning to change. Now don't tell me that fat-free products don't taste good. If you don't like one brand, try another. Different brands really do taste different. Take advantage of the great variety of fat-free food out there and make it easier on yourself to lose weight, lower your cholesterol, and eat healthier.

In 1980, if anyone suggested cooking without salt, fat, and sugar, people would have laughed. Back then we were told to substitute margarine for butter, because butter was supposed to clog your arteries. Well, that's still true about butter, but now we know that margarine is not good for us either. Why? Because margarine has just as much fat as butter and just as many calories. It can also raise your triglyceride levels (liquid fat in the blood) and stimulate the circulation of free radicals, which are known to cause some types of cancer, in the body. The partially hydrogenated oils in margarine are also believed to increase your cholesterol. This goes for potato chips or anything made with partially hydrogenated oils. Believe it or not, even hard candy can raise your triglyceride levels. If you eat more sugar than you can assimilate, your body will convert it to fat.

During the past fifteen years, a lot of partially true claims have been made that oat bran is the answer to getting rid of cholesterol. But now we know that oat bran, though it does carry away cholesterol, is not the sole secret to good health. You have to do more than just eat oat bran. Scientists and nutritionists keep studying, and we all keep learning about what's healthy and what isn't, and sometimes we feel a little out of control. We don't know what our apples were sprayed with, or whether some toxic chemical was sucked up by our vegetables, or if antibiotics or hormones were fed to cattle that become our hamburgers, or if mercury was in last night's fish.

I was recently the keynote speaker for a Cardiopulmonary Community Educational Series at a hospital near my home. I assured patients, some who had just had open-heart surgery, that a healthy lifestyle can actually be fun and delicious. I eat this way and I don't feel deprived, and I feel that this is one of the few things in my life I can control. Even when I eat out in restaurants I ask them to cook my food my way, and if they bring it to me with calorie-loaded oil all over my salad, or with calorie-loaded cream and butter sauce all over my fish, I ask them to take it back and bring me another dinner the way I asked for it. They always do it, usually with good humor. I even challenge New Orleans chefs and they come up with some really creative stuff. People look over at my plate enviously because it looks good, and it is good, and they don't charge me any more for it either. At parties, I bring something I can eat, like fruit, or mock stuffed eggs, or taco dip and chips.

"But what about fats? Why are you talking about calories? Aren't fats what you have to watch out for?" asked a skeptical lady at that talk at the hospital. I could tell that she was angry with me for complicating things by bringing up calories. Yes, you have to eliminate as much fat as you can. I had a bag of baked corn chips and dip with me that night. This lady picked up the bag and read the Nutrition Facts, and although there was no oil in the ingredients, a serving of chips still had two grams of fat. "These have fat in them," she said, rather bewildered. "How can that be?" I said, "They're made of corn and corn has oil in it. You know—corn oil." If you eat any meat or fish or chicken and even some vegetables, you're going to get some fat. The challenge is to control how much fat you consume at a given meal.

Everyone asks me how I got into healthy cooking and eating. I don't dislike rich, fatty foods at all. I just dislike what they do to my body. People tell me all the time, "Oh be happy. Let loose once in a while. Cheat a little. One time won't hurt."

Well, first of all, I am happy. I weigh 115 pounds and I love getting whistled at even though I am fifty-nine years old. I don't have high blood pressure or diabetes and I'm in pretty good shape. And one time does hurt, because cheating once usually leads to cheating twice and on it goes. I'm very sociable and I go out to lunch with friends at least three times a week. I belong to garden clubs and political clubs and historical clubs and I like the luncheons and dinners. My husband and I eat out a lot when we're home and when we travel. If I do decide to have something fattening, I choose how I'm going to spend calories very consciously. Once in a while I'll eat a fried soft-shell crab sandwich, but even then, I'm choosing my calories, not letting a restaurant choose them for me.

I got into this type of cooking because several years ago my husband Ray was in terrible shape. If the diabetes didn't get him, his high blood pressure would, so he went into the hospital.

The doctors put Ray on a no-salt, no-sugar, no-fat diet, known as the Pritikin diet, but it was much more than that. It turned out the diet was also a no honey, no molasses, no egg yolks, no cheese (to speak of), no butter, no margarine, no mayonnaise, no oils of any kind, no alcohol, no avocados, no coconuts, no coffee, no tea (except herb teas), no soft drinks with or without sugar, no caffeine, no organ meats, no barbecue, no nuts, except water chestnuts and chestnuts, no potato skins, no black or white pepper, and no artificial sweeteners.

When Ray and I first got married I cooked the traditional New Orleans style with lots of butter. If something needed liquid, I used melted butter. My cooking tasted good, but it was killing my husband.

At one point I took Ray off starches, thinking he would lose weight. I gave him big steaks, vegetables, but no starches and he developed gout because his body produced too much uric acid from eating too much meat. By the time he was thirty-five he was falling apart. The doctor reduced his meat intake to 3.5 ounces a day and ordered that starches be added to his diet.

Unfortunately, Ray really needed an even more restrictive diet. By the time he was forty-five he was a borderline diabetic. He also had high blood pressure, was very overweight, and still occasionally suffered from gout. So he checked back into the hospital to be put on the Pritikin diet—otherwise, he knew he wasn't going to last long. On the new eating plan his cholesterol, triglycerides, blood pressure, and weight came down fast.

At first, I didn't think I was going to be able to go along with the restrictions of Ray's new diet. I struggled to adjust to it, but after a while, it got easier, and here I am, many years later, still cooking that way. It really isn't that difficult and it's good, regular food—not weird food. I still cook the dishes I made when I was first married, except I just prepare them differently. For example, I use chicken stock, vegetables, water, wine, or apple juice concentrate instead of butter or oil. The results are sometimes even better than the original recipes!

Other people are able to keep on cooking like this, too. A lady who lost twenty-one pounds cooking the recipes out of my first book told me, "This is the first diet I've ever been on where I don't feel like I'm going crazy." She had had two open-heart surgeries and had just had another heart attack; if she didn't lose weight she was going to have to be opened up again. It made me feel good to think my book was helping her, and I decided that I would like to help more people who had been given a directive by their doctor without being given any instructions or guidance. If I can help people find tasty methods of cooking healthy food, that's got to be a good deed.

Order ID: 102-0530439-1335426

Thank you for buying from goodwill-industries-northern-mi on Amazon Marketplace.

Shipping Address:
Heidi L Grondahl
PO Box 79
Williston, ND 58802-0079

Order Date: Jan 15, 2010
Shipping Service: Standard
Buyer Name: Heidi Grondahl
Seller Name: goodwill-industries-northern-mi

Quantity	Product Details
1	Cooking the Fat-Free, Salt-Free, Sugar-Free, Flavor-Full Way by Williams... **Merchant SKU:** A-2-0895948583 **ASIN:** 0895948583 **Listing ID:** 1202E57JPAK **Order-Item ID:** 36511804591506 **Condition:** Used - Good **Comments:** WE SHIP DAILY!!! COVER HAS SOME WEAR, AND PAPERS EDGES HAVE A FEW STAINS

Thanks for buying on Amazon Marketplace. To provide feedback for the seller please visit
www.amazon.com/feedback. To contact the seller, please visit Amazon.com and click on "Your Account" at the top of
any page. In Your Account, go to the "Orders" section and click on the link "Leave seller feedback". Select the order or
click on the "View Order" button. Click on the "seller profile" under the appropriate product. On the lower right side of
the page under "Seller Help", click on "Contact this seller".

CHAPTER 1

Cooking My Way

"No sugar, no salt, no fat, no fun," the lady said, and she wasn't kidding. Another person said, "No salt, no sugar, no fat; no good." Both he and his wife came to hear me lecture at a hospital. They were both recovering from recent open-heart surgery. The gentleman would not even try my carrot cake or taco dip. He said, "It'll all taste like cardboard." It was not a mystery to me why he was in such bad shape—his mind was totally closed. His wife didn't say anything but I didn't see her try my cooking either. So be warned, if you do start cooking my way, you may be accused of being a wet blanket. Stick to your guns—you have to be a little bit assertive.

Of course, you can't refuse to eat at a dinner party. If bringing food with you isn't possible, try to eat as wisely as you can. If you can't resist the desserts, just take a very small piece of the best one. If you have to, close your eyes when the desserts are passed—or don't go near the buffet table where they are displayed. Sometimes you have to play mind games with yourself and sometimes you will feel deprived. Remember, deprivation is relative. Feeling slightly deprived does not keep you from having fun—nor does it keep you from eating well.

I hear this argument all the time: "Years ago people didn't know that fat, sugar, or sodium caused health problems. My grandma used to cook everything in bacon grease and she did okay." Your grandma might have lived a long time, but let me tell you about the time I looked up my great-great grandfather, Numa Hubert, in the New Orleans Library. I looked through the death records in New Orleans starting in 1850, to find out where he was buried and I never found one person who lived past the age of sixty. The greatest number of deaths were of children. Many people died in their twenties. It looked to me as if most people back then didn't live long enough to get a chronic sickness that many people over forty face today (high blood pressure, heart disease, and diabetes). The ones who did grow old probably had wonderful genes.

"No salt, no sugar, no fat, no food." This is another remark you may hear. Remember, you are eating all the same foods everybody else eats when you leave out the salt, sugar, and fat—it's just that your cooking methods are different. You'll still get custard when you want custard, and vegetable soup when you want vegetable soup, and pot roast when you want pot roast.

The alternatives for sugar are fruits and concentrated fruit juices. For whipped toppings you will use gelatin mixed with baked bananas and skimmed evaporated milk instead of heavy cream and sugar. For salt, you will use juice concentrates, wine, and sometimes a bit of vinegar or lemon juice. Pepper helps, too. Instead of using oil, you will use nonstick pots and pans, stocks and water or juice concentrates, or other liquids—sometimes vegetables or fruits that contain a lot of water like zucchini squash and bananas, as I did in the crab cake recipe and the bananas in the corn bread recipe. Bananas also double in those recipes for taste. I could go into a lot of examples here, but I think you get the idea. Try the recipes and you will be surprised that you can achieve the same results you are used to.

What makes you keep to the diet?

For one thing, your terror of dying, and for another, avoiding pain. However, a person in good health who goes on this type of diet ordinarily will not have the same motivation as the person who has just had open-heart surgery.

Yet I know people who have had two open-heart surgeries who were great about their diets and exercise for about a year. Then they slid back into their old habits…until they had another heart attack. If that one didn't kill them, they tightened up for a while again. When people get to feeling better, they forget they are in danger.

For me, pain is a great motivator. A while ago for four days I felt my heart bumpity bumping as if I were in love. The only person I had around to be in love with was my husband Ray, and we had been married twenty-three years. I called my doctor. He found I had an extra heartbeat, probably caused by stress and caffeine. One of my sons had been in a car wreck and had an operation. With nothing else to do but chew my fingernails at the hospital, I drank several cups of coffee a day, even though I knew it wasn't good for me. When I cut out all coffee and tea, I got better. But later, I allowed myself one cup of real tea a day, and sometimes I sneaked two. When I started drinking a cocktail once in a while, I started having stomach pains. This turned out to be a hiatal hernia. Then I was diagnosed with cystic breast disease when I went for a routine mammogram, which is affected by caffeine too. I got off all alcohol and caffeine, and the pains in my stomach and breasts went away and I had no more bumpity-bumping heart (sorry Ray). When you can see and feel the immediate effects that certain foods have on you, you are more likely to stay away from them.

The problem is that people with heart disease are in a more dangerous position than I was. Ray can't tell when either his blood pressure or blood sugar is up, and he certainly can't feel the cholesterol building up in his veins.

If you don't have physical symptoms, but you know you need to lose weight, a future special event can keep you motivated. Plan a high-school reunion six months ahead of time and plan to look great for it, and to continue to look great after you've achieved your goal.

I make it a rule in my house that anything I cook is cooked without salt, sugar, or fat. If Ray brings anything he is not supposed to eat into the house (which he does occasionally), I can't stop him, but any food he gets from me is going to be cooked properly. When we're home he eats the right kinds of foods for breakfast, lunch, and dinner, and so do I. Things might not be perfect when we go out, but we do our best.

Eating Out

When I give talks to groups in restaurants, the owners often come out to meet me and practically grab my books away from me. They tell me they have customers coming in all the time wanting their meals cooked without salt, fat, and sugar. Many excellent cooks have no idea what contains cholesterol or what is high in sodium. For instance, they think olive oil is not fattening, and if you object to it they'll look at you with big eyes and say, "But it's virgin!" Like that somehow magically takes the calories out.

INGREDIENTS

How much sodium is okay?

I'm always astounded when I figure out how much sodium is in a serving, even if I didn't put any salt in the dish, or use any ingredients containing salt! The American Heart Association recommends that a healthy adult should consume 3,000 milligrams of sodium a day. For people with high blood pressure they recommend 2,000 milligrams a day, sometimes lower. Some of my entrées contain as much as 300 to 350 milligrams of sodium. That might sound like a lot of sodium, but considering 1 teaspoon of salt has a spectacular 2713 milligrams of sodium, 300 for a main serving of something doesn't sound so bad.

Remember that every time you use salt, the sodium content goes sky high. You will find numerous substitutes in the following recipes that will give you plenty of flavor without the sodium.

How much fat do we need?

I hear these arguments all the time: If you don't eat at least three teaspoons of oil or some kind of fat a day, you aren't getting enough fat. If you look at the nutrient values at the bottom of each of the recipes in this book you will be hard-pressed to find a recipe that does not contain some fat, even though I add no oils, grease, margarine, or butter, except in a few recipes where I use a nonstick spray.

The point is, cave men could not go down to a store and buy oil or margarine; they obtained the fats they needed from whatever foods they ate, without adding any more. You can, too. So you *are* getting fat in your diet whether you add three teaspoons of oil a day to your diet or not.

The American Heart Association says that no more than 30 percent of a person's daily calories should come from fat. The Pritikin program says that no more than 10 percent of one's daily calories should come from fat.

What about vitamins A and E?

Many people worry that nonfat diets won't provide enough vitamins A and E because these vitamins are fat-soluble. But remember, you *are* getting *some* fat in your diet, no matter how hard you try to avoid it. If you eat carrots, dark green and deep yellow vegetables, and deep yellow fruit for vitamin A, and green leafy vegetables, broccoli, legumes (beans), whole grains like oatmeal, fortified cereals, and milk for vitamin E, you will be fine. Egg yolks contain vitamin E but not egg whites, by the way, so if you aren't eating the yolks because of all the fat in them, you'll need to get your vitamin E from other sources. Getting enough vitamin E is essential because its antioxidant properties tie up those free radicals, preventing the cell damage that can cause cancer. Vitamin E is also good for your heart. The FDA recommends that adults consume 400 international units of vitamin E a day.

What about sugar?

Most of us know by now that eating too much refined sugar can rot your teeth, make you fat, and can eventually lead to serious conditions such as obesity and diabetes. But don't despair! The recipes for sweets in this book don't call for refined sugar of any kind. You can use fruits and fruit juices and get the same delicious results.

And there's more good news! Does your herb tea taste bland? Try adding a little honey, molasses, fructose or a grain syrup to it. If you are on a 2,000 calorie-a-day diet, you can have 2 tablespoons of the above-mentioned sweeteners a day and you'll be okay. Check with your doctor first though if you're a diabetic. Incidentally, for heart patients on Cumadin, the vitamin K found in herb tea is not soluble in water, so all herb teas are safe.

Apple Juice Concentrate: Apple juice concentrate is frozen, undiluted concentrated juice without any sugar added. Check to see if it contains any sugar. I use whatever amount I need, cover the top with a plastic sandwich bag, and store it in the freezer. Although the advice on the can says you should not defrost the concentrate, it seems to be okay if you refreeze it while it is still cold.

Get acquainted with herbs and spices

I've always used herbs and spices because my mama did, and I have loved exploring the more exotic stuff that is so readily available today. I'm always surprised when I meet a person who owns my cookbooks who says she didn't cook this or that because they didn't have this herb or spice. If you look in your kitchen cabinet right now, and all you find is salt and pepper, you need to take a trip to the grocery store and get yourself a selection of herbs and spices.

My kids tell me some people don't buy herbs and spices because they are expensive, which is true in the case of saffron that goes for $6.00 for .03 ounces, but that .03 ounces will be enough to make every recipe containing saffron in this book, and you will still have some left over.

One way to keep dried herbs and spices fresher is to put the containers into something airtight and store them in the freezer. (Weevils do the Mexican hat dance when they find themselves a bottle or can of chili powder.) Incidentally, you can get salt-free chili powder. Just check the different ingredients lists before you buy.

You will notice I don't insist on fresh herbs. This is because I have a hard time finding them in New Orleans. I've tried to grow them and they all die on me. I've had some house plants for twenty years, but I can't grow one fresh herb, not even thyme or parsley.

If you want to use fresh herbs, you have to use about three times as much as the dried ones. In some cases, like parsley and basil, you need even more. Frankly, I can't guarantee how these recipes will come out if you substitute fresh herbs because I haven't tried them. I advise you to follow these recipes pretty closely, especially the first time you make them, because they are finely tuned for ultimate flavor and texture. (I'm not trying to brag, it's just that I've experimented with them over and over until I got them just right.)

Here is a complete list of every herb and spice you will find in the recipes in this book in the order of the most used to the least used. If you can't afford to buy them all at one time, just buy two or three a week.

Red pepper flakes (sometimes called crushed red pepper)
Cayenne pepper
Garlic powder, preferably granulated
Onion flakes
Parsley flakes
Thyme
Bay leaves
Sage
Marjoram
Saffron
Basil
Cumin (cumino)
Oregano
Chili powder

Turmeric
Paprika
Curry powder
Mustard seed
Coriander
Dill seeds
Celery seed
Dill weed
Cloves
Cinnamon
Allspice
Mace
Tarragon
Dried chives
Caraway seeds

Staples you will need

Don't worry if you don't have every ingredient listed in my book. I don't even have everything for every recipe in my books either. Decide what you want to cook for a few days or a week, and then make a list of what you will need for each recipe, and it's off to the grocery store. There *are* some things you will want to keep on hand so you can get right to the fun of cooking:

Oat bran
Cornmeal
Elbow macaroni (whole wheat and/or semolina)
Instant brown rice
Thin spaghetti (whole wheat and/or semolina)
All-purpose unbleached flour
Whole wheat flour
Bread flour (bromated flour)
Cornstarch
Rapid rise yeast
Whole wheat bread
Skimmed evaporated milk
Sapsago cheese
One percent fat cottage cheese or fat-free cottage cheese
Jumbo-size eggs

Frozen apple juice concentrate
Salt-free canned tomatoes
Salt-free tomato paste
Salt-free tomato sauce
Baking soda
Low-sodium baking powder
Unflavored dry gelatin
Vinegar (apple cider and something fancier if you like)
Low-sodium soy or tamari sauce
Celery
Green peppers
Yellow or white onions
Potatoes
Tabasco® sauce
Inexpensive medium red hot sauce
Red Rosé wine
Vanilla extract

Supplies you will need, continued

Nonstick spray (plain, butter-flavored and olive oil-flavored)

Apple pectin powder

Your favorite all-fruit spreadable fruit

Your favorite sugar-free pear and apple spread

Frozen Chuck Wagon-style corn (a mixture of whole kernel corn, onions, tomatoes, green and red bell peppers)

You may have a questions about a few items in the staple list:

Oat Bran: It is not the *only* answer to ending a high cholesterol problem, but it is helpful because it's high in fiber, makes wonderful muffins, is light and delicious and can be added to bread dough. Nowadays you will see a variety of oat bran products in your grocery store: plain oat bran, flakes, or others. Quaker and Mother's make plain oat bran. If by mistake you buy one of the multi-grain hot cereal products that contains some barley flakes and wheat bran, don't worry. It's a little coarser than plain oat bran but will work just fine for the muffin recipes. You can also buy oat bran at health food stores and natural food co-ops.

Bread Flour or Bromated Flour: I use bromated flour especially for making bread. Two brands I use are Pillsbury and Gold Medal. The labels will say something like "bread flour" or "better for bread," and will have the word "bromated" printed somewhere on the package.

Is bromated flour healthy? I checked into it just to make sure, because there is no way Honest to God Pizza (page 116) or Dr. Vanselow's Rye Bread (page 74) is going to come out right (not like a rock) without using bromated bread flour. The Pillsbury Company sent me this information: Bromation increases the protein in the flour from 10 1/2 percent to 12 percent and gives the bread more elasticity. Potassium bromate allows for proper gluten development.

According to Bill Friedrich at the FDA in Washington, D.C., naturally white, bromated bread flour contains 50 parts per million of potassium bromate, or less than 1,000th of a percent.

The pharmacist at my local drug store, Alex Capace, R. Ph., said that the *mate* on potassium bromate means that 70 percent of the substance goes straight through the body, or in other words, is not absorbed. He said probably none of it is absorbed, and the little that might be is not harmful anyway.

Whole Wheat Flour and Unbleached White Flour: Most of the time you should try use whole wheat flour, but sometimes a recipe won't come out right unless you use unbleached white flour, so go ahead and use it. You can add a little oat bran cereal to it to give it some extra fiber, but don't get yourself all hung up. If nothing but unbleached white flour is what you need, just eat more vegetables to get the extra fiber.

Whole Wheat Bread: All whole wheat breads contain some salt, and most contain some honey or molasses. If you can find Pritikin Bread that is sweetened with fruit, get it. You won't be using that much commercial whole wheat bread anyway. I buy a sliced loaf, put it in the freezer, pull off what I need, then put the rest back in the freezer. A loaf might last me six months. In such small amounts, the honey or molasses is nothing to fret about.

Low-Sodium Baking Powder: There are several brands of low-sodium baking powder available in the diet section of your supermarket or health food store. I usually use Featherweight Brand, but I find that it loses its strength pretty quickly.

Red Hot Sauces: If you already have your own favorite brand, go ahead and use it in the recipes that call for hot sauce, but be careful. Many popular brands are *so* hot they will overpower the other flavors in some of these dishes.

When you squirt red hot sauces on for extra flavor after you have everything on your plate, figure you are adding about 25 mg of sodium per 1/4 teaspoon of the inexpensive sauces and about 7 mg of sodium for 1/4 teaspoon of most hot sauces.

Fat-free Cheeses: If you're going to eat fat-free you couldn't have picked a better time to start. It used to be hard to find anything fat-free that tasted good, but now the selection is enormous. You do have to look, though, to see if the fat-free items are also sugar-free and salt-free. All the fat-free cheeses contain a little salt, and milk has a good bit of sodium in it anyway, but if you don't go overboard and just melt a little over vegetables or a baked potato, you'll be fine. Try different brands until you find the ones you like.

I use fat-free cream cheese in my cheese cake and no one can tell the difference. It comes out very creamy and light. You can also use it on crackers or bread and add an all-fruit jelly or jam. Use it as an hors d'oeuvre, on a plate with an all-fruit preserve over it with crackers around to spread it on.

I haven't yet found a really delicious, fat-free Parmesan cheese. I find they don't have much flavor or texture. Until they come out with a good one, I suggest you use sapsago cheese, which is a dead ringer for Parmesan cheese (which is too fatty). But don't bite into it—*always* use it grated.

Sapsago cheese is a hard green cheese from Switzerland flavored with melilot, a kind of clover. It's getting easier to find in many supermarkets, but if you can't find it locally, contact Otto Roth, 14 Empire Blvd., Moonachie, NJ 07074, phone 201-440-3600. Otto Roth does not distribute in Hawaii, Alaska, England, New Zealand, or Australia, so if you live in one of those places you'll have to do some research to get it through another distributor.

The nutrient values for 1 tablespoon of sapsago cheese are 13.68 calories; 1.80 g protein, 0.00 g fat, 0.00 g saturated fat; 0.00 mg cholesterol; 0.00 g carbohydrates; 100.59 mg sodium; 0.00 g fiber. Compare this to 1 tablespoon

Parmesan cheese which has 40 calories, 4 g protein, 4.5 g fat, 280 mg sodium, 0 g fiber.

There is also fat-free cottage cheese and a hoop cheese that is something like cottage and they are both excellent.

Fat-free Sour Cream and Fat-Free Yogurt: A friend of mine told me she couldn't even find regular sour cream at her grocery store—all of them were either fat-free or low-fat. I have included recipes for making them from scratch, though, just in case the fat-free craze goes away and you can't find what you need.

Why Jumbo Eggs? I use jumbo eggs in all recipes containing egg whites, simply because they have bigger, fluffier whites and they make the recipes come out better. If you can't find them, extra large eggs will do just about as well, but don't go smaller than that.

Apple Pectin Powder: Apple pectin powder, not tablets, is wonderful for making the jellies in this book. It is one item you will probably have to get at your health food store. The kind I get is salt- and starch-free with no sugar added. It's made by the Solgar Co., Inc., Lynbrook, N.Y. 11563. I called them to find out about the availability of apple pectin powder. They told me you can get it all over the United States, including Hawaii. In Alaska you can get it in Anchorage at Roy's Health Food Store. If you can't find it at your local health food store you can call toll free: 1-800-645-2246. In London you can find apple pectin powder at Body Active, Unit C 11 London Pavilion No. 1 Picadilly. Solgar doesn't sell to any stores in Australia or New Zealand; however, if you write to them they can direct you to a new source.

Fruit Spreads: I have included recipes for jellies and preserves but the commercial fruit spreads are really delicious. They are more expensive than if you make them yourself, but they save lots of time and work.

Nonfat Mayonnaise: There are quite a few excellent fat-free mayonnaise dressings available now. They usually have a little sugar and salt in them, so use just a little. As with other nonfat items, try different brands until you find one that you like.

Nonfat Margarine: I think it's awful and it doesn't melt very successfully, but my husband and daughter-in-law like it and you may find a brand that you like. I took a tub of it to my pharmacist and he looked over the ingredients and didn't find anything harmful in it.

Low-Sodium Tamari or Soy Sauce: These are interchangeable. If you can't find one of the low-sodium varieties, just use half the amount of the regular sauce called for in a recipe. So, if the recipe calls for 2 teaspoons of low-sodium soy or tamari sauce, just use 1 teaspoon of the regular sauce. Then add 1 teaspoon of water per teaspoon of sauce. The sodium content and taste will be about the same.

Red Rosé Wine: Red Rosé wine tastes best in cooking. Use your favorite, and remember, never cook with a wine you wouldn't drink by the glass.

Instant Brown Rice: In some recipes I use instant brown rice because it's fast, easy, delicious, and convenient. I suggest regular brown rice in some recipes for the purists, but I think the instant tastes better than regular brown rice! If you can't find instant brown rice in your supermarket in the U.S., you can call: 1-800-431-1003.

A 1/3-cup serving of instant brown rice contains 80 calories; 2 g protein; .66 g fat; 0 mg cholesterol; 17.3 g carbohydrates; 3.3 mg sodium; 1.3 g fiber. I couldn't find any information on the saturated fat.

Canned Tomatoes and Tomato Paste and Sauce: If you can't find the salt-free varieties, you can substitute ones containing salt.

Chuck Wagon-Style Corn: Chuck wagon-style frozen corn is simply a mixture of whole kernel corn, green bell pepper, red bell pepper, chopped onion, and sometimes chopped tomato. I find it convenient for making all sorts of dishes. If you can't find it, use 1 part whole kernel corn, 1 part frozen or fresh chopped green peppers, and 1 part frozen or fresh chopped onions. Add to that about 1/2 or more of a medium chopped tomato for color.

Green Bell Peppers: My sister-in-law who was raised close to the Texas border thinks green peppers are some kind of hot Mexican peppers, but that's not what I'm talking about when I say green pepper. The green peppers I'm talking about are squatty and sweet, and are not hot at all. They are also known as bell peppers or sweet bell peppers.

Equipment

Get yourself a really good food processor that can knead bread dough. You will also need a blender and an electric mixer because you're going into the business of serious cooking.

I love my slow cooker, too, because it frees me up to go out all day. I use a 5-quart, with the ceramic pot that lifts out of the metal, electric part. It's easy to wash, easy to put in the microwave if I need to, and easy to put in the refrigerator to store or to cool a soup or stew prior to skimming the grease off.

I like to have several glass measuring cups, in different sizes. I mix and cook in them, as well as use them for measuring. They do very well in the microwave because they are glass and have handles.

I also have a set of metal measuring cups, because it's easier to measure 1/4 cup in something that is only 1/4 cup; the same for 1/2, 1/3, and 1 cup.

I have two sets of measuring spoons, mainly because I don't like washing and drying them while I'm putting a recipe together. Try to find sets that have a 1/8 teaspoon measure.

I always use nonstick pots and pans. I have two frying pans, two 5-quart soup pots, and an array of smaller saucepans. You will also need a chopping board, a good set of knives, a hand grater that has small holes for grating sapsago cheese, wooden spoons, a colander, a salad dressing bottle, nonstick muffin tins—miniature and large—two large nonstick baking pans, two 9-inch by 13-inch baking dishes, two 8-inch square baking dishes, two 1 1/2-quart casserole dishes, 2 nonstick bread pans, and one large roasting pan with a cover, a salad bowl, two flan pans, a potato masher, a large kitchen spoon and fork, custard cups, a food scale, plastic wrap, zip-lock storage bags, and aluminum foil.

Of course, all this is pretty basic. I'm sure you already have most of these things in your kitchen.

Cooking Techniques

Some people ask me if it takes longer to cook the way I do. If you compare my way of cooking to opening up a TV dinner, yes it does take longer, but if you cook from scratch, it won't take you any longer.

Cooking Without Fats: Since you can't use any fat, you are going to have to learn how to cook without it. You are also going to be doing some serious degreasing of stews, soups, things like that. I'll start with sautéing.

Sautéing without oil: You will need nonstick pots. You won't need chicken stock or water or anything wet when you sauté vegetables because the steam that will result interferes with the caramelizing process produced by the natural sugars in the vegetables. Just toss your chopped veggies into the nonstick pan or pot over medium-high heat. When they begin to sizzle, use your wooden spoon to toss them until they are a bit brown around the edges and look a little shiny. Then add whatever liquid you need.

When sautéing red meats, place them in a nonstick pan or pot over medium-high heat and stir until the meat has browned on all sides. In the case of chicken, it will still look pale, but that's okay.

Degreasing or skimming: When you make stocks, gravies, stews, or soups, some fat and grease floats to the top. If you are in a hurry, just spoon off as much of the fat as possible, then float a lettuce or cabbage leaf on the surface of the liquid to absorb the rest. Or you can touch the bottom of a paper or a china plate to the surface and it will pick up grease.

Another way to degrease hot liquids is to let them cool first to room temperature, then refrigerate them for several hours, or overnight. The grease will rise to the top where it can be lifted off and discarded. Forget about those see-through pitchers that are supposed to be separators. You end up losing half the good stuff you want to keep and there will still be grease floating on the top.

A quick way to degrease hamburger meat is to put a paper towel in the pan with the meat when it is almost browned, and then stir the paper towel around the meat as it finishes browning. I usually have to use three or four towels to get all the grease out.

A more conventional way to degrease hamburger is to brown it, then drain it in a colander, and then drain it on paper towels. Wipe or wash the grease out of the pan, add the drained meat, and continue to cook to desired doneness. (I skip the colander part and just use a lot of paper towels so I don't have to wash the colander.)

Using Nonstick Sprays and Baking Pans: The nonstick sprays now come in butter and olive oil flavors. I use them even in nonstick bread pans and muffin tins because there are so few calories in these sprays that I'd rather use them than take a chance that my baked goods won't come out of the pans. If the pans are brand new or are in extremely good shape, they don't need any spray. But, if I'm cooking something with flour or other starchy ingredients, I'll usually spray even a nonstick dish.

Rinsing Salted Canned Goods: Some products like canned crab, shrimp, and some vegetables like hominy, are packed in salted water. If you drain and rinse them thoroughly you can get rid of a tremendous amount of the salt and sodium. In fact, with canned shrimp, crab, or clams you can reduce each can from about 1,140 mg of sodium to about 177 mg. To drain: open the can, hold your hand over the top, and turn it over; let the liquid drain through your fingers. Fill the can with water with the product still in it, and drain again. With canned shrimp, crab, or clams, repeat the process.

Don't Omit Ingredients

My cousin (third once removed) told me she made my Crawfish Etouffée from my first cookbook. I asked her how she liked it. "Umm, okay," she replied without much enthusiasm. That answer disturbed me because she should have said, "Wonderful!" It turned out that she didn't include the apple juice concentrate—just 1 tablespoon plus 1 teaspoon, because it didn't seem very important to her. But believe me, the difference between that little bit of juice concentrate and none, was the difference between "Wonderful!" and "Umm, okay."

Everything, down to 1/16 teaspoon of something in the recipes in this book, is there because it is *absolutely needed.* You don't have much leeway when you can't add salt and butter or margarine, so you have to take advantage of every taste-enhancing trick that is available.

Putting the dishes together: I've already advised that these recipes must be followed exactly as they are written and the order each ingredient is added is equally important. If a recipe says to cook certain vegetables first, then add fish and cook some more; don't think if you put all the vegetables and fish in at the same time and cook it all together that the dish will come out tasting good. It might be a disaster.

DECODING NUTRITIVE VALUES

For each recipe you will find a list of the nutritive values of each serving. This information was taken from The Food Processor Nutrition and Fitness Software from ESHA Research (P.O. Box 13028, Salem, OR 97309), which is based on the most recent USDA data, and from product manufacturers. I also consulted the United States Department of Agriculture, Home and Garden Bulletin, Number 72. Keep in mind that the nutrient data should be viewed as a guide and not as an exact representation of the nutrient values of each and every food. Many recipes, for example, call for an onion or a green pepper, and the exact values of these will vary depending on size. Where possible in cooked dishes, I have used cooked instead of raw values for foods. Also, I have rounded off all nutrient values to the nearest whole number, except in the case of calories and sodium, in which case I rounded off to the nearest five.

To figure some values you might have to do a little arithmetic depending on what you're trying to measure so here's a chart that might help:

Equivalents by Capacity or Volume (all measures level)

1 quart = 4 cups
1 cup = 8 fluid ounces = 1/2 pint = 16 tablespoons
5 tablespoons + 1 teaspoon = 1/3 cup
4 tablespoons = 1/4 cup
1 tablespoon = 3 teaspoons
2 tablespoons = 1 fluid ounce

Equivalents by Weight

1 pound = 16 ounces
3.57 ounces = 100 grams
1 ounce = 28.35 grams

Note: 1 tablespoon of sapsago cheese weighs 5 grams. That information might help you if you come across something of similar texture that you find measured only in grams.

EXCHANGES

You may be on a diet that counts exchanges instead of calories. I think the exchange system works best if the foods are not mixed together. It's easier to measure an apple by itself rather than a fruit compote, or measure a cup of milk by itself rather than blended with fruit, or a piece of meat by itself rather than in a stew, if you are trying to measure by exchanges.

One-third cup cooked brown rice is considered 1 bread exchange and 1/2 cup of mashed potatoes is considered 1 bread exchange, 1/4 cup no-fat cottage cheese is considered a dairy exchange, 1 small apple is considered 1 fruit exchange, and so on. When I developed these recipes, I kept exchanges in mind, so when, for instance, I used no-fat or low-fat cottage cheese and made something amounting to 6 servings I used 1 1/2 cups of cottage cheese; that would work out to 1 dairy exchange for each serving. Following is the exchange list used by the Pritikin diet which lists many of the foods you will eating:

How To Use These Charts

For a 1,000-calorie-a-day diet, eat six complex carbohydrate servings (starchy foods, such as beans, corn, potatoes, cereals, rice), twelve vegetable servings, three fruit servings, and two dairy servings. You can eat only three ounces of meat, fish, or poultry a week); on those days count the meat as a dairy serving.

If you want to maintain your weight on a 2,000-calorie-a-day diet, eat eighteen servings of complex carbohydrates, fifteen vegetable servings, five fruit servings (one of which should be citrus), two dairy servings (or one dairy serving if meat is eaten that day). You are allowed 3 to 4 ounces of meat, poultry, or fish a day, not to exceed 1 1/2 pounds a week. Limit shrimp, crab, crayfish (crawfish), or lobster servings to 1 3/4 ounces cooked weight per day because of their high cholesterol content.

If you looked at the charts below, you will see how large the servings are for each item. As you plan your food for the day, check the recipes you plan to use, as a single recipe may contain, for example, two milk servings or two fruit servings.

Complex Carbohydrate Exchanges

Each portion provides approximately 80 calories.

Vegetables

Beans, dried cooked	1/3 cup
Beans, lima, fresh	1/2 cup
Chestnuts	6
Corn, kernels	1/2 cup
Corn on the cob	6 inches long
Corn, popped, no oil or salt added	3 cups
Hominy	1/2 cup
Lentils, cooked	1/3 cup
Parsnips	2/3 cups (1 small)
Peas, black eyes, split cooked	1/3 cup
Peas, fresh	1/2 cup
Potato, white, baked	1 (2-inch diameter)
Potato, white, mashed	1/2 cup
Potato, sweet	1/3 cup
Pumpkin, cooked	3/4 cup
Squash, winter	3/4 cup
Yams, baked	1/3 cup

Breads and crackers (whole grain: wheat, rye, or sourdough)

Bagel, water	1/2
Bread, whole wheat, rye, sourdough	1 slice
Breadsticks	2 (4 inches long)
Bun, hamburger, whole wheat	1/2
English muffin	1/2
Matzo cracker, plain	3/4 ounce
Pita, whole wheat	1/2 of a 6-inch pocket
Rice cakes	3/4 ounce
Rice crackers	3/4 ounce
Roll, whole wheat, rye, sourdough	1 (2-inch diameter)
Rye crackers, no salt	4
Tortilla, corn	1 (6-inch diameter)

Flours

Arrowroot	2 tablespoons
Buckwheat flour	3 tablespoons
Cornmeal	3 tablespoons
Cornstarch	2 tablespoons
Matzo meal	3 tablespoons
Potato flour	2 1/2 tablespoons
Rice flour	3 tablespoons
Rice flour, dark	4 tablespoons
Whole wheat flour	3 tablespoons

Complex Carbohydrate Exchanges, continued

Grains, Cereals, and Pasta

Barley, cooked	1/2 cup
Cornmeal, dry	2 1/2 tablespoons
Cracked wheat (bulgar), cooked	1/2 cup
Flake cereal	1/2 cup
Nugget cereal	3 tablespoons
Grits, cooked	1/3 cup
Kasha (buckwheat groats), cooked	1/3 cup
Macaroni, whole wheat	1/2 cup
Noodles, rice, cooked	1/2 cup
Noodles, whole wheat, cooked	1/2 cup
Oatmeal, cooked	1/2 cup
Pasta, enriched white, cooked	1/2 cup
Rice, brown, cooked	1/3 cup
Rye cereal, cooked	1/2 cup
Shredded wheat biscuit cereal	1 large biscuit
Shredded wheat biscuit, or spoon-size	1/2 cup
Steel-cut oats, cooked	1/2 cup

Vegetable Exchanges

Each portion provides approximately 25 calories. 1 cup of raw vegetables equals 1/2 cup of cooked.

Artichoke, whole base, and ends of leaves	1 small
Asparagus	1 cup
Beans, green or yellow	1 cup
Beets	1 cup
Bok choy	1 cup
Broccoli	1 cup
Brussels sprouts	1 cup
Cabbage	1 cup
Carrots	1 medium
Cauliflower	1 cup
Celery	1 cup
Celery root	1 cup
Cilantro	1 cup
Chayote (mirliton)	1 cup
Chicory	1 cup
Chilies	1 cup
Chinese cabbage	1 cup
Chives	1 cup
Coriander (cilantro)	1 cup
Cucumber	1 cup
Eggplant	1 cup
Endive	1 cup
Escarole	1 cup
Greens, beet, collard, chard	1 cup
Jerusalem artichokes	1 cup
Jicama	1 cup
Kale	1 cup
Leeks	1 cup
Lettuce	1 cup
Lima beans, baby	1/4 cup
Mint	1 cup
Mushrooms	1 cup
Okra	1 cup
Onions, all types	1 cup
Parsley	1 cup
Pea pods, Chinese	1 cup
Peppers, red and green	1 cup
Pimento	1 cup
Radishes	1 cup
Romaine lettuce	1 cup
Rhubarb	1 cup
Rutabagas	1 cup

Vegetable Exchanges, continued

Shallots	1 cup
Spinach	1 cup
Sprouts, assorted	1 cup
Squash, zucchini, spaghetti, summer	1 cup
Tomato	1 medium
Tomatoes canned in juice, unsalted	1 cup
Tomato juice, unsalted	2/3 cup
Tomato paste, unsalted	3 tablespoons
Tomato sauce, unsalted	1/2 cup
Vegetable juice, unsalted	2/3 cup
Water chestnuts	4 medium
Watercress	1 cup

Fruit Exchanges

Fresh, dried, frozen, or canned with sugar or syrup. Each portion provides approximately 60 calories.

Apple	1 small (2-inch diameter)
Apple juice or cider	1/3 cup
Applesauce, unsweetened	1/2 cup
Apricots, fresh	1 medium
Apricots, dried	2 halves
Banana	1/2 medium
Berries, boysenberries, blackberries, raspberries, blueberries	3/4 cup
Cantaloupe	1/3 (5-inch diameter)
Cherries	12 large
Cranberries, unsweetened	1 cup
Crenshaw melon	2-inch wedge
Dates	2 1/2 medium
Date sugar	1 tablespoon
Figs, fresh	2 (2-inch diameter)
Fruit cocktail	1/2 cup
Fruit juice concentrate	2 tablespoons (1 ounce)
Grapefruit	1/2 medium
Grapefruit juice	1/2 cup
Grapes	15 small
Guava	1 1/2
Honeydew melon	1/8 medium
Kiwi	1 large
Kumquats	5
Lemon juice	1/2 cup
Lime juice	1/2 cup
Loquats	13
Mandarin oranges	3/4 cup
Mango	1/2 small
Nectarine	1 (1 1/2-inch diameter)
Orange	1 (2 1/2-inch diameter)
Orange juice	1/2 cup
Papaya	1 cup
Passionfruit	1
Passionfruit juice	1/3 cup
Peach	1 (2 3/4-inch diameter)
Pear	1 small
Persimmon, native	2 medium
Pineapple, fresh	3/4 cup
Pineapple, canned without sugar	1/3 cup
Pineapple juice	1/2 cup
Plantain	1/2 small

Fruit Exchanges, continued

Plums	2 (2-inch diameter)
Pomegranate	1/2
Prunes, fresh	2 medium
Prunes, dried	3
Prune juice	1/3 cup
Raisins	2 tablespoons
Strawberries	1 1/4 cup
Tangerine	2 (2 1/2-inch diameter)
Watermelon	1 1/4 cup

Dairy Exchanges

Each portion contains approximately 90 calories and is 1 percent fat or less by weight (15 percent of calories, or less from fat).

Nonfat milk	1 cup
Nonfat buttermilk	1 cup
Nonfat yogurt	3/4 cup
Evaporated nonfat milk	1/2 cup
Dry-curd cottage cheese or hoop cheese	1/4 cup
1% or less low-fat cottage cheese	1/4 cup
Nonfat cottage cheese	4 ounces
Nonfat cream cheese	approximately 2 1/2 ounces
Nonfat sour cream	3 ounces
Nonfat powdered milk	1/3 cup

High-Protein Exchanges

Each portion provides approximately 35 to 55 calories per ounce. High-protein exchanges are controlled because of their fat and cholesterol content. Although soybeans and tofu do not contain any cholesterol, they are higher in fat than any other legumes; 40 to 50 percent of their calories come from fat. You may select soybeans or tofu in place of fish, fowl, or meat on the Pritikin diet.

In the chart below, note the total fat, cholesterol, and calories contents, as well as the percentage of calories from fat, in 3 1/2-ounce, cooked servings of the foods.

RECOMMENDED HIGH PROTEIN FOODS

Meat or Fish (3 1/2 ounces cooked)	Fat (g)	Chol. (mg)	Calories	% Calories from Fat
Shrimp, which appears between the solid and dashed lines, is recommended in 2-ounce portions. Foods that appear below the dashed line are not recommended.				
Abalone	0.3	54	49	4.0
Lobster, northern	0.6	72	98	5.4
Pike	0.9	50	113	7.0
Flounder	1.0	46	129	7.0
Cod, Atlantic	0.9	55	105	7.4
Haddock	0.9	55	112	7.5
Sole	0.8	42	68	10.0
Scallops	1.4	52	112	11.0
Clams	2.0	67	148	12.0
Red Snapper, mixed species	1.7	47	128	12.1
Crab, Alaskan king	1.5	53	97	14.0
Tuna, white water-packed	2.5	42	136	16.0
Turkey, white meat	3.2	69	157	18.0
Sea bass	2.6	53	124	19.0
Halibut	2.9	41	140	19.0
Chicken, white meat	3.6	85	165	20.0
Oysters	2.2	50	90	22.0
Mussels, blue	4.5	56	172	23.0
Trout	4.3	74	151	26.0
Beef, top round	5.4	84	184	26.0
Pork, tenderloin, lean only	4.8	93	166	26.1
Swordfish	5.1	50	155	30.0
Beef, flank, lean only	7.3	90	195	34.0
Lamb, lean leg	7.0	93	184	34.0
Salmon, sockeye	11.0	81	178	61.0

High-Protein Exchanges, continued

Meat or Fish (3 1/2 ounces cooked)	Fat (g)	Chol. (mg)	Calories	% Calories from Fat
Sardines, Pacific, water-packed, unsalted	12.0	81	178	89
Shrimp	1.1	133	99	9.8
(Shrimp is recommended in 2 ounce portions only.)				
The following high-protein foods are not recommended:				
Crayfish	1.4	178	114	10.7
Chicken, dark, without skin	9.7	93	205	43.0
T-bone steak, lean	10.4	80	214	44.0
Veal, rump and round	11.2	101	215	46.0
Turkey, dark, without skin	11.5	89	221	47.0
Pork loin, top	14.9	94	258	52.0
Beef, lean ground, broiled	17.6	101	280	57.0
Beef, chuck, (pot roast), fat and lean	24.4	99	337	65.0

Instead of four food groups, we now have five. If you look on cereal or cracker boxes you can find the Food Guide Pyramid. Fats are now a food group. It will give you a good idea of which foods you should eat more of and which less.

Serving Sizes

Item	Raw Weight	Serving Size	Cooked Weight (edible portion)
Chicken breast	5 oz.	1	3 1/2 oz.
Clams (in shell)	36 oz.	16	3 1/2 oz.
Mussels (in shell)	15 oz.	33	3 1/2 oz.
Oysters (raw)	4 oz.	7	—
Scallops	4 oz.	18 to 20	3 1/2 oz.
Shrimp, boiled, medium size	—	9	2 oz.
Soybeans, cooked (37 calories/oz.)	—	2/3 cup	—
Tofu (21 calories/oz.)	—	6 oz.	—
Ultra low-fat cheese (less than 34% of calories fat, 67 calories/oz.)	—	2 oz.	—

Miscellaneous Foods

In addition to the exchanges, here are recommendations for the following food items:

Item	Quantity	Calories
Egg whites	7/week	16 each
Garlic	As desired	Negligible
Gelatin, plain	1 oz/week (4 envelopes)	95/oz.
Horseradish, prepared no salt added	1 Tbsp./day	7/Tbsp.
Sapsago (green) cheese	1–2 Tbsp./week	20/Tbsp.
Seeds (as seasoning only)	Less than 1/8 tsp./day	Negligible
Soy sauce (low-sodium)	1 tsp./day	Negligible
Teas: selected herbal	Moderate amount	Negligible
Unprocessed bran	1–3 Tbsp./day as needed	9/Tbsp.

THE WEIGHT-LOSS, KEEP-AT-IT-DIET

That's what this is, other than being an extremely healthy diet. You notice I don't call it "The Weight-Loss, Keep-It-Off-Diet," because you really need to keep at it to keep it off. Once you get down to your goal-weight you may think you can eat anything without thinking about what's in it. You can't do that and expect to keep your figure or your health. Sorry. You must be vigilant for the rest of your life. I'm not even going to qualify that statement. If you fall off—get back on and don't fall off very often.

Exercise

You must exercise. When you first go on a diet you will probably lose weight quickly, but after a week or so, you stop losing if you don't exercise. That's because your body will think you are starving and it keeps lowering your metabolism even though you keep on eating less, so you keep on not losing weight. The best, easiest, and least expensive thing I've found, if my weight is at my ideal weight, is to get outside and walk for at least forty minutes every other day. If I go over my ideal weight, I walk every day. Be sure to wear jogging shoes to walk in even if you don't jog (advice from my podiatrist) because the wrong shoes will discourage you from exercising. Exercise fools your body, keeping your metabolism up, so you continue to lose weight. I like to go first thing in the morning rather than at the end of the day when it's easy to find excuses not to do it. In one hand I carry a spray bottle full of water and liquid crab boil to keep any loose neighborhood dogs away and a bottle of drinking water for me in the other hand. I heat the drinking water to warm my hands in the winter. The two full bottles also provide weight to firm my arms.

Weighing Yourself

Contrary to what most diets recommend, I think you should weigh yourself every day. If you wait a week you could pick up five to ten pounds and not even realize it. If you weigh in every day you will see you gained a pound yesterday and you can watch yourself for a day or two until it comes off, which isn't as hard as losing five or ten pounds. I have a scale in my closet and I weigh myself first thing in the morning nude, before I eat or drink anything. I even take the curlers out of my hair. I keep a chart and pencil on the wall by the scale and mark the date, how much I weigh, and "bbbe" or "abbe," which means "before bowel before eating" and "after bowel before eating," because they can make a difference in your weight.

Your self-image

Who are you? When you start to become healthy and begin to lose weight, you have to be careful about what you are saying to yourself and asking yourself. When I started losing weight after recovering from a broken leg and no exercise a few years ago (I had gotten up to 134), I would look in the mirror and see this thin person and ask, "Who is that?" I'd feel my hips and they didn't feel squashy anymore, and I'd ask, "Who is this?" And I felt a little frightened because I'd lost some of myself. I wasn't who I was before, even though I looked better and felt better. I was tempted to try to get my old fat self back. Sometimes I'd eat fattening food just to prove to my self that I could gain weight and that I wasn't losing weight because of some terrible illness. You might tell yourself you're wearing yourself out with exercise. But if you can get past all this nonsense and convince yourself that you are you, fat or thin, sick or healthy, you will finally get to know yourself and get used to yourself as a slim, attractive, healthy person.

CHAPTER 2

A Few Basics: Stocks, Gravies, Sauces, Preserves

I include beef, poultry, and fish stocks here because they are the foundation of my cooking.

Gravies are also great additions that have helped me to develop this style of cooking, and the Piquante Sauce has changed my life, it's so handy and delicious. These are the kinds of special things that make a meal worth eating. I don't think my husband and I could have stayed on this program without our Roast Beef Gravy, our Brown Turkey Gravy, and our Italian Tomato Sauce.

I like to buy the commercially available all-fruit preserves, but sometimes I can't find them. I was thrilled to come up with absolutely delicious all-fruit jellies after experimenting with apple pectin powder. They add so much to a sugar-free diet, and apple pectin powder is loaded with fiber but you can't even tell it's there.

The recipes in this chapter will help you to make your food taste delicious, and add to your enjoyment of life.

BROWN BEEF STOCK

YIELD: ABOUT 4 QTS.

Nutrition Facts

Amount Per Serving	
Calories 40	Calories from Fat 0

	% Daily Value*
Total Fat 0g	0%
Saturated Fat 0g	0%
Cholesterol 0mg	0%
Sodium 590mg	25%
Total Carbohydrate 8g	3%
Dietary Fiber 2g	6%
Sugars 4g	
Protein 2g	

Vitamin A 160%	•	Vitamin C 10%
Calcium 2%	•	Iron 2%

I don't like the stock made from raw beef because I think it lacks flavor and it's very difficult to season well. I always make my beef stock from browned, roasted meat or browned beef neck bones.

1 to 2 pounds of neck bones or leftover roast beef
2 carrots
1 large onion, peeled and quartered
2 celery ribs and leaves cut in halves
1/4 cup Red Rosé wine
Water

To brown the neck bones, put them in a 5-quart Dutch oven or heavy, lidded pot and cook in the oven at 450 degrees F., until they are nearly burned. If you use leftover roast beef, there is no need to brown it first. Add the vegetables, fill to the top with water, and simmer on top of the stove, uncovered.

After the stock has simmered for several hours, remove the vegetables and place the stock in the refrigerator to cool. All the fat will rise to the top and harden so it can be skimmed off. If you want perfectly clear stock, you can strain it through cheesecloth, which should trap any leftover grease. If the stock is cold enough, though, you should be able to get every bit of it off without this step. Use the cooked meat and vegetables in soup.

STOCK FROM UNCOOKED TURKEY OR CHICKEN

YIELD: ABOUT 2 QTS.

Nutrition Facts

Amount Per Serving

Calories 50	Calories from Fat 15

	% Daily Value*
Total Fat 1.5g	**2%**
Saturated Fat 0g	**0%**
Cholesterol 20mg	**7%**
Sodium 25mg	**1%**
Total Carbohydrate 1g	**0%**
Dietary Fiber 0g	**0%**
Sugars 0g	
Protein 9g	

Vitamin A 0%	•	Vitamin C 2%
Calcium 2%	•	Iron 2%

This information assumes that homemade stock is similar in value to degreased, canned, salt-free chicken stock. The nutritive values of this stock will vary according to its strength.

You can use this stock in any recipe that calls for chicken stock or turkey stock, as opposed to stock made from roasted turkey or chicken.

1 to 2 pounds turkey or chicken parts (1 or 2 turkey wings) or
    2 chicken backs, 2 necks, and 4 wing tips)
2 carrots
1 large onion, quartered
2 celery ribs, including leaves
Water

Take any parts of raw turkey or chicken and put them in a 5-quart stockpot with the carrots, onion, and celery. Fill the pot with water. Bring to a boil, then lower the heat and simmer for about 5 hours. If you want especially strong stock, simmer the stock longer, until much of the liquid has evaporated. If you need stock in a hurry, cook at a fast boil, uncovered, for 20 to 25 minutes, then set aside to cool. When the liquid is cool, remove the meat and bones and vegetables. Set the remaining liquid in the refrigerator until the grease rises to the top and hardens. Skim and use as directed.

Pick the cooked chicken meat or turkey meat off the bones and use it to make dishes using either chicken or turkey meat.

CONCENTRATED CHICKEN STOCK

Nutrition Facts

Amount Per Serving

Calories 10	Calories from Fat 5

	% Daily Value*
Total Fat 0.5g	**1**%
Saturated Fat 0g	**0**%
Cholesterol 0mg	**0**%
Sodium 690mg	**29**%
Total Carbohydrate 1g	**0**%
Dietary Fiber 0g	**0**%
Sugars 1g	
Protein 1g	

Vitamin A 0%	•	Vitamin C 0%
Calcium 0%	•	Iron 0%

I use Concentrated Chicken Stock in place of olive oil, butter, or margarine, because it makes a good wetting and binding agent and adds a lot of flavor.

2 chicken necks plus 1 back, skin removed
1 quart of water

Place the chicken in a 2-quart saucepan. Add a quart of water and set on the stove, uncovered. Bring to a boil, then lower the heat and simmer for about one hour. It's okay for some of the water to evaporate. You want to end up with one cup of stock, not including the fat. Remove chicken pieces and place the stock in the refrigerator until the grease hardens on the top. Skim and use as directed.

STOCK FROM ROASTED CHICKEN OR TURKEY

YIELD: ABOUT 2 QTS.

Nutrition Facts

Amount Per Serving	
Calories 10	Calories from Fat 5

	% Daily Value*
Total Fat 0.5g	1%
Saturated Fat 0g	0%
Cholesterol 0mg	0%
Sodium 630mg	26%
Total Carbohydrate 1g	0%
Dietary Fiber 0g	0%
Sugars 1g	
Protein 1g	

Vitamin A 0%	•	Vitamin C 0%
Calcium 0%	•	Iron 0%

This information assumes that homemade stock is similar in value to degreased, canned, salt-free chicken stock. The nutritive values of this stock will vary according to its strength.

I've found over the years that the stock made from the leftover bones of roasted chickens or turkey breasts is far superior to that made from raw chicken or turkey. You can use this for any recipe in this book requiring stock. To roast a chicken, skin it, sprinkle it with 1/4 plus 1/8 teaspoon garlic powder, 1/8 teaspoon cayenne pepper, and 1 1/2 tablespoons dried minced onion, in that order. For Roasted Turkey Breast, follow the recipe on page 149.

Microwave Directions: Cook the chicken, uncovered, at 80 percent power or on "roast" for 30 to 40 minutes. With a sharp knife, pierce the chicken in the very meaty part of the thigh near where it is connected to the back. If any red juice comes out, cook the chicken for 5 to 6 minutes longer.

Oven Directions: Roast the chicken for 1 hour at 350 degrees F. with an aluminum foil tent over the chicken. When the legs are loose and easy to lift up and down, the chicken is done. Just to make sure, pierce the meaty part of the thigh near where it is connected to the back. If any red or pink juice runs out, cook the chicken a little longer.

Save the pan drippings or any leftover gravy in the refrigerator and degrease. Place leftover bones in a large stockpot with the degreased drippings or gravy. Fill the pot with water and simmer for 5 to 6 hours. For especially strong stock, simmer longer, until quite a bit of the liquid has evaporated. Remove the bones and meat and refrigerate the stock to allow the fat and grease to rise to the top and harden. Skim and use as directed. You will have a beautifully seasoned stock, which can be frozen in individual airtight containers so you always have some on hand.

Pick the cooked chicken or turkey off the bones and save for recipes using turkey or chicken meat.

FISH STOCK

YIELD: ABOUT 4 QTS.

Nutrition Facts

Amount Per Serving

Calories 45	Calories from Fat 15
	% Daily Value*
Total Fat 2g	3%
Saturated Fat 0g	0%
Cholesterol 0mg	0%
Sodium 370mg	15%
Total Carbohydrate 2g	1%
Dietary Fiber 0g	0%
Sugars 1g	
Protein 5g	

Vitamin A 50%	•	Vitamin C 4%
Calcium 2%	•	Iron 0%

To make fish stock, you can really use any part of the fish. The heads are cheap and sometimes free at the fish market or from your butcher.

2 or 3 raw fish heads, or back bones and tails
2 carrots
1 large onion, quartered
2 celery ribs, including leaves
Sprig fresh parsley (optional)
Water

Place all the ingredients in a 5-quart stockpot and fill it with water. Bring to a boil, then simmer, uncovered, for 5 to 6 hours. For stronger, more flavorful stock, simmer longer, until quite a bit of the liquid has evaporated. Remove the heads and/or bones, then strain to remove any other debris. This will make a beautifully seasoned stock, which can be frozen in individual airtight containers so that you always have some on hand.

SHRIMP STOCK

YIELD: 1 2/3 CUPS

Nutrition Facts

Amount Per Serving

Calories 30	Calories from Fat 0
	% Daily Value*
Total Fat 0g	0%
Saturated Fat 0g	0%
Cholesterol 0mg	0%
Sodium 25mg	1%
Total Carbohydrate 7g	2%
Dietary Fiber 2g	6%
Sugars 4g	
Protein 1g	

Vitamin A 0%	•	Vitamin C 10%
Calcium 2%	•	Iron 2%

Shrimp stock can be used in any shrimp dish that uses water. It will intensify the flavor of the dish.

Peels of 1 to 2 pounds of shrimp
4 cups water
1 rib of celery including leaves, roughly chopped
1 small onion, coarsely chopped

In a nonstick 5-quart stockpot, sauté the shrimp shells over high heat by turning them over and over. First they will steam, and then they will smoke and give off a marvelous aroma. Continue stirring for 2 minutes, then immediately add the water. Stir, bring to a boil (don't let it boil over), then cook uncovered, over low heat until the liquid reduces to 1 2/3 cups, or whatever the recipe calls for. Strain. If you have a little too much, boil it down a little more. If you have too little, add enough water to make it the amount you need. Throw the shells away or dig them into your garden or your compost pile.

ROAST BEEF GRAVY I

It is hard to predict exactly how much gravy this will make, because some meat is juicier and produces a generous amount of drippings. You may end up with more than 4 cups. I freeze the gravy in small amounts for adding to other recipes. It adds meat flavor without the meat.

4 or 5 pound eye of round or rump roast
2 cups Beef Stock (page 43) or water
5 tablespoons whole wheat flour
2 tablespoons onion flakes
1/2 cup fresh, chopped parsley
3 or 4 fresh, sliced mushrooms
Mock Kitchen Bouquet (page 58) or 1 teaspoon real Kitchen Bouquet
2 or 3 tablespoons apple juice concentrate
2 bay leaves
1/2 teaspoon crumbled or powdered dried thyme
1/2 teaspoon garlic powder
1/4 to 1/2 teaspoon cayenne pepper

Preheat the oven to 400 degrees F.

To make a flavorful gravy, start with a well-seasoned roast. Be sure to cut off any visible fat. Either stuff fresh garlic pieces into little holes you make with a knife into the roast or sprinkle with garlic powder. Then sprinkle with onion powder and cayenne pepper. Place the roast in a roasting pan and bake at 400 degrees F. until the outside is brown. Lower the heat to 350 degrees F. and roast 18 to 20 minutes per pound for a medium-rare roast, including the initial browning time. A meat thermometer registers 175 degrees F. for medium-rare, and 180 degrees F. for well-done. Add 2 inches of water to the pan and continue to cook uncovered, until desired doneness, basting occasionally. Remove the roast to a serving platter and set the pan of drippings in the refrigerator. The next day, all the fat and grease will have risen to the top and hardened. Just pop it off and discard.

Pour the water from the drippings pan into a blender, add the flour, and blend. Place your roasting pan on the stove, covering 2 burners, if necessary, and add all the seasonings, mushrooms, and blended stock mixture. Boil over high heat, stirring until the gravy achieves the desired thickness.

Slice up the roast beef and store in 1 1/2-ounce packages in your freezer.

If you don't want to use a whole roast for this, place 2 pounds of beef neck bones in a roasting pan and sprinkle with garlic powder, onion powder, and cayenne pepper. Place them in a preheated 400 degree F.-oven and let them get very, very brown. Add about 2 inches of water and place on top of the stove over 2 burners, if necessary. Simmer covered for about 1/2 hour to 45 minutes. As the water evaporates, add some occasionally so that there is always at least an inch of water in the pan. Remove the neck bones and give them to your dog or your neighbor's dog if you don't have one. Place the drippings in the refrigerator overnight and discard the hardened grease that will have risen to the top. Place the water in a blender, add the flour, and blend. Place your roasting pan on the stove covering 2 burners, if necessary. Add all the other seasonings, mushrooms, and blended stock mixture. Boil over high heat, stirring until the gravy achieves the desired thickness.

ROAST BEEF GRAVY II

Nutrition Facts

Amount Per Serving	
Calories 40	Calories from Fat 0

	% Daily Value*
Total Fat 0g	0%
Saturated Fat 0g	0%
Cholesterol 0mg	0%
Sodium 320mg	13%
Total Carbohydrate 6g	2%
Dietary Fiber less than 1 gram	3%
Sugars 2g	
Protein 1g	

Vitamin A 0%	•	Vitamin C 6%	
Calcium 2%	•	Iron 2%	

4 to 5 pound roast
2 cloves garlic, sliced, or 1/2 teaspoon garlic powder
1/4 cup onion flakes or dried chopped onions
Cayenne pepper, to taste
4 to 5 mushrooms, sliced
1/4 cup water
2 tablespoons cornstarch
2 celery ribs and leaves
1/2 cup Red Rosé wine

Use any kind of very lean roast, and remove all visible fat before cooking.

Place in a slow cooker or a roasting pan. Pierce the roast with a sharp knife and stuff fresh garlic slices into the holes, or sprinkle the roast with garlic powder and cayenne pepper. Then sprinkle it generously with dried onion flakes or dried chopped onions. Cut the celery ribs half way through crosswise and drape them over the roast.

Slow Cooker Directions I: The very best way to do this is covered in a slow cooker. Do not add any water at this time. Turn it on the high setting. When the roast is brown, add about 2 inches of water and 1/4 cup wine. Continue to cook until fully done, about 4 hours. Remove the roast and set the drippings in the refrigerator.

Slow Cooker Directions II: Place the roast in the slow cooker and cover. Add 2 inches of water and 1/4 cup wine. Turn it on low setting and cook for 6 hours. Remove the roast and set the drippings in the refrigerator.

Oven Directions: Preheat oven to 400 degrees F. Place the seasoned roast on the middle shelf of the oven to brown. When brown, add about 2 inches of water to the plan, lower the heat to 350 degrees F. and roast, basting occasionally, to the desired doneness. Bake 18 to 20 minutes per pound for a medium-rare roast. A meat thermometer registers 175 degrees F. for medium-rare, and 180 degrees F. for well-done. Remove the roast from the pan and set the drippings in the refrigerator. The next day remove it and discard the hardened fat and grease.

Heat the drippings on the stove top, using two burners if necessary, and add the mushrooms. Cook the mushrooms over medium heat until they darken. Thoroughly combine the cornstarch with 1/4 cup water and the remaining wine. Add to the drippings and cook over medium heat, stirring constantly until the cornstarch thickens the gravy. Add a little more water if the gravy is too thick.

CHICKEN OR TURKEY GRAVY BASE FROM STOCK

Nutrition Facts

Amount Per Serving	
Calories 40	Calories from Fat 0

	% Daily Value*
Total Fat 0g	0%
Saturated Fat 0g	0%
Cholesterol 0mg	0%
Sodium 230mg	10%
Total Carbohydrate 8g	3%
Dietary Fiber 1g	4%
Sugars 4g	
Protein 1g	

Vitamin A 2%	•	Vitamin C	4%
Calcium 2%	•	Iron	6%

I always make this recipe ahead and freeze it to add to my Thanksgiving skimmed turkey drippings so that I have plenty of instant gravy when I need it. Or I freeze it in cup-size containers to add to skimmed chicken drippings when it is just for me and Ray.

5 cups Strong Chicken Stock (page 45) or Turkey Stock (page 46)
10 tablespoons whole wheat flour
5 tablespoons onion flakes
1 tablespoon celery flakes
2 tablespoons dried parsley
1 1/2 teaspoons dried sage
1 1/2 teaspoons powdered or crumbled thyme
1/4 teaspoon marjoram
1 1/2 teaspoons garlic powder
1/2 teaspoon cayenne pepper
1/3 cup Red Rosé wine
5 tablespoons apple juice concentrate
2 1/2 cups sliced mushrooms
2 teaspoons medium red hot sauce
1/4 cup Mock Kitchen Bouquet (page 58) or 1 1/2 teaspoons commercial Kitchen Bouquet

In a large stockpot, add 3 cups of the stock and set aside.

Pour the remaining 2 cups of stock and the flour into a blender. Mix the flour in with a spoon to wet it, then blend on high setting until the flour and stock are thoroughly combined. Add this mixture to the stockpot, and then add the onion flakes, celery flakes, parsley, sage, thyme, marjoram, garlic powder, cayenne, wine, juice concentrate, mushrooms, and hot sauce. Cook over high heat, stirring constantly. When the mixture starts to bubble, stir and continue to cook for 1 minute. Then reduce the heat to low and add the Kitchen Bouquet. Cover and simmer for 45 minutes, stirring occasionally.

BROWN TURKEY GRAVY

Nutrition Facts

Amount Per Serving

Calories 25	Calories from Fat 0

	% Daily Value*
Total Fat 0g	**0**%
Saturated Fat 0g	**0**%
Cholesterol 0mg	**0**%
Sodium 130mg	**6**%
Total Carbohydrate 5g	**2**%
Dietary Fiber less than 1 gram	**2**%
Sugars 2g	
Protein 1g	

Vitamin A 2%	•	Vitamin C 6%
Calcium 0%	•	Iron 2%

Drippings and juice from a roasted turkey, degreased
2 cups of turkey or chicken stock or water
1/4 cup Red Rosé wine
5 tablespoons whole wheat flour
2 tablespoons dried onion flakes
1/2 cup chopped, fresh parsley
1 cup sliced mushrooms
**Mock Kitchen Bouquet (page 58) or 1 teaspoon real Kitchen
 Bouquet**
3 to 4 tablespoons apple juice concentrate
1/2 teaspoon dried sage
1/2 teaspoon powdered or crumbled thyme
1/2 teaspoon marjoram
1/2 teaspoon garlic powder
1/4 to 1/2 teaspoon cayenne pepper

Place the drippings from a turkey in a saucepan. Add the turkey stock or water and wine to the pan. Mix well and add the whole wheat flour, then pour mixture into a blender. Blend and then return to the pan. Add all other ingredients and cook over medium heat, stirring constantly until the mushrooms have darkened and the gravy is the desired thickness.

FAST ITALIAN TOMATO SAUCE

**YIELD: 12 SERVINGS
1/4 CUP = 1 SERVING**

Nutrition Facts

Amount Per Serving	
Calories 20	Calories from Fat 0
	% Daily Value*
Total Fat 0g	**0%**
Saturated Fat 0g	**0%**
Cholesterol 0mg	**0%**
Sodium 75mg	**3%**
Total Carbohydrate 4g	**1%**
Dietary Fiber less than 1 gram	**4%**
Sugars 1g	
Protein 1g	

Vitamin A 6%	•	Vitamin C 8%
Calcium 0%	•	Iron 2%

1 16 ounce can low-fat, low-sodium tomato sauce
1/2 cup water
1 cup sliced mushrooms
1 onion, chopped
1/4 teaspoon garlic powder
2 teaspoons Italian seasoning
1 tablespoon dried parsley

Cook covered, over medium heat 30 minutes. Stir frequently.

CHINESE MUSTARD SAUCE

YIELD: 2 SERVINGS

Nutrition Facts

Amount Per Serving	
Calories 15	Calories from Fat 10
	% Daily Value*
Total Fat 1g	**2%**
Saturated Fat --g	**--%**
Cholesterol --mg	**--%**
Sodium 0mg	**0%**
Total Carbohydrate 1g	**0%**
Dietary Fiber 0g	**0%**
Sugars --g	
Protein 1g	

Vitamin A 0%	•	Vitamin C 0%
Calcium 0%	•	Iron 2%

This tastes just like the kind you get in Chinese restaurants.

2 teaspoons ground mustard
1 tablespoon water

Mix 2 teaspoons ground mustard with 1 tablespoon water. Just multiply the mixture by 2, 4, or more for more sauce.

ITALIAN TOMATO SAUCE

**YIELD: 4 1/2 CUPS
1/4 CUP = 1 SERVING**

Nutrition Facts

Amount Per Serving

Calories 50	Calories from Fat 10

	% Daily Value*
Total Fat 1g	1%
Saturated Fat 0g	0%
Cholesterol 0mg	0%
Sodium 130mg	5%
Total Carbohydrate 9g	3%
Dietary Fiber 2g	8%
Sugars 3g	
Protein 2g	

Vitamin A 60%	•	Vitamin C 45%
Calcium 2%	•	Iron 6%

This recipe is made basically from scratch.

1 large onion, coarsely chopped
1 large green pepper, coarsely chopped
1 medium carrot, finely diced
1 rib celery with leaves, finely diced
7 large mushrooms, sliced
2 cups water
1/2 cup Red Rosé wine
1/2 cup Roast Beef Gravy I or II (pages 48 and 50)
1/2 cup salt-free tomato paste
1 tablespoon apple juice concentrate
1 teaspoon oregano
2 teaspoons dried parsley or 1/2 cup chopped fresh parsley
1/2 teaspoon red pepper flakes
1/2 teaspoon cumin
1/2 teaspoon garlic powder or 5 cloves, chopped
1 1/2 teaspoons basil

Place all of the vegetables in a nonstick 5-quart pot and turn the heat on high. Sauté until the onions look brown around the edges and a little transparent. Add the water and stir. Turn down the heat to low, then add the wine, beef gravy, tomato paste, and juice concentrate. Then add oregano, parsley, red pepper flakes, and cumin. Cover and cook on low heat for 2 hours. Check and stir frequently. Add more water if mixture becomes too thick. During the last 10 minutes of cooking, add the garlic powder and basil. If you use fresh garlic, add it 20 minutes before the sauce is done.

PIQUANTE SAUCE

1 medium onion
1 fresh jalapeño pepper
1 can (4 ounces) roasted, peeled, mild green chili peppers, rinsed and chopped by hand
2 cans (15 ounces each) salt-free tomato sauce
1/2 teaspoon salt-free chili powder
2/3 cup apple cider vinegar
2 tablespoons apple juice concentrate
1/8 teaspoon garlic powder
1/3 cup water

Mince the onion and jalapeño pepper in a food processor or very finely by hand. In a 2-quart stockpot, combine the onion, jalapeño pepper, green chili peppers, tomato sauce, chili powder, vinegar, juice concentrate, and garlic powder. Rinse the food processor with the water and add the water to the pot. Bring to a boil, cover, and simmer for 10 minutes. Remove the cover and simmer for 35 to 40 minutes, stirring occasionally.

Cool and serve with Toasted Tortilla Chips, or commercial baked tortilla chips. Compare the nutritional values of different brands. You can also use this as a sauce to spice up almost any dish. This recipe can be doubled, tripled, or quadrupled and frozen in small containers.

SWEET AND SOUR SAUCE

4 teaspoons sugar-free pear and apple spread
1 1/2 teaspoons apple cider vinegar
1 teaspoon water

Mix all the ingredients together until smooth, and serve.

HOMEMADE SKIM MILK YOGURT

YIELD: 1 QUART
1/2 CUP = 1 SERVING

Nutrition Facts

Amount Per Serving

Calories 50	Calories from Fat 0

	% Daily Value*
Total Fat 0g	0%
Saturated Fat 0g	0%
Cholesterol 5mg	1%
Sodium 85mg	3%
Total Carbohydrate 7g	2%
Dietary Fiber 0g	0%
Sugars 7g	
Protein 5g	

Vitamin A 6%	•	Vitamin C 2%
Calcium 20%	•	Iron 0%

I cannot tell you the feeling of power I experienced the first time I made yogurt. There it was, after 6 hours, quivering in little cups. And it wasn't so difficult or fussy as I thought it would be. The first time I tried to make it, I got everything together and already had it warming up when I discovered I had added only half the culture. I was frantic but I didn't do anything, and it still came out!

To make your first batch you will need to buy a dry yogurt culture from your health food store. The next batch can be made with 3 tablespoons of the yogurt from your first batch. (You can use the yogurt from the grocery store to do this if it contains live cultures.) After you have made six or seven batches, use a new package of the dry yogurt culture because the yogurt will become more tart with each batch.

1 quart skim milk
1 teaspoon plain gelatin
3 tablespoons hot water
3 tablespoons instant, nonfat, dry milk powder
1 package of dry yogurt culture, or 3 tablespoons of your most recent batch of yogurt or live-cultured commercial yogurt

In a saucepan that has been rinsed in very cold water, scald the milk by placing over high heat until tiny bubbles begin to form around the edges of the pan and the temperature of the milk is 180 degrees F.; or you can scald the milk in a microwave safe glass container in the microwave oven on high 15 to 20 seconds.

In a separate bowl, mix the gelatin with the hot water. Remove the milk from the heat and stir in the nonfat dry milk and gelatin. When it cools to between 90 and 120 degrees F., stir in the culture, or 3 tablespoons of previously made yogurt. Pour the mixture into a blender or food processor and blend thoroughly. Pour into 1 cup crocks, small jars or even coffee cups.

You now have one of three choices; you have to incubate the yogurt, which means keeping it between 105 degrees F. and 115 degrees F.

Method 1: First, heat up a 5-quart slow cooker on low setting for 10 minutes, then turn it off. Take a pie pan that will fit and place it upside down in the bottom of the cooker. Cover the cups or jars with aluminum foil and place them in the cooker. Replace the cover on and let the yogurt sit for 45 minutes. Turn the cooker on low for 10 minutes and then turn it off. Keep doing this for 5 or 6 hours, letting the yogurt sit for 45 minutes between heatings.

Method 2: Pour the yogurt mixture in a bowl or in small crocks or cups and cover. Place in a gas oven with only the pilot lit. Let sit for 5 or 6 hours.

Method 3: Pour the yogurt mixture into crocks or cups and place in an electric yogurt maker. Follow manufacturer's instructions.

Store your homemade yogurt in the refrigerator in airtight containers.

BAKED BANANA

In addition to using a baked banana for a treat by itself, I use it to sweeten my recipes, just like I used to use sugar. When a banana is baked it becomes very soft, so I beat it with a fork or a whisk in its baking liquid and add it to whatever I'm making. Sometimes it takes the place of salt and the taste and supplies the texture of fat as well. The secret is to always use very ripe bananas.

1/2 very ripe banana, peeled
1 teaspoon water

Microwave Directions: Place the banana in a container with high sides. Add the water. Cover and bake on high for 1 minute 30 seconds to 1 minute 50 seconds, until the banana looks collapsed.

Conventional Oven Directions: Place the banana in a small baking dish. Add 1 teaspoon of water and cover. Set the temperature at 400 degrees F. and bake for 20 minutes.

MOCK KITCHEN BOUQUET

Nutrition Facts

Amount Per Serving	
Calories 35	Calories from Fat 0

	% Daily Value*
Total Fat 0g	**0%**
Saturated Fat 0g	**0%**
Cholesterol 0mg	**0%**
Sodium 5mg	**0%**
Total Carbohydrate 9g	**3%**
Dietary Fiber 0g	**0%**
Sugars 7g	
Protein 0g	

Vitamin A 0%	•	Vitamin C 2%
Calcium 0%	•	Iron 2%

When Creole cooks used open fireplaces or hearths in kitchens that were separate from the plantation houses, they often thrust a whole onion, skin and all, into the burning coals. When it began to brown, they would pull it out, dust off the ashes, and toss it into a soup or gravy to give it a rich brown color.

If you are worried about the caramel sugar in store-bought Kitchen Bouquet when you want to color a sauce or gravy, you can use this old-fashioned method.

Peel of 4 yellow onions
Water
1/4 teaspoon garlic powder
1/2 teaspoon onion powder
1 tablespoon apple juice concentrate

Peel the onions, wash the peels if they look dirty, and dry them. Place them on a cookie sheet or a sheet of aluminum foil with the edges folded up. Place them on the bottom rack of your oven and turn it to 500 degrees F. Let the onion peels bake for about 10 minutes. Check them to see if any of them have turned almost black, which means they are done. If they have not darkened, continue to bake for another 5 minutes but check them every 2 minutes.

Place the browned onion peels in a small saucepan. Cover with water over high heat, and boil until the liquid has reduced by about three fourths. Strain the remaining liquid into a cup or bowl, discard the peels, and add the garlic powder, onion powder, and juice concentrate.

When you use this in any recipe, be sure to add 3 tablespoons of concentrated apple juice to counter the bitter taste.

CREAMY HORSERADISH

Nutrition Facts

Amount Per Serving

Calories 5	Calories from Fat 0

	% Daily Value²
Total Fat 0g	**0%**
Saturated Fat 0g	**0%**
Cholesterol 0mg	**0%**
Sodium 0mg	**0%**
Total Carbohydrate 2g	**1%**
Dietary Fiber 0g	**0%**
Sugars 1g	
Protein 0g	

Vitamin A 0%	•	Vitamin C 15%
Calcium 0%	•	Iron 0%

Horseradish root, of course, may not come in exactly 2 1/4-ounce pieces, so if the roots you find in the produce section of the grocery store are a little heavier or lighter, add more or less of the other ingredients, as needed. The roots themselves look rather formidable—dried up and unattractive. When you get up the courage to use them you'll find that they aren't much harder to peel than a potato.

2 1/4 ounces fresh horseradish root
2 tablespoons apple cider vinegar
1/4 cup water
2 teaspoons apple juice concentrate

Wash and peel the roots, then wash them again. Place them in a blender or a food processor. Add the vinegar, water, and juice concentrate and process until creamy. You may have to scrape down the sides a few times, and process again. When you scrape the contents down, stand back—don't lean over the container! The fumes will not only clear your sinuses, they might put them out of commission. This is powerful stuff.

Store in an airtight jar. When serving, keep the jar covered as much as possible to retain the flavor. You can freeze it in small amounts.

HORSERADISH SAUCE

YIELD: 1/2 CUP
1 TBSP. = 1 SERVING

Nutrition Facts

Amount Per Serving

Calories 15	Calories from Fat 5

	% Daily Value*
Total Fat 0.5g	**1%**
Saturated Fat 0g	**0%**
Cholesterol 5mg	**1%**
Sodium 55mg	**2%**
Total Carbohydrate 1g	**0%**
Dietary Fiber 0g	**0%**
Sugars 0g	
Protein 2g	

Vitamin A 2%	•	Vitamin C 0%
Calcium 2%	•	Iron 0%

My husband thinks this stuff is mild, but he eats jalapeño peppers plain and doesn't drink water afterward, so be warned! But if you think it's too mild, increase the amount of Creamy Horseradish.

1/2 cup nonfat cottage cheese
2 tablespoons Creamy Horseradish (page 59)
1/8 teaspoon dried dillweed (optional)

Combine the cottage cheese and Creamy Horseradish in a blender until very smooth. Scoop out a tiny bit to taste. Then scoop out a little more and sprinkle it with a little dillweed and taste it, to see if you like the dill. If you do, add it and blend again. I like the dill, but it's a very personal spice. It's a good idea to try it sparingly at first.

This is great with Easy Corned Beef or cold chicken; it is also a super dip for raw vegetables.

Variation: EASY HORSERADISH SAUCE

Combine 1/4 cup Kraft fat-free mayonnaise dressing, 2 tablespoons Creamy Horseradish, and 1/8 teaspoon dried dillweed (optional) in a bowl and mix thoroughly.

CREOLE CREAM CHEESE

When I was a child I ate what is called Creole Cream Cheese, as distinguished from the thicker, Philadelphia style cream cheese. Of course I had to quit eating it because it contained cream. However, I once read that if you put yogurt in a colander lined with cheesecloth and let it drip, it made some kind of cheese. When I tried to make it, it turned out to be Creole Cream Cheese! Use a little fructose to sweeten it. It's also a dead ringer for sour cream—perfect on a baked potato. It doesn't hold its shape as well as sour cream, so it is not as good for mixing with things to make dips, but by itself it makes a delicious dip for fresh vegetables or toasted, homemade tortilla chips, or spread thickly on whole wheat bread.

1 quart Skim Milk Yogurt (page 56)

Line a colander with a piece of cheesecloth and place it over a bowl. Add the yogurt and cover loosely, to keep things from falling in it. Refrigerate overnight. The next day the whey will have dripped out and there is Creole Cream Cheese.

To make 1/2 cup of cheese for baked potatoes, use a paper coffee filter to line an orange juice strainer with 1 cup of yogurt in it, and then set it in the refrigerator to drip. You can use the whey as part of the water the next time you make bread.

FRUIT PATRICIAN

Nutrition Facts

Amount Per Serving	
Calories 130	Calories from Fat 0

	% Daily Value*
Total Fat 0g	**0**%
Saturated Fat 0g	**0**%
Cholesterol 0mg	**0**%
Sodium 10mg	**0**%
Total Carbohydrate 31g	**10**%
Dietary Fiber 2g	**8**%
Sugars 28g	
Protein 1g	

Vitamin A 10%	•	Vitamin C 15%
Calcium 2%	•	Iron 2%

Delicious and refreshing by itself, or served cold over Cantaloupe Ice Cream, hot over Whole Wheat Pancakes, and with Brown or Brown and Wild Rice.

You can usually find 16-ounce bags of mixed frozen fruit in the frozen food section of your grocery store. You should also be able to find both kinds of melons mixed in a bag, too, but if you can't, just buy packages of the separate fruits and use equal parts of each to make up about 4 cups in all.

1 package (16 ounces) of mixed frozen fruit
1 cup frozen honeydew and cantaloupe, mixed
1 1/3 cup water
1/2 cup apple juice concentrate
2 tablespoons cornstarch

Defrost the fruit to room temperature. Place the water and apple juice concentrate into a 1 1/2 quart saucepan and then add all the fruit except the strawberries. Set the saucepan over high heat and bring to a boil. Sprinkle 1 tablespoon of the cornstarch over the mixture, first by patting it in with the back of the spoon, then blending thoroughly. Sprinkle the remaining table-spoons of cornstarch over the mixture using the same method. Keep stirring until the mixture becomes clear and begins to thicken. If you want it thicker, just add another tablespoon of cornstarch. If you want it sweeter, add more apple juice concentrate.

BLUEBERRY JELLY

Nutrition Facts

Amount Per Serving	
Calories 25	Calories from Fat 0
	% Daily Value*
Total Fat 0g	**0%**
Saturated Fat 0g	**0%**
Cholesterol 0mg	**0%**
Sodium 5mg	**0%**
Total Carbohydrate 7g	**2%**
Dietary Fiber 0g	**0%**
Sugars 5g	
Protein 0g	
Vitamin A 0% • Vitamin C 6%	
Calcium 0% • Iron 0%	

1/4 cup water
1/2 cup apple juice concentrate
5 tablespoons grape juice concentrate
1 tablespoon apple pectin powder
1 cup fresh or frozen blueberries

Combine the water and juice concentrates in a blender. Add the pectin and mix it in slightly with a spoon. Blend on high setting for about 2 minutes, then pour the mixture into a small saucepan. Warm the mixture over high heat, stirring constantly. When it begins to foam and steam, boil for 3 minutes, stirring constantly and, if necessary, lifting the pot off the heat slightly to keep it from boiling over. Remove the pan from the heat and add the blueberries. Return the pan to high heat and stir constantly for 1 minute, again, lifting the pan if it starts to boil over. Pour the mixture into a container, cover, and allow it to cool for about 2 hours, then refrigerate.

CHERRY PRESERVES

Nutrition Facts

Amount Per Serving

Calories 25	Calories from Fat 0

	% Daily Value*
Total Fat 0g	**0%**
Saturated Fat 0g	**0%**
Cholesterol 0mg	**0%**
Sodium 5mg	**0%**
Total Carbohydrate 6g	**2%**
Dietary Fiber 0g	**0%**
Sugars 4g	
Protein 0g	

Vitamin A 2%	•	Vitamin C 6%
Calcium 0%	•	Iron 2%

1 can (16 ounces) pitted, tart, unsweetened, red cherries
1/4 cup water
1/2 cup grape juice concentrate
5 tablespoons apple juice concentrate
1 tablespoon apple pectin powder

Drain the cherries, discarding the canning liquid, and set aside.

Combine the water and juice concentrate in a blender. Add the pectin and mix it in slightly with a spoon. Blend on high setting for about 2 minutes, then pour the mixture into a small saucepan. Warm the mixture over high heat, stirring constantly. When the mixture begins to foam and steam, boil it for 3 minutes, stirring constantly and, if necessary, lifting the pot off the heat to maintain a steady rolling boil and prevent it from boiling over. Remove the pan from the heat and add the cherries. Return the pan to high heat and stir constantly for 1 1/2 minutes, again, lifting the pan if it starts to boil over. Pour the mixture into a container, cover, and set aside for about 2 hours, then refrigerate.

PINEAPPLE PRESERVES

Nutrition Facts

Amount Per Serving	
Calories 25	Calories from Fat 0

	% Daily Value*
Total Fat 0g	**0%**
Saturated Fat 0g	**0%**
Cholesterol 0mg	**0%**
Sodium 0mg	**0%**
Total Carbohydrate 6g	**2%**
Dietary Fiber 0g	**0%**
Sugars 5g	
Protein 0g	

Vitamin A 0%	•	Vitamin C 8%
Calcium 0%	•	Iron 0%

1 can (20 ounces) crushed, unsweetened pineapple
1/4 cup water
1/2 cup plus 5 tablespoons pineapple juice concentrate
1 tablespoon apple pectin powder

Drain the pineapple in a colander for about 20 minutes and press with a spoon to squeeze out any remaining juice. Save the juice for another use.

Combine the water and pineapple juice concentrate in a blender. Add the pectin and mix it in slightly with a spoon. Turn the blender on high for about 2 minutes. Pour the mixture into a small saucepan and stir constantly over high heat. When the mixture begins to foam and steam, boil for 3 minutes, stirring constantly and lifting the pot off the heat slightly to keep the pot from boiling over and the bottom of the pan from scorching, as necessary. Remove the pan from the heat and add the pineapple. Return the pan to high heat and stir constantly for 1 1/2 minutes, holding the pan off the burner almost the whole time. Pour the mixture into a covered container. Cool for about 2 hours; then store in the refrigerator.

Note: You can buy apple pectin powder at your supermarket's canning section.

MINT JELLY

**YIELD: 3/4 CUP
1 TBSP. = 1 SERVING**

Nutrition Facts

Amount Per Serving	
Calories 50	Calories from Fat 0
	% Daily Value*
Total Fat 0g	**0%**
Saturated Fat 0g	**0%**
Cholesterol 0mg	**0%**
Sodium 15mg	**1%**
Total Carbohydrate 12g	**4%**
Dietary Fiber less than 1 gram	**2%**
Sugars 8g	
Protein 0g	
Vitamin A 0% • Vitamin C 4%	
Calcium 2% • Iron 6%	

1/4 cup water
1/2 cup plus 5 tablespoons apple juice concentrate
1 tablespoon orange juice concentrate
2 tablespoons apple pectin powder
1 tablespoon dried mint leaves

Combine the water and juice concentrates in a blender. Add the pectin and mix it in slightly. Blend on high setting for about 2 minutes. Pour the mixture into a small saucepan, add the mint leaves, and cook over high heat, stirring constantly. When the mixture begins to foam and steam, boil for 3 minutes, stirring constantly and lifting the pot off the heat slightly to keep the pot from boiling over. Pour into a container, cover, and let it cool for about 2 hours; then refrigerate.

To serve, cut it into chunks or heat it to soften it and make it more like a sauce.

To make orange jelly, you can omit the mint leaves. This is good served heated over chicken.

CHAPTER 3

Breakfast Foods, Muffins, and Breads

How about a slice of Banana Bread with Cherry Jelly, and perhaps fat-free cream cheese for breakfast? Now, who would have thought you could enjoy goodies like these on a salt-free, sugar-free, fat-free diet?

You can make big batches of muffins, pancakes, and breads, and freeze them so you don't have to be up early every morning rummaging around in the kitchen when you should be getting ready for work or school, or whatever else you may have to do. And you will be amazed at how inventive you can be when making muffins by adding different fruits.

If you long for a piece of toast in the morning you can use an all-fruit spread without added sugar, but when you are on this type of diet, you won't be eating much toast. Mainly you will eat cereals such as shredded wheat, hot cracked wheat, and even hot oatmeal with milk. Southerners like grits, which are nice with a tablespoon or two of roast beef gravy over them.

To cook these cereals, just read the directions and leave out any salt or butter. For sweetness add fruit to the cereal. Fresh fruit is preferred to juice because of its fiber content and herbal tea is preferable to black tea or coffee.

You will definitely lose weight faster if you stick to the cereal, milk, fruit, herb tea combination.

Once or twice a week you might vary your diet with one of the recipes in this chapter, but don't go overboard. One pancake please, or two pieces of French toast. Don't forget that the Fruit Patrician (page 62) has to be considered a fruit serving, depending how much you use.

MICROWAVE OATMEAL

Rolled oats are plain oatmeal, in other words, oatmeal that is not instant, not 1-minute, or any kind of precooked, or quick oats. You should be able to get them in your grocery store, but of course when you look at the oatmeal section, the variety is staggering. There are all kinds of flavored oats, and variously timed oats in every kind of box imaginable. The rolled oats probably won't be labeled as such. Quaker, for instance, calls them "Old Fashioned Quaker Oats." It may be simpler to buy oatmeal at a health food store.

1/3 cup rolled oats
1/8 teaspoon cinnamon
1/4 large Baked Banana (page 57)
2 tablespoons apple juice concentrate
Water
1/4 cup skim milk

In a cereal bowl, combine the oatmeal and cinnamon.

In a 1-cup measure, beat the banana in its baking liquid with a fork until it is liquefied. Add the juice concentrate to the banana mixture and then add enough water to make 2/3 cup. Stir this mixture into the oatmeal. Place uncovered in the microwave and cook on high setting, uncovered, for 2 minutes. Stir and cook for 1 minute. Stir again, cover, and let sit 2 minutes. While cereal is sitting, heat the milk on high setting in the microwave for 40 seconds. Pour the milk over the oatmeal.

OMELET CHARLYN

Nutrition Facts

Amount Per Serving

Calories 50	Calories from Fat 0

	% Daily Value*
Total Fat 0g	0%
Saturated Fat 0g	0%
Cholesterol 0mg	0%
Sodium 420mg	17%
Total Carbohydrate 4g	1%
Dietary Fiber less than 1 gram	4%
Sugars 2g	
Protein 8g	

Vitamin A 4%	•	Vitamin C 10%
Calcium 2%	•	Iron 4%

My very good friend Charlyn, who shares my enthusiasm for healthy cooking, gave me the idea for this recipe, so I named it after her.

2 jumbo egg whites
1 teaspoon skim milk
1/4 cup chopped scallions
1/4 cup chopped green pepper
1/4 cup chopped tomato
1/4 cup chopped mushrooms
1 teaspoon low-sodium soy sauce (optional)
Cayenne pepper

In a mixing bowl, beat the egg whites with the milk and set aside.

Spray a nonstick pan with butter-flavored nonstick spray. Place the vegetables in the pan and sauté over high heat, stirring constantly. After 1 or 2 minutes, add the soy sauce and continue stirring. When the vegetables are fairly soft and the onions look somewhat transparent, sprinkle with a little cayenne pepper, lower the heat to medium, and stir.

Pour the beaten egg whites over the vegetables. When the eggs have partially set, push all the ingredients towards the center of the pan and continue to cook over medium heat. Turn over and cook until eggs are done. Sprinkle with more cayenne pepper, if desired. Serve with toast on the side.

FRENCH TOAST

If you decide to use commercial bread, use only 2 slices since these will be about twice the size of slices of homemade bread in this book.

2 jumbo egg whites
1/2 cup skim milk
4 slices whole wheat bread or oat bran bread

In a small bowl, whisk together the egg whites and milk until thoroughly combined. Place 1 slice of bread in the mixture at a time and pierce with a fork to distribute the liquid evenly through the bread. Turn over and pierce the other side.

Spray a nonstick frying pan with butter-flavored nonstick spray. Preheat the pan over medium heat for a few minutes and "fry" each slice of toast, turning once when the first side is brown. It is finished when both sides are brown.

HASH BROWN POTATOES

2 large potatoes
1 large white onion, coarsely chopped
Cayenne pepper

Spray a nonstick pan with butter-flavored nonstick spray.

Peel potatoes, then grate with the grater blade of a food processor. Combine with the onion and spread evenly in a nonstick frying pan. Lightly sprinkle the top with cayenne pepper. Place over medium heat. Do not stir or cover. When the potatoes are brown on the bottom (check by carefully lifting a corner with a spatula), turn the whole thing over and cook the other side. If you can't turn them over whole, divide into 4 or 5 sections and turn each section over separately. Sprinkle with more pepper and cook until brown. Serve immediately.

HUEVOS CON PAPAS (EGGS AND POTATOES)

YIELD: 8 SERVINGS

Nutrition Facts

Amount Per Serving

Calories 100	Calories from Fat 0

	% Daily Value*
Total Fat 0g	**0%**
Saturated Fat 0g	**0%**
Cholesterol 0mg	**0%**
Sodium 140mg	**6%**
Total Carbohydrate 18g	**6%**
Dietary Fiber 2g	**9%**
Sugars 4g	
Protein 7g	

Vitamin A 10%	•	Vitamin C 60%
Calcium 2%	•	Iron 6%

This colorful dish is perfect to serve at a buffet brunch. The turmeric turns the egg whites a natural egg-yellow color. Fresh tomato slices drizzled with apple cider vinegar on the side are a must to give this dish just the right tanginess, or serve it with Piquante Sauce for some fire on the tongue.

1/2 cup Chicken Stock (page 45)
4 cups sliced potatoes (1/4-inch thick)
1 1/2 cups chopped onion
1/2 medium green pepper, chopped
12 jumbo egg whites
3 tablespoons grated sapsago cheese
1/4 teaspoon turmeric
1/8 teaspoon dried basil
1/4 teaspoon dried oregano
1/2 teaspoon dried parsley
1/8 teaspoon cayenne pepper
1/2 teaspoon medium red hot sauce
1 jar (4 ounces) pimento pieces

In a 5-quart stockpot, combine the chicken stock, potatoes, onion, and green pepper. Cover and bring to a boil; then simmer over very low heat for about 50 minutes until the potatoes are soft. There's no need to stir. Drain the liquid, and reserve for soup.

In a 2-quart mixing bowl, combine egg whites, 2 tablespoons of the sapsago cheese, and all of the turmeric, basil, oregano, parsley, cayenne, and red hot sauce. Beat with an electric mixer or wire whisk until the eggs begin to froth. Add the cooked vegetables to the egg mixture and combine thoroughly.

Preheat oven to 350 degrees F.

Spray a 3-quart baking dish with butter-flavored nonstick spray and pour the egg mixture into it. Chop the pimento pieces in a small bowl to keep from losing their juice, and then pour them with their juice over the top of the egg mixture. Mix them in slightly—you want them to stay near the top because the dish looks so pretty when it comes out of the oven. Bake uncovered, on the middle rack of the oven for 40 minutes, or until the top browns.

WHOLE WHEAT BREAD

1/4 cup white grape juice concentrate
1 cup warm water
1 package or 1 tablespoon of dry baker's yeast
4 cups whole wheat flour

In a mixing bowl thoroughly combine the juice concentrate and warm water. The mixture should feel just warm to your finger. Add the yeast and stir until it dissolves. Set in a warm place, such as the top of your water heater, freezer, or refrigerator for 5 or 10 minutes until froth has formed on top, which means the yeast mixture is ready.

In your food processor fitted with the plastic dough blade, add the flour. Pour the yeast mixture in all at once and process until the dough forms. If the mixture seems dry and won't form a ball, add up to 1/4 cup water, a little at a time, until the dough picks up all the flour.

When the dough has formed a ball, turn it out onto a clean, dry, lightly floured work surface, and knead it by hand until it is elastic and smooth and bounces back when you poke it with your finger. This should take about 10 minutes.

Place the dough in a bowl, cover the surface with plastic wrap, and set it in a warm place to rise until it has doubled in bulk or until it is twice the size it was when you started. This will take about 1 1/2 hours. Remove the dough from the bowl and place it on your work surface. Punch the dough down until all the air has escaped and it is flat.

Spray two 9 x 5 x 2 1/2-inch bread pans with butter-flavored nonstick spray. Even nonstick bread pans must be sprayed.

Divide the bread dough in half, shape into loaves roughly the length of your pans, and place a loaf in each pan. Take two pieces of plastic wrap and spray each with the nonstick spray. Place them over the bread dough spray-side down, then set them in a warm place. Check them in a half hour to see if the dough has risen to the tops of the pans. If not, check again every 15 minutes or so until they rise to just that height.

Preheat oven to 450 degrees F.

Remove the plastic carefully and bake loaves for about 20 minutes on the middle rack of the oven. When the tops are nice and brown, they are done and can be turned out on a cooling rack. The extra loaf can be frozen once it has cooled completely.

DOCTOR VANSELOW'S RYE BREAD

YIELD: 32 SLICES

Nutrition Facts

Amount Per Serving

Calories 80	Calories from Fat 0

% Daily Value*

Total Fat 0g	0%
Saturated Fat 0g	0%
Cholesterol 0mg	0%
Sodium 0mg	0%
Total Carbohydrate 16g	5%
Dietary Fiber 2g	6%
Sugars 2g	
Protein 2g	

Vitamin A 0%	•	Vitamin C 0%
Calcium 0%	•	Iron 4%

When I was a judge for the New Orleans Dietetic Association's 3rd Annual Culinary Heart's Cookoff in New Orleans, I was seated beside fellow judge Dr. Neal A. Vanselow, Chancellor of Tulane University Medical School, and his wife, Mary. Dr. Vanselow told me that he loved to bake yeasted breads, rye being one of his favorites, and that the secret to achieving a good textured rye bread is to use medium-ground rye flour. Fine-ground flour makes the bread too heavy. Mary was kind enough to send me her husband's recipe which I have adapted slightly to meet the salt-free, sugar-free, fat-free guidelines.

Look for medium-ground rye flour at health food stores, and if you can't find it, call your local bread bakeries—they might have it to sell or will be able to tell you where you can order it.

2 bottles (12 ounces each) of alcoholic or nonalcoholic beer
1/4 cup apple juice concentrate
2 envelopes or 2 tablespoons dry baker's yeast
3 1/8 to 3 1/4 cups unbleached bromated bread flour, divided
1 tablespoon caraway seeds
2 cups medium-ground rye flour

In a medium saucepan, bring the beer to a boil, then lower the heat and simmer for 5 minutes. Pour 2 cups of the beer into a large mixing bowl and discard the rest. Add the apple juice concentrate. Cool the mixture until it is just warm, but not hot to the touch. Sprinkle the yeast over the mixture and whisk until it is dissolved. Set the bowl in a warm place for about 5 minutes, or until the mixture looks foamy.

Using a wire whisk or fork, beat in 2 cups of the bread flour until batter is smooth. Add caraway seeds and combine, then add the rye flour, and mix thoroughly. Gradually work in the remaining bread flour, adding just enough to form a sticky but workable dough.

When the dough forms a ball, knead briefly in the bowl. Turn the dough out onto a lightly floured surface and knead for about 3 minutes, dusting with bread flour if it gets sticky. It's ready when you poke the dough with your finger and it bounces back.

Return the dough to the mixing bowl. Spray a piece of plastic wrap with a nonstick spray and place it loosely, spray-side down, over the dough. Set the dough in a warm place and leave it for about 1 hour, or until it has doubled in volume.

Preheat the oven to 375 degrees F.

Turn the dough out onto a lightly floured surface and knead for about 1 minute. Divide the dough in half and form 2 long, narrow loaves. Spray either nonstick French bread pans or nonstick baking sheets with nonstick spray. Place the loaves in the French bread pans or diagonally on the baking sheets. Spray plastic wrap with nonstick spray and place loosely, spray-side down, over the loaves. Set the loaves in a warm place for about 45 minutes until they are doubled in volume. Remove the plastic wrap.

Place the pans on the middle and top racks of the oven and bake for 25 to 35 minutes. The loaves are done when they are lightly brown, both top and bottom, and sound hollow when tapped. Cool on wire racks. Slice with an electric knife or a serrated bread knife.

OAT BRAN BREAD

1/4 cup apple juice concentrate
1 cup warm water
1 package or 1 tablespoon of dry baker's yeast
3 1/2 cups white unbleached, bromated flour
1/2 cup oat bran cereal

In a mixing bowl, combine the juice concentrate and warm water. (The mixture should feel just warm to your finger.) Add the yeast and stir until it dissolves. Set in a warm place, such as the top of your water heater, freezer, or refrigerator for between 5 and 10 minutes, or until froth has formed on top, which means the yeast mixture is ready.

In a food processor fitted with the plastic dough blade, first add the flour and oat bran cereal. Then pour the yeast mixture in all at once and process until the dough forms. If the mixture seems dry and won't form a ball, add up to 1/4 cup water, a little at a time, until the mixture is moist enough to form a ball. You can mix your dough in a large bowl, and if necessary, add up to 1/4 cup warm water until the dough picks up all the flour and oat bran. If your processor is small, you may have to divide the ingredients in half and process the dough in batches.

When the dough has formed into a ball, turn it out onto a clean, dry, lightly floured surface and knead until it is elastic and smooth and bounces back when you poke it with your finger. This should take about 10 minutes.

Place the dough in a bowl and set it in a warm place to rise until it has doubled in bulk or is twice the size it was when you started. This will take about 1 1/2 hours. Place the dough on your work surface. Punch the dough down until all the air has escaped.

Spray two 9 x 5 x 2 1/2-inch bread pans with butter-flavored nonstick spray. Even nonstick bread pans must be sprayed. Divide the bread dough in half, shape into loaves roughly the length of your pans, and place a loaf in each pan. Take two pieces of plastic wrap and spray each with the nonstick spray. Place them over the bread dough spray-side down, then set them in a warm place to rise again. Check them in a half hour to see if the dough has risen to the tops of the pans. If not, check again every 15 minutes or so until they have risen to just that height.

Preheat oven to 450 degrees F.

Remove the plastic carefully and bake loaves for about 20 minutes on the middle rack of the oven. When the tops are nice and brown, they are done and can be turned out on a cooling rack. The extra loaf can be frozen once it has cooled completely.

FRENCH ROLLS

These are so good they don't need any butter or jam.

1/4 cup apple juice concentrate
1 cup warm water
1 package or tablespoon of dry baker's yeast
2 cups white unbleached flour
2 cups whole wheat flour

In a mixing bowl, combine the juice concentrate and warm water. The mixture should feel just warm to your finger. Add the yeast and stir until it is dissolved. Set in a warm place for 5–10 minutes, or until froth forms on top. Then the yeast mixture is ready.

Place the flour in a food processor fitted with a plastic dough blade. If your processor is small, you may have to divide the ingredients in half and process the dough in batches. Add the yeast mixture all at once and process until the dough forms. If the mixture seems dry and won't form a ball, add up to 1/4 cup water, a little at a time, until the mixture forms a ball. If you don't have a food processor, you can mix your dough in a bowl. If, after you mix it, the dough does not pick up all the flour, add up to 1/4 cup warm water. Turn the dough out onto a clean, dry, lightly floured work surface and knead by hand until it is elastic and smooth. This should take about 10 minutes. The dough should bounce back when you poke it with your finger.

Set the dough, covered, in a warm place to rise until it doubles in bulk. This will take about 1 1/2 hours. When the dough is twice the size as when you started, turn it back out onto your work surface. Punch it down until all the air has escaped and the dough is flat.

Use 2 nonstick cookie sheets or spray regular cookie sheets with a nonstick spray. Break off pieces of the dough about the size of golf balls and roll each one between your palms to form balls. Place them about 2 inches apart on the cookie sheets and set the cookie sheets, uncovered, in a warm spot for about 20 minutes. Preheat oven to 450 degrees F. When the dough balls are about twice their original size bake them for about 15 minutes. Check after 10 minutes. When the rolls look brown, they are done. Loosen them with a spatula if any have stuck. Let them cool on the pans.

Freeze in sealed plastic bags.

ONION ROLLS

YIELD: 17 ROLLS

Nutrition Facts

Amount Per Serving

Calories 110	Calories from Fat 0

	% Daily Value*
Total Fat 0g	0%
Saturated Fat 0g	0%
Cholesterol 0mg	0%
Sodium 15mg	1%
Total Carbohydrate 22g	7%
Dietary Fiber less than 1 gram	4%
Sugars 2g	
Protein 3g	

Vitamin A 0%	•	Vitamin C 2%
Calcium 0%	•	Iron 10%

These are delicious dunked in roast beef or chicken gravy or as a spicy snack with hot herb tea.

1/4 cup apple juice concentrate
1 1/4 cup warm water
1 package or 1 tablespoon dry baker's yeast
3 1/3 cups unbleached bread flour
1/2 cup oat bran cereal
1 teaspoon medium red hot sauce
1/4 cup dried minced onions
1/4 teaspoon dried red pepper flakes

In a mixing bowl, combine the juice concentrate and water. Add the yeast and stir until it dissolves. Set in a warm place for 5 to 10 minutes, or until the top looks foamy.

In a food processor fitted with a plastic dough blade, combine the flour and oat bran cereal. If your processor is small, you may have to divide the ingredients in half and process the dough in batches. Add the hot sauce to the yeast mixture, then pour that mixture all at once into the food processor, and process until the dough forms. If the mixture seems dry and won't form a ball, add up to 1/4 cup water, a little at a time, until the mixture is moist and forms a ball.

Turn the dough out onto a clean, dry work surface, lightly floured if the dough is sticky. Flatten the dough out and sprinkle it with about 1/3 of the onion and red pepper flakes. Fold the dough, working the onions and pepper into it. Flatten the dough again, and add more onions and pepper. Repeat a few times until all the onions and pepper are folded into the dough.

If you don't have a food processor, you can mix the dough in a large bowl. If the dough does not pick up all the flour and oat bran, add up to 1/4 cup warm water. Turn the dough out onto a clean, dry, work surface, lightly floured if the dough is very sticky. Knead the dough until it begins to feel elastic and smooth, then start adding and working in the onions and peppers. Kneading should take about 10 minutes. The dough should bounce back when you poke it with your finger.

Place the dough in a bowl. Cover the surface with plastic wrap. Set the dough in a warm place to rise until it doubles in bulk, about 1 1/2 hours.

Turn the dough out on your work surface. Punch it down until all the air has escaped and it is flat. Break off pieces of the dough about the size of golf balls and roll between your palms to form balls. Place each dough ball about

2 inches apart on a large nonstick cookie sheet or regular cookie sheet that has been sprayed with nonstick spray. Set the cookie sheet in a warm spot, uncovered, for about 20 minutes, until the rolls have doubled in size.

While the rolls are rising, preheat the oven to 450 degrees F., then bake for 15 minutes, but check after 10 minutes. When the rolls look brown, they are done. Cool on the cookie sheet.

Freeze extras in sealed plastic bags. Defrost at room temperature, or in the microwave on high for about 20 seconds, or place in a preheated 450 degree F.-oven for 4 to 5 minutes.

OAT BRAN MUFFINS

Though it's not the magical cure-all ingredient that experts once thought, oat bran does absorb cholesterol. On the other hand, if you eat a lot of fruits, vegetables, and whole grains you don't need oat bran.

2 1/2 cups oat bran cereal
1 1/4 cups plus 2 tablespoons apple juice concentrate or grape juice concentrate
1 tablespoon low-sodium baking powder
4 jumbo egg whites, beaten
1/2 cup raisins

Preheat oven to 425° F.

Spray miniature muffin pans (found at gourmet kitchen equipment stores) with nonstick spray. In a mixing bowl, thoroughly combine the oat bran, juice concentrate, baking powder, and egg whites. Then fold in the raisins. Pour the batter into the muffin cups, leaving a little room in each cup for the muffins to rise. Bake on the center rack for 15 to 17 minutes, or until golden brown. Check in 10 minutes as these muffins burn easily.

Remove from oven and let the muffins sit in the pans for about 10 minutes, then turn them out on paper towels to cool further. The towels will absorb the oil from the nonstick spray.

Extra muffins can be stored in the freezer in a sealed plastic bag. Remove the muffins one at a time for snacks. Defrost at room temperature or in the microwave for 5 to 10 seconds.

BANANA BRAN MUFFINS

YIELD: 12 MUFFINS

Nutrition Facts

Amount Per Serving

Calories 110	Calories from Fat 5

% Daily Value*

Total Fat 0.5g	**1**%
Saturated Fat 0g	**0**%
Cholesterol 0mg	**0**%
Sodium 240mg	**10**%
Total Carbohydrate 25g	**8**%
Dietary Fiber 2g	**6**%
Sugars 18g	
Protein 2g	

Vitamin A 2%	•	Vitamin C 6%
Calcium 6%	•	Iron 15%

2 1/2 cups oat bran cereal
1 teaspoon baking soda
2 teaspoons low-sodium baking powder
1 1/4 cups plus 2 tablespoons apple juice concentrate
2 jumbo egg whites, slightly beaten
2 medium to large bananas

Preheat the oven to 400 degrees F.

Spray nonstick muffin pans with nonstick spray.

Combine oat bran cereal, baking soda, and baking powder in a large mixing bowl. Add the juice concentrate and egg whites and combine thoroughly. Slice the bananas into 1/4-inch slices and fold into the batter. Spoon into the muffin cups, making sure there are banana slices in each muffin. Bake on the middle rack of the oven for 15 to 20 minutes, until golden brown and not too dark around the edges. Let muffins cool in the pans for 10 minutes, then turn them out onto a wire rack to cool.

Freeze extras in a sealed plastic bag and reheat in microwave for about 1 minute on high setting.

BRAN-CHERRY MUFFINS

Nutrition Facts

Amount Per Serving	
Calories 25	Calories from Fat 0

	% Daily Value*
Total Fat 0g	0%
Saturated Fat 0g	0%
Cholesterol 0mg	0%
Sodium 60mg	2%
Total Carbohydrate 5g	2%
Dietary Fiber 0g	0%
Sugars 3g	
Protein 1g	

Vitamin A 0%	•	Vitamin C 0%
Calcium 2%	•	Iron 6%

These moist and delicious oat bran muffins are made with black cherry, all-fruit preserves that you can buy in most health food stores and many groceries.

2 1/2 cups oat bran cereal
1 tablespoon low-sodium baking powder
4 jumbo egg whites, slightly beaten
1 jar (10 ounces) or 1 cup black cherry all-fruit preserves
6 tablespoons apple juice concentrate

Preheat the oven to 425 degrees F.

Spray 3 nonstick miniature muffin pans with nonstick spray.

In a large bowl, mix the oat bran cereal and baking powder. Add the eggs, preserves, and juice concentrate and combine thoroughly. Fill each muffin cup almost to the top. Bake on middle rack of the oven for 10 to 12 minutes. When the muffins begin to brown around the edges they are done. Turn the muffins out onto wire racks to cool. Refrigerate or freeze in a sealed plastic bag or airtight container.

WHOLE WHEAT RAISIN MUFFINS

Nutrition Facts

Amount Per Serving	
Calories 180	Calories from Fat 5

	% Daily Value*
Total Fat 0.5g	1%
Saturated Fat 0g	0%
Cholesterol 0mg	0%
Sodium 125mg	5%
Total Carbohydrate 40g	13%
Dietary Fiber 3g	11%
Sugars 21g	
Protein 4g	

Vitamin A 0%	•	Vitamin C 2%
Calcium 2%	•	Iron 8%

1 1/2 cups whole wheat flour
1 cup unbleached, bromated flour
1 teaspoon baking soda
2 teaspoons low-sodium baking powder
1 1/4 cups plus 2 tablespoons apple juice concentrate
2 jumbo egg whites, beaten
3/4 cup raisins

Preheat the oven to 400 degrees F.

Spray one muffin pan with nonstick spray. In a mixing bowl, thoroughly combine the flour, baking soda, baking powder, juice concentrate, and eggs. Fold the raisins into the batter. Fill nonstick muffin cups 3/4 full and bake 15 to 20 minutes until brown. Let cool for about 5 minutes and then turn muffins out on a wire rack to finish cooling.

Store in the freezer in an airtight container or sealed plastic bag. Defrost at room temperature or heat them in the microwave for one minute.

PINEAPPLE-BLUEBERRY BRAN MUFFINS

YIELD: 12 MUFFINS

Nutrition Facts

Amount Per Serving

Calories 230	Calories from Fat 0

	% Daily Value*
Total Fat 0g	0%
Saturated Fat 0g	0%
Cholesterol 5mg	2%
Sodium 200mg	8%
Total Carbohydrate 50g	17%
Dietary Fiber 5g	20%
Sugars 30g	
Protein 11g	

Vitamin A 15%	•	Vitamin C 45%
Calcium 10%	•	Iron 10%

The first time I made these, I gave four to my friend Margie to take with to her exercise class to meet our mutual friend Gerry. Margie was supposed to share the muffins with Gerry, but when I asked Gerry later how she liked them, she knew nothing about them. Later Margie 'fessed up. Gerry wasn't at exercise class that day so guess what happened to the muffins?

2 1/2 cups oat bran cereal
1 tablespoon low-sodium baking powder
4 jumbo egg whites, beaten lightly
1 cup pineapple juice concentrate
1 can (20 ounces) crushed unsweetened pineapple, drained
1/2 cup frozen or fresh blueberries

Preheat oven to 425 degrees F.

Spray nonstick muffin pans with a nonstick spray.

In a mixing bowl, combine the oat bran cereal and baking powder. Add the egg whites and pineapple juice concentrate, then add the pineapple and blueberries and combine thoroughly. Spoon the mixture into the cups. Bake on the middle rack of the oven for about 20 minutes, until brown nubbins appear on the tops. If you wait until the muffins are totally brown on top, they will be burned on the bottom. Turn out onto a wire rack to cool.

CRANBERRY BREAD

My friend and neighbor, Peggy Stanford, shared her grandmother's recipe with me which I adjusted to Pritikin-style cooking. Peggy, who is from Pennsylvania, insists she is a Yankee and says Yankees are the only folks who know what to do with cranberries, and I have to agree after tasting this bread! I never would have believed cranberries could taste this good.

1 1/2 cup coarsely chopped fresh or frozen cranberries
1 cup oat bran cereal
1 cup whole wheat flour
1 1/2 teaspoons low-sodium baking powder
1/2 teaspoon baking soda
2 jumbo egg whites, lightly beaten
1/3 cup orange juice concentrate
3/4 cup apple juice concentrate
1 teaspoon grapefruit zest

Preheat oven to 350 degrees F.

Spray a 9 x 5-inch nonstick bread pan with nonstick spray.

In a food processor, chop the cranberries very coarsely, leaving some whole. Set aside.

In a mixing bowl, combine the oat bran cereal, flour, baking powder, and baking soda. Add the eggs, orange juice, apple juice, and grapefruit zest and combine thoroughly. Mix in the cranberries and pack the mixture into the bread pan. Shake the pan from side to side to spread the batter out evenly. Bake for 1 hour. Cool on a wire rack for 10 minutes. Loosen the sides with a rubber spatula and lift the bread a little, then turn the bread out onto a wire rack to finish cooling. It's also delicious hot. Slice with an electric knife or serrated bread knife.

CORNBREAD

YIELD: 8 WEDGES

Nutrition Facts

Amount Per Serving	
Calories 230	Calories from Fat 0

	% Daily Value*
Total Fat 0g	**0%**
Saturated Fat 0g	**0%**
Cholesterol 5mg	**2%**
Sodium 200mg	**8%**
Total Carbohydrate 50g	**17%**
Dietary Fiber 5g	**20%**
Sugars 30g	
Protein 11g	

Vitamin A 15%	•	Vitamin C 45%
Calcium 10%	•	Iron 10%

This is delicious with beans, or any dish containing gravy. It's also very good spread with all-fruit preserves.

2 cups yellow cornmeal
1 tablespoon low-sodium baking powder
1/2 very large Baked Banana (page 57)
Approximately 1/4 cup apple juice concentrate
4 jumbo egg whites, lightly beaten
1 cup water

Preheat oven to 400 degrees F.

Spray a 1 1/2-quart or 2-quart round casserole dish with nonstick, butter-flavored spray.

Combine the cornmeal and baking powder in a mixing bowl. Pour the baked banana and baking juices into a 1-cup measure, then pour in enough apple juice concentrate to make 1/2 cup. Add the egg whites, water, banana, and juice concentrate to the cornmeal mixture and combine thoroughly. Pour batter into the casserole dish. Shift from side to side to spread the batter evenly. Place the casserole on the middle shelf of the oven and bake for 30 to 35 minutes, or until the top is golden brown and a toothpick inserted into the center comes out clean. Serve immediately, directly from the dish in 8 equal wedges. Refrigerate leftovers and rewarm in the microwave (covered) for about 30 seconds on high setting.

BANANA BREAD

Nutrition Facts

Amount Per Serving

Calories 90	Calories from Fat 0

	% Daily Value*
Total Fat 0g	**0**%
Saturated Fat 0g	**0**%
Cholesterol 0mg	**0**%
Sodium 160mg	**7**%
Total Carbohydrate 21g	**7**%
Dietary Fiber 2g	**9**%
Sugars 9g	
Protein 3g	

Vitamin A 0%	•	Vitamin C 4%
Calcium 4%	•	Iron 4%

2 cups whole wheat flour
2 teaspoons low-sodium baking powder
1 teaspoon baking soda
1/2 large Baked Banana (page 57)
Approximately 3/4 cup apple juice concentrate
1 cup mashed, ripe banana (2 medium bananas)
4 jumbo egg whites, beaten until almost foamy

Preheat the oven to 350 degrees F.

Spray an 8 x 4-inch nonstick bread pan with butter-flavored nonstick spray.

Sift the flour into a large bowl, and add the whole wheat kernels that are left behind in the sifter. Add the baking powder and baking soda and combine thoroughly.

Pour the baked banana and baking liquid into a 1-cup measure. Add enough apple juice concentrate to come up to the 1-cup measure mark. Thoroughly combine the baked banana and juice concentrate, then pour the mixture into the bowl with the flour. Add the mashed bananas and the egg whites. First blend with a spoon until ingredients are wet, then beat with an electric mixer for about 2 minutes until the mixture is smooth. Pour into the pan and place in the middle rack of the oven. Bake for 1 hour, or until a toothpick inserted into the center comes out clean. Cool in the pan for 10 minutes, loosen around the edges with a rubber spatula, then turn onto a wire rack to cool completely. For best results slice with an electric knife or a bread knife.

GRANNY'S RAISIN BREAD

Nutrition Facts

Amount Per Serving

Calories 120	Calories from Fat 0

	% Daily Value*
Total Fat 0g	0%
Saturated Fat 0g	0%
Cholesterol 0mg	0%
Sodium 110mg	4%
Total Carbohydrate 28g	9%
Dietary Fiber 1g	4%
Sugars 18g	
Protein 2g	

Vitamin A 0%	•	Vitamin C 2%
Calcium 6%	•	Iron 8%

The Granny Smith apples in this recipe give it an apple pie taste.

1 1/2 cups unbleached bromated white flour
1/4 cup oat bran cereal
1 tablespoon low-sodium baking powder
1/4 teaspoon cinnamon
2 jumbo egg whites
1 1/4 cups apple juice concentrate
1 Granny Smith apple, peeled, cored, and sliced
1 cup raisins

Preheat the oven to 325 degrees F.

Spray an 8 x 4-inch bread pan with a butter-flavored nonstick spray.

In a large mixing bowl, combine the flour, oat bran cereal, baking powder, and cinnamon. Beat in the egg whites and juice, and then add the apple slices. Add the raisins last and combine thoroughly. Pour the batter into the pan and place on the middle rack of the oven. Bake for 1 hour and 20 minutes. Loosen around the edges with a spatula and turn out onto a wire rack to cool. Slice with an electric knife or a serrated bread knife.

CRÊPES

Nutrition Facts

Amount Per Serving

Calories 90	Calories from Fat 0

	% Daily Value*
Total Fat 0g	**0**%
Saturated Fat 0g	**0**%
Cholesterol 0mg	**0**%
Sodium 220mg	**9**%
Total Carbohydrate 17g	**6**%
Dietary Fiber less than 1 gram	**2**%
Sugars 4g	
Protein 5g	

Vitamin A 4%	•	Vitamin C 2%
Calcium 20%	•	Iron 8%

3/4 cup unbleached white flour
1/4 cup oat bran cereal or 1/4 cup unbleached flour
2 teaspoons low-sodium baking powder
1 2/3 cups skim milk
2 jumbo egg whites

In a blender, mix the flour, oat bran, and baking powder. Add the egg whites and skim milk and combine thoroughly.

Pour some cooking oil on a paper towel and rinse it under the faucet. Wring it out and wipe a nonstick frying pan with it before you begin cooking the crêpes, and repeat every third crêpe. Even with the nonstick pan you will probably have to do this but don't worry, the amount of fat is negligible.

Preheat the pan for just a few minutes over high heat. Pour in 1/3 cup of the batter and tilt the pan in all directions to fill the bottom of the pan. When little bubbles form on top of the crêpe, continue to cook for a little longer, then try to lift an edge with a spatula. If it seems like it will stick, continue to cook. Sometimes, when the crêpe is ready to turn over, one edge will curl up a little. When you can lift an edge with a spatula, look underneath. If it looks tan, slide the spatula under the crêpe and grasp the edge with your thumb and forefinger, then turn it over with the help of the spatula. (This is much easier than flipping it in the air and if you wreck the first one, don't despair—it's always the hardest to cook.) If you are an experienced pancake or crêpe maker, leave the heat on high, lowering it if the pan starts to smoke, and turning it back up when the pan starts to cool. But if things seem to be getting ahead of you, turn the heat to medium. It might take you longer, but you won't burn all your crêpes.

Serve crêpes on a hot plate with your favorite filling or topping.

WHOLE WHEAT PANCAKES

**YIELD: 7–8 PANCAKES
1 PANCAKE = 1 SERVING**

Nutrition Facts

Amount Per Serving	
Calories 1290	Calories from Fat 60

	% Daily Value*
Total Fat 7g	10%
Saturated Fat 2g	10%
Cholesterol 10mg	4%
Sodium 1900mg	79%
Total Carbohydrate 264g	88%
Dietary Fiber 35g	140%
Sugars 79g	
Protein 63g	

Vitamin A 30%	•	Vitamin C 45%
Calcium 170%	•	Iron 70%

**2 cups whole wheat flour
1 tablespoon low-sodium baking powder
2 jumbo egg whites
2 1/2 cups skim milk
2 bananas, cubed or 2 cups blueberries (optional)**

Spray a nonstick frying pan with butter-flavored nonstick spray.

In a large mixing bowl, thoroughly combine the flour and baking powder. Add the egg whites and combine, and finally add the milk. Beat until batter is smooth (free of lumps). Add either the bananas or the blueberries.

Preheat the frying pan over medium heat for 1–2 minutes. To make large pancakes, pour a disk about 5 inches in diameter into the pan, then tilt the pan in all directions; the batter on top will drip over the sides and widen the pancake. When little bubbles begin to appear on top of the pancake, turn it over. Cook on the other side until you can see it has turned brown when you peek under the edge with a spatula. Remove it to a warm plate. Be sure to scrape any crusty leavings out before pouring your next pancake. If your pancakes begin to smoke, lower the heat. If they begin to stick, pour a little cooking oil on a paper towel; wet the paper towel, then ring it out and wipe the pan with it. Repeat after every third pancake. Be sure to stir the batter between each batch of three.

Top with Fruit Patrician, or you can melt one of the all-fruit preserves in the microwave or in a saucepan over low heat, to use for syrup.

These pancakes freeze beautifully so you can double the recipe and freeze the extras. Place plastic wrap between each pancake and store in an airtight container. Reheat while still frozen in the microwave for about 1 minute or heat on an oven proof plate in a preheated conventional oven at 350 degrees F. for about 5 or 6 minutes or on a piece of aluminum foil in a toaster oven for 3 or 4 minutes.

Variation: WAFFLES

Make the same batter as for pancakes. Use a nonstick waffle iron, and follow the manufacturer's directions. Spray the waffle iron with a nonstick spray several times during cooking. Waffles may also be frozen successfully and reheated using the same methods as for pancakes.

SOUTHERN BRUNCH

YIELD: 8 SERVINGS

Nutrition Facts

Amount Per Serving

Calories 230	Calories from Fat 20

	% Daily Value*
Total Fat 2g	3%
Saturated Fat 0.5g	3%
Cholesterol 20mg	6%
Sodium 710mg	30%
Total Carbohydrate 29g	10%
Dietary Fiber 2g	7%
Sugars 4g	
Protein 21g	

Vitamin A 15%	•	Vitamin C 15%
Calcium 50%	•	Iron 10%

I call this southern, because the casserole contains grits. Grits are like cornmeal, but with a distinctively different taste and texture. They are made by grinding and sifting cleaned white corn kernels and then removing the corn bran and germ. It looks coarser than cornmeal, but it doesn't cook up as solid as cornbread. If your grocer doesn't have grits, ask him to contact Martha White Foods, Inc., P. O. Box 58, Nashville, Tenn. 37202.

This dish is nice for a crowd and can be served as a main meal at dinner or as a 2 a.m. breakfast after a dance or party. You can have it all put together in the refrigerator, then pop it in the oven when you get home.

8 jumbo egg whites
4 cups Chicken Stock (page 45)
1/8 teaspoon cayenne pepper
1/4 teaspoon turmeric
1 cup finely chopped onion
1 1/2 cups uncooked quick (5-minute) grits
1 cup (7 ounces) cooked or uncooked chopped white chicken meat
2 cups nonfat cheddar cheese
2 teaspoons dried parsley
2 to 4 tomatoes, sliced (enough to cover the top of the casserole)
1 can (4 ounces) green chilies
2 tablespoons grated sapsago cheese

Preheat oven to 350 degrees F.

In a large bowl, beat the egg whites, chicken stock, cayenne pepper, and turmeric with an electric mixer or wire whisk until well blended. Add the onion, grits, chicken, cheddar cheese, and parsley. Combine thoroughly. Pour into a nonstick 9 x 13-inch glass baking dish, spreading out the ingredients evenly. Slice the tomatoes and distribute them over the top of the casserole, edges touching. Slice the chilies into thin strips and arrange the slices over the top and then sprinkle with the sapsago cheese.

Place the uncovered casserole on the middle rack of the oven and bake for 1 hour. Remove and let the casserole sit uncovered for 15 minutes to absorb the juices. Serve hot.

MURIEL'S SOFT-CENTERED SPOON BREAD

YIELD: 5 SERVINGS

Nutrition Facts

Amount Per Serving	
Calories 110	Calories from Fat 5

	% Daily Value*
Total Fat 0.5g	1%
Saturated Fat 0g	0%
Cholesterol 0mg	0%
Sodium 150mg	6%
Total Carbohydrate 22g	7%
Dietary Fiber 2g	8%
Sugars 8g	
Protein 5g	

Vitamin A 2%	•	Vitamin C 2%
Calcium 15%	•	Iron 8%

My cousin Muriel gave me this wonderful recipe. It has a soft, almost pudding-like center, and a bit of a crust on the outside. It's great plain with some herb tea, but it's even better with some all-fruit preserves or with one of the jellies in the last chapter. Try it in a bowl with some sliced bananas and/or strawberries and a little hot milk poured over it. It's also wonderful for sopping up the gravy from your roast beef.

Note: Regular cornmeal won't work in this recipe.

1/2 cup corn tortilla meal (masa harina)
1/4 cup whole wheat flour
1 teaspoon low-sodium baking powder
2 jumbo egg whites
1/4 Baked Banana (page 57)
3 tablespoons apple juice concentrate
1 cup skim milk

Preheat the oven to 375 degrees F.

Spray an 8-inch-square nonstick baking pan with butter-flavored nonstick spray.

In a large bowl, combine the tortilla meal, flour, and baking powder. Set aside.

In a small bowl, beat the egg whites with an electric mixer or wire whisk until they are very frothy. In a separate bowl, beat the banana and baking liquid together with the juice concentrate. Pour the eggs and the juice mixture into the tortilla meal mixture. Add 1/2 cup of milk. Beat on high speed with an electric mixer for 2 1/2 minutes or vigorously by hand, until the batter is very smooth. Pour the batter into the pan and shift it back and forth a little to spread the batter evenly.

Place on the middle rack of the oven. In order not to disturb the surface of the batter, reach in and slowly pour the remaining 1/2 cup of milk evenly over the top. Bake for 25 to 30 minutes, until you see the paper thin edges curling up and turning a medium brown. The bread will not be soupy, so to dish it up, use a knife to cut it and a pie server or spatula to serve it.

CHAPTER 4

Meat Entrées

Although meat should be eaten in small portions, it's still easy to make those portions delicious through the addition of vegetables, starches, wine, and seasonings.

At first, I thought 3 1/2- to 4-ounce portions of meat would be so small they wouldn't be worth eating, but now a 3 1/2-ounce portion of meat seems quite normal. When I go into a steakhouse and I see an order of prime rib on someone else's plate I almost faint! To me, it looks like a whole roast!

For the most part, these recipes use meat as an addition to other foods, but sometimes it's wonderful to have meat out there by itself where you can really taste it, so I've included a few of those recipes too. After all, you don't have to stop living just because you cook a little differently. Eat and enjoy!

HOME-STYLE BEEF STEW

Nutrition Facts

Amount Per Serving

Calories 270	Calories from Fat 35

	% Daily Value*
Total Fat 4g	6%
Saturated Fat 1.5g	8%
Cholesterol 55mg	19%
Sodium 70mg	3%
Total Carbohydrate 33g	11%
Dietary Fiber 5g	21%
Sugars 10g	
Protein 26g	

Vitamin A 360%	•	Vitamin C 50%
Calcium 4%	•	Iron 20%

1 1/2 pounds very lean stew meat
3 medium onions, chopped
1 small green pepper, chopped
3 tablespoons whole wheat flour
Water
4 medium potatoes, peeled and cut in large pieces
5 large carrots cut in 1-inch pieces
6 large mushrooms, sliced
1 tablespoon dried parsley
1 teaspoon garlic powder
2 bay leaves
1/2 teaspoon cayenne pepper
1 tablespoon apple juice concentrate
1/2 cup fresh or frozen green peas
1/2 teaspoon dried thyme

Remove and discard any visible fat from the meat and cut into about 1-inch cubes. Place enough pieces of meat to cover the bottom of a 5-quart nonstick stockpot without allowing the pieces to touch each other. Over medium-high heat brown the meat on the bottom moving it around while it is browning. Turn the meat over and brown the other side. If the pot starts to smoke, lower the heat to medium. When brown, remove the meat to a bowl and add the remaining meat to the pot to brown. Cook the same way as the first batch. If the meat doesn't brown fast enough over medium heat, set the heat on high so that the meat doesn't steam, which it will do if the heat is too low. Remove the meat to the bowl and set aside.

Pour off any grease in the pot and wipe out with a paper towel. Add the onions and green pepper to the pot and begin to sauté them. After they have begun to brown and the onions look transparent, sprinkle with the flour and mix by turning them over constantly over high heat. When the flour begins to smoke, continue turning the flour and vegetables over for about 20 seconds more. Add some water immediately and lower the heat. Add more water, a little at a time, stirring constantly. When enough water has been added so it is not boiling rapidly, add the meat, potatoes, carrots, mushrooms, peas, and all the seasonings except the thyme. Add enough water to cover everything and cover with a lid. Simmer for 2 to 3 hours until the meat is very tender, stirring occasionally. Add the thyme and simmer for 30 minutes. Skim the fat off the top before serving.

SLOW COOKER BEEF

Nutrition Facts

Amount Per Serving

Calories 340   Calories from Fat 170

	% Daily Value*
Total Fat 19g	29%
Saturated Fat 8g	41%
Cholesterol 115mg	39%
Sodium 70mg	3%
Total Carbohydrate 4g	1%
Dietary Fiber 0g	0%
Sugars 2g	
Protein 36g	

Vitamin A 0%	•	Vitamin C 4%
Calcium 2%	•	Iron 25%

A slow cooker is a wonderful way to have roast beef for dinner and still be able to go out during the day. Even if you have to cook the roast for an hour more than recommended, it will still be all right. I slice the mushrooms and mix up the cornstarch, water, juice concentrate, and wine before I leave home and refrigerate them, and when I get home, I add them to the pot.

3 or 3 1/2 pound eye of round or rump roast, fresh or frozen
1/4 teaspoon cayenne pepper
1/2 teaspoon garlic powder
1/4 cup dried minced onion or onion flakes
2 ribs celery and leaves
2 cups water
3 tablespoons cornstarch
1/4 cup Red Rosé wine
1 tablespoon apple juice concentrate
2 cups sliced mushrooms
1 tablespoon dried parsley

Defrost the roast slightly if it is frozen, then trim off any visible fat, and place it in a 5-quart slow cooker.

Slow Directions: Sprinkle with the cayenne, garlic powder, and dried onion, letting some of the onion fall into the bottom of the pot. Cut the celery ribs in half and place on top of the roast. Add 1/2 cup of the water. Cover and turn the setting to low. Cook for 8 hours. Mix up the cornstarch, remaining water, wine, and juice concentrate. Pour it into the pot. Add the mushrooms and parsley, and cook on high setting for another 30 minutes, stirring occasionally. The roast should be very tender.

Quick Directions: Sprinkle with the cayenne, garlic powder, and dried onion, allowing some of the onion fall into the bottom of the pot. Cut the celery ribs in half and place on top of the roast. Do not add the water. Cover and cook on high setting for 4 1/2 hours. Mix up the cornstarch, water, wine, and apple juice concentrate. Add to the pot. Add the mushrooms and parsley, and cook for another 30 minutes, stirring occasionally. The roast should be very tender. Remove the roast from the pot to a serving platter and cover. Skim the fat off the gravy. Serve with brown or white rice. Pour 1/4 cup of the gravy over each serving of the rice and meat. Each serving will contain about 4 ounces of meat.

BOEUF EN BROCHETTE

Nutrition Facts

Amount Per Serving

Calories 250	Calories from Fat 70

	% Daily Value*
Total Fat 7g	11%
Saturated Fat 3g	16%
Cholesterol 75mg	25%
Sodium 250mg	10%
Total Carbohydrate 19g	6%
Dietary Fiber 3g	12%
Sugars 11g	
Protein 29g	

Vitamin A 10%	•	Vitamin C 90%
Calcium 4%	•	Iron 25%

Use either metal or bamboo skewers. If you use bamboo skewers, be sure to soak them in a little water first. This will prevent them from splintering when you skewer the meat.

12 ounces very lean sirloin, filet mignon, or rib-eye steak cut into bite-size pieces
8 mushrooms, cut in half
2 medium onions, quartered and separated
2 medium tomatoes, cut in 8 wedges
1 medium green or yellow sweet bell pepper, chopped in 10 to 12 pieces
4 teaspoons low-sodium soy sauce
6 tablespoons water
Juice of 2 limes
1/2 teaspoon garlic powder
2 tablespoons apple juice concentrate
1/4 teaspoon cayenne pepper

Spear the meat and vegetables with the skewers, alternating the meat, onions, peppers, tomatoes, and mushrooms, with at least 4 cubes of meat on each skewer. Try to get one piece of onion and one piece of pepper on either side of the meat as you go. Set aside.

Make the marinade in a cup by combining the soy sauce, water, lime juice, garlic powder, juice concentrate, and cayenne.

Place the skewered meat and vegetables in a shallow pan. Add the marinade, cover, and set in the refrigerator to marinate for 2 hours. Baste with the marinade every 30 minutes.

Preheat oven or broiler.

Place the brochettes in a metal baking pan and set it about 4 inches from the heat source of the broiler. Reserve the marinade. Broil for 4 minutes. Check a couple of times so you don't scorch the top of the vegetables. Turn the brochettes over and baste them with the marinade. Broil for about 5 minutes, checking frequently, until the meat looks nice and brown. Serve immediately. If the meat is totally fat-free, pour some pan juices over. Each serving will contain 3 ounces of meat.

SWISS STEAK

YIELD: 5 SERVINGS
WITH 2/3 CUP RICE

Nutrition Facts

Amount Per Serving

Calories 350   Calories from Fat 50

	% Daily Value*
Total Fat 6g	9%
Saturated Fat 2.5g	11%
Cholesterol 75mg	25%
Sodium 210mg	9%
Total Carbohydrate 39g	13%
Dietary Fiber 4g	16%
Sugars 3g	
Protein 34g	

Vitamin A 0%	•	Vitamin C 4%
Calcium 4%	•	Iron 20%

1 (1 pound) round steak about 1/2 inch thick
1/3 cup whole wheat flour
Cayenne pepper
Water
1 bay leaf
Scant 1/2 teaspoon dried thyme
4 teaspoons low-sodium soy sauce
1 large onion, chopped

Trim off as much fat off the steak as possible. Place in a nonstick frying pan and sauté on both sides until very brown. Lower the heat and sprinkle the flour over the steak and into the pan. Turn the steak over and add enough water to almost cover it. Move the steak around in the water until the flour works itself smoothly into the mixture. Add the pepper, bay leaf, thyme, and soy sauce, and stir. Sprinkle with the onion (some on the steak and some in the water) and cover. Cover and simmer for at least 2 hours. Check, stir, and move the steak around frequently. Add more water as it evaporates. Slice into serving-size portions and serve with the gravy. For a 1 1/2-ounce serving, cut off a section 1 inch by about 3 inches and weigh. If you are really very scrupulous about the fat, let the pan with meat and gravy sit in the refrigerator overnight. The next day, skim off every bit of grease, then serve. It might taste even better than it would have the first day.

GRILLADES AND GRAVY

Nutrition Facts

Amount Per Serving

Calories 630	Calories from Fat 50

	% Daily Value*
Total Fat 6g	9%
Saturated Fat 2g	11%
Cholesterol 70mg	24%
Sodium 65mg	3%
Total Carbohydrate 103g	34%
Dietary Fiber 6g	22%
Sugars 9g	
Protein 39g	

Vitamin A 170%	•	Vitamin C 70%
Calcium 4%	•	Iron 45%

Grillades (pronounced gree-ahds) means "grilled meat" and is an old-time favorite here in New Orleans, usually for breakfast over grits, but also for dinner over rice. If you use grits, the instant or regular varieties are fine. Just follow the package directions but leave out the salt.

3/4 pound round steak, about 1/4 inch thick
1 1/2 cups chopped onions
1 cup chopped green pepper
1/3 cup whole wheat flour
2 2/3 cups water
1 large carrot, sliced
1/8 teaspoon cayenne pepper
1 bay leaf
1/8 teaspoon garlic powder
1/2 teaspoon dried thyme
1 tablespoon apple juice concentrate
2 tablespoons Red Rosé wine

Remove any fat from the meat and discard. Cut the meat into 1-inch squares. Combine the steak pieces, onion, and green pepper in a nonstick frying pan. Sauté over high heat until the meat looks brown. Add the flour and toss with the meat and vegetables for about 25 seconds. Add the water, stirring until thoroughly combined. Add the carrot, cover, and cook over low heat for 2 hours, stirring often and adding a little water if the mixture starts to dry out. Add the cayenne, bay leaf, garlic powder, thyme, juice concentrate, and wine. Simmer covered, for 30 minutes more, until the meat is very tender. Don't forget to stir every so often. Each serving should contain 3 ounces of meat.

EASY CORNED BEEF

Nutrition Facts

Amount Per Serving

Calories 210 Calories from Fat 70

	% Daily Value*
Total Fat 8g	12%
Saturated Fat 3.5g	17%
Cholesterol 85mg	29%
Sodium 70mg	3%
Total Carbohydrate 3g	1%
Dietary Fiber 0g	0%
Sugars 3g	
Protein 30g	

Vitamin A 0%	•	Vitamin C 2%
Calcium 2%	•	Iron 20%

This is a great New Year's Day dish which you can cook a day ahead and reheat. I like to cook corned beef in a slow cooker so I can go off and forget it, but you can cook it on top of the stove very easily, too. Serve the corned beef with Horseradish Sauce, or with just plain Creamy Horseradish. On New Year's Day cabbage is for money and black-eyed peas are for good luck. You carry the cabbage into every room of the house. This is an old German New Orleans custom which everyone takes part in.

3-pound sirloin tip, or eye of the round, or rump roast
5 cups water
1 large onion, quartered
1 celery rib, cut in thirds
1/2 cup apple cider vinegar
4 tablespoons apple juice concentrate
1 pouch commercial crab boil, or Homemade Crab Boil (page 170)

Slow Cooker Directions: Cut all visible fat off the roast and place it in a 5-quart slow cooker. Add the water, onion, celery, vinegar, juice concentrate, and bag of crab boil. Cover, cook for 5 hours on high setting, or until the meat is very tender. Remove 1 cup of liquid and refrigerate until any fat hardens and rises to the top. Discard it. Meanwhile, keep the meat warm on a low setting. To serve, reheat the liquid to pour over the meat. Slice the roast with an electric knife if you have one.

Stove Top Directions: Cut all visible fat off the roast and place it in a 5-quart stockpot. Add the water, onion, celery, vinegar, juice concentrate, and bag of crab boil. Cover, bring to a boil, then simmer for 5 hours, or until the meat is very tender. You shouldn't have to add water, but check and maintain the water level by adding water, if necessary. Remove 1 cup of liquid and refrigerate until any fat rises to the top and hardens. Discard. Meanwhile, keep the meat warm on simmer. To serve, reheat the liquid to pour over the meat. Slice the roast with an electric knife if you have one.

When I cook this on New Year's Eve to serve the next day, I just slice the roast, put it in an ovenproof serving dish, and pour the juice over it after it has been degreased. I let it sit in the refrigerator covered that way. On New Year's Day, I put the whole thing in the microwave, covered with plastic wrap for about 10 to 15 minutes on high setting, or I cover the dish with aluminum foil and reheat at 300 degrees F. for about 30 minutes in the oven. Each serving should contain about 3 1/2 ounces of meat.

HAMBURGER

Nutrition Facts

Amount Per Serving

Calories 170   Calories from Fat 80

	% Daily Value*
Total Fat 9g	14%
Saturated Fat 3.5g	18%
Cholesterol 35mg	12%
Sodium 75mg	3%
Total Carbohydrate 1g	0%
Dietary Fiber 0g	0%
Sugars 0g	
Protein 20g	

Vitamin A 40%	•	Vitamin C 2%
Calcium 2%	•	Iron 10%

7 ounces very lean ground round or flank steak
2 tablespoons finely grated carrot
1/16 teaspoon cayenne pepper
1/8 teaspoon dried parsley
1/8 teaspoon garlic powder

In a mixing bowl, combine the ground meat with the carrot, cayenne, parsley, and garlic powder. Form into 2 patties and place them in a nonstick frying pan. Fry over high heat for 5 minutes after the meat starts to sizzle. Turn the patties over and reduce the heat to medium-low. Turn the patties often to keep down the smoke. Cook for about 15 minutes altogether. Serve with coleslaw. Each serving should contain 3 1/2 ounces of meat.

SULLEY'S GROUND MEAT HASH

Nutrition Facts

Amount Per Serving

Calories 250	Calories from Fat 60

	% Daily Value*
Total Fat 7g	11%
Saturated Fat 3g	14%
Cholesterol 30mg	9%
Sodium 60mg	3%
Total Carbohydrate 28g	9%
Dietary Fiber 3g	12%
Sugars 6g	
Protein 18g	

Vitamin A 6%	•	Vitamin C 60%
Calcium 4%	•	Iron 15%

My mother-in-law, Erneth, taught me this old German recipe which her grandmother, Pauline, brought with her from Germany when she and her husband immigrated to Louisiana in the late 1800s.

I named this for my daughter-in-law, Sulley, because she now continues the tradition of making my husband's favorite hash for his birthday and Father's Day, something I used to do. A daughter-in-law is a wonderful thing to have.

1 pound very lean ground beef or flank steak
2 medium onions, chopped
1 small green pepper, chopped
5 cups water
4 cups peeled, diced potatoes
1 1/2 teaspoons dried thyme
2 bay leaves
1/4 teaspoon cayenne pepper or more, to taste
1 tablespoon dried parsley or 1/4 cup chopped fresh parsley
2 tablespoons plus 1 teaspoon orange juice concentrate
1 teaspoon Tabasco

Brown the ground beef in a nonstick 5-quart stockpot over high heat. Drain the meat, remove to a plate, and pat it with paper towels to absorb the grease, then wipe out the pot with more paper towels. In the same pot, combine the onions and green pepper. Sauté over high heat until the onions look brown around the edges and a little bit transparent. Add the water, potatoes, meat, thyme, bay leaves, cayenne, parsley, juice concentrate, and Tabasco. Bring to a boil, then lower the heat to medium, and cook for 45 minutes, uncovered, stirring occasionally. Stir frequently during the last 10 minutes. Serve hot. Each serving should contain 2 2/3 ounces of meat.

SALISBURY STEAK

Nutrition Facts

Amount Per Serving

Calories 210   Calories from Fat 80

	% Daily Value*
Total Fat 9g	**14**%
Saturated Fat 3.5g	**18**%
Cholesterol 35mg	**12**%
Sodium 75mg	**3**%
Total Carbohydrate 7g	**2**%
Dietary Fiber less than 1 gram	**3**%
Sugars 4g	
Protein 21g	

Vitamin A 2%	•	Vitamin C 6%
Calcium 2%	•	Iron 15%

Five 3 1/2-ounce patties of very lean ground top round beef or flank steak
1/8 teaspoon cayenne pepper
2 cups water
1/2 cup Red Rosé wine
1 tablespoon apple juice concentrate
1 teaspoon medium hot sauce
1 very large onion or 2 medium onions, sliced in rings
1 tablespoon cornstarch

Place the meat patties in a nonstick frying pan and sprinkle with cayenne. Over high heat, brown the patties, turning them over once or twice to brown both sides. Remove the patties to a plate. Pour out any grease left in the pan and wipe the pan clean with paper towels. Return the patties to the pan. Reduce the heat to medium-low. Add the water, wine, juice concentrate, and hot sauce. Distribute the onion rings over the patties. Cover and cook over moderate to low heat for about 25 minutes, moving the patties around occasionally, but don't turn them over. After 25 minutes, uncover, sprinkle with the cornstarch, then turn the patties over and move them around in the pan to mix the cornstarch into the liquid. Cook for 10 minutes, uncovered, over medium-high heat, stirring constantly. Each serving should contain 3 1/2 ounces of meat.

CREOLE-STYLE MEATLOAF

YIELD: 10 SERVINGS

Nutrition Facts

Amount Per Serving

Calories 430	Calories from Fat 90

	% Daily Value*
Total Fat 10g	**15**%
Saturated Fat 3.5g	**18**%
Cholesterol 35mg	**11**%
Sodium 140mg	**6**%
Total Carbohydrate 56g	**19**%
Dietary Fiber 5g	**20**%
Sugars 7g	
Protein 29g	

Vitamin A 20%	•	Vitamin C 50%
Calcium 6%	•	Iron 30%

If you don't like meatloaf because it's always dry, you haven't eaten Creole-Style meatloaf like my mama used to make. Always juicy and delicious, my kids love this one and yours will too.

For the Meatloaf:
2 pounds very lean ground beef
2 jumbo egg whites
Water
2 slices Pritikin or commercial whole wheat bread
1/8 teaspoon cayenne pepper
1/2 teaspoon garlic powder
1/4 teaspoon dried basil
1/4 teaspoon dried oregano
1/8 teaspoon ground cumin
1/4 teaspoon dried marjoram
1/4 Baked Banana (page 57)

For the Sauce:
2 cups sliced mushrooms
2 medium onions, chopped
1 large green pepper, chopped
3 cups water
1 can (12 ounces) or 1 1/4 cups salt-free tomato paste
1/2 teaspoon garlic powder
1 1/2 teaspoons dried oregano
1/2 teaspoon dried basil
1 tablespoon dried parsley, or 1/2 cup chopped fresh parsley
1/4 teaspoon cayenne pepper
1/8 teaspoon ground cumin
2 tablespoons apple juice concentrate
1/4 cup white Chablis

Place the meat in a large bowl and add the egg whites. Wet the bread with water and squeeze the water out of it. Break up the wet bread and add it to the meat and egg whites. Sprinkle with the spices and banana. Mix the meat and seasonings gently with your hands until everything is well blended. Don't overwork the meat or it will be tough. Place the meat mixture in a 9 x 13-inch baking dish and form it gently into a nice, stocky loaf, about 8 x 4 x 4 inches. Smooth the loaf by patting it gently all over.

Microwave Directions: Place the loaf in the microwave and bake uncovered for 25 minutes at 70 percent power, to brown.

Oven Directions: Place the loaf on the middle rack. Set the temperature at 400 degrees F, and bake uncovered for about 25 minutes until brown. Tip the dish and spoon out any fat or grease. Then wipe the dish around the loaf with paper towels.

To make the sauce: place the mushrooms, onions, and green pepper in a nonstick frying pan and sauté over high heat, until the onions look a little transparent and brown around the edges. Remove the pan from the heat and add the water, tomato paste, garlic powder, oregano, basil, parsley, cayenne, cumin, juice concentrate, and wine. Stir to combine, return the pan to the heat, cover, and simmer for 1 hour, checking and stirring every 10 to 15 minutes. Add a little water if the liquid starts to dry out. Pour the sauce over the browned loaf.

Microwave Directions: Place the loaf in the microwave, uncovered. Bake on simmer or 50 percent power for 30 minutes. Baste at 15 minutes.

Oven Directions: Cover the baking dish with aluminum foil and place on the middle rack of the oven. Set the heat at 325 degrees F. Bake for 1 hour, basting occasionally.

There should be 3 ounces of meat in each serving.

STUFFED GREEN PEPPERS

Nutrition Facts

Amount Per Serving	
Calories 270	Calories from Fat 45

	% Daily Value²
Total Fat 5g	8%
Saturated Fat 2g	9%
Cholesterol 15mg	5%
Sodium 115mg	5%
Total Carbohydrate 40g	13%
Dietary Fiber 6g	25%
Sugars 10g	
Protein 17g	

Vitamin A 20%	•	Vitamin C	250%
Calcium 4%	•	Iron	15%

3 ounces very lean ground beef
1 cup chopped onions
1/2 teaspoon low-sodium soy sauce
1 cup cooked Brown Rice (page 256) or Brown and Wild Rice (page 255), or instant cooked brown rice
1/4 teaspoon cayenne pepper
1/2 teaspoon garlic powder
1 teaspoon dried parsley flakes or 1 tablespoon fresh chopped parsley
1/2 teaspoon chili powder
1/3 cup water
1 jumbo egg white
2 large green peppers, stemmed and seeded but left whole
Sapsago cheese

Brown the meat in a nonstick frying pan. When it is almost brown, toss in a paper towel and stir it around to absorb the grease as you continue to brown the meat. Replace soaked paper towels with clean ones until all the grease is removed. Add the onions and soy sauce, and sauté with the beef over high heat. When the onions look a little brown at the edges and a little bit transparent, lower the heat to medium. Add the rice, cayenne, garlic, parsley, chili powder, and water. As you mix everything together be sure to incorporate the caramelized leavings at the bottom of the pan. Stir in the egg white and remove from the heat.

Stuff the mixture into the cavity of each pepper. Sprinkle with sapsago cheese. Place in a nonstick pan and bake uncovered at 350 degrees F. for 30 minutes. Cover loosely with aluminum foil and bake 15 minutes more.

Each serving contains 1 1/2 ounces of meat.

Variation: MEATLESS STUFFED PEPPERS

Substitute 1/2 cup nonfat cottage cheese for the meat. Mix it with the other ingredients just before stuffing the peppers.

EGGPLANT SORRENTO

Something about this pasta dish reminds me of the quaint mountainside town of Sorrento, Italy, which clings to the cliffs high above the Mediterranean Sea, directly across the Bay of Naples from the Isle of Capri. Perhaps it's the fragrance of the oregano, cumin, basil, and tomato. It is said that smells last longer in our memories than any other sensual experience, and the aroma of this dish takes me back to that magical little town.

4 ounces very lean ground top round beef or flank steak
1 large onion, chopped
1 large green pepper, chopped
1 can (15 ounces) salt-free tomato sauce
1 cup water
1/4 teaspoon garlic powder
1 1/2 teaspoons dried oregano
1/4 teaspoon dried red pepper flakes
1/2 teaspoon dried basil
1/4 teaspoon ground cumin
1 large eggplant
6 ounces uncooked semolina or whole wheat spaghetti
  (about 2 cups cooked)
4 tablespoons grated sapsago cheese

Brown the ground beef in a nonstick 5-quart stockpot, over high heat, then remove and drain on paper towels, then pat the meat with more paper towels to absorb any grease. Wipe out the pot. Combine the onion and green pepper in the stockpot and sauté over high heat by turning the vegetables, until the onions look transparent and a little brown around the edges. Remove the pot from the heat and add the tomato sauce. Rinse the tomato sauce can with 1 cup of water, and add the rinse water to the pot. Add the garlic powder, oregano, red pepper flakes, basil, and cumin. Stir and set the pot over medium-low heat, covered. Peel the eggplant and cut it into approximately 1-inch-square chunks. Add the eggplant to the pot, cover, and cook over low heat for about 45 minutes, stirring occasionally.

About 25 minutes before the eggplant is cooked, heat the water for the spaghetti. When it comes to a rolling boil, add the spaghetti. Cook semolina spaghetti for about 10 minutes and whole wheat spaghetti for about 15 minutes. Drain the spaghetti and set aside.

When the eggplant is very tender, chop it up a little more with the edge of a spoon, then add the spaghetti to the pot and mix everything together. Serve immediately as a full meal. Sprinkle 1 tablespoon of sapsago cheese over each serving. Each serving will contain a little over 1 ounce of meat.

CAJUN-STYLE SHEPHERD'S PIE

Nutrition Facts

Amount Per Serving

Calories 300	Calories from Fat 40

	% Daily Value*
Total Fat 4.5g	7%
Saturated Fat 1.5g	8%
Cholesterol 15mg	5%
Sodium 60mg	3%
Total Carbohydrate 50g	17%
Dietary Fiber 7g	26%
Sugars 11g	
Protein 17g	

Vitamin A 160%	•	Vitamin C 120%
Calcium 6%	•	Iron 15%

When my husband and I were last in London, we stopped to eat lunch in an outdoor café not a half block from the London Bridge near the Tower of London. As we sat, watching the boats glide by and taking in the marvelous sight of the ancient castle walls of the Tower of London across the river, we enjoyed Shepherd's pie. I liked the concept, but I just had to Cajunize it when I came home.

4 medium to large potatoes, peeled
1 large carrot, sliced
Water
6 ounces very lean ground round beef or flank steak
1 cup chopped onion
1 cup chopped green peppers
1/4 cup skim milk, approximately
1/2 teaspoon dried basil
1 1/2 teaspoons dried parsley
1 tablespoon onion powder
1/8 plus 1/16 teaspoon cayenne pepper, divided
1 cup frozen or fresh green peas
2 tablespoons sapsago cheese

Place the potatoes in a 2-quart saucepan, with water to cover. Bring to a boil and cook until tender when pierced with a sharp knife, about 25 minutes. Drain and set aside.

Microwave Directions: Pour 1/4 cup water into a narrow, high-sided 3-cup container and cover. Cook on high setting for 25 seconds. Add the carrots, cover, and cook on high setting for 5 minutes. Drain, reserving the cooking liquid, and set both the liquid and carrots aside.

Stove Top Directions: Pour 1/2 cup water into a 1-quart saucepan and bring to a boil over high heat. Add the carrots, cover tightly, bring back to a boil over high heat, and cook for 5 minutes, until tender. Drain, reserving the cooking liquid. Set both the liquid and carrots aside.

While the potatoes and carrots are cooking, sauté the ground meat in a nonstick frying pan over high heat, stirring until nice and brown. Remove the meat from the pan, and drain it on paper towels, patting with more paper towels to absorb all the grease. Wipe out the pan with paper towels. Add the onions and green pepper to the pan. Sauté the vegetables over high heat, until the onion looks brown around the edges and a little transparent. Remove the pan from the heat and set aside.

Mash the potatoes with enough skim milk to make them creamy, about 1/4 cup. Add basil, parsley, onion powder, 1/8 teaspoon cayenne, the green peas, and the reserved cooking liquid from the carrots, and combine.

In the frying pan, combine the meat, carrots, onions, and green pepper, green peas, and the remaining 1/16 teaspoon of cayenne. Set aside.

In an 8-inch-square nonstick casserole dish or pan, layer half the potato mixture, then all of the meat mixture, then the remaining potato mixture. Sprinkle sapsago cheese on top. Bake on the middle rack of the oven for 35 minutes. Switch to broil and broil for 3 minutes to brown the top, watching carefully to be sure it doesn't burn. Each serving should contain 1 1/2 ounces of meat.

MOUSSAKA

Nutrition Facts

Amount Per Serving	
Calories 390	Calories from Fat 100

	% Daily Value*
Total Fat 11g	**18**%
Saturated Fat 4.5g	**22**%
Cholesterol 45mg	**15**%
Sodium 450mg	**19**%
Total Carbohydrate 34g	**11**%
Dietary Fiber 5g	**21**%
Sugars 10g	
Protein 39g	

Vitamin A 15%	•	Vitamin C 30%
Calcium 15%	•	Iron 25%

Before I heard about the Pritikin diet, my husband and I used to eat at a cute little restaurant on Decatur Street in New Orleans called Mr. Gyro's. They have the most unusual moussaka I have ever eaten. The potato base and meringue topping are really special. I did not actually get their recipe, but I figured out what was in it and then adjusted the recipe to fit the guidelines of salt-free, fat-free, sugar-free eating. It turns out beautiful and delicious and Ray asks me when I'm going to make it all the time.

For the Meat Mixture:
2 large potatoes
1 large eggplant
2 pounds lean ground beef
1/2 teaspoon cayenne pepper, divided
1 cup chopped onions
1 can (6 ounces) salt-free tomato paste
3/4 cup water or Beef Stock (page 43)
1/2 teaspoon garlic powder
1/2 teaspoon ground cinnamon
3/4 teaspoon dried oregano
4 slices commercial whole wheat bread made into crumbs (use a food processor or blender), divided

Boil or bake potatoes, let cool, and peel.

While the potatoes are cooking, slice the eggplant lengthwise into 1/4-inch-thick slices. Do not peel. Place the slices on a nonstick pan and sprinkle with 1/4 teaspoon of the cayenne pepper. Broil until lightly brown in the oven or broiler. Turn once. Check every few minutes. (I set my timer for 3 minutes so I won't forget.)

While the potatoes and eggplant are cooking, sauté the ground beef in a nonstick frying pan and drain off any grease, then toss a paper towel into the pan and continue to sauté, stirring the paper towel around to remove any remaining grease. Use several paper towels, discarding them as they become soaked. Remove the meat and wipe the pan with more paper towels. Add the onions and sauté over high heat until they look a little transparent. Add the meat back to the pan and stir in the tomato paste, water or stock, garlic powder, cinnamon, oregano, and the remaining 1/4 teaspoon of cayenne pepper.

Spray a 9 x 13-inch baking dish or nonstick baking pan with a nonstick spray, preferably olive oil-flavored. Slice the potatoes about 1/8 to 1/4 inch thick. Cover the bottom of the pan with the potato slices. Sprinkle them with half of the bread crumbs. Place half the eggplant slices over the potatoes and crumbs. Spread the meat mixture over the eggplant. Place the remaining eggplant slices over the meat. Sprinkle with the remaining bread crumbs. Set aside and prepare the cheese topping.

The Cheese Topping:
8 egg whites
2 cups skim milk
5 tablespoons whole wheat flour
1/2 teaspoon nutmeg
1 cup plus 3 tablespoons nonfat cottage cheese
1/4 cup grated sapsago cheese

Beat the egg whites until stiff and set aside.

Combine the milk, nutmeg, and flour in a blender until mixture is smooth.

Microwave Directions: Pour the milk mixture into a 2-quart container. Cook for 5 minutes on high setting, stirring after each minute, until smooth and thickened.

Stove Top Directions: Pour the milk mixture into a 2-quart saucepan or double boiler, and cook over a medium heat, stirring constantly, until thickened.

Add the cottage cheese and sapsago cheese to flour-milk mixture. If you leave out the sapsago or Parmesan, just add a little more cottage cheese to the flour-milk mixtures. Fold mixture into egg whites gently. Spread over top of casserole. Set the oven temperature at 350 degrees F. Bake for about 40 minutes, until top browns. Serve in squares and sprinkle with the sapsago cheese. If you can't find sapsago cheese, Parmesan can be substituted if you can afford have just a little fat in your diet.

This dish freezes beautifully. Refrigerate first, then cut into individual serving squares. With a spatula, slide the squares into sandwich bags and freeze. To reheat in a microwave, place on a serving plate, cover with plastic wrap, and heat on a medium setting for 10 minutes. Or reheat covered with aluminum foil in a conventional oven at 350 degrees F. for 20 to 30 minutes. There is no need to defrost first.

Divided into 8 servings, each portion contains 4 ounces of meat.

TACOS

People won't believe this is a diet recipe. If you want to cheat, you can use Kitchen Bouquet. It has a little sugar and salt in it, but not that much.

YIELD: 6 SERVINGS

Nutrition Facts

Amount Per Serving

Calories 540   Calories from Fat 120

	% Daily Value*
Total Fat 14g	21%
Saturated Fat 5g	24%
Cholesterol 60mg	21%
Sodium 360mg	15%
Total Carbohydrate 71g	24%
Dietary Fiber 4g	17%
Sugars 19g	
Protein 33g	

Vitamin A 45%	•	Vitamin C 35%
Calcium 25%	•	Iron 25%

For the Meat and Seasoning:
1 1/2 pounds very lean ground beef
1 3/4 cups water, divided
1/4 cup yellow oatmeal
1 new potato peeled or 1/4 cup firmly packed cooked potatoes
1 tablespoon onion powder
1 teaspoon garlic powder
1/2 teaspoon paprika
2 teaspoons chili powder
Mock Kitchen Bouquet (page 58) or 1 teaspoon commercial Kitchen Bouquet
8 drops Tabasco® sauce
2 teaspoons low-sodium soy sauce
1/4 teaspoon cayenne pepper
1/4 cup plus 2 tablespoons apple juice concentrate

For the Taco Sauce:
1 tablespoon cornstarch
3/4 cup water
3 tablespoons salt-free tomato paste
1 1/2 teaspoons plus 7 drops Tabasco®
3 tablespoons vinegar
4 1/2 tablespoons apple juice concentrate
4 1/2 teaspoons chili powder
1 1/2 teaspoons garlic powder
3/4 teaspoon onion powder

The Tortillas:
24 fresh or frozen corn tortillas

The Vegetable and Cheese Filling:
1 large onion, diced
2 medium tomatoes, diced
1 head of lettuce, shredded
1 3/4 cups nonfat cottage cheese

For the meat and seasoning, brown the beef in a nonstick pan and drain off all the grease. Place the meat in a colander and drain, then lay the meat on some paper towels to drain further. Pat all over with more paper towels.

Wipe or wash the pan out to remove any remaining grease. Return the meat to the pan.

Combine 3/4 cup water with all the other ingredients in a blender or food processor, and liquefy. Combine with meat in the pan. Add 1 cup of water to the blender or food processor and swirl it around to remove any remaining seasoning, and add to the pan with the meat. Repeat if there is still a little more seasoning left in the blender. Simmer, uncovered, stirring every 5 to 10 minutes, for 30 minutes. Add more water if the mixture begins to dry out. It should be fairly thick.

Microwave Directions for Taco Sauce: In a 1-quart container combine the cornstarch and water, blending until the mixture is free from lumps. Place in microwave for 1 1/2 minutes on high setting, and stir. Return to the microwave for another 1 1/2 minutes, and stir again. Measuring carefully, add all other ingredients and combine thoroughly before serving.

Stove Top Directions for Taco Sauce: In a small saucepan, combine the cornstarch and water, blending it until the mixture is free from lumps. Cook over high heat, stirring constantly. (The mixture will look like it isn't going to do anything, but all of a sudden it will become thick and almost clear.) Cook for 20 to 25 seconds more, stirring constantly, and then remove from heat. Add all the other ingredients, combine, and serve.

For the tortillas, preheat oven to 300 degrees F. Line every other wire in your oven rack with aluminum foil to make them a little fatter. Bend each defrosted tortilla over a foil-covered rack with the ends hanging down. Bake until toasted, about 3 to 5 minutes. Check them before 5 minutes because they burn easily. The ones closest to the heat will toast first.

Sometimes the tortillas break off and fall to the bottom of the oven, which is very annoying. If the tortillas crack at the edges when you bend them over the oven racks, they will probably break as they begin to toast. If this is the case, I suggest simply laying them flat across your oven racks to make flat tacos or tostados. Just pile everything on top. You can skip lining the racks with aluminum foil, too, and I promise, they are just as good as tacos.

For the vegetable and cheese filling, arrange the vegetables on a platter and mound the cottage cheese in the center and garnish with parsley. Everybody can assemble their taco as they please. I suggest filling the toasted tortillas with the meat filling, then lettuce, tomatoes, onions, cottage cheese, then with taco sauce.

Each taco contains 1 ounce of meat if the meat and seasoning is divided among 24 taco shells.

Variation: MEXI-TACO CASSEROLE

Preheat oven to 350 degrees F. Combine the Meat and Seasoning recipe with 7 egg whites and place in a 1 1/2-quart casserole dish. Bake uncovered until the egg whites solidify.

This is great with Hash Browns (page 71) and a vegetable; or, chop up some lettuce, tomatoes, and onions as you would for tacos and arrange on top. Make up one recipe of Taco Sauce (page 112) or Piquante Sauce (page 55) and pour over the casserole. Top with a dollop of nonfat cottage cheese.

Serves 8 and each serving contains 3 ounces of meat.

JAMBALAYA AU CONGRI

YIELD: 12 (1 CUP) SERVINGS

Nutrition Facts

Amount Per Serving

Calories 160   Calories from Fat 20

	% Daily Value*
Total Fat 2g	3%
Saturated Fat 0.5g	4%
Cholesterol 5mg	2%
Sodium 15mg	1%
Total Carbohydrate 27g	9%
Dietary Fiber 3g	13%
Sugars 2g	
Protein 9g	

Vitamin A 0%	•	Vitamin C 0%
Calcium 2%	•	Iron 10%

Although Jambalaya is a traditional Cajun dish which is always "something mixed with rice," its origins are international. Reminiscent of Spanish arroz con pollo (chicken and rice), it was copied and transformed into Jambalaya by the New Orleans Creole population, who are of both French and/or Spanish descent. Of course, the African-American population in New Orleans have had their influence on Jambalaya, too when they brought it with them from Haiti when thousands fled to Louisiana during the slave uprisings of the mid-eighteenth century. Traditionally, Jambalaya au Congri is a mixture of rice, cow peas, onions, ham, and salted meat. The Haitian refugees brought their religion voodooisn with them, and used congri in their offerings during religious ceremonies. Until the 1940s, it wasn't uncommon to find offerings of congri with coins around them, carefully set beneath the trees in Congo Square in the French Quarter where worshippers used to dance.

Black-Eyed Peas (page 270)
4 cups cooked Brown Rice (page 256)
6 ounces lean ground beef

Combine the hot cooked black-eyed peas and rice in a large pot and keep hot. Sauté the ground beef in a nonstick frying pan, over high heat, until very brown. Toss paper towels into the pan and stir them around to absorb all the grease out of the meat. Then add the meat to the peas and rice and combine thoroughly. (It will be rather soupy.) Serve with some whole wheat bread for sopping up the gravy. Green peas, carrots, and cabbage also go well with this dish. There is 1/2 ounce of meat in each 1-cup serving.

HONEST-TO-GOD PIZZA

Nutrition Facts

Amount Per Serving

Calories 330   Calories from Fat 35

	% Daily Value*
Total Fat 4g	6%
Saturated Fat 1.5g	7%
Cholesterol 15mg	5%
Sodium 170mg	7%
Total Carbohydrate 51g	17%
Dietary Fiber 4g	18%
Sugars 4g	
Protein 20g	

Vitamin A 25%	•	Vitamin C 70%	
Calcium 4%	•	Iron 25%	

I had to make this dough five different ways before I got it right, but now I think the crust is perfect. My husband, who never eats pizza crust, loves this crust.

Let me make a suggestion: Start the dough first, then make the filling and refrigerate it until you are ready to bake the pizza. I give directions for weighting the pizza down, but each time I've made this recipe, it hasn't puffed up, so weighting it is just insurance. Be sure you use bromated bread flour.

Pizza Dough:
4 cups bromated flour
3 tablespoons (3 envelopes) "rapid rise" dry baker's yeast
2 cups plus 2 tablespoons tepid water
12 ounces very lean ground beef
1 medium onion, chopped
1/2 large green pepper, chopped
1/2 cup Red Rosé wine
1 can (12 ounces) salt-free tomato paste (1 1/4 cups)
1 cup water
1/2 teaspoon dried oregano
1/8 teaspoon cayenne pepper
1 teaspoon dried parsley
1/8 teaspoon dried basil
1/4 teaspoon garlic powder

Topping:
1 1/2 cups (12 ounces) nonfat cottage cheese
2 tablespoons grated sapsago cheese
1/2 cup chopped onion
1 cup fresh mushrooms, sliced
1/2 large green pepper, cut in strips
1 jar (4 ounces) pimentos, cut in strips

Combine the flour and yeast in a large bowl. Make a hole in the center of the flour and add the 2 cups of water. First mix with a spoon to blend in the water, then, with one hand, turn the dough over and over in the bowl, poking your fingers into it to distribute the water evenly and handling the dough gently. If the dough still looks dry after handling it about 15 or 16 times, pour 1 tablespoon of water over it, and pick up the rest of the flour in the bowl with the dough; then, if there is still flour in the bottom of the bowl, add the other tablespoon of water and mix. The dough will be slick, but don't worry, it will be fine. Lightly flour a zip-lock-type 1-gallon plastic bag, place the dough in it, and squeeze out all the air. Seal the bag, put it in bowl, and set in a warm place, like on top of the refrigerator or freezer, until doubled in bulk or for 5 to 6 hours.

Meanwhile, prepare the meat sauce: In a nonstick frying pan, sauté the beef until brown. Remove the meat to drain on paper towels and pat with more paper towels to remove the grease. Wipe any remaining grease out of the pan. Combine the onion and green pepper in the pan, and sauté over high heat, turning the vegetables until the onion pieces look brown around the edges and a little transparent. Remove the pan from the heat. Add the wine, tomato paste, water, oregano, cayenne, parsley, basil, and garlic powder and combine thoroughly. Return the pan to high heat and cover. When the liquid begins to bubble, stir, and set the heat to low. Cover and cook for 30 minutes, stirring occasionally.

When ready, the dough will look like a festering blob from outer space ready to take over the planet. But don't let that distract you. Preheat the oven to 450 degrees F., then spray a 12-inch-wide nonstick pizza pan with a nonstick spray.

The only way to remove the dough from the bag is to squeeze it onto the pan, and don't worry if you can't squeeze all of it out. Just squeeze out as much as you can. Wet your hands and spread the dough to the edges of the pan. Wet your hands a couple of times if you have to. Spread the meat sauce on top of the dough, then spread the cottage cheese over the meat sauce. Sprinkle with the sapsago cheese. Arrange the mushroom slices over the cheese, then top with alternating slices of green pepper and pimento, radiating out from the center of the pizza.

The pizza is now ready for the oven, and I would suggest that you weight the center of the pizza down to keep the center of the dough from puffing too much and to keep the topping moister. Here's how: Cut a piece of aluminum foil into a disk, about 10 inches in diameter. Spray the foil with nonstick spray and place it spray-side down in the middle of the pizza. Weight it generously with aluminum pie weights, which you can buy at gourmet stores, or use pebbles or clam shells, anything that won't explode, break, burn, or melt in the oven.

Place the pie on the middle rack of the oven and bake for 40 to 60 minutes, until the crust around the edges looks puffed and golden, almost brown. Ease the pizza off the pan with a spatula, onto a wooden board, and slice. Sprinkle with red pepper flakes, if desired. Each slice will contain 1 1/5 ounces of meat.

GYRO SANDWICHES

**YIELD: 13
SANDWICHES**

Nutrition Facts

Amount Per Serving	
Calories 330	Calories from Fat 80

	% Daily Value*
Total Fat 8g	**13**%
Saturated Fat 3g	**14**%
Cholesterol 25mg	**9**%
Sodium 470mg	**20**%
Total Carbohydrate 42g	**14**%
Dietary Fiber 6g	**24**%
Sugars 4g	
Protein 24g	

Vitamin A 8%	•	Vitamin C 15%
Calcium 4%	•	Iron 20%

1 pound very lean ground beef
1/2 cup finely chopped onion
1/4 Baked Banana (page 57)
1/4 teaspoon allspice
1/4 teaspoon nutmeg
1/4 teaspoon anise seeds
1/4 teaspoon sage
1/4 teaspoon cayenne pepper
1/4 teaspoon basil
1/4 teaspoon paprika
1 teaspoon parsley flakes
1/2 teaspoon garlic powder or dried chopped garlic
1 jumbo egg white
1 slice commercial whole wheat or Pritikin bread, moistened with
   water, and then with the water squeezed out of it
6 pita breads
Tomatoes
Lettuce
Imitation Mayonnaise (page 305)

Place all the ingredients except the pita, tomatoes, lettuce and imitation mayonnaise in a food processor and blend until it looks like liver spread. Form into a loaf and place in a baking pan.

Microwave Directions: Place the baking dish in a microwave oven uncovered, and set it on bake at 60 percent power or a medium setting. Bake for 45 minutes.

Conventional Oven Directions: Preheat oven to 350 degrees F. Place the baking dish, uncovered, in the oven and bake for about 1 hour, until cooked through.

In the meantime, shred some lettuce and slice some tomatoes. This recipe will make 6 gyro sandwiches containing 2 ounces of meat each, so decide how many sandwiches you want to make and prepare as much lettuce and tomatoes as you will need. Also make some Imitation Mayonnaise. If you want to make 6 sandwiches all at once, make 5 batches of the Imitation Mayonnaise.

When the meat is done, remove from the oven and let it sit for about 10 minutes, then slice very thin slices across the top. Do not slice down. If you have ever seen cooks in restaurants slicing the meat for gyros, you will have noticed that they sliced off the side of the loaf. Their loaf is on a spit in an upright position. Yours is horizontal so their side is your top. Weigh the slices if you are on a strict diet. Cut the pita bread in half. I use bread that is

5 or 6 inches in diameter. Stuff some meat in each pocket, then some lettuce and tomato and finally a dollop of Imitation Mayonnaise. I like only the meat hot. My husband likes to put the whole sandwich in the microwave for 40 seconds on high, to heat it through. You can heat them in a covered dish in a preheated 350-degree conventional oven, but it takes 15 to 20 minutes. Serve with steamed spinach on the side and some peas and whole kernel corn mixed together.

To freeze, slice up 2-ounce servings and seal in small plastic bags, and store in one large zipper-lock bag.

ENCHILADA CASSEROLE

When chopping the vegetables, I keep a soup pot handy and whatever vegetables are extra after measuring, I put in the soup pot and make vegetable soup at the same time I am making this casserole. (Just add whatever else you need to complete the soup.)

1/2 cup finely chopped cauliflower
1 cup finely chopped carrots
1/2 cup finely chopped celery
1/2 cup finely chopped yellow squash
1/2 cup finely chopped zucchini squash
1/2 cup finely chopped mushrooms
1/2 cup peeled and finely chopped cucumbers
2 1/2 cups water
9 ounces very lean ground top round beef or flank steak
1 large onion, chopped
1/2 large green pepper, chopped
1 can (12 ounces) salt-free tomato paste (1 1/4 cups)
1/4 cup salt-free chili powder
1/4 teaspoon garlic powder
1/8 teaspoon cayenne pepper
12 fresh or frozen soft corn tortillas
3 1/2 cups (24 ounces) nonfat cottage cheese, divided
1 can (4 ounces) whole, roasted, peeled mild green chili peppers
1 very large onion or 2 medium onions, chopped, divided
1 teaspoon Tabasco® sauce
1 tablespoon skim milk
1 cup no-fat shredded cheddar cheese (optional)
2 tomatoes, chopped

Microwave Directions: Combine the cauliflower, carrots, celery, yellow squash, zucchini, mushrooms, and cucumbers in a 1 1/2- to 2-quart container. Add 1/2 cup water and cover. Microwave on high setting for 7 to 8 minutes, until the vegetables are tender-crisp. Drain, reserving the cooking liquid. Toss the vegetables together to combine.

Stove Top Directions: Combine the cauliflower, carrots, celery, yellow squash, zucchini, mushrooms, and cucumbers in a 1 1/2- to 2-quart saucepan. Add 1/2 cup water and cover. Bring to a boil and cook for 5 to 7 minutes, until the vegetables are tender-crisp. Drain, reserving the cooking liquid. Toss the vegetables together to combine.

Sauté the ground beef in a nonstick frying pan over high heat, stirring constantly until the meat is brown. Remove the beef from the frying pan to a plate lined with paper towels to absorb the grease. Pat with more paper towels, then wipe any grease out of the pan with paper towels. Add the onion and green pepper to the pan and sauté, until the onion looks transparent and the edges begin to brown. Remove the pan from the heat. (If you don't, when you add the tomato paste it will bubble and spit all over the place.) Add 1 cup of water, the reserved cooking liquid, and tomato paste to the onions and green pepper mixture. Add 1 cup of water to the tomato paste can, stir and add to the pan. Stir again, then add the chili powder, garlic powder, and cayenne. Cover and cook on a low heat for about 30 minutes, stirring occasionally until the vegetables are tender. Add a little water if the mixture becomes too dry or too thick.

In the meantime, stack the tortillas and cut them into approximately 1-inch squares. This makes it easier to serve the casserole after it is cooked.

In a 9 x 13-inch baking dish layer the sauce, then the tortillas, then the cooked vegetables, then 1 3/4 cups of the nonfat cottage cheese, then the sauce again, then the tortillas, then the remaining sauce. (Hint: When layering the sauce, it's hard to judge exactly 1/3 of the sauce for each layer, so be rather skimpy with the sauce on the bottom layer, saving the most sauce for the top layer.) Drain and briefly rinse the chili peppers, then cut the chili peppers in strips and arrange over the top of the casserole. Cover the casserole with aluminum foil and place it on the middle rack of the oven. Set the temperature at 350 degrees and bake for 30 minutes.

To make the topping, combine 1 3/4 cups of the cottage cheese, 2 tablespoons of the uncooked chopped onion, the Tabasco® sauce, and skim milk in a blender or food processor. Blend until the mixture is very smooth. Spread the topping evenly on top of the baked, hot casserole. If desired, sprinkle on the cheddar cheese, then sprinkle the remaining chopped onions and chopped tomatoes all over the top. Cut into squares and serve immediately. Each serving will contain 1 1/8 ounces of meat.

FRENCH ONION SOUP

Nutrition Facts

Amount Per Serving	
Calories 150	Calories from Fat 15

	% Daily Value*
Total Fat 2g	3%
Saturated Fat 0g	0%
Cholesterol 0mg	0%
Sodium 1090mg	45%
Total Carbohydrate 28g	9%
Dietary Fiber 3g	12%
Sugars 12g	
Protein 8g	

Vitamin A 2%	•	Vitamin C 8%
Calcium 4%	•	Iron 8%

1 quart water or beef stock
1/3 cup Roast Beef Gravy, I or II (pages 48 and 50)
1/2 teaspoon Tabasco® sauce
1 teaspoon low-sodium tamari or soy sauce
3 tablespoons plus 1 teaspoon apple juice concentrate
5 small onions, sliced thinly
1/4 cup grated sapsago cheese
Mock Kitchen Bouquet (page 58) or 1 teaspoon commercial Kitchen
   Bouquet
Whole wheat or Pritikin bread

Pour water or beef stock into a 1 1/2- or 2-quart saucepan. Add the gravy, Tabasco® sauce, tamari or soy sauce, and apple juice concentrate. Add the onions to the water and stock, cover, and bring to a boil. Lower the heat to medium and cook, covered, for 10 minutes, then add the cheese. Stir, cover, and simmer for 5 or 6 minutes, or until the onions are very tender. Add the Kitchen Bouquet. Simmer for 5 minutes more. Taste. If the soup tastes at all bitter, add more apple juice concentrate.

Ladle the soup over a slice of bread or toast in each bowl.

BASIC VEGETABLE SOUP

Nutrition Facts

Amount Per Serving

Calories 45	Calories from Fat 5

	% Daily Value*
Total Fat 0.5g	**1%**
Saturated Fat 0g	**0%**
Cholesterol 0mg	**0%**
Sodium 260mg	**11%**
Total Carbohydrate 10g	**3%**
Dietary Fiber 3g	**13%**
Sugars 6g	
Protein 2g	

Vitamin A 150%	•	Vitamin C 45%
Calcium 4%	•	Iron 4%

This soup really needs no spices except pepper, and can be considered a free food on most diets, because it has no starches.

2 medium unpeeled turnips, diced
1/2 medium cabbage, finely chopped
3 medium onions, coarsely chopped
5 medium carrots, finely chopped
1 large or 2 small yellow squash, finely chopped
1 medium zucchini, finely chopped
1 cup Roast Beef Gravy I or II (page 48 and page 50)
5 cups of Turkey or Chicken Stock (page 44)
2 ribs of celery, finely chopped
1 cup chopped fresh parsley
1 large tomato, chopped
1 tablespoon apple juice concentrate
1/2 teaspoon cayenne pepper
Water to cover

Combine all ingredients in a 5-quart stockpot, except the water. Add the water to cover the vegetables and then add another inch or so more water. Cover and simmer for 2 to 3 hours, adding water if the water goes down. Or simmer in a crock pot or slow cooker for about 4 hours.

STUFFED PORK CHOPS

Nutrition Facts

Amount Per Serving	
Calories 420 Calories from Fat 150	
	% Daily Value¹
Total Fat 17g	26%
Saturated Fat 6g	28%
Cholesterol 85mg	28%
Sodium 670mg	28%
Total Carbohydrate 39g	13%
Dietary Fiber 5g	18%
Sugars 8g	
Protein 28g	

Vitamin A 6%	•	Vitamin C 8%
Calcium 20%	•	Iron 20%

4 center-cut pork chops, 1/2-inch thick
1 small to medium onion, finely chopped
4 large mushrooms, sliced
1 rib celery, finely chopped
1/4 teaspoon garlic powder
1 1/2 cups of crumbled Cornbread (page 86)
1 tablespoon dried parsley
3/4 cup Chicken Stock (page 44)

For the Coating:
4 slices of Pritikin or commercial whole wheat bread
1 teaspoon dried thyme
1 teaspoon dried marjoram
1/4 teaspoon cayenne pepper
1 jumbo egg white
Skim milk

Trim every bit of fat off the pork chops, and discard it. Lay the chops on a cutting board, slice them open at the 1/4-inch point, cutting all the way to the bone. This will form the pocket where you will put the stuffing in. Set aside.

Combine the onion, mushrooms, and celery in a nonstick frying pan. Sauté over high heat until the onions look brown around the edges. Remove the pan from the heat. Add the garlic powder, cornbread, parsley, and chicken stock and combine thoroughly. Stuff the mixture into the pockets in the pork chops. Secure the openings with toothpicks. Set aside.

To make the coating, break up the bread slices and combine them in a food processor or blender with the thyme, marjoram, and cayenne. Process to make bread crumbs. Transfer to a shallow bowl or tray. In a separate container, measure the egg white, and mix it with an equal amount of milk.

Dip the stuffed pork chops, one at a time, into the egg-milk mixture by holding each one pinched with your hand to keep the pocket closed. Splash some on top with a spoon or your hand. Messy, I know, but it's hard to keep the stuffing from falling out if you try turning the chops over or use utensils. Place each chop on a bed of the crumbs, and sprinkle crumbs over the top. Do not turn the chop over. Place each chop on a nonstick baking pan. Add any extra crumbs to the top of each chop. Place on the top rack or upper middle section of the oven and set the temperature at 450 degrees F. Bake for 25 minutes. Do not turn. Remove the toothpicks and serve immediately with a wedge of lemon. Each serving will contain about 3 1/3 ounces of meat.

BREADED PORK CHOPS

Nutrition Facts

Amount Per Serving

Calories 190   Calories from Fat 50

	% Daily Value*
Total Fat 6g	**9**%
Saturated Fat 2g	**9**%
Cholesterol 65mg	**22**%
Sodium 160mg	**7**%
Total Carbohydrate 10g	**3**%
Dietary Fiber 1g	**6**%
Sugars 2g	
Protein 25g	

Vitamin A 2%	•	Vitamin C 2%
Calcium 6%	•	Iron 10%

Isn't it nice to know you don't have to give up your breaded pork chops?

4 slices of Pritikin or whole wheat bread
1 teaspoon dried thyme
1 teaspoon dried marjoram
1/4 teaspoon cayenne pepper
1 egg white
Skim milk
6 center-cut pork chops (1/2-inch thick)

Break up the bread slices and mix them in a blender or food processor with the thyme, marjoram, and pepper to make bread crumbs. Transfer to a shallow bowl or tray.

Measure the egg white. Combine with an equal amount of milk in a bowl.

Trim all the fat off the pork chops, dip them in the egg-milk mixture, then dip them in the crumbs, and pat the crumbs in on both sides. Place the chops on a nonstick baking pan. Press any extra crumbs onto the tops of the chops.

Take a piece of aluminum foil about 2 feet by 1 foot and wad it up to make a roll about a foot long. Place it on the back of the rack in the oven to form a "pillow." Place the pan of pork chops in the oven with the "pillow" under one end so the pan is tilted. This is so that any fat left on the meat will collect at the front of the pan and the chops won't be sitting in it. Set the oven temperature at 450 degrees F, and bake on the middle shelf for about 25 minutes, turning once.

Each chop will contain 3 1/2 to 4 ounces of meat. There is no way to measure exactly unless you cut the meat from the bone and weigh it, thus more or less ruining the effect of the breaded pork chop. But, if you are on a very strict diet, it will taste wonderful to you even if it is off the bone. Go ahead and bread your 1 1/2-ounce portion.

SLOW COOKER LAMB

Nutrition Facts

Amount Per Serving

Calories 200	Calories from Fat 70

	% Daily Value*
Total Fat 8g	12%
Saturated Fat 3.5g	18%
Cholesterol 85mg	29%
Sodium 75mg	3%
Total Carbohydrate 2g	1%
Dietary Fiber 0g	0%
Sugars 0g	
Protein 28g	

Vitamin A 0%	•	Vitamin C 2%
Calcium 2%	•	Iron 10%

I'm told that mint jelly is considered something of a culinary cliché. Be that as it may, but when something tastes perfect with a particular dish, why change? I still love mint jelly with lamb. I created a sugar-free recipe for Mint Jelly (page 66) so I wouldn't have to do without it. Save any leftover roast for Lamb Stew (page 127).

3 or 3 1/2 pound lamb leg (bone in)
1/4 teaspoon garlic powder
1/16 teaspoon cayenne pepper
1 celery rib
1 tablespoon cornstarch
Water

Remove every bit of fat from the lamb and discard it, then place the lamb in a 5-quart slow cooker. Sprinkle with garlic powder and cayenne. Cut the celery rib into 2 or 3 pieces and lay them over the lamb. Cover and cook on high setting for about 5 hours.

To make the gravy, remove the cooked lamb and refrigerate it, covered, until the next day, or cover with aluminum foil and keep it warm in a 150 degree-oven. Pour the pan drippings in a medium saucepan and refrigerate for about 1 hour to chill. Remove any fat and grease that has risen to the top and hardened. Add the cornstarch and whisk it in. Add about as much water as there are drippings in the pan. Mix, then heat, stirring constantly until the mixture comes to a boil. Let it boil as you stir for about 30 seconds until the cornstarch thickens.

Each serving should have 1/4 cup of gravy over the lamb. The lamb will weigh 4 ounces.

LAMB STEW

Nutrition Facts

Amount Per Serving	
Calories 280	Calories from Fat 45

	% Daily Value*
Total Fat 5g	**8**%
Saturated Fat 2.5g	**11**%
Cholesterol 50mg	**17**%
Sodium 440mg	**18**%
Total Carbohydrate 34g	**11**%
Dietary Fiber 4g	**18**%
Sugars 11g	
Protein 20g	

Vitamin A 330%	•	Vitamin C 30%
Calcium 6%	•	Iron 15%

Leftover lamb gravy and enough water to make 5 cups of liquid
10 ounces cubed roasted leg of lamb
1 large onion, chopped
2 cups sliced mushrooms
3 celery ribs, chopped
1 lamb bone
4 medium carrots, cut in big chunks
2 very large or 4 to 5 small potatoes, diced
1/4 teaspoon garlic powder
1 tablespoon dried parsley
1/2 teaspoon dried mint
1/4 teaspoon cayenne pepper
2 tablespoons apple juice concentrate
3 teaspoons low-sodium soy sauce
1/2 cup Red Rosé wine
2 tablespoons cornstarch

Measure your leftover gravy and add enough water to equal 5 cups of liquid. If you don't have any gravy, just measure 5 cups of water. Set aside.

Combine the onion, mushrooms, and celery in a 5-quart nonstick pot. Sauté over high heat by turning the vegetables over and over until the onions look a little transparent and brown around the edges. Add the gravy and water mixture, the lamb, and the lamb bone. Reduce the heat to medium-low. Add the carrots and potatoes, stir, and cover. Reduce the heat to low and simmer for about 1 hour, stirring occasionally. Add the garlic powder, parsley, mint, cayenne, juice concentrate, soy sauce, and the Red Rosé wine. Cover and simmer for 30 minutes more, until the carrots and potatoes are tender, stirring occasionally. Remove the pot from the heat.

Remove 1/2 cup of the liquid and let it cool for a few minutes. Add the cornstarch and whisk until the mixture is smooth. Stir the mixture into the stew. Return to the stove and cook over low heat for 3 to 4 minutes, or until the gravy thickens, stirring frequently. Each serving will contain 2 ounces of lamb.

CHAPTER 5

Poultry Entrées

At first I thought a 3 1/2 or 4 ounce portion of chicken or turkey would not be worth eating, but over the years this size portion seems quite normal. Now I nearly faint when I go into a restaurant and see an order of half a good-sized chicken on someone's plate.

I think you will be surprised at the traditional-sounding recipes in this book. You don't have to stop living just because you cook a little differently. Eat and enjoy. And think of all the money you will save.

OVEN-FRIED CHICKEN

YIELD: 4 SERVINGS

Nutrition Facts

Amount Per Serving

Calories 430	Calories from Fat 35

	% Daily Value¹
Total Fat 4g	**6**%
Saturated Fat 1g	**5**%
Cholesterol 135mg	**46**%
Sodium 190mg	**8**%
Total Carbohydrate 35g	**12**%
Dietary Fiber 6g	**22**%
Sugars 3g	
Protein 63g	

Vitamin A 4%	•	Vitamin C 6%
Calcium 8%	•	Iron 20%

If you get a yen for some good old fried chicken, try this. It's not greasy, but it definitely has that fried chicken taste.

4 chicken breasts, about 3 1/2 to 4 ounces each, cut in half
1/2 cup skim milk
1 jumbo egg white
3 to 4 drops Tabasco® sauce
1 1/2 cups whole wheat flour
1/4 teaspoon cayenne pepper
1/4 teaspoon dried sage
1/2 teaspoon onion powder
1/4 teaspoon dried thyme

Remove the skin from the chicken pieces, as well as every little bit of fat.

In a bowl, mix together the milk, egg whites, and Tabasco® sauce. Put the flour in a plastic bag with the cayenne pepper, sage, onion powder, and thyme and shake to combine. Dip each piece of chicken, one at a time, in the milk mixture, then add to the bag, and shake in the flour until coated. Remove each piece and place on a nonstick baking sheet or pan. Take a piece of aluminum foil about 2 feet by 1 foot and wad it up to make a roll about a foot long. Set the oven temperature at 350 degrees F. Place it at the back of the rack in the oven to form a "pillow." Place the pan in the oven with the "pillow" under one end. Any fat or grease left in the chicken will roll towards the opposite end from the "pillow" and the chicken won't be sitting in grease. Bake about 1/2 hour or a little longer, until tender. Turn halfway through cooking. One chicken breast is equal to about 3 1/2 to 4 ounces of meat. If you are on a very strict diet, you might want to skin and bone 1/2 a breast and weigh it. The meat will come to about 2 ounces. Trim off meat until you get the 1 1/2 ounces, then flour and bake your chicken according to the recipe.

BAKED CHICKEN

Nutrition Facts

Amount Per Serving

Calories 270   Calories from Fat 45

	% Daily Value*
Total Fat 5g	8%
Saturated Fat 2g	9%
Cholesterol 15mg	5%
Sodium 115mg	5%
Total Carbohydrate 40g	13%
Dietary Fiber 6g	25%
Sugars 10g	
Protein 17g	

Vitamin A 20%	• Vitamin C 250%
Calcium 4%	• Iron 15%

My husband and kids love chicken prepared this way. They don't miss the salt at all. You can leave the skin on while the chicken bakes because it's been found that the fat from the skin does not penetrate the meat as it cooks, but it imparts flavor to the chicken.

1 whole (3 1/2 pound) chicken
Cayenne pepper
Garlic powder
Onion powder

Place the chicken in a baking dish and sprinkle lightly with the seasonings.

Microwave Directions: Bake, uncovered, at 80 percent power or on roast for 30 to 40 minutes. With a very sharp knife, pierce the chicken in the very meaty part of the thigh near where it is connected to the back. If any red or pink juice comes out, cook the chicken for 5 to 6 minutes longer.

Oven Directions: Preheat the oven to 350 degrees. Bake for 1 hour with an aluminum foil tent over the chicken, which is removed for the last 20 minutes. When the legs are loose and easy to lift up and down, the chicken is done. Just to make sure, pierce the meaty part of the thigh near where it is connected to the back. If any red or pink juice runs out, bake the chicken a little longer.

Remove the skin before you serve the chicken, but save it to flavor chicken stock. One breast is equal to 3 1/2–4 ounces of meat. One whole leg is about the same.

SLOW COOKER CHICKEN DINNER

Nutrition Facts

Amount Per Serving

Calories 240   Calories from Fat 15

	% Daily Value*
Total Fat 2g	3%
Saturated Fat 0g	0%
Cholesterol 70mg	23%
Sodium 380mg	16%
Total Carbohydrate 23g	8%
Dietary Fiber 5g	19%
Sugars 8g	
Protein 31g	

Vitamin A 350%	•	Vitamin C 60%
Calcium 6%	•	Iron 15%

This makes a delicious one-dish meal. If you are out, it can cook for an hour longer on high than the time I specify. Or, cook it on low setting, adding an additional cup of water if you have to be gone for 6 to 8 hours. You can even put the chicken in the pot frozen if you cook it longer than 4 hours.

3 chicken breasts, bone-in, skins removed
1/4 teaspoon garlic powder
2 tablespoons dried onion flakes
1/4 teaspoon cayenne pepper
3 large carrots, cut into chunks
2 cups sliced mushrooms
1 teaspoon celery flakes
1 green pepper, chopped
2 cups thickly sliced potatoes
1/4 cup Red Rosé wine
1 tablespoon dried parsley or 1/4 cup chopped fresh parsley
1 can (15 1/2 ounces) salt-free cut green beans, drained

Place the chicken in a 5-quart slow cooker. Sprinkle with the garlic powder, then the onion flakes, then the pepper. Add the carrots, then the mushrooms. Sprinkle with the dried celery, then the green pepper. Add the potato slices, then pour the wine over the potatoes, and sprinkle with the parsley. Cover and cook on high setting for 3 1/2 hours. Or, if you are not going to be home all day, in order to keep the pot from drying out, add 1/2 cup of water and cook covered, on low setting all day. During the last half hour, add the green beans and cover. Each serving will contain 1 3/4 ounces of chicken.

CHICKEN FRICASSÉE

Nutrition Facts

Amount Per Serving	
Calories 320	Calories from Fat 35

	% Daily Value*
Total Fat 4g	6%
Saturated Fat 1g	5%
Cholesterol 75mg	24%
Sodium 100mg	4%
Total Carbohydrate 37g	12%
Dietary Fiber 5g	20%
Sugars 16g	
Protein 32g	

Vitamin A 25%	•	Vitamin C 110%
Calcium 8%	•	Iron 20%

"Fricassée" is a French word, which means "hash," so perhaps this favorite Creole recipe was created on Martinique or Haiti, which were once French possessions.

During the slave rebellions in the late 1700s, many French and Africans, both free and slaves, fled to New Orleans from St. Domingue (Haiti). One of my ancestors, Guillaume Hubert, brought twenty loyal African slaves to Louisiana with him from St. Domingue. One of them, Lapalu, saved Guillaume's life by hiding him in the jungle, then getting him off the island. For doing that, Lapalu is written up as a hero in Kendal's History of New Orleans. Lapalu's wife or one of the other African women in Guillaume's household probably brought the recipe for Chicken Fricassée with her from St. Domingue and the recipe was passed down through the generations of African cooks.

My grandmother didn't know how to cook because she always had cooks in her household. It wasn't until about 50 years ago in New Orleans that white women of her class started cooking. My mother came along with her interest in the old traditions learned from the cooks in her mother's kitchen.

Albertina, who took care of me when I was little, later became our cook. I remember Mama and Albertina in the kitchen chopping onions and peeling potatoes, drinking coffee and gossiping, and I would watch them and wait for them to give me a chore to do. Chicken Fricassée was a once-a-week event when I was a child, and I think of it as a dish that links my family to past generations.

4 chicken breast fillets cut into pieces, skin removed
1 large green pepper, chopped
2 medium onions, chopped
1 1/4 cups sliced mushrooms
2 celery ribs, chopped
4 cups water
2 cups cubed zucchini (1 medium to large zucchini)
3/4 cup coarsely chopped fresh parsley
1 bay leaf
1 teaspoon dried thyme
1/2 teaspoon dried sage
1/4 teaspoon cayenne pepper
5 tablespoons apple juice concentrate
2 tablespoons dry vermouth

Place half the chicken pieces in a 5-quart nonstick stockpot to just cover the bottom of the pot with no pieces touching each other. Sauté over high heat until lightly brown, stirring frequently. Remove the browned pieces from the pot and add the rest of the chicken. Sauté as you did the first batch. If the pot starts to smoke, reduce the heat. When the last batch is brown, remove from the pot, turn off the heat, and wipe out any grease left in the pot.

Combine the green pepper and onion in the stockpot. Sauté over high heat until the onion is a little brown around the edges and somewhat transparent. Add the mushrooms and celery; continue sautéing until the mushrooms turn dark and limp. Lower the heat and add the water, zucchini, parsley, bay leaf, thyme, sage, cayenne, juice concentrate, and vermouth. Stir to combine and return the chicken to the pot. Add enough water to almost cover the chicken. Cover, set the heat on low and simmer for 1 1/2 hours, stirring occasionally. Each serving contains about 3 1/2 ounces of chicken.

CHICKEN R. B.

Nutrition Facts

Amount Per Serving

Calories 510   Calories from Fat 130

	% Daily Value*
Total Fat 15g	23%
Saturated Fat 4g	21%
Cholesterol 95mg	31%
Sodium 130mg	5%
Total Carbohydrate 55g	18%
Dietary Fiber 11g	45%
Sugars 7g	
Protein 44g	

Vitamin A 130%	•	Vitamin C 120%
Calcium 10%	•	Iron 25%

This recipe is named after my son R. B. (Raymond Benton), who is a very good cook himself. (He says he learned to cook because he raised himself. While that's not exactly true, I did let all my boys cook whenever they wanted to.)

4 chicken breasts, skin removed
1/8 teaspoon garlic powder
1/16 teaspoon cayenne pepper
1 medium carrot, sliced
1 medium green pepper, sliced
1 cup sliced fresh mushrooms
1 celery rib, chopped
1 /3 cups skim milk
2 tablespoons whole wheat flour
1/4 teaspoon dried red pepper flakes
1 teaspoon dried oregano
1/2 teaspoon dried basil
1/4 teaspoon garlic powder
1 teaspoon onion powder
1 tablespoon dried parsley
1 jar (4 ounces) chopped pimentos and juice
1 cup fresh or frozen green peas (rinsed, if frozen)
4 cups cooked (9 ounces before it's cooked) very thin spaghetti or vermicelli
1 medium zucchini, sliced
2 tablespoons grated sapsago cheese

Place the chicken breasts in a 9 x 13-inch baking dish. Sprinkle with the garlic powder and cayenne. Place the baking dish on the middle rack of the oven. Set the oven temperature to 400 degrees F. and bake for 25 minutes; turn once. Remove the chicken to another dish and set aside. Wipe out any grease left in the baking dish, and set the dish aside.

Combine the carrot, green pepper, mushrooms, and celery in a nonstick frying pan. Sauté over high heat until the green peppers develop a nice aroma and look shiny. Remove the pan from the heat and set aside.

To make the sauce, pour 5 tablespoons of the skim milk into a cup. Add the whole wheat flour, and mix until there are no lumps. Pour the rest of the skim milk into the cup, combine, and set aside.

Set the pan with the vegetables over medium heat. Add the skim milk-flour mixture, the red pepper flakes, oregano, basil, garlic powder, onion powder, parsley, and pimentos. Cook and stir constantly until the mixture begins to bubble, then add the peas. Remove the pan from the heat and set aside.

Preheat the oven to 350 degrees F.

Cook the spaghetti in plenty of boiling water until tender, drain, then combine with the sauce in the frying pan. Layer half the spaghetti-sauce mixture in the bottom of the 9-inch-by-13-inch baking dish. Arrange the zucchini slices over the top, then layer the chicken over the zucchini slices. Top with the remaining spaghetti. Cover the dish with aluminum foil and place it on the middle rack of the oven. Bake for 30 minutes. Serve hot and sprinkle 1/2 tablespoon of sapsago cheese over each serving. Each serving should contain about 3 1/2 ounces of chicken.

COUNTRY CHICKEN STEW

My mother used to make the best chicken stew. To this day I can remember how it smelled, simmering on her kitchen stove. That tender, juicy chicken and rich gravy over rice was just wonderful. I use many of her techniques and ingredients plus some of my own for this stew and it tastes almost identical.

8 chicken pieces (mixed)
1/4 teaspoon cayenne pepper
2 medium to large onions, chopped
1 medium to large green pepper, chopped
6 tablespoons whole wheat flour
Water or Chicken Stock (page 44)
4 cloves garlic, chopped
1 teaspoon dried thyme
2 bay leaves
1/8 teaspoon ground turmeric
1/2 teaspoon dried sage
1/4 cup dry vermouth
1 1/2 teaspoon medium red hot sauce
1 tablespoon dried parsley or 1/4 cup fresh, chopped, loosely packed
1/4 cup apple juice concentrate

Remove the skin and as much fat as possible from the chicken pieces. Place as many pieces of chicken as you can in a large nonstick stockpot without stacking them. Sprinkle with a little of the cayenne pepper. Brown the chicken pieces on all sides over high heat, moving them around frequently. Turn them over to brown them on the other side. Remove them to a plate or bowl. If the pot is smoking by this time, lower the heat to medium and quickly add more chicken. Brown as you did the first batch. Increase the heat if the chicken seems to be browning too slowly, or if it looks as though it is steaming instead of browning. Lower the heat again if the pot starts to smoke. Continue in this manner until all the chicken is brown. Remove the chicken from the pot and set aside.

Pour off any grease that has accumulated in the pot and dab the rest of the grease out of the pot with a paper towel, but do not wipe away the caramelized juices. Return the pot to the stove and add the onions and green pepper. Over high heat, sauté until fairly brown. If they begin to smoke, lower the heat a little. Sprinkle the flour over the vegetables and continue to sauté, turning the vegetables over and over. When the flour begins to smoke, continue to sauté for about 20 seconds more, stirring constantly. Immediately, add 2 cups of water a little at a time, while you continue to stir until the mixture is smooth. Add the garlic. Reduce the heat to low and add the remaining ingredients.

Return the chicken to the pot, and add more water or stock if needed to cover the chicken. Simmer covered, for 1 1/2–2 hours. Stir occasionally and add a little more water if the gravy cooks down to more than 1/4-inch below the chicken pieces. The gravy should be a little thicker than melted ice cream. Set aside to cool, then refrigerate overnight. The next day, remove any grease that has hardened on the surface. Reheat to serve the chicken.

Variation: CHICKEN AND DUMPLINGS

Combine 1/2 cup whole wheat flour and 1/2 teaspoon low-sodium baking powder. Then add 1 egg white and 6 tablespoons skim milk and combine thoroughly.

Have your chicken stew and gravy just simmering on the stove. Drop the flour-egg-milk mixture into the simmering gravy. Poach for about 10 minutes or until little air bubbles or holes appear on top of each dumpling. Cook just a few moments longer to make sure they are cooked through. Serve at once with the stew. These dumplings are shaped like little inflated pancakes. If you try to add more flour so you can roll them into the shape of a conventional dumpling, they will be tough.

Yield: 6 dumplings.

CHICKEN ALEXANDER

Nutrition Facts

Amount Per Serving	
Calories 360	Calories from Fat 40

	% Daily Value*
Total Fat 4.5g	7%
Saturated Fat 1g	6%
Cholesterol 40mg	13%
Sodium 400mg	17%
Total Carbohydrate 57g	19%
Dietary Fiber 8g	31%
Sugars 12g	
Protein 26g	

Vitamin A 90%	•	Vitamin C 20%
Calcium 25%	•	Iron 15%

Chicken Alexander is named after my youngest son Alex, who is very health conscious. He's a long distance runner, lifts weights, and likes to cook good food for himself and his wife, Sulley.

2 cups Roasted Chicken Stock (page 46)
1 medium onion, chopped
1 medium zucchini, diced
1 medium carrot, diced
1/4 cup chopped green pepper
1 tablespoon dried celery flakes
1/8 teaspoon cayenne pepper
1/16 teaspoon dried marjoram
1/16 teaspoon ground cumin
1/8 teaspoon dried sage
1/4 teaspoon plus 1/8 teaspoon dried thyme
1/4 cup cornstarch
1 can (12 ounces or 13 ounces) evaporated skim milk
1 1/2 cups cooked, diced white chicken meat

In a 1 1/2-quart saucepan, combine the chicken stock, onion, zucchini, carrot, green pepper, celery flakes, cayenne, marjoram, cumin, sage, and thyme. Bring to a boil, then continue to boil over medium heat, uncovered, for 15 minutes. Remove the pot from the heat, and set aside.

In a small bowl, add the cornstarch to the milk, a little at a time, blending it until it is free of lumps. Add the milk mixture and chicken to the pot. Cook over medium heat for 2 to 4 minutes, stirring constantly, until the mixture is thickened. Serve immediately. Each serving will contain about 1 3/5 ounces of chicken.

SLOW COOKER CHICKEN CACCIATORE

Nutrition Facts

Amount Per Serving

Calories 670	Calories from Fat 40

	% Daily Value*
Total Fat 4g	6%
Saturated Fat 1g	5%
Cholesterol 75mg	24%
Sodium 140mg	6%
Total Carbohydrate 117g	39%
Dietary Fiber 11g	42%
Sugars 7g	
Protein 40g	

Vitamin A 40%	•	Vitamin C 60%
Calcium 10%	•	Iron 25%

4 pieces chicken, breasts or legs, skin removed
1/4 teaspoon garlic powder
1/16 teaspoon cumin
2 1/2 tablespoons minced dried onion
1/4 teaspoon dried red pepper flakes
1/8 teaspoon dried basil
2 teaspoons dried celery flakes
1 teaspoon dried oregano
2 tablespoons dried chopped green pepper
1 tablespoon dried parsley flakes
3 cans (8 ounces each) salt-free tomato sauce
1 cup water
3 tablespoons cornstarch
2 tablespoons apple juice concentrate
1/4 cup Red Rosé wine
4 tablespoons grated sapsago cheese

Place 2 pieces of the chicken in a 5-quart slow cooker. Sprinkle with half of the garlic powder, cumin, onion, pepper, basil, celery, oregano, green pepper, and parsley. Place the other 2 pieces of chicken on top of the first two pieces. Sprinkle with the remaining garlic powder, cumin, onion, pepper, basil, celery, oregano, green pepper, and parsley. Cover and set the heat on high setting. Cook for 3 hours.

Pour the tomato sauce over the chicken. Add the water to 1 can, then pour the water from can to can to get every drop of tomato sauce. To the last can full of water, add the cornstarch and mix until smooth. Pour the mixture around the sides of the chicken pieces, not on top of them. Then pour the juice concentrate and wine around the sides of the chicken. Cover and cook 3 more hours. Stir once or twice during cooking.

Sprinkle a tablespoon of sapsago cheese over each serving. Each serving will contain about 3 1/2 ounces of chicken.

POULET À LA GREEN STORE

The Spanish-descended residents of St. Bernard Parish, near New Orleans, do not adjust well to change. Many of them have ancestors who came from the Canary Islands between 1779 and 1785, and still fly the Spanish flag over their shrimp boats at the annual blessing of the fleet. The King of Spain even comes to visit them occasionally. They are proud of their role in history and still talk as if the pirate Jean Lafitte were still around to help Andrew Jackson win the Battle of New Orleans.

When my son Guillaume and I recently passed through historic St. Bernard Parish on our way to Pointe à la Hache, he said to me, "Mom, we have to turn left at The Green Store." This local landmark at the crossroads has belonged to the same family for about 100 years and has always been painted green.

A few years ago, the owner of the store painted it brown. This caused tremendous confusion, No one could find their way to Pointe à la Hache because the St. Bernardians kept telling everyone to turn left at the green store which was now brown. Finally, the owner repainted his store green and even went a step further: he painted in black building-size letters on the side of the store: THE GREEN STORE. I just had to name a recipe in honor of St. Bernard Parish's Green Store.

1 medium zucchini, sliced, or 1 medium cucumber, peeled and sliced
2 celery ribs, chopped
1 medium onion, chopped
1 1/2 cups cooked white chicken meat
1/2 cup Chicken Stock (page 44)
1 1/2 cups Roasted Chicken Stock (page 46)
1/4 teaspoon garlic powder
1/8 teaspoon cayenne pepper
1 1/2 teaspoons onion powder
1/2 teaspoon dried thyme
1/2 teaspoon dried sage
1 cup sliced mushrooms
1 medium ripe tomato, chopped
1 cup chopped celery
2 tablespoons apple juice concentrate
2 tablespoons unbleached flour

Microwave Directions: In a 1 1/2-quart baking dish, layer the zucchini or cucumber, celery, onions, and chicken. Add 1/2 cup chicken stock. Cover and cook for 8 minutes on high setting. Pour the sauce over the cooked layered vegetables and chicken in the casserole dish. Cover the casserole and cook for 5 minutes on high.

Stove Top Directions for Sauce: Pour the chicken stock into a medium saucepan. Add the garlic powder, cayenne, onion powder, thyme, sage, mushrooms, tomato, celery, and juice concentrate. Cover, and bring to a boil. Lower the heat and simmer covered, for 5 minutes, stirring occasionally. Add the flour by sprinkling it over the mixture 1 tablespoon at a time, and mixing thoroughly each time. Cook uncovered for 2 minutes over low heat, stirring constantly.

Oven Directions for Chicken and Sauce: Layer the zucchini, 2 chopped celery ribs, onion, chicken, the celery, mushrooms and tomato in a 1 1/2-quart casserole dish. Pour all of the chicken stock into a small bowl or large measuring cup. Mix in the garlic powder, cayenne pepper, onion powder, thyme, and sage. Add the juice concentrate. Mix in the flour, 1 tablespoon at a time, until well blended. Pour the mixture over the vegetables and chicken in the casserole. Cover and bake at 350 degrees F. for 45 minutes, and then let it sit in the oven for 15 minutes with the oven off.

Each serving will contain about 2 ounces of chicken.

CHICKEN TROPICANA

Nutrition Facts

Amount Per Serving

Calories 390   Calories from Fat 80

	% Daily Value*
Total Fat 8g	**13**%
Saturated Fat 2.5g	**11**%
Cholesterol 90mg	**30**%
Sodium 90mg	**4**%
Total Carbohydrate 42g	**14**%
Dietary Fiber 2g	**7**%
Sugars 38g	
Protein 28g	

Vitamin A 2%	•	Vitamin C 35%
Calcium 4%	•	Iron 15%

3 1/2 pound chicken
1/4 plus 1/16 teaspoon cayenne pepper, divided
1/4 teaspoon curry powder, divided
2 1/2 cups unsweetened pineapple juice, divided
1/4 cup plus 2 tablespoons apple juice concentrate, divided
1/3 cup brandy, whiskey, or rum, divided
1 large onion, chopped
1/3 cup raisins
1 cup drained unsweetened crushed pineapple, fresh or canned
1/4 teaspoon dried basil
1 tablespoon arrowroot or cornstarch

Remove the skin and as much fat as possible from the chicken. I like to skin my chicken whole, starting at the bottom of the breast. I just keep cutting underneath and pulling. Then I cut up the chicken, and remove any skin that may be left, as well as any pockets of fat.

Microwave Directions: Place the chicken pieces in a 9 x 13-inch baking dish. Sprinkle the chicken with 1/8 teaspoon of the cayenne pepper and 1/8 teaspoon of the curry powder. Bake on high setting for 15 minutes to brown. Turn the chicken over in the pan and add 1 1/2 cups of the pineapple juice, 1/4 cup of the juice concentrate, and the brandy, whiskey, or rum. Stir in the onion, raisins, and pineapple. Sprinkle with 1/16 teaspoon of the cayenne pepper and 1/4 teaspoon basil. Bake for 15 minutes on high setting, basting every so often, then set the heat to low and simmer for 15 minutes.

Remove the chicken from the pan and keep warm. Sprinkle the arrowroot or cornstarch into the pan and pat it into the liquid with the back of your spoon, then stir it into the pan juices until smooth. Add the remaining 1 cup pineapple juice, 2 tablespoons juice concentrate, and 1/8 teaspoon cayenne pepper and 1/8 teaspoon curry powder. Bake on high setting for 7 minutes, stirring frequently. If the mixture doesn't thicken, stir in a little more arrowroot or cornstarch. If it becomes too thick, add more pineapple juice and a little more juice concentrate. It doesn't have to be very thick, you just don't want it watery.

Conventional Oven Directions: Preheat the oven to 400 degrees F. Place the chicken pieces in a 9 x 13-inch baking dish. Sprinkle with 1/8 teaspoon cayenne pepper and 1/8 teaspoon curry powder. Cover loosely with aluminum foil, leaving some air holes on the side, and bake for 20 to 25 minutes to brown the chicken. Turn the chicken over in the pan and add 1 1/2 cups of the pineapple juice, 1/4 cup of the juice concentrate and the brandy, whisky, or rum. Stir in the onion, raisins, and pineapple. Sprinkle with 1/16 teaspoon cayenne pepper and 1/4 teaspoon basil. Lower the oven temperature to 250 degrees F. and bake loosely covered with aluminum foil until the chicken is done, about 25 minutes, basting every so often.

Remove the chicken from the pan and keep warm. Sprinkle the arrowroot or cornstarch into the pan and pat it with the back of your spoon, then stir it in the pan juices until smooth. Add the remaining 1 cup pineapple juice, 2 tablespoons juice concentrate, 1/8 teaspoon cayenne, and 1/8 teaspoon curry powder. Bake at 400 degrees F. for 5 minutes, stirring frequently. If the mixture doesn't thicken, stir in a little more arrowroot or cornstarch and bake for a few minutes more. If it becomes too thick, add more pineapple juice and a little more juice concentrate.

One chicken breast equals 3 1/2 to 4 ounces. One leg equals 3 1/2 to 4 ounces. If you are on a very strict diet and can have only 1 1/2 ounces of meat, remove the meat from a piece of cooked breast and cut it in half. Weigh to be sure you have just 1 1/2 ounces of meat. Serve on a plate with warm sauce from the baking dish poured over the chicken.

POULET SAUCE BLANC (CHICKEN IN WHITE GRAVY)

Nutrition Facts

Amount Per Serving

Calories 320	Calories from Fat 50

	% Daily Value*
Total Fat 5g	8%
Saturated Fat 1.5g	7%
Cholesterol 35mg	11%
Sodium 580mg	24%
Total Carbohydrate 47g	16%
Dietary Fiber 5g	20%
Sugars 16g	
Protein 23g	

Vitamin A 10%	•	Vitamin C 8%
Calcium 30%	•	Iron 15%

You can pour the chicken and gravy over whole wheat toast or over corn bread for a delicious main meal. You could even pour this over spaghetti. This recipe is much easier in a microwave than on top of the stove.

1 large onion, sliced in rings
1 cup Strong Roasted Chicken Stock (page 46)
3 tablespoons cornstarch
1/4 Baked Banana (page 57)
1/4 teaspoon cayenne pepper
1/2 teaspoon dried parsley
1/4 teaspoon dried thyme
1/4 teaspoon dried sage
1 cup (8 ounces) chopped cooked white chicken meat
1 can (12 ounces) evaporated skim milk
Paprika

Microwave Directions: Place the onion rings in a 2-quart microwave dish. Blend the chicken stock with the cornstarch until perfectly smooth and add it to the onion rings. Cover and cook on high setting for 2 minutes. Stir, then cover again and cook on high setting for 5 minutes. Stir, cover, and cook on high setting for 3 minutes more. The onions should be cooked and the liquid thickened; if not, microwave for another 2 minutes.

In a separate container, mash the baked banana. Add the banana and baking juices, the cayenne, parsley, thyme, and sage and combine thoroughly. Add the chicken pieces and combine. Then add the milk and combine everything together. Cover and cook on high setting for 5 minutes. Sprinkle with paprika.

Stove Top Directions: Combine the onion and chicken stock, cayenne, parsley, thyme, and sage, in a medium saucepan. Bring to a boil, cover, and cook over high heat for 5 minutes. Remove from the heat. Combine the milk, banana, and cornstarch in a blender or processor. Blend until smooth. Add the milk mixture and chicken to the saucepan. Return the pot to the heat, cover, and cook over medium heat, stirring constantly, for 3 minutes, or until the mixture thickens. Sprinkle with paprika. Each serving will contain 2 ounces of chicken.

CHICKEN IN WINE SAUCE

1 cup Red Rosé wine
1/4 teaspoon dried tarragon
1/4 teaspoon garlic powder
1/8 teaspoon cayenne pepper
11 tablespoons apple juice concentrate
2 tablespoons dried onion flakes
4 chicken breasts, skins removed
2 tablespoons cornstarch
2 nectarines, sliced (do not peel)

Combine the wine, tarragon, garlic, cayenne, juice concentrate, and onion in an 8-inch-square baking dish. Place the chicken breasts, meat-side-down in the mixture. Cover and place in the refrigerator for at least an hour to marinate. (If you like, you can leave it much longer, until you are ready to cook it.)

When you are ready to cook, remove the chicken to another dish, and add the cornstarch to the marinade. Stir until smooth. Add the nectarines, distributing them evenly in the baking dish. Place the chicken breasts, meat-side-down into the marinade.

Microwave Directions: Cook on high, uncovered, for 20 minutes. Move the chicken around to stir the sauce. Cook on high setting for 5 minutes more, still uncovered. Remove from the oven and let sit for 5 minutes before serving.

Serve meat-side-up with the sauce and nectarines on top. Delicious! Each serving will contain about 3 1/2 ounces of chicken.

CHICKEN CRÊPES

Nutrition Facts

Amount Per Serving	
Calories 300	Calories from Fat 45

	% Daily Value*
Total Fat 5g	**8**%
Saturated Fat 1.5g	**7**%
Cholesterol 50mg	**17**%
Sodium 210mg	**9**%
Total Carbohydrate 39g	**13**%
Dietary Fiber 3g	**14**%
Sugars 15g	
Protein 25g	

Vitamin A 190%	•	Vitamin C 60%
Calcium 15%	•	Iron 15%

1/3 cup chopped onion (1 medium onion)
1/3 cup chopped green pepper (1 small green pepper)
2 cups water
1/2 cup chopped carrot
4 ounces lean cooked chicken breast, diced
1/8 teaspoon cayenne pepper
1/4 teaspoon garlic powder
1 1/2 teaspoons orange juice concentrate
4 1/2 teaspoons apple juice concentrate
1/2 teaspoon dried parsley flakes
1/4 teaspoon powdered or crumbled thyme
1 teaspoon low-sodium soy sauce
2 tablespoons unbleached white flour
2 Crêpes (page 89)

Combine onions and green pepper in a nonstick 1 1/2-quart saucepan. Sauté over high heat for 3 to 4 minutes until the onion is tender. Add the water, carrot, chicken pieces, cayenne pepper, garlic powder, orange juice concentrate, apple juice concentrate, parsley, thyme, and soy sauce. Bring to a rapid boil and boil uncovered to reduce the mixture by about half, about 8 minutes. Strain the liquid from the vegetables into a measuring cup. Add enough water to make 1 cup, if necessary. Pour the liquid back into the vegetables, return the pot to the stove, and bring to a boil again. Sprinkle in about 1/3 tablespoon of the flour at a time. Pat it into the boiling mixture and combine thoroughly. Keep adding flour until it is all mixed in. Boil for about 1/2 minute or until the mixture thickens, stirring constantly. It will not be extremely thick, but it does make a nice gravy. Keep warm while you prepare the crêpes.

To serve, spread the filling on each crêpe, then fold the crêpes like a half a sandwich and pour the remaining filling on top. Each serving will have 2 ounces of chicken. For very strict diets, use only 3 ounces of chicken for this recipe so each serving will have 1 1/2 ounces of meat.

ROASTED TURKEY BREAST

YIELD: 14 SERVINGS

Nutrition Facts

Amount Per Serving	
Calories 270	Calories from Fat 15

	% Daily Value²
Total Fat 1.5g	2%
Saturated Fat 0g	0%
Cholesterol 160mg	54%
Sodium 150mg	6%
Total Carbohydrate 1g	0%
Dietary Fiber 0g	0%
Sugars 0g	
Protein 59g	

Vitamin A 0%	•	Vitamin C 0%
Calcium 2%	•	Iron 15%

Now you can buy just the turkey breast frozen. I'm not talking about turkey roll, or pressed turkey. I'm talking about the whole breast which has been cut from the turkey that is still on the bone. It's very nice for company or just for the convenience.

6-pound turkey breast
1/4 plus 1/16 teaspoon garlic powder
1/16 teaspoon cayenne pepper
1/4 teaspoon dried sage
3 cups water, divided
1/2 cup Chicken or Turkey Stock (page 44)
1/4 cup Red Rosé wine
2 cups or more Chicken or Turkey Gravy Base (optional) (page 51)
1 tablespoon cornstarch
1/8 teaspoon dried thyme
1/8 teaspoon dried sage

Defrost the turkey breast just enough so you can remove the skin and fat. Place the breast in a roasting pan. Sprinkle with the garlic powder, cayenne, and sage. Cover the breast (but not the whole pan) with an aluminum foil tent. Place on the middle rack of the oven. Set the oven temperature to 350 degrees F. and roast undisturbed for 1 hour. Add 1 cup of water to the pan and roast for 1 more hour. Baste the turkey breast with some of the chicken or turkey stock and add another cup of water and the wine to the pan. Recover with the tent and roast for another hour. Baste again, using all the remaining chicken stock, and add 1 more cup of water. Cover, and roast for 30 minutes. (Roast for 3 1/2 hours in all.)

Remove the breast from the pan to a serving platter and keep covered and warm.

To make the gravy, skim off any remaining grease floating in the roasting pan. Skim first with a spoon and then use a lettuce or cabbage leaf over the top to get the last of it, or place a paper plate on top and remove and discard. Repeat if necessary. Sprinkle the cornstarch over the liquid left in the pan, and combine until free of any lumps. Add the thyme and the remaining 1/8 teaspoon of sage. Heat the gravy in the oven at 400 degrees F. for about 5 or 6 minutes, until the cornstarch thickens the gravy. Stir 2 or 3 times. If you have some chicken or turkey gravy base, heat it and add it to the gravy. Each serving will contain 3 1/3 ounces of turkey.

TURKEY HASH

Nutrition Facts

Amount Per Serving	
Calories 180	Calories from Fat 30

	% Daily Value*
Total Fat 3g	5%
Saturated Fat 1g	5%
Cholesterol 35mg	12%
Sodium 480mg	20%
Total Carbohydrate 22g	7%
Dietary Fiber 3g	11%
Sugars 5g	
Protein 17g	

Vitamin A 110%	•	Vitamin C 50%
Calcium 4%	•	Iron 15%

What to do with the leftover holiday turkey? Make some stock and have a wonderful hash, of course.

1 turkey carcass (to yield 3 1/2 cups stock plus 2 cups chopped white meat)
Water
1 medium onion, chopped
1 large green pepper, chopped
1 1/2 cups sliced fresh mushrooms
1 large carrot, sliced
3 cups diced potatoes (about 4 medium potatoes)
1 cup chopped fresh parsley
1/4 teaspoon garlic powder
1/4 teaspoon dried sage
1/2 teaspoon dried thyme
1 bay leaf
1 teaspoon medium red hot sauce
1 tablespoon apple juice concentrate
1/4 teaspoon cayenne pepper
1 tablespoon cornstarch

To make turkey stock: Immerse a turkey carcass in a large stockpot three-quarters full of water. Boil uncovered over medium heat for about 3 hours. Remove the carcass to a separate container and refrigerate. Chill the stock in the refrigerator until the grease rises and hardens on top. Remove the grease. Measure 3 1/2 cups of stock and freeze the rest for future use. Pick all the meat off the carcass. Measure 2 cups (14 ounces) of meat and dice. Freeze the rest of the meat.

Place the onion and green pepper in a 5-quart nonstick pot. Sauté over high heat until the onions brown around the edges and begin to look a little transparent. Add the mushrooms and continue sautéing until the mushrooms look limp. Lower the heat and add the turkey stock, carrot, and potatoes. Then increase the heat to high and bring to a boil. Lower the heat to medium and cook, uncovered, for 25 minutes. Add the parsley, garlic powder, sage, thyme, bay leaf, hot sauce, juice concentrate, and cayenne. Combine thoroughly. Sprinkle with the cornstarch and mix it in well. Cook for 15 minutes more over medium heat, uncovered, stirring occasionally. The gravy should be slightly thick and the liquid should be reduced enough that you can eat it on a plate (as opposed to a bowl). Cook longer to reduce the liquid, if necessary. Serve hot. This freezes well in individual containers for future meals. Each serving will contain 2 ounces of meat.

TURKEY STUFFING

Nutrition Facts

Amount Per Serving

Calories 150	Calories from Fat 20

	% Daily Value*
Total Fat 2.5g	**4**%
Saturated Fat 0.5g	**3**%
Cholesterol 0mg	**0**%
Sodium 620mg	**26**%
Total Carbohydrate 28g	**9**%
Dietary Fiber 5g	**22**%
Sugars 6g	
Protein 6g	

Vitamin A 15%	•	Vitamin C 90%
Calcium 8%	•	Iron 15%

6 slices of Pritikin or commercial whole wheat bread
1 large onion, chopped
3 celery ribs, chopped
1 large green pepper, chopped
2 cups Turkey or Chicken Stock (page 44)
1/2 cup fresh parsley, chopped
1 teaspoon dried thyme
1 teaspoon dried sage
1 teaspoon dried marjoram
1 teaspoon garlic powder
Red pepper flakes, to taste

Process the bread into crumbs in a blender or a food processor, and set aside.

Combine the onions, celery, and green pepper in a nonstick frying pan and sauté over high heat by turning the vegetables until the onion looks a little brown around the edges and somewhat transparent. Add the chicken or turkey stock. Cover and cook over medium heat for about 5 or 6 minutes, until the vegetables are tender. Add the parsley, bread crumbs, spices, and pepper, and combine. Taste for more seasoning. Place in an 8-inch-by-8-inch nonstick cake pan. Set the oven temperature to 350 degrees F. and bake for 20 minutes.

If you want to get really fancy, buy some fresh oysters in a jar of liquid. A dozen will do. Measure the liquid and add enough turkey or chicken stock to make 2 cups and add it and the oysters to the stuffing. You could also use any size can of oysters that have not been smoked. Weigh drained oysters for exact meat serving size.

Spoon turkey gravy over the stuffing.

TURKEY GUMBO

Nutrition Facts

Amount Per Serving

Calories 260	Calories from Fat 20

	% Daily Value*
Total Fat 2.5g	**4**%
Saturated Fat 0.5g	**3**%
Cholesterol 70mg	**23**%
Sodium 480mg	**20**%
Total Carbohydrate 29g	**10**%
Dietary Fiber 3g	**11**%
Sugars 4g	
Protein 28g	

Vitamin A 4%	•	Vitamin C 30%
Calcium 4%	•	Iron 10%

Turkey gumbo is a wonderful and traditional New Orleans solution to, "What do I do with all this leftover turkey?"

1 large onion, coarsely chopped
1 medium green pepper, coarsely chopped
2 ribs celery including leaves, coarsely chopped
1 quart Turkey Stock (page 44)
4 cups (16 ounces) roasted, diced turkey meat
1/4 teaspoon cayenne pepper
1 teaspoon dried sage
1/2 teaspoon garlic powder or 4 cloves, chopped
1 bay leaf
1/2 teaspoon dried thyme, or 2 sprigs fresh thyme
1 teaspoon parsley flakes, or 2 tablespoons chopped fresh parsley
4 teaspoons apple juice concentrate
1/4 cup Red Rosé wine
Filé, for thickening and flavor (optional)

Combine the onions, green pepper, and celery in a 5-quart, nonstick stockpot. Sauté the vegetables over high heat, turning them constantly. When the onions look brown around the edges and somewhat transparent, add the stock and stir. Add all the rest of the ingredients and bring to a boil. Cover, lower the heat, and simmer for at least 1 hour.

Add about 1/2 teaspoon of filé (*fee-lay*) to each bowl, if desired. Each serving will contain a little over 2 ounces of turkey.

ZUCCHINI SOUR CREAM BAKE

Nutrition Facts

Amount Per Serving	
Calories 250	Calories from Fat 25

	% Daily Value*
Total Fat 3g	**5%**
Saturated Fat 0.5g	**4%**
Cholesterol 10mg	**4%**
Sodium 1140mg	**48%**
Total Carbohydrate 36g	**12%**
Dietary Fiber 5g	**20%**
Sugars 6g	
Protein 22g	

Vitamin A 10%	•	Vitamin C 15%
Calcium 10%	•	Iron 15%

2 slices Pritikin or commercial whole wheat bread
1 medium zucchini, thinly sliced
1/4 cup nonfat cottage cheese
3/4 cup Brown Chicken or Turkey Gravy (page 46)
1/4 cup Mock Sour Cream (page 338)

Place bread slices next to each other on an ovenproof dinner plate. Arrange the zucchini over the bread.

Microwave Directions: Place in the microwave for 1 minute on high setting.

Conventional Oven Directions: Preheat oven to 350 degrees F.

Bake for 5 minutes, until zucchini begins to wilt. Spread cottage cheese over the zucchini. Bake on the top shelf for about 10 minutes.

Meanwhile, heat the gravy. Pour the hot gravy over the melted cottage cheese. Top with the Mock Sour Cream, and serve.

HEARTY SQUASH SOUP

Nutrition Facts

Amount Per Serving

Calories 100   Calories from Fat 10

	% Daily Value*
Total Fat 1g	1%
Saturated Fat 0g	0%
Cholesterol 0mg	0%
Sodium 135mg	6%
Total Carbohydrate 20g	7%
Dietary Fiber 5g	18%
Sugars 5g	
Protein 4g	

Vitamin A 8%	•	Vitamin C 45%
Calcium 4%	•	Iron 6%

2 small patty pan squash, chopped (no need to peel or seed)
1 small yellow squash, chopped
1 1/2 cups fresh or frozen green peas
1 large onion, sliced
3 celery ribs, chopped
1/2 cup frozen or fresh corn
1 cup Turkey Stock (page 44) (or Chicken Stock, but Turkey Stock is better)
Water to cover
1 cup cooked brown rice (page 256)
Cayenne pepper

Microwave Directions: In a 5-quart container, combine the vegetables and stock. Add water to cover. Cover and cook on high setting for 16 minutes. Cook on medium setting for 10 minutes, or until the vegetables are tender.

Stove Top Directions: In a 5-quart stockpot, combine the vegetables and stock. Add water to cover. Cover the pot and bring to a boil. Lower the heat and simmer until vegetables are tender, about 10 minutes more. Add the rice and heat through just before serving. Add cayenne pepper to taste and serve.

CARROT CREAM CHOWDER

Nutrition Facts

Amount Per Serving

Calories 80	Calories from Fat 0

	% Daily Value*
Total Fat 0g	**0**%
Saturated Fat 0g	**0**%
Cholesterol 0mg	**0**%
Sodium 280mg	**12**%
Total Carbohydrate 14g	**5**%
Dietary Fiber 2g	**6**%
Sugars 8g	
Protein 4g	

Vitamin A 160%	•	Vitamin C 10%
Calcium 15%	•	Iron 2%

3 large carrots, chopped
2 ribs celery, chopped
1 large onion, chopped
2 large potatoes, peeled and diced
2 1/2 cups Chicken Stock (page 44)
1/4 cup dry white wine
1 can (12 ounces) evaporated skim milk (or 1 1/2 cups skim milk)
1/4 teaspoon cayenne pepper or more, to taste

Microwave Directions: Combine the carrots, celery, onion, and potatoes in a 5-quart container with the chicken stock and wine. If the liquid does not cover the vegetables, add either more stock or water. Cook, covered, on high setting for 16 minutes. Stir. Turn the microwave to a medium setting and cook covered, for another 10 minutes, or until the vegetables are tender. Stir in the milk and pepper and heat through.

Stove Top Directions: Combine the carrots, celery, onion, and potatoes in a 5-quart stockpot with the chicken stock and wine. If the liquid does not cover the vegetables, add either more stock or water. Bring to a boil, then lower the heat to medium, and cook, covered, until vegetables are tender, about 10 minutes after the water starts to boil. Stir once during cooking. Stir in the milk and pepper and heat through.

EGG DROP SOUP

YIELD: 1 SERVING

Nutrition Facts

Amount Per Serving

Calories 45	Calories from Fat 10

	% Daily Value*
Total Fat 1g	**1**%
Saturated Fat 0g	**0**%
Cholesterol 0mg	**0**%
Sodium 790mg	**33**%
Total Carbohydrate 4g	**1**%
Dietary Fiber less than 1 gram	**2**%
Sugars 2g	
Protein 4g	

Vitamin A 2%	•	Vitamin C 8%
Calcium 2%	•	Iron 2%

Rice flakes are hard and dry like any dry pasta. They are about the size of a potato chip and about as thin. Leave them whole for cooking. If they are broken badly in the package, just judge how many would be equal to the size of 7 or 8 big potato chips. You should be able to find them at an Asian market. If you can't find them, use 1/8 cup of dry noodles or 1/8 cup broken, dry spaghetti.

7 or 8 uncooked rice flakes
3 or 4 scallions or 1 small white onion, chopped
1 cup Turkey or Chicken Stock (page 44)
1 1/2 cups water
1/4 teaspoon dried parsley
1/8 teaspoon cayenne pepper
1 jumbo egg white
1/2 teaspoon apple juice concentrate

In an uncovered 1 1/2-quart pot, combine the rice flakes and onions with the turkey stock and water. Bring to a boil, then lower the heat to medium and cook until the water reduces to about 1 cup, about 9 or 10 minutes. Add parsley, pepper, raw egg white, and apple juice concentrate. Cook for about 1/2 minute more, or until the egg turns white. Pour into a thermos for lunch and take along some popcorn, carrots or celery, some fruit, and perhaps some Oat Bran bread (page 76). I always take an Oat Bran Muffin (page 80), too, for a fiber-rich snack, and my herb tea in another thermos.

CHAPTER 6

Fish and Shellfish Entrées

For all of you folks in my home town of New Orleans, who will see fish "fillets" all through this chapter, I've never seen this spelling either, until recently, but you have to understand that this book goes all over the world and the rest of the world spells it "fillet" for everything except beef. It's still "filet mignon."

Fish and shellfish are excellent sources of protein without as much fat as red meat or poultry. They do have quite a bit of sodium, however, from the iodine present particularly in shellfish, so be careful and check the nutritional levels as you plan your menus.

As with most other foods, fresh is best when it comes to fish. If you're lucky enough to live in an area where fresh fish and shellfish are readily available be adventurous and try some varieties that you may not be familiar with. Frozen fish and shellfish, except for shrimp which are ruined when frozen, are fine to use when fresh is unavailable, but canned fish or shellfish should be used judiciously because they are virtually unavailable without salt.

SHRIMP JAMBALAYA

YIELD: 5 SERVINGS

Nutrition Facts

Amount Per Serving	
Calories 260	Calories from Fat 25

	% Daily Value*
Total Fat 2.5g	**4%**
Saturated Fat 0.5g	**3%**
Cholesterol 65mg	**22%**
Sodium 350mg	**14%**
Total Carbohydrate 45g	**15%**
Dietary Fiber 4g	**17%**
Sugars 10g	
Protein 14g	

Vitamin A 20%	•	Vitamin C 80%
Calcium 6%	•	Iron 20%

You must have fresh shrimp to make this recipe. Frozen or canned just won't do. Be sure to save the shells from the shrimp to make Shrimp Stock.

**1 1/4 pounds unpeeled large shrimp including the heads, or
  30 large unpeeled shrimp without heads (12 ounces or about
  1 1/2 cups, peeled)**
2 bay leaves
1 2/3 cups Shrimp Stock (page 47)
1/3 cup Red Rosé wine
1 large onion, chopped coarsely
1 medium green pepper, chopped
3 ribs celery and leaves, chopped
3 medium tomatoes, diced
3 tablespoons salt-free tomato paste
3 cloves fresh garlic finely chopped
1 teaspoon dried thyme
1/2 teaspoon ground cumin
1 teaspoon parsley flakes or 2 tablespoons chopped fresh parsley
1/2 teaspoon dried basil
1/2 teaspoon red pepper flakes
3 tablespoons apple juice concentrate
1 tablespoon low-sodium soy sauce
1 cup uncooked long grain white rice

Peel and devein the shrimp. Start the shrimp stock according to the recipe, and add the bay leaves and the wine to the shrimp stock as you cook it.

While the stock is cooking, combine the onion, green pepper, and celery in a nonstick 5-quart stockpot. Sauté over high heat by turning the vegetables until the onion looks a little brown and transparent. If the stock is not ready yet, remove the vegetables from the heat and set aside until the stock is ready. When the stock is ready, strain and measure it. You want to have 1 2/3 cups of liquid, including the wine that was added to it. Add water if necessary. Pour the stock and wine mixture into the pot. Add the tomatoes, tomato paste, garlic, thyme, cumin, parsley, basil, pepper, juice concentrate, and soy sauce. Stir and cover. Bring to a boil, then simmer for 5 minutes over low heat. Add the rice and stir to combine. Cover and cook on the lowest possible heat for 35 minutes. Gently add the shrimp. Cover and continue to cook on low heat for 20 minutes. Remove from the heat and let stand covered, for 25 minutes. Fluff all the ingredients with a fork. Be careful not to mash the rice. Each 1-cup serving contains 4 ounces of shrimp. Serve with mixed steamed broccoli, cauliflower, and mushrooms.

SHRIMP CREOLE

Nutrition Facts

Amount Per Serving

Calories 170   Calories from Fat 10

	% Daily Value*
Total Fat 1g	1%
Saturated Fat 0g	0%
Cholesterol 40mg	13%
Sodium 125mg	5%
Total Carbohydrate 34g	11%
Dietary Fiber 5g	21%
Sugars 12g	
Protein 8g	

Vitamin A 60%	•	Vitamin C 150%
Calcium 6%	•	Iron 15%

I remember when I was a child, if my mother wanted to give me a treat, she would cook this. She is the only person I ever knew who put potatoes in this recipe. The potatoes sop up all that good gravy and makes it taste wonderful. They thicken it, too, without adding flour. If you use fresh, unpeeled shrimp, save the peels for making shrimp stock.

1 cup plus a little more, chopped onion
1 1/2 cups chopped green pepper
1 1/4 cups chopped celery, stalks and leaves
1/4 cup finely chopped carrot
2 cups water
1 1/4 cups chopped tomato
2 bay leaves
2 1/2 cups cubed white potatoes
12 ounces unpeeled fresh shrimp (6 ounces fresh, peeled shrimp or 15 large fresh shrimp), or 2 cans (4 1/2 ounces each) of shrimp
1 cup Shrimp Stock (page 47) or water
1 teaspoon dried parsley flakes
4 teaspoons salt-free tomato paste
2 tablespoons apple juice concentrate
1/8 teaspoon cayenne pepper
1/2 teaspoon low-sodium soy sauce
1/8 teaspoon garlic powder
1 teaspoon dried thyme or 4 sprigs fresh thyme
1/8 teaspoon ground allspice
2 teaspoons fresh lemon juice

Combine the onion, green pepper, celery, and carrot in a large, nonstick frying pan. Sauté over high heat for about 6 minutes until the onion is a little brown on the edges and slightly transparent. Add the water and reduce the heat to low. Add the tomato, bay leaves, and potatoes. Cover and simmer for 1 hour, stirring occasionally.

If you are using fresh shrimp, peel and devein the shrimp and make the Shrimp Stock (page 47). Refrigerate the peeled shrimp. When the vegetable mixture has simmered for 1 hour, add the shrimp stock or water. Simmer for 12 minutes uncovered. Add the parsley, tomato paste, apple juice concentrate, cayenne pepper, soy, garlic powder, thyme, allspice, and lemon juice. Stir and simmer for 3 minutes uncovered. Add the shrimp and simmer for 30 minutes uncovered, stirring occasionally. Add a little water if needed. Remove from the heat, set aside to cool, then refrigerate for 3 to 4 hours to mingle seasonings. Reheat and serve. Each serving has 1 1/2 ounces of shrimp each.

OVEN-FRIED SHRIMP

You could cut this recipe in half to serve a smaller group. Serve with fresh lemon wedges to squeeze over them, or some Horseradish Sauce (page 60) on the side, or Piquante Sauce (page 55), or if you want to cheat a little, some ketchup. By the way, after you peel your shrimp, don't wash them because you will wash the flavor away.

1 cup yellow cornmeal
1/4 teaspoon dried marjoram
1/4 teaspoon dried thyme
1/4 teaspoon cayenne pepper
1/4 teaspoon dried sage
1 pound fresh peeled shrimp, about 20 large shrimp (1 3/4 pounds if weighed unpeeled)

Spray a nonstick pan with nonstick spray.

In a plastic or paper bag, combine the cornmeal, marjoram, thyme, cayenne, and sage. Shake well to mix. Add a few shrimp at a time into the bag with the seasoned cornmeal, and shake to coat. Place the shrimp, not touching each other, in the pan. Place on the middle rack of a conventional oven, set the temperature at 400 F., and bake for 15 minutes. Serve immediately.

STUFFED ARTICHOKES PALERMO

**YIELD: 2 SERVINGS
WHOLE ARTICHOKES**

Nutrition Facts

Amount Per Serving

Calories 570   Calories from Fat 60

	% Daily Value*
Total Fat 7g	11%
Saturated Fat 1.5g	8%
Cholesterol 135mg	44%
Sodium 1290mg	54%
Total Carbohydrate 84g	28%
Dietary Fiber 12g	46%
Sugars 10g	
Protein 37g	

Vitamin A 20%	•	Vitamin C 35%
Calcium 35%	•	Iron 60%

You will swear that these artichokes contain olive oil. For a real olive oil effect, rub the plate you serve these on with some highly aromatic olive oil but try to resist licking your fingers.

You can prepare these artichokes two ways: Either stuff them and leave them whole, or remove each leaf and serve them as individual "bon bites" ("a little something good in the mouth"; an old Creole-French-English expression) at a party.

**29 medium fresh or canned shrimp, or 3 1/2 ounces peeled
2 large artichokes
1 medium onion
1 rib celery
3 large mushrooms
1 cup Concentrated Chicken Stock (page 45)
1/4 cup dry vermouth
1 tablespoon dried parsley flakes or 1/4 cup finely chopped fresh
   parsley
1/2 teaspoon dried thyme
1 teaspoon medium red hot sauce
1/2 teaspoon garlic powder
1/8 teaspoon cayenne pepper
1 1/2 teaspoons dried oregano
Water
1 1/2 cups whole wheat bread crumbs
2 tablespoons plus 1 teaspoon grated sapsago cheese**

If you are using canned shrimp, rinse and soak them for 20 minutes or longer in ice water. If you are using fresh shrimp, wash, peel, and devein them, and set aside.

Steam the artichokes in about an inch of water in a large pot, with the cover on. Bring the water to a boil first, then lower the heat and simmer for about 25 to 30 minutes. Be careful not to overcook them. After 20 minutes, test for doneness. If a leaf pulls off easily and the flesh from the bottom of the leaf is tender, the artichoke is done. Remove from water and set aside to cool.

For the Filling: The onions, celery, and mushrooms can be chopped in a food processor or by hand. Place the chopped vegetables in a nonstick frying pan. Place the fresh shrimp in the food processor and chop, but not too finely—you want little chunks of shrimp. If you are using canned shrimp, *do not* put them in the food processor. They should be broken up later with the edge of a wooden spoon in the pan.

Sauté the celery, mushrooms, and onions over high heat. When the onion looks brown around the edges and a bit transparent, add the shrimp pieces, or break up canned ones, Concentrated Chicken Stock, dry vermouth, parsley flakes, thyme, hot sauce, garlic powder, cayenne pepper, and oregano. Add a little water to the food processor bowl, swirl it around and add it to the frying pan. Cover the pan and lower the heat. Simmer until the onions and celery are tender and the shrimp are cooked, about 10 minutes. Add the cracked wheat or oat bran bread crumbs and the sapsago cheese, and combine. You should have a nice, moist stuffing. If it looks a little dry and crumbly, add some water. If it is too wet, add a few more bread crumbs. You don't want too many bread crumbs, though.

To stuff an artichoke: Begin by gently pulling back the leaves of the artichoke after it is cooked and cooled. Start from the outer leaves and move toward the middle. When you reach the center leaves, start removing them to make a cavity or cup in the center of the artichoke. When you have pulled enough leaves you will see the "choke" part or hairy section on top of the heart. Carefully pull the little hairs out. They will come out in clumps. This leaves the heart exposed. Cut off the sharp points of the leaves if you want to, but it's not necessary. Cut off the stem carefully so the artichoke can sit flat. Dig out the soft, edible part of the stem, chop, and add to the filling. Fill up the cavity of the artichoke with filling and then put about a teaspoon of filling at the base of each leaf. Sprinkle a few bread crumbs on top of each section of filling. Serve at room temperature.

To stuff individual leaves: After the artichokes are cooked and cooled, pull off all the leaves. Save the sturdiest ones. Remove the choke from the heart. Chop the heart up and dig out the soft middle of the stem and add it to the pan with the rest of the filling ingredients. Follow cooking instructions above.

When the filling is ready, fill the base of each reserved leaf with about 1 teaspoon of the filling. Arrange them on a platter and sprinkle a few bread crumbs over the filling of each leaf. Serve cold or at room temperature.

Note: If for some reason you should happen to get bitter artichokes, as I have on occasion, add 1 to 3 teaspoons of apple juice concentrate to your filling mixture to counteract the bitter taste.

PAELLA

Nutrition Facts

Amount Per Serving

Calories 260   Calories from Fat 25

	% Daily Value*
Total Fat 3g	**5%**
Saturated Fat 1g	**4%**
Cholesterol 65mg	**22%**
Sodium 240mg	**10%**
Total Carbohydrate 36g	**12%**
Dietary Fiber 3g	**13%**
Sugars 7g	
Protein 18g	

Vitamin A 10%	•	Vitamin C 70%
Calcium 8%	•	Iron 40%

One summer my husband and I traveled all over Spain. The food, contrary to what we expected, was not Mexican or Southwestern; there was not a tortilla nor taco to be found. It was closer to New Orleans Creole, tasty, not very peppery, but more seasoned than the food we had in France. They even have boiled crawfish to eat as snacks in the bars. One of the most popular dishes that you can get everywhere is Paella. It is very similar to New Orleans Jambalaya except for the saffron, which makes it traditionally and uniquely Spanish.

Mussels are wonderful in this dish, but you could use fresh clams. I think you need some fresh shellfish in the shell to make it right. Sometimes we had it with broiled crawfish or langostinos (small lobsters) in it, which made it very colorful, and sometimes we had it with a little chicken in it, too.

1 cup uncooked white rice
1 1/4 cup onion, chopped
1 cup green pepper, chopped
3 cups diced patty pan (3 small squash)
1 cup water
1/2 cup Red Rosé wine
1 tablespoon apple juice concentrate
2 teaspoons dried parsley
1/2 teaspoon garlic powder
1/8 teaspoon cayenne pepper
1 cup frozen green peas
1/4 teaspoon string saffron, packed tightly
1 can (4 1/2 ounces) small shrimp, drained and rinsed
1 can (8 ounces) whole oysters
2 cups sliced fresh mushrooms
1 pound fresh mussels in the shells (about 26 mussels)

Combine the rice, onion, and green pepper in a 5-quart nonstick stockpot. Sauté over high heat until the rice looks white and opaque. Remove the pot from the heat. Add one at a time and stirring after each addition: the squash, water, wine, juice concentrate, parsley, garlic powder, cayenne, peas, saffron, shrimp, oysters, and mushrooms. Stand the mussels up straight here and there with the hinged end stuck into the rice. Return the pot to high heat and bring to a boil. Immediately turn the heat to the lowest setting, cover, and cook without stirring for about 1 hour. Check after 45 minutes and taste the rice to see if it is soft. When the rice is soft, remove from the heat and let sit covered, for 20 minutes. Serve hot with a green vegetable and/or salad.

SHRIMP-STUFFED WHITE SQUASH

Nutrition Facts

Amount Per Serving

Calories 250	Calories from Fat 25

	% Daily Value*
Total Fat 3g	4%
Saturated Fat 0.5g	3%
Cholesterol 65mg	21%
Sodium 430mg	18%
Total Carbohydrate 41g	14%
Dietary Fiber 6g	24%
Sugars 8g	
Protein 17g	

Vitamin A 15%	•	Vitamin C 110%
Calcium 15%	•	Iron 25%

This is a tasty, old-fashioned, Creole dish. Even the skins of the squash are edible because the sugars in the skins become caramelized and sweet with baking.

3 large whole patty pan squash
1 medium onion, coarsely chopped
1 medium green pepper, coarsely chopped
1 cup whole wheat or Pritikin bread crumbs
1/2 teaspoon dried thyme
1/4 teaspoon cayenne pepper
1 can (4 1/2 ounces) well-rinsed shrimp or
**   18 large or 30 small fresh peeled shrimp**
1/2 teaspoon medium red hot sauce
2 jumbo egg whites

Microwave Directions: With a knife, pierce the top of the squash in several places. Set on a plate and bake for 15 minutes on high setting. Test with a knife for tenderness. If they are still hard, cook another 2 minutes. They should be very soft, but if not, keep cooking and testing every 2 minutes. Remove squash from oven, place on a nonstick baking pan, and set aside to cool.

Stove Top Directions: Place the squash in a saucepan. Cover the squash with water, and cook over medium-low heat for about 45 minutes. Test with a knife for tenderness and continue cooking until tender. Remove squash carefully from pot and place on a nonstick baking pan and set aside to cool.

Combine the onion and green pepper in a nonstick frying pan. Sauté the vegetables over high heat until the onions look transparent and slightly limp. Remove pan from heat and set aside.

When the squash are cool, cut circles out of the tops of each squash as you would if you were preparing pumpkins to make jack-o-lanterns. Lift out the circular sections. Scrape the flesh of the squash "tops" into the pan with the sautéed vegetables. Discard the "tops" after scraping them clean. With a teaspoon, carefully scrape the flesh out of the rest of the squash into the pan. You don't need to deseed. Add the remaining ingredients to the saucepan and combine thoroughly. Spoon the mixture into the squash shells. If you like, sprinkle extra bread crumbs on top and spray with nonstick butter-flavored spray. Set the oven temperature at 350 degrees F. Place on the middle rack of the oven and bake for 25 to 30 minutes and serve.

Each serving contains about 1 1/2 ounces of shrimp, depending on the size of the shrimp. Weigh in advance to exact measurement. If you use a 4 1/2-ounce can of shrimp, the serving size will be a little over 1 ounce of shrimp per person. You may substitute 6 ounces of nonfat cottage cheese for the shrimp.

OYSTERS MARDI GRAS

YIELD: 4 SERVINGS

Nutrition Facts

Amount Per Serving	
Calories 160	Calories from Fat 20

	% Daily Value*
Total Fat 2g	3%
Saturated Fat 0g	0%
Cholesterol 35mg	12%
Sodium 290mg	12%
Total Carbohydrate 24g	8%
Dietary Fiber 8g	32%
Sugars 4g	
Protein 12g	

Vitamin A 15%	•	Vitamin C 45%
Calcium 8%	•	Iron 35%

Some of my loveliest memories of growing up in New Orleans are luncheons to honor brides-to-be debutantes at Corinne Dunbar's Restaurant on St. Charles Avenue. The old Victorian house with its elegant, quiet dining rooms, was an uptown landmark. There was no menu, but we always enjoyed Corinne Dunbar's most memorable dishes: Oysters Mardi Gras and Banana Fritters.

Corinne Dunbar's is just a memory now, of vétivèrt cologne, and ladies who wore hats and white gloves to lunch, when uptown New Orleans was a small city unto itself, hardly conscious of the rest of the world, or even of the rest of the city.

4 fresh artichokes
1/2 cup finely chopped onion
1/4 cup chopped fresh parsley or cilantro
2 cups mushrooms, sliced
1 bay leaf
Oyster water
Chicken stock from Roasted Chicken (page 46)
15 to 19 fresh oysters or 1 jar (10 ounces) of fresh unwashed oysters
1/4 teaspoon Tabasco® sauce
1 large clove garlic, peeled and chopped
1 tablespoon cornstarch
1 teaspoon apple juice concentrate
1 teaspoon Worcestershire sauce
1 tablespoon dry vermouth

Place the artichokes on their sides in a 5-quart stockpot. (There is no need to trim them in any way.) Add about 1 inch of water. Cover and cook over medium heat for 45 minutes, or until leaves pull out easily and the meat at the bottom of the leaves is soft. Check occasionally to make sure the water has not boiled away and add more water if necessary. Drain and set aside to cool.

Place the onion, parsley or cilantro, mushrooms, and bay leaf in a 1 1/2-quart saucepan. Pour the oyster water into a measuring cup, then add enough chicken stock to it until you have 1 cup of liquid in all. Add the mixture to the pot. Bring the liquid to a boil and cook covered, over high heat, until the pot starts to boil. Uncover, stir, and cook until the onion is tender, a total of about 6 minutes. Watch closely so that the pot doesn't dry out and stir occasionally. Remove the pot from the heat.

In the meantime, deleaf the artichokes, saving the prettiest and strongest leaves. Remove and discard the choke, or the hairy part of the bottom of the artichoke. Slice the stem off and squeeze out any part of it and add it to the pot. Discard the tough part of the stem. Lay the weaker leaves on a plate and scrape across the soft part with a knife and add the pulp to the pot. Discard the scraped leaves. Reserve the whole bottoms.

Place the oysters and any remaining oyster juice in a blender or food processor. Add the Tabasco® sauce, garlic, cornstarch, juice concentrate, and Worcestershire sauce. Pulse on and off, 5 times. Add the oysters to the pot. Pour the vermouth into the blender or food processor. Swirl it around to rinse and add to the pot. Bring to a boil over high heat. Let the mixture boil for about 1 1/2 minutes, stirring constantly.

Set the artichoke bottoms in the centers of 4 rimmed soup bowls, one per bowl, or plates if you don't have the rimmed soup bowls. Surround the artichoke bottoms with leaves, the points of the leaves up, or toward the edges of the plate, and layered, like the artichoke grows. Ladle the oyster mixture over the bottoms. Serve warm with whole wheat toast points. Each serving will contain 2 1/2 ounces of oysters.

OYSTERS ROCKEFELLER CASSEROLE

Nutrition Facts

Amount Per Serving

Calories 350	Calories from Fat 70

	% Daily Value*
Total Fat 7g	11%
Saturated Fat 1.5g	8%
Cholesterol 100mg	33%
Sodium 650mg	27%
Total Carbohydrate 41g	14%
Dietary Fiber 6g	25%
Sugars 5g	
Protein 33g	

Vitamin A 110%	•	Vitamin C 60%
Calcium 15%	•	Iron 80%

Normally, this dish consists of oysters on the half-shell with a spicy spinach concoction on top, but due to the fact that you need a lot of butter to keep the oysters moist, I decided to make this as a casserole.

1 package (10 ounces) frozen chopped spinach
8 slices Pritikin or commercial whole wheat bread
1/8 teaspoon ground cumin
1/8 teaspoon garlic powder
1/4 teaspoon cayenne pepper
1/2 teaspoon dried parsley
1/2 teaspoon dried oregano
1/2 teaspoon dried basil
12 to 18 fresh unwashed oysters and juice
6 jumbo egg whites
1/4 Baked Banana (page 57)
Skim milk
2 tablespoons grated sapsago cheese

Cook the spinach according to package directions, drain and set aside.

Place the bread in a food processor or blender and process to make bread crumbs. Add the cumin, garlic powder, cayenne, parsley flakes, oregano, and basil to the bread crumbs, and process until the spices are blended into the crumbs.

Drain the oysters, reserving the juice. Pour the oyster juice into a 2-cup measure and add the egg whites, banana and baking liquid. Then add enough skim milk to make 1 1/2 cups. Beat the oyster juice, egg whites, banana, and milk together thoroughly. Gently combine the oysters with the cooked spinach, then mix 1/2 of the oyster juice mixture with the oysters and spinach.

Spread half the bread crumbs in the bottom of an 8-inch-square nonstick baking pan. Spread the oysters and spinach mixture over the bread crumbs. Top with the remaining bread crumbs. Poke holes all over the top with a fork. Pour the remaining oyster juice mixture very slowly over the top, patting the top gently to encourage the liquid to seep through the bread crumbs. Sprinkle with sapsago cheese. Cover the baking pan very loosely with aluminum foil, not letting it touch the bread crumbs, and slash the foil in several places to let out steam. Let the casserole sit in the refrigerator for 2 hours or more. Set in the oven, set the temperature at 325 degrees F., and bake for 1 hour. Serve immediately. There are about 2 1/2 ounces of oysters per serving.

OYSTER SOUP

Nutrition Facts

Amount Per Serving

Calories 270   Calories from Fat 90

	% Daily Value*
Total Fat 10g	15%
Saturated Fat 4.5g	22%
Cholesterol 50mg	16%
Sodium 360mg	15%
Total Carbohydrate 26g	9%
Dietary Fiber 1g	5%
Sugars 17g	
Protein 17g	

Vitamin A 10%	•	Vitamin C 40%
Calcium 50%	•	Iron 40%

This delicate, rich soup can be served as a main dish with toasted French Rolls (page 77).

2 dozen fresh oysters and juice (or large, fresh clams and juice)
1/4 pound (6 to 8) scallions, chopped, including tops
1/3 cup chopped fresh parsley
1 can (12 ounces) evaporated milk
Skim milk
Cayenne pepper

Into a 2-quart saucepan, combine the oyster juice, scallions, and parsley. Cover and over high heat, bring to a boil. Lower the heat to medium and cook gently for about 5 minutes.

Pour the canned milk into a quart-size measuring cup or container. Add enough skim milk to make 1 quart and then pour into a saucepan. Cook over high heat to scald the milk, which is when tiny bubbles form around the edges of the pan and the temperature of the milk is 180 degrees F. (Do not boil oyster juice and milk together as the oyster juice may curdle the milk.) Pour the scalded milk into the saucepan with the oyster juice and onions and add the oysters. Set on medium heat, stirring constantly, and continue cooking until the edges of the oysters curl. This happens quickly, so be careful not to overcook. Add the cayenne pepper. Serve immediately with rolls for dunking. If divided into 3 servings, each serving will contain about 2 ounces of oysters.

HOMEMADE CRAB BOIL

What is crab boil and what do you do with it? Well, in Louisiana we don't eat our boiled crabs, crawfish, and shrimp on plates. We eat them in mountains, piled on newspapers. And we boil them out in the yard in big kettles with crab boil. The spices for the crab boil come in perforated plastic bags that get tossed into the boiling water with the seafood, with some garlic, onions, lemons, and sometimes chili powder. We even use crab boil with lobster. You should be able to find crab boil in a gourmet shop if you can't find it at your grocery store. But it's not that much trouble to make your own.

6 tablespoons mustard seeds
5 tablespoons coriander seeds
2 bay leaves
4 allspice berries
4 whole cloves
1/4 teaspoon dried red pepper flakes

Mix all the seasonings together in a bowl.

To make the bag for the spices, cut three 1-foot squares of cheesecloth. (You can get cheesecloth in the automotive section of the grocery store, but check to see if it says not to be used in cooking.) Cut another strip of cheesecloth for tying the bag closed. Lay the pieces of cloth on top of each other. Pour the spices on top of the cheese cloth. Pull the ends of the cloth up around the spices and tie with the strip of cheesecloth. Submerge the bag of spices in the water with whatever seafood you may be cooking. After everything is cooked, just throw the whole bag away.

The nutritive values of spices are negligible.

CRAB QUICHE WITH MEDITERRANEAN SAUCE

YIELD: 4 SERVINGS

Nutrition Facts

Amount Per Serving

Calories 270	Calories from Fat 30

	% Daily Value*
Total Fat 3.5g	**5%**
Saturated Fat 1g	**4%**
Cholesterol 35mg	**12%**
Sodium 700mg	**29%**
Total Carbohydrate 35g	**12%**
Dietary Fiber 5g	**19%**
Sugars 9g	
Protein 26g	

Vitamin A 8%	•	Vitamin C 8%
Calcium 35%	•	Iron 15%

8 slices commercial whole wheat or Pritikin bread
2 cups sliced fresh mushrooms
1/4 cup sliced scallions
1/3 cup firmly packed crabmeat
1/4 cup nonfat cheddar cheese
1 cup skim milk
6 jumbo egg whites
1 teaspoon dried parsley or 3 tablespoons finely chopped fresh parsley
1/8 teaspoon cayenne pepper
1/8 teaspoon garlic powder or 1 fresh garlic clove, chopped
2 tablespoons grated sapsago cheese
1 1/2 cups Mediterranean Sauce (next page)

Spray an 8 x 8-inch nonstick pan with butter-flavored nonstick spray.

Remove the crusts from the bread. Place 4 of the slices in the bottom of the baking pan. Fill in any gaps between them with the crusts. Layer the mushrooms over the bread, then the onions, then the crabmeat, then the cheese. Cover with the 4 remaining slices of bread. Fill in gaps with more crusts. Combine the milk, egg whites, parsley, pepper, and garlic in a blender. Pour the milk mixture slowly over the top layer of bread. Let it soak in as you go or it will run right off the top and spill on the counter. Sprinkle with sapsago cheese. Cover with aluminum foil but don't let the foil touch the bread. Cut gashes in the foil to let out steam. Set the oven temperature at 350 degrees F. and bake in the oven for 40 minutes. Remove from the oven and let the quiche sit covered, for about 10 minutes before serving. About 15 or 20 minutes before serving time, prepare the Mediterranean Sauce.

To serve, cut the quiche into squares and pour on the warm Mediterranean Sauce. For best results, the Mediterranean Sauce should not be reheated, but if necessary, reheat it on the stove over medium heat. Add a little more milk if it is too thick. Stir constantly until it is just hot, then immediately remove it from the heat, and serve. Each person will get 1 1/2 ounces of crabmeat.

MEDITERRANEAN SAUCE

Nutrition Facts

Amount Per Serving	
Calories 80	Calories from Fat 5
	% Daily Value²
Total Fat 1g	1%
Saturated Fat 0g	0%
Cholesterol 30mg	10%
Sodium 320mg	14%
Total Carbohydrate 7g	2%
Dietary Fiber 0g	0%
Sugars 5g	
Protein 10g	

Vitamin A 6%	•	Vitamin C 6%	
Calcium 15%	•	Iron 4%	

If you double this recipe, it will cover 6 slices of toast and make a lovely main meal.

1 cup Concentrated Chicken Stock (page 45)
1/2 cup sliced scallions
1 tablespoon unbleached flour
1 can (13 ounces) evaporated skim milk
1/2 can (6 ounces) white crabmeat, drained and rinsed
1/8 teaspoon cayenne pepper

Pour the chicken stock into a medium saucepan and add the scallions. Bring the stock to a boil over high heat and continue to boil, uncovered, for 6 minutes until the liquid has almost disappeared. Stir in the flour immediately and lower the heat to medium. Slowly stir in the milk. Continue to cook for 4 minutes, stirring constantly. Add the crabmeat and pepper and cook for 1 minute more. Serve immediately.

OVEN-FRIED SOFT-SHELLED CRABS

YIELD: 6 SERVINGS

Nutrition Facts

Amount Per Serving	
Calories 420 Calories from Fat 160	
	% Daily Value*
Total Fat 18g	28%
Saturated Fat 4.5g	22%
Cholesterol 45mg	15%
Sodium 1120mg	47%
Total Carbohydrate 49g	16%
Dietary Fiber 2g	7%
Sugars 0g	
Protein 13g	

Vitamin A 2%	•	Vitamin C 2%
Calcium 6%	•	Iron 15%

Our Louisiana soft-shelled crabs are small, about 4 to 6 inches across the top of the shell and shed their hard shells, usually in July and August. Then they hide in grasses in warm and shallow water until their shells harden up again, which they do quickly if left in the water. The trick is to catch them when they have just shed and then keep them out of the water. The crabs will stay in that delectable soft state if refrigerated or frozen. Prepared this way, you can eat the whole crab, claws, shell, and everything. But don't even think about using Alaskan crabs or those huge Dungeness crabs they have in San Francisco.

To clean, set them on a board top-side up. Lift one side of the shell where it points. You will see the gray, finger-like lungs attached to both sides of the crab, growing from where the legs attach. Just pull them all off. Cut off the eyes and mouth. If any part of the crab feels papery and not soft and smooth and rubbery, it means the shell has already started to harden. Pull any papery parts off. (They will come off as if the crab had been wrapped in cellophane.)

1 cup yellow cornmeal
1/4 teaspoon dried marjoram
1/4 teaspoon dried thyme
1/4 teaspoon cayenne pepper
1/4 teaspoon ground sage
6 cleaned soft-shelled crabs

Spray a nonstick pan with nonstick spray.

In a plastic or paper bag, combine the cornmeal, marjoram, thyme, cayenne, and sage. Shake to combine. Wet the crabs and, one at a time, add them to the bag of seasoned cornmeal, seal, and shake to coat. Place the crabs on the pan, not touching each other, top-side up. Place in a conventional oven on the middle rack, set the temperature at 400 degrees F., and bake for 15 minutes. Turn the crabs over and bake for 5 minutes more. Serve immediately with lemons, Piquante Sauce (page 55), or a little ketchup.

CRAB CAKES

YIELD: 6 SERVINGS

Nutrition Facts

Amount Per Serving

Calories 90	Calories from Fat 10

	% Daily Value*
Total Fat 1g	2%
Saturated Fat 0g	0%
Cholesterol 20mg	6%
Sodium 190mg	8%
Total Carbohydrate 14g	5%
Dietary Fiber 2g	9%
Sugars 4g	
Protein 8g	

Vitamin A 2%	•	Vitamin C 25%
Calcium 4%	•	Iron 6%

Zucchini and banana, while adding good taste, also give the right amount of moistness and texture to make these perfect. If you like you could stuff this mixture into oven-proof crab shell forms, or real shells, to make stuffed crabs.

4 slices Pritikin whole wheat or commercial whole wheat bread
1/2 teaspoon garlic powder
1 teaspoon dried parsley
1/4 teaspoon cayenne pepper
1/2 teaspoon dried thyme
1/2 cup finely chopped onions
1 celery rib, finely chopped
1 cup finely chopped zucchini
1/4 Baked Banana (page 57)
2 jumbo egg whites
Juice of 1 medium lemon
1 can (6 ounces) crabmeat, white or claw, rinsed

In a blender or food processor, combine the bread, garlic powder, parsley, basil, cayenne, and thyme to make seasoned bread crumbs.

Combine the onions, celery, and zucchini in a nonstick frying pan and sauté over high heat by turning the vegetables until the zucchini looks limp. Remove the pan from the heat and set aside to cool. Add the seasoned bread crumbs.

In a separate bowl, combine the banana and egg and beat with a fork. Add the banana-egg mixture to the vegetables and then add the lemon juice and crabmeat.

Spray a nonstick pan with a nonstick butter-flavored spray because these cakes tend to stick. Form 6 crab cakes about the size of hamburgers, and place them on the pan. Place on the middle rack of the oven, set the temperature at 350 degrees F., and bake uncovered for 15 minutes. Turn over and bake for 10 to 15 minutes more until brown. Serve immediately with lemon wedges.

CRAB SOUFFLÉ

2 patty pan squash
2 slices whole wheat or Pritikin bread
1 large onion, chopped
1 large green pepper, chopped
1/4 teaspoon garlic powder
1 tablespoon dried parsley
1/4 teaspoon dried red pepper flakes
1/2 teaspoon dried thyme
2 tablespoons dry vermouth
1/4 Baked Banana (page 57)
1 can (6 1/2 ounces) crab claw meat, rinsed
6 jumbo egg whites at room temperature
1 tablespoon grated sapsago cheese

Microwave Directions: With a knife, pierce the tops of the squash in several places. Baked uncovered, on high setting for 15 minutes. Check them, and if they are still hard, cook another 2 minutes or more. Remove the squash from the microwave and set aside to cool.

Stovetop Directions: In a large stockpot, cover the squash with water and cook over medium heat for about 45 minutes. Test with a knife for tenderness and continue cooking until tender, if necessary. Remove the squash from the stockpot and set aside to cool.

While the squash is cooling, make bread crumbs by processing the bread in a food processor or blender and set aside.

Place the onions and green peppers in a nonstick 5-quart pot. Sauté over high heat by turning the vegetables until the onions look transparent and are a little brown around the edges. Remove the pot from the heat.

Cut the tops off the squash and scrape the pulp from the insides, including the seeds, and add the pulp and seeds to the onions and green peppers. Add the garlic powder, parsley, pepper, thyme, vermouth, banana and baking juices, and the crabmeat. Mix, then add the bread crumbs and mix everything thoroughly.

Beat the egg whites with an electric mixer until they form stiff peaks. Fold the egg whites into the crabmeat mixture and put the mixture in a 2-quart soufflé dish or an 8-inch-square baking dish. Sprinkle with sapsago cheese. Place in the oven on the top shelf, set the temperature at 350 degrees F., and bake, uncovered, for 40 to 45 minutes. When the top is brown, it's done. Serve immediately.

CRAWFISH ÉTOUFFÉE

Nutrition Facts

Amount Per Serving	
Calories 120	Calories from Fat 10

	% Daily Value*
Total Fat 1g	2%
Saturated Fat 0g	0%
Cholesterol 75mg	24%
Sodium 170mg	7%
Total Carbohydrate 15g	5%
Dietary Fiber 4g	14%
Sugars 4g	
Protein 13g	

Vitamin A 8%	•	Vitamin C 80%	
Calcium 6%	•	Iron 10%	

If you don't live in Louisiana, and you can't get fresh crawfish (and believe me, Louisiana crawfish are the best), you may be able to buy Louisiana crawfish frozen at your grocery, fishmonger, or gourmet shop. I have used frozen tails in this recipe and I can guarantee that they are positively super.

But be warned—if you decide to catch your own be sure to cook them first. If you try to use them uncooked they will be wiggling around while you try to peel them, and might even bite you. Trust me. You have to cook them first! If you can't get crawfish, you may substitute nine ounces of shrimp, clams, oysters, crabmeat, or chunks of any firm-fleshed white fish.

Étouffée (Cajunized) is pronounced "ae-too-fay." If you make this with shrimp it is Shrimp Étouffée, etc. The word "étouffée" means "to smother," which describes the sauce or gravy that the crawfish or shrimp are served in.

Many people in New Orleans think that "étouffée" means "stuffed." This goes back to the days when ladies wore tight corsets. In hot weather they would suffocate, or smother because they were "stuffed" into their corsets. Some people who order étouffée in a restaurant are disappointed when they can't find any stuffed crawfish in their étouffée.

9 ounces fresh or frozen, peeled, cooked, crawfish tails, or 70 medium-size live crawfish
1 large onion, chopped
1 large green pepper, chopped
5 ribs celery, chopped
2 teaspoons low-sodium soy sauce
1/4 cup whole wheat flour
Water
5 cloves garlic, chopped
2 teaspoons dried parsley flakes or 1/4 cup fresh parsley chopped
2 bay leaves
1 teaspoon dried thyme
1 tablespoon plus 1 teaspoon apple juice concentrate
3 tablespoons Red Rosé wine
Cayenne pepper, to taste

To cook live crawfish, first, you must purge them in salt water. Place the crawfish in a pail with enough water to cover them. Add about 2 cups of salt to the water and stir. Let the crawfish sit for about 30 minutes. This cleans a lot of the dirt out of them. In the meantime, put a large pot on the stove about 2/3rds full of water and bring to a rapid boil. Add the crawfish and boil for 20 minutes; then remove from the heat but allow them to cool in their own water. Peel and devein as you would shrimp. Refrigerate.

Combine onion, green pepper, and celery in a room-temperature, nonstick frying pan. Set the heat on high. Add tamari or soy sauce and sauté the vegetables until the onion looks transparent. Add the flour and stir until it begins to smoke. Continue to stir for about 20 seconds, then immediately add a little water and continue stirring. Lower the heat to medium. Add the garlic and more water, a little at a time, stirring constantly and smoothing out any lumps in the flour. Continue adding water and stirring until you have added enough water too cover the vegetables plus a little bit more. Cook, stirring constantly, until the mixture thickens. The exact amount of liquid is not important. You are making a nice, thick gravy about the consistency of, or just a little thicker than melted ice cream. For now, though, make it thinner than that, because it is going to cook down and you want to have enough liquid to allow for evaporation. Add the parsley, bay leaves, thyme, apple juice concentrate, and wine. Crawfish, fish, shrimp, oysters, or clams should *not* be added at this time. Simmer the mixture covered for 2 hours. Stir often. Add water if needed.

Fifteen minutes before you plan to serve, add the crawfish, fish, shrimp, oysters, or clams, and simmer for just 15 minutes. *Do not overcook* or the seafood will shrink to nothing or become mushy.

The serving size is 3 ounces of crawfish per person if you serve 3 people. For the regression diet, reduce the amount of peeled crawfish to 4 1/2 ounces, but use the same amount of other ingredients or add a little more chopped celery (1 to 1 1/2 cups) to fill out the volume. The crawfish or other fish will be sparse but you will still have enough gravy for the rice. Or, you can make this dish as is and pick out 5 or 6 crawfish and weigh them to be exact. Broken up fish will be harder to pick out than shrimp or crawfish so just use the 4 1/2 ounces of fish to start with, and then you won't have to worry about getting more than 1 1/2 ounces of meat.

CRAWFISH PIE

YIELD: 12 SERVINGS

Nutrition Facts

Amount Per Serving

Calories 260   Calories from Fat 10

	% Daily Value*
Total Fat 1.5g	**2**%
Saturated Fat 0g	**0**%
Cholesterol 40mg	**13**%
Sodium 290mg	**12**%
Total Carbohydrate 50g	**17**%
Dietary Fiber 5g	**22**%
Sugars 7g	
Protein 14g	

Vitamin A 6%	•	Vitamin C 80%
Calcium 6%	•	Iron 10%

My brother brought home some boiled crawfish when I was twelve years old, and that's when my love affair with crawfish began.

Deep in Cajun country, Palmetto, Louisiana, to be exact, all neatly picked crawfish tails in 1-pound portions are packed. There are two kinds of packaged crawfish—washed and unwashed. The washing gets rid of the fat. If you can't get any other kind of crawfish except those with fat, just put the crawfish in a colander and rinse them. If all you can find is live or cooked, unpeeled crawfish, it takes 8 to 8 /18 pounds of unpeeled to equal 1 pound of peeled crawfish. Note: It has been recently discovered that crawfish fat is not really fat.

Potato Base:
6 medium potatoes
5 slices Pritikin or commercial whole wheat bread in crumbs
1 1/2 cups frozen or fresh green peas

Filling:
1 pound cooked, peeled, washed crawfish tails (2 cups packed, or about 125 tails)
1 large onion, chopped
1 large green pepper, chopped
5 celery ribs, chopped
2 cups Stock from Roasted Chicken or Turkey (page 46)
2 bay leaves
1/4 teaspoon cayenne pepper
1 teaspoon garlic powder
1 teaspoon dried thyme
2 teaspoons dried parsley
2 teaspoons low-sodium soy sauce
3 tablespoons Red Rosé wine
4 jumbo egg whites

Topping:
7 medium potatoes, peeled and quartered
6 tablespoons nonfat cottage cheese
1/4 Baked Banana (page 57)
5 tablespoons evaporated skim milk
1/4 teaspoon red pepper flakes
1 tablespoon grated sapsago cheese
Fresh lemon wedges

To make the potato base: boil or bake 6 potatoes in their skins. Set aside to cool, then peel, and slice. In a 9 x 13-inch baking dish, arrange a layer of the potato slices.

Process the bread in a food processor or blender to make bread crumbs. Sprinkle the crumbs over the potato slices. Then sprinkle the green peas over the bread crumbs.

Pick through the crawfish tails and remove any black veins, and set aside.

Filling: combine the onions, green pepper, and celery in a nonstick frying pan and sauté over high heat by turning them until the onions look a little transparent and the edges turn a bit brown. Lower the heat to medium-low. Add the stock, bay leaves, cayenne, garlic powder, thyme, parsley, soy sauce, and the wine and stir. Cover and simmer for 15 minutes over low heat, stirring occasionally. Remove from the heat and let the mixture cool for 20 minutes. Stir in the egg whites. Add the crawfish tails. Pour the crawfish mixture over the potato base.

Topping: cover the remaining 7 potatoes in water and boil until very tender, 10 to 15 minutes. Pierce with a knife to test.

While the potatoes are cooking, process the cottage cheese, banana and its baking juices, and milk in a blender or food processor until smooth.

Drain the potatoes and mash. Add the cottage cheese-milk mixture and continue to mash until the potatoes are fluffy and creamy. Spread the potato mixture over the crawfish mixture in the baking pan. Sprinkle with red pepper flakes and sapsago cheese.

Place the crawfish pie in the oven on the middle rack, set the temperature at 350 degrees F., and bake for 40 minutes. Place under broiler for 5 minutes to brown the top. Let sit outside the oven for 10 minutes, then serve in squares with 1 fresh lemon wedge on each plate. Each serving will contain 1 1/3 ounces of crawfish.

SCALLOPS IN CREAM SAUCE

Nutrition Facts

Amount Per Serving

Calories 240   Calories from Fat 15

	% Daily Value*
Total Fat 2g	3%
Saturated Fat 0.5g	3%
Cholesterol 40mg	14%
Sodium 420mg	17%
Total Carbohydrate 27g	9%
Dietary Fiber 2g	8%
Sugars 11g	
Protein 29g	

Vitamin A 8%	•	Vitamin C 35%
Calcium 30%	•	Iron 8%

1 1/2 cups uncooked cauliflower, chopped
1/3 cup Chicken or Turkey Stock (page 44)
1 bay leaf cut in half
3 tablespoons cornstarch
1/4 teaspoon garlic powder
1/8 teaspoon cayenne pepper
1 can (12 ounces) evaporated skim milk
1 pound scallops
2 slices commercial whole wheat bread in crumbs
3 tablespoons grated sapsago cheese

Spray and 8 x 8-inch baking dish with a nonstick spray and set aside.

Combine the cauliflower, stock, and bay leaf in a 1 1/2-quart saucepan. Cover, bring to a boil, and boil for about 3 minutes over high heat, until the liquid is almost evaporated. Watch closely.

Place the cornstarch, garlic powder, and cayenne in the baking dish and add the milk. Stir until the cornstarch is dissolved. Cut the scallops into 4 pieces if they are very large, then add the scallops, cauliflower, and bay leaf, plus 2 tablespoons of the cheese to the cornstarch mixture. Sprinkle with the bread crumbs, and then sprinkle with the remaining tablespoon of cheese. Bake uncovered in an unpreheated oven at 400 degrees F. on the middle rack for 30 minutes. Turn the temperature of the oven down to 150 degrees F. and let the casserole sit in the oven for 20 minutes before serving.

COQUILLE ST. JACQUES

Coquille St. Jacques is one of my favorite dishes served at the many famous French restaurants of New Orleans. Naturally, these are usually prepared with lots of butter, heavy cream, and salt; but here I have "Pritikinized" the recipe and my husband Ray laps up every last bit whenever I make it.

1 cup Turkey Stock (page 44)
8 scallions, chopped
1 tablespoon whole wheat flour
4 tablespoons whole wheat or Pritikin bread crumbs, divided
1/2 teaspoon dried thyme
1/8 teaspoon red pepper flakes
1/8 teaspoon cayenne pepper or more to taste
2 jumbo egg whites
10 large scallops (about 7 ounces)
2 teaspoons fresh lemon juice
2 cups Cheesy Mashed Potatoes (page 229)
2 tablespoons grated sapsago cheese
Paprika for garnish

In a saucepan, combine the turkey stock and chopped scallions or green onions and bring to a boil. Lower the heat to medium and cook covered, stirring occasionally, for about 5 or 6 minutes, until the onions are soft. Sprinkle the flour over the mixture and pat it in with the back of a wooden spoon, then stir over medium heat until smooth. Add 3 tablespoons of the bread crumbs, the thyme, red pepper flakes, and 1/8 teaspoon of the cayenne and taste. You might want another 1/8 teaspoon of cayenne. Stir in the 4 egg whites. Remove from the heat and add scallops and lemon juice. Divide the mixture between 2 shells or small casseroles. Sprinkle the remaining 1 tablespoon of bread crumbs over the mixture. Set the oven at 400 degrees F., then place the shells on a baking pan and place in the oven and bake for 10 minutes.

If you have a pastry bag, fit it with a large decorator tip. Fill the bag with the potatoes and flute the potatoes all around the edges of little casseroles or around the edge of the shells. Leave the center empty. Use a spoon if you don't have a pastry bag. Make little peaks in the potatoes as you would with meringue. Sprinkle with the sapsago cheese and a little paprika. Return to the oven and bake for 10 minutes more. Then move them to the broiler and broil for 3 minutes, until the tips of the potatoes are brown. Serve immediately with a lemon wedge, a green vegetable on the side, and a salad.

This is about 3 1/2 ounces of scallops per person. For exact measurements, weigh scallops before cooking them.

POACHED FISH

Nutrition Facts

Amount Per Serving	
Calories 180	Calories from Fat 20

	% Daily Value*
Total Fat 2g	3%
Saturated Fat 0g	0%
Cholesterol 65mg	21%
Sodium 120mg	5%
Total Carbohydrate 14g	5%
Dietary Fiber 2g	7%
Sugars 10g	
Protein 27g	

Vitamin A 15%	•	Vitamin C 20%
Calcium 6%	•	Iron 8%

This is a tasty dish flavored with the spices of crab boil. If you don't want to bother making your own, you can buy packaged crab boil. Have your fishmonger scale and gut the fish for you and tell him to leave the head on. The head and bones make for good juice.

2 1/2 quarts water
1 pouch prepared salt-free crab boil or Homemade Crab Boil (page 170)
1 tablespoon salt-free chili powder
1/2 cup apple cider vinegar
1 large onion, peeled and quartered
2 celery ribs, cut in halves
1/4 cup apple juice concentrate
2 1/2 pound white-fleshed fish, weighed before being scaled and gutted
1 lemon

Pour the water into a roasting pan that just fits the fish nicely. In other words, not too large a pan. Add the pouch of crab boil, chili powder, vinegar, onion, celery, and juice concentrate. Bring the mixture to a boil uncovered on top of the stove. Reduce the heat to medium and simmer uncovered for 35 minutes. Put the fish in the pan. If you need more water to cover the fish, add it, but as little as is possible. Simmer the fish uncovered over medium-high heat for 20 minutes. Turn off the heat and squeeze the lemon over the fish and cooking liquid. Drop the peels into the liquid. Let sit for 30 minutes to marinate.

BRONZED CATFISH GUILLAUME

YIELD: 2 SERVINGS

Nutrition Facts

Amount Per Serving

Calories 160	Calories from Fat 80

	% Daily Value*
Total Fat 9g	**13%**
Saturated Fat 2g	**10%**
Cholesterol 55mg	**18%**
Sodium 240mg	**10%**
Total Carbohydrate 1g	**0%**
Dietary Fiber 0g	**0%**
Sugars 0g	
Protein 18g	

Vitamin A 2%	•	Vitamin C 10%
Calcium 2%	•	Iron 4%

This recipe was named for my son Guillaume, who once called home wanting this recipe while he was in college at Louisiana State University.

2 teaspoons low-sodium soy sauce
3 tablespoons water
Juice of 1 medium lemon or 2 tablespoons frozen concentrated
  pure lemon juice
1/4 teaspoon garlic powder
1/8 teaspoon cayenne pepper
2 catfish fillets, 4 ounces each
1/2 teaspoon dried parsley
1/4 cup water

For the sauce, mix the soy sauce, 3 tablespoons of water, lemon juice, garlic powder, and cayenne in a small container.

Add 2 tablespoons of the sauce in a nonstick pan. Set the heat on high. When the sauce begins to steam, add the fillets, and then turn them over to coat them with sauce. Shake the pan back and forth, to move the fillets around. Leave space between the fillets, and turn them often. After cooking for 3 minutes, add 2 more tablespoons of sauce and sprinkle with the parsley. Continue to cook for 3 minutes more, shaking the pan and turning the fish. Add any extra sauce to the pan as the fish cooks. Press on the fish with the edge of your spatula. When the fish seems like you could cut right through it with the spatula, it's done. Remove to a warm plate and cover.

Add 1/4 cup of water to the pan and deglaze the juices over high heat moving the juices back and forth in the pan with the spatula. When the juices have been reduced by about half and look like a nice butter sauce, pour over the fish. If you double this recipe, do not double the 1/4 cup of water for the sauce.

STUFFED CATFISH

Nutrition Facts

Amount Per Serving	
Calories 220 Calories from Fat 45	
	% Daily Value*
Total Fat 5g	8%
Saturated Fat 1.5g	6%
Cholesterol 75mg	25%
Sodium 450mg	19%
Total Carbohydrate 20g	7%
Dietary Fiber 3g	11%
Sugars 5g	
Protein 25g	
Vitamin A 4% • Vitamin C 35%	
Calcium 6% • Iron 10%	

1 medium onion, finely chopped
3 slices commercial whole wheat or Pritikin bread
1/2 cup Turkey Stock (page 44)
1/8 teaspoon dried thyme
1 teaspoon parsley flakes
1/4 plus 1/8 teaspoon garlic powder
1/8 teaspoon dried sage
1/16 teaspoon celery seed
1/8 teaspoon ground bay leaf
1/2 teaspoon medium red hot sauce
1/8 plus 1/16 teaspoon Tabasco® sauce
Juice of 1 lemon
3 tablespoons water
2 teaspoons low-sodium soy sauce
3 (4 1/2-ounce) catfish fillets

Spray an 8-inch-by-8-inch baking dish with a nonstick spray.

Sauté the onion in a nonstick frying pan over high heat, turning the onion until it looks a bit transparent and brown around the edges. Remove from the heat. Break up the bread and add it to the pan, then add the thyme, parsley, sage, celery seed, bay leaf, and 1/8 teaspoon of garlic powder. Mix in the turkey stock, medium hot sauce, and 1/16 teaspoon of Tabasco® sauce, making sure the bread is well combined. Divide the stuffing equally among the catfish fillets. Fold each fillet in half over the stuffing and secure the open ends of the fillets with toothpicks. Place the fillets in the baking dish.

Make a sauce by combining the lemon juice, water, soy sauce, the remaining 1/8 teaspoon of Tabasco® sauce, and the remaining 1/4 teaspoon garlic powder.

Place the baking dish, uncovered, on the middle rack of the oven. Set the temperature at 350 degrees F. Baste with half the sauce, and bake for 35 minutes. Baste with the remaining sauce and bake for 5 minutes more. Serve immediately with the sauce poured over the fillets.

EASY OVEN-FRIED CATFISH

YIELD: 6 SERVINGS

Nutrition Facts

Amount Per Serving

Calories 150   Calories from Fat 30

	% Daily Value*
Total Fat 3.5g	5%
Saturated Fat 1g	4%
Cholesterol 65mg	22%
Sodium 50mg	2%
Total Carbohydrate 9g	3%
Dietary Fiber less than 1 gram	4%
Sugars 0g	
Protein 20g	

Vitamin A 2%	•	Vitamin C 2%
Calcium 2%	•	Iron 6%

Try to find the small catfish. The great big ones are liable to be strong-tasting. The best catfish are the whole ones that are no longer than 12 inches, including the head.

1/2 cup yellow cornmeal
1/16 teaspoon cayenne pepper
1/2 teaspoon dried thyme
1/2 teaspoon ground sage
3 whole cleaned catfish (7 to 8 ounces each), skin and heads removed
Water

Preheat the oven to 400 degrees F.

Spray a large nonstick baking pan with nonstick spray. In a plastic or paper bag, combine the cornmeal, cayenne, thyme, and sage. Seal, then shake the bag to mix the spices.

Cut each catfish in half making the tail ends longer since the part nearest the head has more meat. You want to have about 3 1/2 ounces of meat per serving, not including the bones. Rinse each of the pieces under cold water, and leaving them wet, place them one at a time in the bag with the cornmeal mixture. Seal the shake to coat. Place each piece on the pan.

Bake the fish on the top rack for 20 to 25 minutes until lightly brown. Turn once if they look like they won't stick when you run a spatula under the pieces. If they appear to be sticking, though, leave them alone. They will be fine. Just serve them brown side up. Serve with fresh lemon wedges. If you don't mind cheating a little, ketchup is good on the side, too. Piquante Sauce (page 55) would not be cheating and is a different experience from the lemon and ketchup. Each piece will have about 3 1/3 ounces of meat.

MAHI MAHI JAMAICA-STYLE

Nutrition Facts

Amount Per Serving

Calories 360   Calories from Fat 25

	% Daily Value*
Total Fat 3g	4%
Saturated Fat 0.5g	3%
Cholesterol 85mg	28%
Sodium 115mg	5%
Total Carbohydrate 55g	18%
Dietary Fiber 6g	24%
Sugars 18g	
Protein 26g	

Vitamin A 15%	•	Vitamin C 80%
Calcium 6%	•	Iron 20%

When my husband and I were last in Jamaica, we were served mahi mahi in a wonderful curry sauce. I added baked bananas as a side dish, and please don't skip making them. They really bring out the flavor of the whole dish.

If you can't find mahi mahi, swordfish, shark, or some fish that has rather heavy, but flaky white meat will do.

1 1/2 pounds mahi mahi fillets
1 1/2 tablespoons fresh lemon juice
1/4 teaspoon garlic powder
3 very ripe bananas
2 tablespoons water
1 medium onion, chopped
1 large green pepper, cut in long, narrow strips
1 1/2 cups water
1/2 cup Red Rosé wine
2 tablespoons apple juice concentrate
4 garlic cloves, chopped
2 tablespoons curry powder
2 large tomatoes, sliced in narrow wedges
1/8 to 1/4 teaspoon cayenne pepper (optional)

Remove the skin from the mahi mahi fillets by slipping a sharp knife under the skin and working back until the skin comes off. Cut the fish into 6 equal sections. Line an 8-inch-square baking dish with aluminum foil, leaving extra foil to fold over the fish. Place the fish fillets on the foil. Sprinkle with lemon juice and then garlic powder. Cut slices off the squeezed lemons and place pulp-side down, over the fish. Fold the foil loosely over the fish. Refrigerate while you prepare the bananas.

Peel the bananas, then cut them in half across the short part of the banana, leaving their full thickness. Place the halves in a separate nonstick baking pan. Sprinkle with 2 tablespoons of water. Cover the pan with foil. (If you don't plan to eat all the mahi mahi—the recipe makes 6—just put as many banana halves as you wish to eat in the pan and add 1 teaspoon of water for each half.)

Put the bananas and the fish in the oven and set the temperature at 350 degrees F. Bake for about 35 minutes, or until the fish is flaky and white.

While the fish and bananas are cooking, combine the onion and green pepper in a nonstick 5-quart stockpot. Sauté over high heat by turning the vegetables until the onion appears transparent and a little brown around the edges. Add the water. Lower the heat to medium. Add the wine and the juice concentrate, then add the garlic and curry powder and combine. Add the tomatoes. Cover and cook for about 15 minutes, or until the tomatoes and onion are tender, stirring occasionally.

When the fish is done, pick it up out of the baking dish in the aluminum foil, holding the top edges of the foil around the fish. Carefully pour any juice from the fish into the pot with the vegetables and combine. Taste. If the curry powder contains no pepper, add cayenne to taste, 1/8 to 1/4 teaspoon for this amount of sauce is about right. Reheat the sauce if necessary.

MAHI MAHI BOUILLI

Nutrition Facts

Amount Per Serving

Calories 150   Calories from Fat 20

	% Daily Value*
Total Fat 2g	3%
Saturated Fat 0g	0%
Cholesterol 40mg	14%
Sodium 170mg	7%
Total Carbohydrate 9g	3%
Dietary Fiber 2g	6%
Sugars 6g	
Protein 20g	

Vitamin A 10%	•	Vitamin C 45%
Calcium 15%	•	Iron 10%

Bouilli (pronounced boo-yee) means boiled in French, so this is really boiled redfish, but boiled gently.

1/2 cup **Strong Chicken Stock from Roasted Chicken (page 46)**
1/2 cup **white Chablis**
1 tablespoon **apple juice concentrate**
1 medium **onion, chopped**
1/2 medium **green pepper, chopped**
1 **celery rib, chopped**
1 large **ripe tomato, hand chopped**
1 **bay leaf**
1/4 teaspoon **garlic powder**
1/2 teaspoon **dried thyme**
1/2 teaspoon **onion powder**
1/2 teaspoon **saffron threads or powder, tightly packed**
1 teaspoon **dried parsley**
1/8 teaspoon **dried red pepper flakes**
4 (3 1/2-ounce) **mahi mahi fillets**

Combine all the ingredients, except the fish, in a saucepan. Bring to a boil, then cover, and reduce the heat to low for 15 minutes, stirring occasionally, until the vegetables are tender. Spoon half the cooked vegetables and liquid into a 1 1/2-quart baking dish. On top of the liquid and vegetables, place the redfish fillets. Then spoon the rest of the cooked vegetables and liquid over the fish. Cover the dish, set the temperature of the oven to 350 degrees F. and bake on the top shelf of the oven for 40 minutes.

Serve over cooked angel hair pasta (or the smallest size semolina spaghetti you can find), with green peas on the side. Each serving will contain 3 1/2 ounces of fish.

BAKED TROUT

Nutrition Facts

Amount Per Serving

Calories 330 Calories from Fat 110

	% Daily Value*
Total Fat 12g	**19**%
Saturated Fat 3.5g	**18**%
Cholesterol 135mg	**45**%
Sodium 260mg	**11**%
Total Carbohydrate 3g	**1**%
Dietary Fiber less than 1 gram	**4**%
Sugars 1g	
Protein 48g	

Vitamin A 15%	•	Vitamin C 35%
Calcium 15%	•	Iron 6%

Shopping tip: Buy a whole trout that weighs about 1/2 pound with the head, which will yield about 3 ounces of meat. Or buy a trout that weighs 1 pound and cut it in half to serve two people. Sometimes the small trout are hard to find. If trout is unavailable, another fresh water fish will do. You could even make this recipe with sections of larger salt water fish that has been cut across the bone, such as swordfish, or shark. (Use baby shark. The big ones don't taste as good.) Do not use tuna or salmon.

2 teaspoons low-sodium soy sauce
3 tablespoons water
1 lemon
1/4 teaspoons garlic powder
1/8 teaspoon cayenne pepper
2 small (1/2 pound each) speckled trout

Mix tamari or soy sauce, water, juice of the lemon, garlic powder, and cayenne pepper in a cup or small bowl. Place fish on a fairly large sheet of aluminum foil. Draw the edges of the foil up around the fish to form a bag. Pour the seasoning over the fish. Tuck the aluminum foil up around the fish leaving an opening about 1 inch wide to let out the steam. Set the oven temperature at 300 degrees F., and place the foil-wrapped fish on a baking pan in the oven and bake for 20 minutes. Open the foil and slash the fish in several places and baste with the cooking juice. Tuck the foil up around the fish as before. Bake for 20 minutes more, and serve.

This dish may seem to have a lot of salt at first glance because of the 2 teaspoons of tamari or soy sauce, but you will see after it cooks that there is so much juice the soy or tamari sauce becomes very diluted. For a much less salty fish, just don't serve the fish with all the sauce.

CLAM AND TUNA CHOWDER

YIELD: 11 SERVINGS

Nutrition Facts

Amount Per Serving	
Calories 70	Calories from Fat 0

	% Daily Value*
Total Fat 0g	0%
Saturated Fat 0g	0%
Cholesterol 10mg	3%
Sodium 180mg	8%
Total Carbohydrate 8g	3%
Dietary Fiber less than 1 gram	3%
Sugars 4g	
Protein 8g	

Vitamin A 40%	•	Vitamin C 10%
Calcium 10%	•	Iron 6%

1 large potato, diced
1 large carrot, sliced
1 1/2 cups chopped celery with leaves
Water
1/4 teaspoon dried red pepper flakes
1 tablespoon dried parsley
1/4 cup white Bordeaux wine
1 can (6 1/2 ounces) minced clams, rinsed
1 can (6 1/2 ounces) tuna packed in water, drained
1 can (12 ounces) evaporated skim milk

Combine the potato, carrot, and celery in a 3-quart stockpot. Cover the vegetables with water. Cover the pot and bring to a boil. Uncover and boil for 5 minutes over high heat. Add the parsley, wine, clams, and tuna. Cover, cook for 2 minutes over medium heat. Add the milk and heat through. Serve hot.

TUNA ON TOAST

YIELD: 3 SERVINGS

Nutrition Facts

Amount Per Serving	
Calories 300	Calories from Fat 35

	% Daily Value*
Total Fat 3.5g	6%
Saturated Fat 1g	4%
Cholesterol 15mg	6%
Sodium 500mg	21%
Total Carbohydrate 47g	16%
Dietary Fiber 8g	31%
Sugars 10g	
Protein 24g	

Vitamin A 4%	•	Vitamin C 20%
Calcium 8%	•	Iron 30%

My friend Charlyn can't believe this is tuna! She thinks it tastes like a crabmeat dish you would get in a fancy restaurant! Now she makes it for her family.

2 cups Chicken or Turkey Stock (page 44)
1 cup chopped onion
3 cups sliced fresh mushrooms
1 bay leaf
1 teaspoon dried thyme, or 2 sprigs of fresh thyme
1/8 teaspoon cayenne pepper
1 teaspoon dried or 2 tablespoons chopped fresh parsley
5 tablespoons whole wheat flour
1 can (6 1/2 ounces) water-packed tuna
1 tablespoon apple juice concentrate
6 slices toasted commercial whole wheat or Pritikin bread

Combine the stock, onions, mushrooms, bay leaf, thyme, cayenne pepper, and parsley in a large saucepan. Bring to a boil, then lower the heat to medium, and cook for 15 minutes, uncovered. As it cooks, sprinkle with about 1/3 tablespoon at a time of the flour and pat it in with the back of a spoon, stirring until smooth. Continue until you have added all the flour and the mixture is smooth and thick. Add the tuna fish and apple juice concentrate and combine.

Serve over toasted commercial whole wheat or Pritikin bread. Pritikin Rye Bread tastes good with this, too. Serve 2 slices of bread to each person. If served on 6 slices of bread, each slice of toast will hold slightly over 1 ounce of tuna.

CODFISH CAKES

Nutrition Facts

Amount Per Serving

Calories 50	Calories from Fat 0

	% Daily Value*
Total Fat 0g	**0%**
Saturated Fat 0g	**0%**
Cholesterol 5mg	**2%**
Sodium 15mg	**1%**
Total Carbohydrate 10g	**3%**
Dietary Fiber less than 1 gram	**3%**
Sugars 2g	
Protein 4g	

Vitamin A 2%	•	Vitamin C 10%
Calcium 0%	•	Iron 2%

When I was a little girl, my mother used to make codfish cakes during Lent. I always thought they were delicious: brown and crisp on the outside, and tender and moist on the inside. When you observe Lent or not, these aren't hard to make and taste just like Mama's.

3 large potatoes, peeled and quartered
6 ounces fresh codfish fillets, rinsed and cut into chunks
2 tablespoons minced dried onions
1 tablespoon dried parsley
2 teaspoons medium red hot sauce
1/2 tablespoon grated sapsago cheese
1/4 Baked Banana (page 57)
1/2 teaspoon dried thyme
1 tablespoon apple cider vinegar
1/8 teaspoon cayenne pepper
1 jumbo egg white

Place the potatoes in a 2-quart saucepan with enough water to cover, and cook over high heat, uncovered, for about 20 minutes until tender. Pierce with a sharp knife to test. Drain off the water and set aside.

Place the fish in a food processor fitted with a cutting blade and process briefly until the fish starts to form a ball, but do not *purée*.

Mash the potatoes. Mix in one ingredient at a time, the fish, onions, parsley, hot sauce, cheese, banana and baking juices, thyme, vinegar, cayenne, and egg white. Taste. If the potatoes were very big, you might want to add a little more cayenne, vinegar, and sapsago cheese. Let the mixture sit, out of the refrigerator, for about 20 minutes. Then make 12 round flat patties about 2 inches in diameter and 1/2-inch thick.

Preheat oven to 200 degrees F. Spray a nonstick frying pan with nonstick spray. Preheat it over high heat until a drop of water dropped on it sizzles. Place patties in a circle, not touching each other, in the pan. Leave the middle of the pan empty. Brown the patties on one side, then turn the patties over and brown on the other side. Remove to a hot ovenproof plate and put in the oven to keep warm. Cook the next batch of patties as you did the first batch. If the pan begins to smoke while you are cooking, lower the heat a bit, turn back up as the pan cools. Try to keep an even high heat. Serve hot with lemon wedges and some steamed carrots and peas.

You can freeze and reheat these. Freeze each patty separately, wrapped in plastic wrap. Use a conventional oven or microwave to reheat. Each cake will contain 1/2 ounce of fish.

NEW ORLEANS-STYLE SEAFOOD GUMBO

Gumbo is a thick, delicious seafood soup served in just about every restaurant and home in the city of New Orleans. The word "gumbo" is thought to be a combination of the Portuguese and African words for okra. It can also be made with chicken, turkey, or sausage, instead of seafood, and while there are probably a thousand recipes for gumbo, when you eat any of them you know you are eating gumbo. If you can't get the shrimp or oysters for this dish, you can substitute fish, but please do try to get the crabs or crabmeat. Without it, it just isn't gumbo! And if you live in San Francisco, or some place like that where you have those enormous Dungeness crabs, 3 crabs will be enough for this recipe. The crabs I use average 5 to 6 inches from tip to tip of the shells. Serve with French Rolls and Cooked Brown Rice or cooked instant brown rice.

2 pounds fresh okra, or frozen okra, but fresh is better
2 large onions, chopped
5 ribs celery, chopped
2 large green peppers, chopped
5 to 6 garlic cloves, chopped, or 2 teaspoons garlic powder
6 tablespoons whole wheat flour
2 cups Fish Stock (page 47) or water
2 cups Chicken or Turkey Stock (page 44)
3 bay leaves
1 cup chopped fresh parsley
1/2 teaspoon cayenne pepper or more, to taste
6 fresh or frozen crabs or 2 cans (6 ounces each) or equal amount frozen crabmeat
2 pounds fresh, unpeeled shrimp or 2 cans (4 1/2 ounces each)
1 pint fresh oysters and juice or 1 can (8 ounces) oysters or 1 can (6 ounces) clams
2 teaspoons dried thyme, or 2 sprigs fresh thyme
1 teaspoon filé per bowl, for thickening and flavor (optional)
Cooked brown rice

Cut off the stem-tips of the okra, then slice. I place 5 or 6 next to each other and slice them straight across. This makes it go very fast and tastes better than if you throw them in the food processor. The other vegetables, however, *can* be chopped in the food processor.

If you are using frozen okra, do not brown it. For fresh okra brown it this way. In a nonstick, room temperature, 5-quart soup pot, add the sliced okra. Over high heat, sauté the okra, turning it over constantly with a wooden spoon. Soon little strings will form between the okra slices. Sautéing helps get some of the stickiness out of the okra. When the edges begin to brown, remove to a bowl. (If you are using frozen okra start with this next step.) Add the onions, green peppers, celery, and garlic to the pot and sauté them, turning them constantly. When they begin to brown and the onions become a little transparent, add the flour. Keep turning the mixture over with your spoon. When the flour begins to smoke, continue to stir for about another 15 to 20 seconds. Immediately, add the 2 cups of fish stock or water a little at a time, mixing it in and smoothing out the flour. Continue stirring and adding until you have added all the fish stock or water. If the mixture is still bubbling madly, add a cup or two of the chicken stock until it calms down. Add the bay leaves, parsley, and pepper. Cover, lower the heat, and simmer.

How to Clean Crabs. If you have fresh, live crabs, soak them in ice water with plenty of ice cubes for about 20 minutes. This anesthetizes them so they can't feel or move.

Hold each live anesthetized crab over a bowl to catch the liquid. There is a little "trap door" on the bottom side of each crab—pull that off. Then hold the crab, eyes facing away from you, with your left-hand thumb pressing down on the crab's left back leg, and your right-hand fingers on top of the shell and your thumb underneath, pull off the shell. Scoop out all of the yellow fat or orange eggs in the top shells and discard the shell. Keep the fat and eggs. If you are extremely cholesterol conscious, don't use the fat. But there is such a little bit in a huge pot, and it adds so much flavor. Pull off the "dead men's fingers," which are the feathery things, off the "breast" of the crab and anything else that isn't crabmeat, and discard. Break the crab in two at its center and toss into the gumbo pot, shell, legs, and all. Add any liquid you caught from the crabs into the pot, too, and rinse the bowl with a little water and add that. If you have canned crabmeat, rinse it and add now. If you have frozen crabmeat, add it.

Return the okra to the pot. Add enough water to come within an inch from the top of the pot. Simmer for 1 1/2 hours, stirring occasionally. Keep covered.

How To Peel Shrimp. While the gumbo is cooking, peel your shrimp. First pull off the head and discard. With your right hand, hold the end of the shrimp's tail. With the forefinger and thumb of your left hand, take hold of the shell that was nearest the shrimp's head and lift it over the top, around to the other side, and off. The next little section will come off the same way. Then just squeeze the last couple of sections with your right thumb and forefinger on the tail, and the shrimp will pop out. Take the little dark vein out of the top of the shrimp with the tip of a sharp knife.

During the last 1/2 hour of cooking, add the shrimp, oysters or clams, thyme, and perhaps some more cayenne pepper. Taste and adjust your seasonings. Add oyster or clam juice if you have it.

Just before serving, toast the French Rolls in the oven for 7 or 8 minutes. The crust will become crunchy and crispy just like New Orleans-style French bread, and you can use it to dunk in your gumbo. Pour the gumbo over about 1/2 cup of rice in individual bowls. If you use small crabs, place half of a crab in each bowl and serve.

If you have been able to find filé, pronounced *fee-lay*, sprinkle about a teaspoon on top of each bowl of gumbo and stir it in. Filé is made from sassafras leaves and it gives extra flavor and thickens the gumbo. However, filé is not necessary to gumbo. Many people prefer not to use it. Note: Do not use fresh sassafras leaves off a tree. I checked with Judith Reagan at the F.D.A. in Washington, D.C. She said that the fresh plant contains saffarole, a substance which is suspected of causing cancer in humans. Commercial filé is required by the F.D.A. to be treated with a solvent that completely removes the saffarole. She assured me that no solvent is left in the commercial filé and that it is perfectly safe to eat.

If you use your ordinary 5-quart soup pot and have it filled to about an inch from the top with liquid, which is how this should come out, you will get about 14 one-cup servings with about 2 to 2 1/2 ounces of seafood in each bowl. It freezes very well. When I know I will be having house guests, I make a big pot of gumbo and freeze it so I won't have to do so much cooking when company comes.

PO-MAN'S GUMBO

One cold day Ray said he wanted gumbo for dinner. Well, I went out to the bayou and checked the crab traps, and no crabs, just a couple of perch. Crabs just don't like to get caught in cold weather—never did, probably never will. I checked the freezer and there was not one shrimp to be found, and no oysters, either. There wasn't even a bag of frozen okra. But Ray insisted. Well, I wasn't about to go all the way to town to go shopping so I scoured my kitchen and came up with the following recipe and Ray never knew the difference. Thus, was created po-man's gumbo.

2 1/2 cups chopped onion
6 celery ribs, with all the leaves, chopped
1 medium zucchini, chopped
1 can (16 ounces) whole peeled salt-free tomatoes
1 can (12 ounces) regular or nonalcoholic beer
1/4 cup apple juice concentrate
1 cup water
6 tablespoons whole wheat flour
4 cups Chicken or Turkey Stock (page 44)
1 can (6 1/2 ounces) minced clams
1 can (6 1/2 ounces) water-packed tuna, drained
3 bay leaves
2 tablespoons chopped fresh garlic
1/4 teaspoon cayenne pepper
2 teaspoons dried thyme
2 tablespoons dried parsley or 1/2 cup fresh parsley, chopped
4 1/3 cups cooked instant brown rice
2 teaspoons filé per bowl for thickening and flavor (optional)

Place the onion in a dry nonstick 5-quart soup pot. Sauté over high heat, tossing constantly until the onion looks a little transparent and brown around the edges. Remove the pan from the heat. Add the celery, zucchini, and tomatoes and their juice. Break up the tomatoes in the pot. Add the beer, and set aside.

Combine the juice concentrate, water and flour in a blender or food processor and blend until smooth. Add the mixture to the soup pot. Add the chicken or turkey stock. (You do not need to brown the flour. It works better this way for this recipe and don't worry, everything will turn out the right color.) Add the clams, tuna, bay leaves, garlic, and cayenne. Stir and cover the pot. Bring to a boil, then lower the heat and simmer for 1 hour, stirring occasionally. After 1 hour, add the thyme and parsley. Simmer, covered, for 1 more hour, stirring occasionally. Serve hot in individual bowls over 1/2 cup cooked instant brown rice. Add filé if you like it. Each serving contains 1 ounce of meat.

BOUILLABAISSE NEW ORLEANS STYLE

YIELD: 4 SERVINGS

Nutrition Facts

Amount Per Serving

Calories 360 Calories from Fat 50

% Daily Value*

Total Fat 6g	**9**%
Saturated Fat 1.5g	**8**%
Cholesterol 55mg	**18**%
Sodium 1020mg	**42**%
Total Carbohydrate 38g	**13**%
Dietary Fiber 6g	**25**%
Sugars 18g	
Protein 32g	

Vitamin A 130%	• Vitamin C 120%
Calcium 15%	• Iron 20%

New Orleans bouillabaisse calls for a combination of redfish and red snapper cooked with onions, then added to a tomato broth. However, when I created the recipe for this book, I couldn't find any redfish (due to scarcity with the popular craze of blackening them), so I substituted speckled trout for the redfish. You can also use other fish, like cod, orange roughy, or flounder.

2 1/2 cups finely chopped onion
1/4 cup finely chopped celery
1 cup Red Rosé wine
4 cups Chicken Stock from Roasted Chicken (page 46)
1/4 cup finely chopped fresh parsley
1 medium carrot, finely chopped
1 can (16 ounces) salt-free tomatoes, chopped (save the juice)
1 large fresh tomato, chopped
2 bay leaves
1 teaspoon dried thyme
1/8 teaspoon cayenne pepper
1/8 teaspoon ground allspice
2 garlic cloves, chopped
1 tablespoon apple juice concentrate
1/4 teaspoon powdered saffron or threads packed tightly
4 teaspoons low-sodium soy sauce
6 tablespoons water
Juice of 2 lemons
1/2 teaspoon garlic powder
1/8 teaspoon cayenne pepper
1/2 pound speckled trout fillets
1/2 pound red snapper fillets
1/4 cup water
3 slices commercial whole wheat bread trimmed and diced, for garnish
4 tablespoons grated sapsago cheese, for garnish
4 tablespoons Rouille Sauce (page 333)

Combine the onions and celery in a 5-quart, nonstick soup pot and sauté over high heat by tossing them constantly until the onions look a little transparent and brown around the edges. Lower the heat to medium and add the wine, chicken stock, parsley, carrot, tomatoes and juice, bay leaves, thyme, cayenne, allspice, garlic, and juice concentrate. Bring to a boil; then cover, lower the heat, and simmer for 1 hour, or until the onions and carrots are soft, stirring occasionally. Add the saffron during the last 15 minutes.

About 30 minutes before the soup is finished cooking, begin preparing the fish: Cut the fish into 2 1/2-inch pieces and set aside.

Make a sauce by combining the soy or tamari sauce, the 6 tablespoons water, the lemon juice, garlic powder, and the pepper in a small bowl. Pour 2 tablespoons of the sauce into a nonstick frying pan and place over high heat. When the sauce begins to sizzle, add half the fish pieces. Turn them over to coat with the sauce. Cook for about 3 minute on one side. Pour 2 tablespoons of the sauce over, and turn the fish over. Cook for about 3 minutes on the second side. The fish should look brown. If it doesn't, keep cooking it, turning it over until it is brown. Remove to a bowl. Pour another 2 tablespoons of the sauce into the pan and add the rest of the fish. Brown it as you did the first batch. Remove it to the bowl. Pour any extra sauce into the pan, plus 1/4 cup of water. Mix it around and let it sizzle uncovered, until the liquid thickens and begins to look like a butter sauce. Add it into the soup. Add the fish to the soup pot and simmer for about 10 minutes, covered. Ladle the bouillabaisse into soup bowls. Sprinkle untoasted, diced, whole wheat bread on top of each serving. Sprinkle 1 tablespoon sapsago cheese and 1 tablespoon of Rouille Sauce over the bread. Serve immediately. Each serving contains 4 ounces of fish.

QUICK AND EASY SEAFOOD GUMBO

YIELD: 14 SERVINGS

Nutrition Facts

Amount Per Serving	
Calories 240	Calories from Fat 25

	% Daily Value*
Total Fat 3g	4%
Saturated Fat 0.5g	4%
Cholesterol 75mg	25%
Sodium 400mg	17%
Total Carbohydrate 35g	12%
Dietary Fiber 4g	17%
Sugars 6g	
Protein 16g	

Vitamin A 8%	•	Vitamin C 35%	
Calcium 10%	•	Iron 25%	

One night, I was pressed for time and I had everything frozen or canned in the house to make gumbo with, I thought, what the heck, I'm just going to dump everything in and let it go. I was amazed. It turned out great! It still took as long to cook, but the preparation time was reduced to 20 minutes, if that. Of course, I had chicken stock already made in the freezer.

2 cups frozen diced onions
1 cup frozen diced green peppers
1 1/2 cups frozen diced celery
5 cups frozen sliced or cut okra (20-ounce package)
6 cups water
3 tablespoons whole wheat flour
4 cups Chicken Stock from Roasted Chicken (page 46)
3 bay leaves
1 tablespoon dried parsley, or 1/4 cup fresh chopped parsley
1/2 teaspoon cayenne pepper
2 teaspoons garlic powder
2 teaspoons dried thyme, 3 sprigs fresh thyme
5 tablespoons apple juice concentrate
1/2 cup Red Rosé wine
2 cans (6 1/2 ounces each) claw or white crabmeat, rinsed
2 cans (4 1/2 ounces each) shrimp, rinsed
1 pint fresh unwashed oysters and juice, or 1 can (8 ounces) oysters, rinsed, or 1 can (6 ounces) clams, rinsed
Instant brown or white rice

In a 5-quart soup pot, combine the onions, green pepper, celery, okra, and 5 1/4 cups of the water. Pour the flour into a blender or food processor. Add the remaining 3/4 cup water and blend. When the mixture is perfectly smooth, mix it slowly into the pot with the vegetables and chicken stock. Set the heat on high and bring to a boil. Lower the heat and simmer for 1 hour, uncovered, stirring occasionally. Add the bay leaves, parsley, cayenne, garlic powder, thyme, juice concentrate, Red Rosé wine, crab, shrimp, oysters, and oyster juice, if they are fresh oysters or clams. Simmer for 30 minutes, uncovered, stirring occasionally. Remove from the heat and let sit for 30 minutes, then reheat. Or if you have time, when the soup is cool, refrigerate for 4 or 5 hours, then reheat. (Letting the gumbo sit allows the flavors to mingle, improving the flavor.) Each serving will contain 2 to 2 1/2 ounces of seafood. Serve in a soup bowl over 1/2 cup of instant brown rice.

Vegetable Side Dishes and Entrées

Eating healthy means eating plenty of vegetables, but don't think that you need to add that dab of butter or margarine to them. You don't. So many vegetables are delicious without it. You might say to yourself, "Oh that little bit of butter—it's nothing." Well that pat of butter or margarine *is* something; it's fat and calories you don't need.

So try these recipes without the margarine or butter. I think you will be surprised how good they are.

In Louisiana we tend to mix our vegetables with everything else. We sort of fancy them up, you might say, or maybe the vegetables fancy up the other foods! What I do when I plan my meals is to serve something like crawfish pie, which has a complicated flavor, with something like plain steamed cabbage on the side. Or I might serve cabbage jambalaya, which has lots of flavor, with plain steamed peas or spinach on the side. Two complex foods will just compete with each other instead of complement each other. So give some thought to which dishes you put together, and don't forget your vegetables!

VEGETABLES THAT NEED VERY LITTLE HELP

Artichokes: Place artichokes in 1 inch of water in a stockpot. Bring to a boil and reduce the heat to low. Cook covered for about 25 minutes, or until you can pull off a leaf easily and the flesh at the base of the leaf is tender.

Asparagus: Cut off the tough ends and steam just a few minutes for baby spears, up to 5 minutes for larger, more mature spears. Serve hot or cold plain or with a little lemon juice drizzled over the top, or a dollop of Kraft-Free Mayonnaise Dressing.

Beets: Pour enough water into a medium-size saucepan to cover the beets. Cover and bring to a boil. Immediately add the beets. Cover and cook over high heat for 6 to 7 minutes, or until tender. Watch carefully. Serve hot as a vegetable or cold in Beet Salad. Reserve the cooking liquid for red food color.

Broccoli: Peel the stems and steam in over boiling water for 4 to 5 minutes for baby florets, and up to 8 or 9 minutes for very large heads. Serve plain or drizzle with a little lemon juice or red or white Balsamic vinegar, and serve hot or cold.

Brussels sprouts: These are better cooked on top of the stove. Place about 2 cups of Brussels sprouts in a 1 1/2-quart saucepan. Add about 1/2 inch of water. Cover, bring to a boil, and cook on medium heat 8 to 10 minutes, or until tender.

Cabbage: There are several types of cabbage now available in most grocery stores: In addition to the familiar white and purple, there is the more delicately flavored Napa cabbage, and the various Asian cabbages, such as bok choy. Cabbages cook very quickly; just steam chopped cabbage covered in 1 inch of boiling water for about 10 minutes before serving hot.

Carrots: Do not peel. Cut as desired. Place carrots in a saucepan and add about 1/4 inch of water. Cover, bring to a boil, and cook over medium heat about 5 minutes.

Cauliflower: Steam the head whole in a saucepan, in about an inch of water, covered, over medium heat 10 to 15 minutes. Test with a sharp knife to see if it is done. Or cut off the florets and place in a saucepan. Add about 1/4 inch of water and cover. Bring to a boil, then cook over medium heat for about 5 minutes, or until tender. (It takes longer to cook the whole head because the heat takes longer to reach the center.)

Corn on the cob: Use a large enough pot to hold the corn and add enough water to cover. Bring the water to a fast boil. Drop the corn in and boil for about 6 minutes, or less according to your taste.

Cucumbers: Are a staple in almost any salad, or by themselves, sliced alongside almost any dish for a refreshing, palette-cleansing flavor. Peel and cut into 1/2-inch thick slices. Marinate, covered, for at least 2 hours in your favorite dressing. Place cucumber slices on a nonstick baking pan and broil for 5 minutes, or until heated through.

Green Peas: Place about 2 cups of peas, or less, in a 1 1/2-quart saucepan. Add 1/2 cup of water. Bring to a boil, cover, and cook over a medium heat for 5 minutes, or less according to your taste.

Spinach: Place about 8 cups of carefully washed spinach in 1/2 inch of water in a covered stockpot. Bring to a boil, cover, and cook over medium heat 8 to 10 minutes. Drain immediately. Serve plain or with lemon drizzled over, or a squirt of Worchestershire sauce.

Squash, Patty-pan: If you use squashes that are no longer than 2 1/2 inches in diameter, you don't need to peel them. Just cut up and cook in 1/2 cup rapidly boiling water, covered, for 5 to 7 minutes, or until just tender. Serve hot plain or with a sprinkle of cayenne.

Squash, Yellow Crook necked: Cut 2 or 3 squashes in chunks and place in a 1 1/2-quart saucepan. Add 1/2 cup of water. Bring to a boil, cover, and cook over medium heat for 5 or 6 minutes. Or, cook whole for about 5 or 6 minutes in a saucepan in 1/2 cup of water; then slice them. They overcook and get too watery if you cut them first.

Zucchini: Cut into chunks. Place zucchini pieces in a 1 1/2-quart saucepan. Add 1/2 cup of water. Bring to a boil, cover, and cook over medium heat for 5 or 6 minutes.

ARTICHOKE CASSEROLE

1 1/2 cups commercial whole wheat or Pritikin bread crumbs (3 slices of bread)
1/4 cup yellow cornmeal
1 medium onion, chopped
1 can (14 ounces) artichoke hearts, packed in water, drained, and rinsed
1 can (8 ounces) sliced water chestnuts, rinsed
1 cup frozen French-style green beans
1/4 teaspoon dried basil
1/4 plus 1/8 teaspoon garlic powder
1/2 teaspoon dried oregano
1/8 teaspoon ground cumin
1/8 teaspoon cayenne pepper
2 tablespoons grated sapsago cheese
2 jumbo egg whites
1/2 teaspoon medium red hot sauce
1 1/4 cups strong Chicken Stock (page 45), cooled
1/2 fresh lemon

In a bowl, mix the bread crumbs with the cornmeal and set aside.

In a large, nonstick frying pan sauté the onions over high heat, until they are transparent and brown around the edges. Remove the pan from the heat. Add the cornmeal and bread crumbs to the onions and combine.

Cut the artichoke hearts into quarters, then add them, the water chestnuts, and green beans to the onion–bread crumb mixture and combine. Finally, add the basil, garlic powder, oregano, cumin, cayenne, and 1 tablespoon of the sapsago cheese, and combine everything thoroughly.

In a large mixing bowl, combine the egg whites, hot sauce, and the cooled chicken stock and beat slightly. Then add to the rest of the ingredients, mixing everything together. Turn the mixture into a nonstick, 8-inch square baking dish, or an ovenproof glass baking dish that has been sprayed with olive oil-flavored nonstick spray. Cover the dish with aluminum foil and place on the middle rack of the oven and bake for 1 hour at 300 degrees F. Remove the foil and bake for another 15 minutes.

Squeeze the lemon over the casserole, sprinkle with the remaining 1 table-spoon of sapsago cheese, and serve immediately with lemon wedges on the side.

BROCCOLI PILAF

Nutrition Facts

Amount Per Serving

Calories 130   Calories from Fat 10

	% Daily Value*
Total Fat 1g	**2%**
Saturated Fat 0g	**0%**
Cholesterol 0mg	**0%**
Sodium 55mg	**2%**
Total Carbohydrate 23g	**8%**
Dietary Fiber 4g	**16%**
Sugars 3g	
Protein 8g	

Vitamin A 25%	•	Vitamin C 110%
Calcium 4%	•	Iron 6%

This is a good recipe to make if you have some leftover cooked rice.

1 1/2 cups cooked Brown and Wild Rice Mixed (page 255)
2 cups cooked chopped broccoli
2 egg whites
1/4 teaspoon cayenne pepper
1 tablespoon dry onion flakes or 1 medium onion, chopped
5 or 6 tomato slices
2 1/2 tablespoons grated sapsago cheese

Preheat oven to 300 degrees F.

Combine the rice, broccoli, egg whites, pepper, and onions in a 1-quart baking dish. Arrange the tomato slices over the top. Sprinkle with the sapsago cheese and bake uncovered, for 40 minutes.

CREAMED BROCCOLI WITH MUSHROOMS AND CARROTS

Nutrition Facts

Amount Per Serving

Calories 80	Calories from Fat 5

	% Daily Value*
Total Fat 0.5g	**1%**
Saturated Fat 0g	**0%**
Cholesterol 0mg	**0%**
Sodium 55mg	**2%**
Total Carbohydrate 16g	**5%**
Dietary Fiber 4g	**17%**
Sugars 7g	
Protein 5g	

Vitamin A 120%	• Vitamin C 100%
Calcium 10%	• Iron 8%

A simple cream sauce enhances the flavor of slightly cooked vegetables, creating a dish that's good enough for company. Double everything except the steaming water for more servings.

2 1/2 cups chopped fresh broccoli
1 1/4 cups sliced fresh mushrooms
1 medium carrot, sliced
1 rib celery, chopped
1/4 cup chopped fresh parsley, loosely packed
1 medium onion, chopped
1 1/2 cups water
2/3 cup skim milk
3 tablespoons whole wheat flour
1/8 teaspoon red pepper
Grated sapsago cheese (optional)

Place all the vegetables in a large stockpot and add the water. Cover, bring to a boil, and cook for 4 to 5 minutes. Drain the vegetables in a colander and place them in a serving dish. Save the cooking water for soup.

While the vegetables are cooking, add the milk to a blender or food processor with the flour and pepper, and blend until smooth. Pour the mixture into a saucepan, set on the stove, and set the heat to high. Stir constantly until the mixture thickens. (It will be quite thick.)

Add the mixture to the cooked vegetables and toss to coat them. Sprinkle with a little sapsago cheese, if desired. Serve immediately.

Variation: CREAMED BROCCOLI, MUSHROOM, AND CARROT SOUP*

Leftovers make a great soup. Place leftover cooked vegetables in a blender or food processor. Cover with skim milk and turn and pulse 4 times very quickly. (You just want to chop the vegetables up a little, not pulverize them.) Heat and eat.

It would be impossible to give the nutritional values for this recipe without knowing exactly how many vegetables or how much skim milk is used.

BROCCOLI MUSHROOM BAKE

Nutrition Facts

Amount Per Serving

Calories 310   Calories from Fat 30

	% Daily Value*
Total Fat 3.5g	5%
Saturated Fat 1g	4%
Cholesterol 10mg	4%
Sodium 1080mg	45%
Total Carbohydrate 47g	16%
Dietary Fiber 9g	34%
Sugars 15g	
Protein 26g	

Vitamin A 50%	•	Vitamin C 150%
Calcium 20%	•	Iron 15%

This dish seemed so plain that I was amazed when my husband announced that this was one of the best things he had ever eaten!

1 medium onion, chopped
1/2 cup nonfat cottage cheese
2 tablespoons skim milk
3 dashes Tabasco® sauce
1 cup chopped broccoli florets
4 large mushrooms, sliced
2 slices Pritikin or commercial whole wheat bread
1/2 cup Turkey Gravy (page 52)

Combine 1/4 of the chopped onion in a blender or food processor with 1/4 cup of the cottage cheese, the skim milk, and the Tabasco® sauce. Blend until smooth and set aside.

Combine the broccoli, onions, and mushrooms in a nonstick pan, and sauté until the broccoli begins to become tender.

Meanwhile, toast the bread lightly and place on an ovenproof dinner plate. Cover the toast with broccoli, onion, mushroom mixture. Spoon the remaining 1/4 cup cottage cheese on top. Set the oven temperature at 400 degrees F. Set the plate on the top shelf of your oven and bake for 10 minutes.

Meanwhile, heat the turkey or chicken gravy. Pour the hot gravy over the broccoli and cottage cheese. Then pour on the puréed cottage cheese and onion from the blender, and serve.

The cottage cheese is considered 2 milk servings.

BROCCOLI CHOWDER

Nutrition Facts

Amount Per Serving

Calories 140	Calories from Fat 5

	% Daily Value*
Total Fat 0.5g	**1%**
Saturated Fat 0g	**0%**
Cholesterol 0mg	**0%**
Sodium 55mg	**2%**
Total Carbohydrate 29g	**10%**
Dietary Fiber 5g	**18%**
Sugars 8g	
Protein 6g	

Vitamin A 25%	•	Vitamin C 150%
Calcium 10%	•	Iron 10%

1 1/4 to 1 1/2 pounds fresh broccoli or 2 packages (10 ounces each) frozen chopped
6 medium to large potatoes, peeled and diced
3 medium onions, chopped
1/2 cup chopped fresh parsley
Water
2 cups skim milk
1/2 teaspoon dried basil
Cayenne pepper, to taste

If you are using fresh broccoli, peel the stems, but do not chop. Place the broccoli in a large stockpot with about 1 1/2 inches of water and cover. Cook over medium heat until tender-crisp, about 10 minutes. Cook frozen broccoli according to package directions. Drain the broccoli, reserve cooking water, and set the broccoli aside to cool.

Microwave Directions: Do not cook the broccoli in the microwave because it doesn't come out well. Follow the directions above for the broccoli. Everything else, however, will cook nicely in the microwave.

Combine the potatoes with the onions and parsley in a 5-quart container and cover with 1/2 inch of the reserved water from the cooked broccoli. Add plain water, if needed. Cover with a lid and cook on high setting for 25 minutes.

When the broccoli has cooled, cut into large chunks and purée in a blender or food processor with the milk, basil, and cayenne pepper. Add the broccoli mixture to the potato mixture, heat through, and serve.

Stove Top Directions: Combine the potatoes with the onions and parsley in a 5-quart stockpot. Add the reserved water from broccoli. Add more water until the vegetables are covered by 1/2 inch of liquid. Cover, bring to a boil, then lower to medium heat, and cook until potatoes and onions are tender, about 10 to 15 minutes.

When broccoli is cool, cut in into large chunks and purée in a blender or food processor with the milk, basil, and cayenne pepper. Add the broccoli mixture to the potato mixture, heat through, and serve.

This soup tastes even better the day after you make it because the onion flavor has time to permeate the chowder. It also freezes beautifully in individual 1-cup containers.

BROCCOLI-SQUASH COMBO

Nutrition Facts

Amount Per Serving

Calories 50	Calories from Fat 5

	% Daily Value*
Total Fat 0.5g	1%
Saturated Fat 0g	0%
Cholesterol 0mg	0%
Sodium 30mg	1%
Total Carbohydrate 8g	3%
Dietary Fiber 4g	17%
Sugars 3g	
Protein 6g	

Vitamin A 35%	•	Vitamin C 180%
Calcium 6%	•	Iron 6%

This combination is so good it needs no extra seasoning, not even pepper.

2 1/2 cups chopped broccoli
1 medium patty pan squash, diced, no need to peel or seed
2 tablespoons grated sapsago cheese

Preheat the oven to 350 degrees F.

Combine the broccoli and squash in a large pot. Add about an inch of water and cover. Bring to a boil and cook over medium heat for 5 to 7 minutes, until tender. Drain, reserving the water for soup. Set the vegetables aside to cool.

When cooled, process the vegetables with the chopping blade of your food processor or cut up very finely with a knife.

Place in a casserole dish and sprinkle with sapsago cheese. Bake until heated through, about 15 minutes.

VARIATION: BROCCOLI SQUASH COMBO WITH CHEDDAR

If you can afford a little sodium, prepare and cook the broccoli and squash together as above. Before baking, sprinkle with 1/4 cup grated nonfat cheddar cheese, and 2 tablespoons sapsago cheese. Bake covered at 350 degrees F. until heated through, about 15 minutes.

Nutrition Facts

Amount Per Serving

Calories 70	Calories from Fat 5

	% Daily Value*
Total Fat 0.5g	1%
Saturated Fat 0g	0%
Cholesterol 0mg	0%
Sodium 150mg	6%
Total Carbohydrate 9g	3%
Dietary Fiber 4g	17%
Sugars 4g	
Protein 10g	

Vitamin A 40%	•	Vitamin C 180%
Calcium 30%	•	Iron 6%

CABBAGE JAMBALAYA

This first part of this recipe, the vegetables, can be served as is, without the rice base, but for a meatless meal, the addition of instant brown rice is terrific. This is also delicious with the addition of chicken or shrimp.

The Vegetables:
2 tablespoons apple juice concentrate
2 medium turnips, diced (do not peel)
1 1/2 cups plus 1 tablespoon Chicken or Turkey Stock (page 44)
1 bay leaf
1 can (16 ounces) salt-free tomatoes and juice
1/2 large cabbage, cut up in small pieces (about 4 cups)
1/4 teaspoon cayenne pepper
1/4 teaspoon dried thyme

The Rice Base:
2 1/4 cups instant uncooked brown rice
1 1/2 cups Chicken Stock (page 44)
1/2 cup salt-free tomato paste

Add the juice concentrate to a nonstick 5-quart stockpot. Cook over high heat until the liquid begins to sizzle. Add the turnips. Let them sit in the liquid to cook for about 2 minutes, or until you see the liquid begins to evaporate. When the liquid begins to evaporate rapidly in the pan, stir the turnips constantly until they are a little bit brown, and continue to cook until all the liquid is gone and the turnips are partially cooked. Add the stock and bring to a boil. Remove the stockpot from the heat. Add the bay leaf, tomatoes, and cabbage. Sprinkle with the cayenne and thyme. Cover with a tightly fitting cover and cook over high heat for 15 minutes, or until the cabbage is tender. Stir all the ingredients together to combine. Serve as is, as a vegetable, or make the rice for jambalaya.

In a 9 x 13-inch baking dish, combine the rice, stock, and tomato paste. Add the cooked cabbage mixture including any liquid left in the pot and combine. Cover with aluminum foil and place on the middle rack of a conventional oven. Set the temperature at 350 degrees F. and bake for 20 minutes. Remove the dish from the oven and let it sit, covered, for 10 minutes, then serve.

CABBAGE EXTRAVAGANZA

1 cup unsweetened pineapple juice
2 tablespoons brandy
1 tablespoon apple juice concentrate
1/3 cup raisins
1 large onion, chopped
8 cups red cabbage cut in chunks (1/2 large red cabbage)
1 teaspoon low-sodium soy sauce
1/4 teaspoon cayenne pepper or more, to taste
1 teaspoon dried basil
2/3 cup chopped apple

In a 5-quart stockpot, combine the pineapple juice, brandy, and apple juice concentrate. Add the raisins and onion. Bring to a boil, cover, and cook over high heat for 5 minutes. Add the cut up cabbage, sprinkle with soy sauce and cayenne pepper. Stir and toss to combine all the ingredients together. Cover, lower the heat to medium-low, and cook until the cabbage is fairly tender, about 3 minutes. Check and stir frequently because the cabbage burns easily. Add the basil and cook for 2 minutes. Add the apple chunks and cook for 5 minutes more. Serve with Chicken Tropicana.

RED CABBAGE WITH TURNIPS

1 small to medium purple turnip, diced
1 medium onion, chopped
1 teaspoon low-sodium soy sauce
2 tablespoons apple juice concentrate
1/8 teaspoon cayenne pepper
1/2 medium red or green cabbage, chopped
3/4 cup water

Combine the turnip and onion with the soy sauce, apple juice concentrate, and cayenne in a nonstick 5-quart stockpot and sauté over high heat until the onions and turnips are fairly brown, about 4 1/2 minutes. Add the cabbage and sauté with the other vegetables for about 5 minutes. Add the water, cover, bring to a boil, and cook for about 3 minutes or until the cabbage is tender. Stir every minute. Add more water if the pot starts to dry out.

CARROTS LYONNAISE

YIELD: 3 SERVINGS

Nutrition Facts

Amount Per Serving	
Calories 70	Calories from Fat 5

	% Daily Value*
Total Fat 0.5g	**1%**
Saturated Fat 0g	**0%**
Cholesterol 0mg	**0%**
Sodium 280mg	**12%**
Total Carbohydrate 14g	**5%**
Dietary Fiber 3g	**12%**
Sugars 9g	
Protein 2g	

Vitamin A 410%	•	Vitamin C 15%
Calcium 4%	•	Iron 4%

I learned to make this lovely French way of preparing carrots when I was first married, and it became a family favorite, but the original recipe called for butter or margarine. However, chicken stock makes a very good substitute and this dish is just as delicious as the original.

1 large onion, sliced in rings
1 cup plus 3 tablespoons Chicken Stock (page 44)
3 large carrots, julienned
1/16 teaspoon cayenne pepper
1 tablespoon unbleached white flour
2 teaspoons apple juice concentrate

Place the onion rings and 1/2 cup of the chicken stock in a frying pan. Cover, bring to a boil, and cook for 8 to 10 minutes over high heat until the onions are soft. In the meantime, julienne the carrots. Pour 1/2 cup of the chicken stock into a 1-quart pot, cover, and bring to a boil. Add the carrots immediately, cover, and cook for about 5 minutes over high heat until the carrots are tender crisp.

When the onions are done, sprinkle with cayenne and flour. Stir over medium heat to blend in the flour. Add the carrots and liquid they were cooked in, plus the remaining 3 tablespoons of chicken stock, and the juice concentrate. Stir until the liquid thickens and makes a nice sauce for the carrots and onions. If too thick, add just a little more chicken stock. Serve immediately.

CAULIFLOWER-SQUASH CHOWDER

YIELD: 4 SERVINGS

Nutrition Facts

Amount Per Serving

Calories 100	Calories from Fat 0

	% Daily Value*
Total Fat 0g	**0%**
Saturated Fat 0g	**0%**
Cholesterol 0mg	**0%**
Sodium 75mg	**3%**
Total Carbohydrate 19g	**6%**
Dietary Fiber 2g	**9%**
Sugars 10g	
Protein 6g	

Vitamin A 8%	•	Vitamin C 40%
Calcium 15%	•	Iron 2%

Use either uncooked vegetables or leftover cooked vegetables. If you use cooked vegetables, use the cooking water in this recipe for the water to cover the vegetables. If you threw the cooking water away, just use plain water.

1 medium potato, peeled and diced
1 medium onion, chopped
1 cup chopped or diced cauliflower
1 very small patty pan squash, chopped (no need to peel or seed)
Water to cover
2 cups skim milk
1/4 teaspoon of cayenne pepper, or more

Microwave Directions: If you use all raw vegetables, combine the potato, onion, cauliflower, and squash in a 5-quart container. Cover with water, then cover the container. Cook on high setting for 5 minutes until vegetables are tender. If you use precooked squash and cauliflower, add them after the potatoes and onions are cooked, to warm them through. Add the skim milk and cayenne. Bring to a boil, and serve.

Stove Top Directions: If you use all raw vegetables, combine the potato, onion, cauliflower, and squash in a 5-quart stockpot. Cover with water and cover the pot. Bring to a boil, then lower the heat to medium, and cook for about 5 minutes, until the vegetables are tender. If you use precooked squash and cauliflower, add them after potatoes and onions are cooked, to warm them through. Add the skim milk and pepper. Bring to a boil, and serve. This dish is even better reheated and eaten the next day.

CAULIFLOWER WITH CARROT TOPPING

YIELD: 4 SERVINGS

Nutrition Facts

Amount Per Serving	
Calories 30	Calories from Fat 0

	% Daily Value*
Total Fat 0g	**0%**
Saturated Fat 0g	**0%**
Cholesterol 0mg	**0%**
Sodium 35mg	**1%**
Total Carbohydrate 6g	**2%**
Dietary Fiber 3g	**11%**
Sugars 3g	
Protein 2g	

Vitamin A 40%	•	Vitamin C 80%	
Calcium 2%	•	Iron 2%	

This cauliflower comes out looking like it has cheddar cheese over it. However, if you want a cheesy taste as well, but also a few more calories, sprinkle with sapsago cheese or nonfat cheddar cheese. For fewer servings, use a smaller pot and half the amounts of the vegetables.

Water
1 large cauliflower
1/4 teaspoon dried dillweed (optional)
4 tablespoons finely grated carrot
Grated sapsago cheese or nonfat cheddar cheese (optional)

Break the cauliflower into florets. Pour about 3/4 inch water into a 5-quart stockpot, cover, and bring to a boil. Place the cauliflower pieces in the boiling water, sprinkle dillweed and the grated carrot over the cauliflower. Cover, bring to a boil, and cook for 5 to 8 minutes, until the cauliflower is tender. Serve hot and sprinkle with a little sapsago cheese or fat-free cheddar cheese, if desired.

CHILIES RELLEÑOS

Nutrition Facts

Amount Per Serving

Calories 70	Calories from Fat 0

	% Daily Value*
Total Fat 0g	**0%**
Saturated Fat 0g	**0%**
Cholesterol 0mg	**0%**
Sodium 480mg	**20%**
Total Carbohydrate 8g	**3%**
Dietary Fiber 2g	**10%**
Sugars 3g	
Protein 8g	

Vitamin A 8%	•	Vitamin C 30%
Calcium 2%	•	Iron 2%

You could eat this for breakfast as well as dinner. It tastes especially good with Mexican Style Red Beans (page 264). Yes, these eggs will come out yellow because of the turmeric.

4 jumbo egg whites
1/16 teaspoon garlic powder
Pinch of cumin (less than 1/16 teaspoon)
1/8 teaspoon turmeric
1/2 teaspoon dried chives
1/8 teaspoon dried red pepper flakes
1/2 cup finely chopped onion
1 can (4 ounces) peeled, green whole chilies, rinsed

Spray a nonstick frying pan with butter-flavored nonstick spray.

In a small mixing bowl, combine the eggs, garlic powder, cumin, and turmeric. Beat with a whisk or an egg beater until they form soft peaks. Stir in the chives, red pepper flakes, and onion. Cut each chili into thirds and arrange, evenly spaced, in the frying pan. Pour the egg mixture over the chilies. Turn the heat on high and cook until the egg on the bottom begins to set, just a few minutes. Divide the mixture in half with a spatula and carefully turn each section over. Cook for a minute or so more until the egg looks cooked. Serve immediately.

If you want to cook more servings, either have another frying pan ready, or plan to wash the one you are using before cooking up another batch. You can keep finished servings warm, covered with aluminum foil, in the oven. Set the oven temperature very low and slit the foil to allow steam to escape.

COLLARDS TCHOUPITOULAS

YIELD: 8 SERVINGS

Nutrition Facts

Amount Per Serving

Calories 60	Calories from Fat 0

	% Daily Value*
Total Fat 0g	**0**%
Saturated Fat 0g	**0**%
Cholesterol 0mg	**0**%
Sodium 25mg	**1**%
Total Carbohydrate 13g	**4**%
Dietary Fiber 5g	**19**%
Sugars 5g	
Protein 2g	

Vitamin A 110%	•	Vitamin C 45%
Calcium 4%	•	Iron 2%

Tchoupitoulas was the name of an Indian tribe and is also the name of a street in New Orleans. With all the mispronunciations of street names in New Orleans, believe it or not, this one is pronounced the same by everyone: chop-a-too-las. Tchoupitoulas Street runs through town along the Mississippi River, through a neighborhood of people who know about collard greens, and how to cook them.

1 large onion, chopped
3 cups (approximately) peeled and diced eggplant (1 small or 1/2 large eggplant)
1 medium carrot, sliced
2 tablespoons apple juice concentrate
2 1/2 cups plus 1 tablespoon water
1/4 teaspoon cayenne pepper
2 cups water
1 bunch collard greens (about 5 quarts), chopped
1 large tomato, chopped
Vinegar

Combine the onion, eggplant, carrot, 1 tablespoon of the juice concentrate, and 1 tablespoon of the water in a nonstick 5-quart stockpot. Sprinkle with 1/8 teaspoon of the cayenne. Turn the heat to high and sauté the vegetables, stirring them frequently. When the eggplant looks a shade darker, add 2 1/2 cups of water and turn the heat to low. Cover and let cook while you prepare the greens.

Wash each leaf separately and cut off the stems. Chop the greens and add them into the pot. Five quarts of greens is only an approximate figure, use whatever you have. Distribute the chopped tomato over the top, then add the remaining 1 tablespoon of the juice concentrate and 1/8 teaspoon of the cayenne. Cover and cook on high heat for 15 minutes, or until the greens are just about tender. Keep checking and add 2 cups of water if it starts to dry out. After the first 15 minutes, combine thoroughly, distributing the eggplant, onions, and carrots through the greens. Cover and cook for another 5 minutes over high heat, or until the greens are tender. Mix again as if tossing salad. Serve hot, sprinkled with wine, apple cider vinegar, or hot sauce.

MEXICORN AND RICE

Nutrition Facts

Amount Per Serving	
Calories 70	Calories from Fat 0

	% Daily Value*
Total Fat 0g	**0**%
Saturated Fat 0g	**0**%
Cholesterol 0mg	**0**%
Sodium 0mg	**0**%
Total Carbohydrate 15g	**5**%
Dietary Fiber 2g	**7**%
Sugars 2g	
Protein 2g	

Vitamin A 2%	•	Vitamin C 35%
Calcium 0%	•	Iron 2%

2 cups frozen chuck wagon-style corn (or any frozen corn that contains whole kernel corn, green and red bell peppers, and onions, sometimes tomatoes)
1 cup cooked Brown Rice and Wild Rice Mixed (page 255)
1 jalapeño pepper, sliced, or less, to taste
1/4 teaspoon garlic powder
1 teaspoon onion powder
3 to 6 tablespoons water

Microwave Directions: Combine all the ingredients in a 1-quart container. Add 3 tablespoons of water. Cook on high setting for 3 minutes, covered. Stir and cook for 3 more minutes. Serve immediately.

Stove Top Directions: Combine all the ingredients in a bowl.

Bring 6 tablespoons of water to a boil in a small saucepan. Add corn mixture and cover. Lower heat to medium and cook for 3 to 4 minutes, until corn is tender. Serve immediately.

CORN ZUCCHINI MIX

1 medium to large zucchini, diced
1 can (16 ounces) whole kernel salt-free, sugar-free corn, or 1
    package (10 ounces) frozen corn or 1 1/2 cups fresh corn off
    the cob
1 tablespoon grated sapsago cheese

Microwave Directions: In a 1 1/2-quart microwave container, combine the zucchini with the corn. Add the water from the canned corn or add about 1/2 inch of water if using fresh corn. Cover and microwave on high setting for 5 or 6 minutes, until the vegetables are tender. Sprinkle with sapsago cheese.

Stove Top Directions: In a 1 1/2-quart saucepan, combine the zucchini and the corn. Add the water from the canned corn or add about 1/2 inch of water if using fresh corn. Cover, bring to a boil, then cook on medium heat 5 to 6 minutes, until the vegetables are tender. Sprinkle with sapsago cheese.

INDIAN CORN WITH PEPPERS

This is an American Indian recipe from the Southwest. It is marvelously simple and tantalizingly good.

1 1/2 cups frozen or fresh corn kernels
1 can (4 ounces) green roasted chili peppers, drained, rinsed and
chopped

Microwave Directions: Place corn in a 1-quart container. Add 2 tablespoons water, cover, and heat on high setting for 3 minutes. Stir in chili peppers. Cover and heat on high setting for 2 to 3 minutes more, until corn is tender. Serve hot.

Stove Top Directions: Place corn in a saucepan. Add 1/2 cup of water. Bring to a boil, cover, and cook for 2 minutes. Add chili peppers. Cook for 2 to 3 minutes, until corn is tender. Serve hot.

STUFFED EGGPLANT

YIELD: 2 SERVINGS

Nutrition Facts

Amount Per Serving

Calories 320	Calories from Fat 25

	% Daily Value*
Total Fat 2.5g	4%
Saturated Fat 0.5g	3%
Cholesterol 5mg	2%
Sodium 540mg	22%
Total Carbohydrate 49g	16%
Dietary Fiber 11g	43%
Sugars 19g	
Protein 23g	

Vitamin A 20%	•	Vitamin C 90%
Calcium 15%	•	Iron 25%

This recipe and its variations are delicious and are a full meal in themselves. All you need is green salad and fruit for dessert.

1 large eggplant
1 large onion, chopped in about 1/4-inch cubes
1 small green pepper, chopped in 1/4-inch dice
4 cloves garlic, minced
3 slices Pritikin or whole wheat bread in crumbs
1/3 cup Red Rosé wine
2/3 cup nonfat cottage cheese
1 teaspoon dried thyme
1/4 teaspoon ground bay leaf
2 egg whites
1/4 cup chopped, fresh parsley
Cayenne pepper, to taste
4 teaspoons grated sapsago cheese

Microwave Directions: Cut the eggplant in half lengthwise and place on a dish with the two halves together. Cook on high setting for 12 minutes. Set aside to cool. Then place the two halves turned face up on a nonstick baking pan. Scoop the pulp out into a bowl. Cutting around the edges of the pulp helps to loosen it. Set the halves and pulp aside.

Stove Top Directions: Place the whole eggplant in a large stockpot and fill with water to cover. Boil for about 25 to 30 minutes until eggplant is tender. Test with a sharp knife but be careful not to tear the skin too much. Remove from the pot very carefully and place on a chopping board to cool. Cut in half lengthwise. Place the two halves turned face up on a nonstick baking pan. Scoop the pulp out into a bowl. Cutting around the edges of the pulp with a very sharp knife helps to loosen it. Set the halves and pulp aside.

Sauté the onion and green pepper until lightly browned in a nonstick frying pan. Add eggplant. Then add all the other ingredients except the sapsago cheese, and combine thoroughly. Pile into eggplant shells and sprinkle with sapsago cheese. Set the oven temperature at 350 degrees F. Bake for 20 to 25 minutes on the middle rack.

Nutrition Facts

Amount Per Serving

Calories 410   Calories from Fat 25

	% Daily Value*
Total Fat 2.5g	**4**%
Saturated Fat 0.5g	**3**%
Cholesterol 175mg	**58**%
Sodium 520mg	**21**%
Total Carbohydrate 54g	**18**%
Dietary Fiber 10g	**40**%
Sugars 19g	
Protein 42g	

Vitamin A 40%	• Vitamin C 230%
Calcium 15%	• Iron 35%

Variation: RICE AND CHILI-STUFFED EGGPLANT

Substitute 1 cup cooked Brown Rice (page 256) for the bread crumbs, leave out the wine and add 1 1/2 peeled and chopped and roasted mild green chilies. Use whole ones and chop them. The whole ones have more flavor than the ones that come already chopped. Rinse the canned chilies if you are very, very strict about your sodium intake. Then add 2 teaspoons of a medium red hot sauce. Use the cottage cheese as in the regular recipe. After you sauté the vegetables, add 1 cup of water and the eggplant and mash with the back of your spoon. Add the seasonings and egg. Set the heat on medium and let the water evaporate, stirring all the while. Then add the rice and cottage cheese. Stuff the eggplant shells and bake as directed above.

MEATLESS MOUSSAKA

Nutrition Facts

Amount Per Serving	
Calories 190	Calories from Fat 10

	% Daily Value*
Total Fat 1.5g	2%
Saturated Fat 0g	0%
Cholesterol 0mg	0%
Sodium 180mg	8%
Total Carbohydrate 34g	11%
Dietary Fiber 7g	27%
Sugars 12g	
Protein 10g	

Vitamin A 320%	•	Vitamin C 50%
Calcium 8%	•	Iron 15%

I grind my bread for crumbs, then my carrots with a cutting blade in a food processor, and mash my tomatoes with a potato masher. I use a lot of dried vegetables, too, which makes this recipe quicker to make. The ground carrots taste like ground meat because the texture is identical.

2 large potatoes, baked or boiled, peeled, and sliced
1 large eggplant
4 slices commercial whole wheat bread, in crumbs (2 cups)
5 large carrots, finely ground
1 can (9 ounces) salt-free cooked tomato, mashed
1 can (6 ounces) salt-free tomato paste
2 cups sliced fresh mushrooms
3 tablespoons dried onions
2 tablespoons dried green bell pepper
1/2 teaspoon dried garlic powder
1/2 teaspoon dried red pepper flakes
1 teaspoon dried parsley
1/2 teaspoon nutmeg
1/2 teaspoon cinnamon
3/4 teaspoon dried oregano
1/2 cup Red Rosé wine
1/2 cup water
8 jumbo egg whites
1/2 cup skim milk
1/4 cup grated sapsago cheese

Preheat oven to 425 degrees F.

Spray a 9-inch-by-13-inch dish with butter-flavored nonstick spray.

Slice the unpeeled eggplant across to make thin disks, then quarter the disks and set aside.

In a 5-quart stockpot, combine the carrots, tomatoes, tomato paste, mushrooms, onions, bell pepper, garlic powder, pepper, parsley, nutmeg, cinnamon, oregano, wine, and water. Bring to a boil, then turn off the heat, leave covered, and set aside.

Layer the potato slices over the bottom of the baking dish. Sprinkle half the bread crumbs over the potatoes. Arrange half the eggplant slices over the bread crumbs.

Beat the egg whites and milk for about 2 minutes, until foamy. Immediately pour the egg mixture over the eggplant. Spread half the tomato sauce mixture from the pot over the egg. Spread the remaining eggplant over the tomato sauce. Spread on the remaining tomato sauce. Sprinkle with the remaining bread crumbs, then sprinkle the cheese over the bread crumbs. Spray one side of a large piece of aluminum foil with butter-flavored nonstick spray. Place spray-side down over the casserole and wrap around the edges. Place the casserole on the middle rack of the oven and bake for 45 minutes. Remove from the oven and let sit covered for 20 minutes before serving.

BREADED EGGPLANT

Nutrition Facts

Amount Per Serving	
Calories 90	Calories from Fat 10

	% Daily Value*
Total Fat 1g	2%
Saturated Fat 0g	0%
Cholesterol 0mg	0%
Sodium 130mg	5%
Total Carbohydrate 17g	6%
Dietary Fiber 4g	15%
Sugars 6g	
Protein 5g	

Vitamin A 4%	•	Vitamin C 2%
Calcium 6%	•	Iron 6%

My mother used to sprinkle sugar over breaded eggplant, but sliced bananas under the bread crumb coating makes them as moist and delicious on the inside as well as just as crisp on the outside.

Butter-flavored nonstick spray
4 slices Pritikin or commercial whole wheat bread
1/8 teaspoon cayenne pepper
1/8 teaspoon garlic powder
1 teaspoon dried parsley
1/4 teaspoon dried marjoram
1 teaspoon dried basil
1 large eggplant
2 jumbo egg whites
Skim milk
1 tablespoon whole wheat flour
1 1/2 bananas, sliced

Preheat the oven to 350 degrees F.

Spray a nonstick baking pan with butter-flavored nonstick spray.

In a blender or food processor, combine the bread, cayenne, garlic powder, parsley flakes, marjoram, and basil, and process to make crumbs. Set aside.

Peel, then slice the eggplant lengthwise into 1/8-inch thick slices. In a 2-cup measuring cup, combine the egg whites and an equal amount of skim milk; then add the flour and mix thoroughly. Dip the eggplant slices, one at a time, into the egg-milk mixture. Using a fork, pierce the eggplant slices all over while they are in the egg-milk mixture. Remove the eggplant slices and coat with the bread crumbs on one side. Place the slices, coated-side down, on the baking pan. Coat the banana slices with the egg-milk mixture and arrange them on top of each slice of eggplant. Sprinkle the tops of the eggplant slices with the remaining bread crumbs. Place on the middle rack of the oven and bake for 25 minutes. Spray the eggplant with butter-flavored spray, bake for 5 more minutes and serve hot from the oven.

If you want to get fancier, served with heated applesauce (with no sugar added), or sprinkle with a little red hot sauce, and/or a dollop of Horseradish Sauce (page 60).

STEWED EGGPLANT

Nutrition Facts

Amount Per Serving	
Calories 230	Calories from Fat 0

	% Daily Value*
Total Fat 0g	**0**%
Saturated Fat 0g	**0**%
Cholesterol 5mg	**2**%
Sodium 200mg	**8**%
Total Carbohydrate 50g	**17**%
Dietary Fiber 5g	**20**%
Sugars 30g	
Protein 11g	

Vitamin A 15%	•	Vitamin C 45%
Calcium 10%	•	Iron 10%

Stewed eggplant is a traditional Creole delight and one of the first dishes I learned to cook. Rice is a must with this to sop up the gravy.

1 medium onion, chopped
1 small green pepper, chopped
1 can (16 ounces) whole tomatoes, or 2 1/2 cups of chopped fresh tomatoes
1 cup water
1 large eggplant, cubed
1 teaspoon dried parsley flakes, or 3 tablespoons fresh chopped parsley
1/2 cup apple juice concentrate
1/8 teaspoon cayenne pepper
1/2 teaspoon dried thyme

Place onion and green pepper in a nonstick stockpot. Turn the heat on high and sauté until the onion looks brown around the edges and a little transparent, and the green pepper begins to look a little shiny. Add the tomatoes, juice, and water. Break up the tomatoes a little with a wooden spoon. Add the eggplant, and then add all the other ingredients and combine. Cover and cook over medium-low heat, stirring frequently, until the eggplant is tender, about 20 to 25 minutes. Keep your eye on it to be sure it doesn't burn and lower heat a bit, if necessary. Serve over instant brown rice along with a small steak and some steamed carrots.

GREEN BEANS

Nutrition Facts

Amount Per Serving

Calories 40	Calories from Fat 0

	% Daily Value*
Total Fat 0g	**0%**
Saturated Fat 0g	**0%**
Cholesterol 0mg	**0%**
Sodium 30mg	**1%**
Total Carbohydrate 9g	**3%**
Dietary Fiber 3g	**14%**
Sugars 3g	
Protein 2g	

Vitamin A 10%	•	Vitamin C 20%
Calcium 6%	•	Iron 6%

These are somewhat challenging to cook successfully without salt, and done this way they are delicious.

2 cups water
3/4 pound fresh green beans, trimmed
3 celery ribs, coarsely chopped
2 tablespoons dried chopped onions
1/16 teaspoon cayenne pepper

Bring the water to a boil in a covered 5-quart pot. Remove the pot from the heat. Add the beans and celery. Sprinkle the onions and cayenne pepper over the top. Cover and cook over high heat for 4 minutes. Stir. Cover and cook over high heat for 4 to 5 minutes more, or until the vegetables are tender. Serve hot.

MUSTARD GREENS

YIELD: 4 SERVINGS

Nutrition Facts

Amount Per Serving

Calories 70	Calories from Fat 0

	% Daily Value*
Total Fat 0g	**0%**
Saturated Fat 0g	**0%**
Cholesterol 0mg	**0%**
Sodium 40mg	**2%**
Total Carbohydrate 14g	**5%**
Dietary Fiber 6g	**23%**
Sugars 7g	
Protein 4g	

Vitamin A 320%	•	Vitamin C 140%
Calcium 15%	•	Iron 10%

Fresh mustard greens taste superior to canned or frozen ones, and they really aren't that much trouble to fix. Washing them is the biggest problem. I hold a bunch by the stems and dunk them up and down in a large pot of cold water so that any sand or dirt sinks to the bottom.

2 medium-size onions, chopped
8 cups fresh mustard greens, destemmed and chopped
2 medium-size carrots, sliced
Water
1/8 teaspoon red pepper flakes

Put the onions in a 5-quart nonstick soup pot, and turn the heat on high. Sauté until they look a little brown around the edges and somewhat transparent. Add about 1/2 inch water to he pot. Add the greens and carrots and sprinkle the red pepper flakes over them. Cover and cook over medium heat for 10 to 20 minutes, or until the greens and carrots are tender. Stir and serve.

STEWED OKRA AND TOMATOES OVER RICE

YIELD: 4 SERVINGS

Nutrition Facts

Amount Per Serving	
Calories 260	Calories from Fat 15

	% Daily Value*
Total Fat 2g	3%
Saturated Fat 0g	0%
Cholesterol 0mg	0%
Sodium 30mg	1%
Total Carbohydrate 57g	19%
Dietary Fiber 8g	34%
Sugars 16g	
Protein 8g	

Vitamin A 30%	•	Vitamin C 120%	
Calcium 15%	•	Iron 10%	

This is a very old New Orleans dish, brought by African slaves who were taken to New Orleans by the white masters who were fleeing slave uprisings in the Caribbean Islands in the late 1700s. Of course, okra originally came from Africa and is still a staple of Caribbean cuisine.

I used to make this dish with ham, but I was very surprised at how good it tastes without the ham. It is a particularly good meatless entrée.

2 cups chopped onions
1 large green pepper, chopped
1 pound fresh okra, sliced
1 can (16 ounces) salt-free tomatoes
1/2 cup water
1/8 teaspoon cayenne pepper
2 3/4 tablespoons apple juice concentrate
Cooked brown or white rice

In a nonstick 5-quart stockpot, combine the onions and green pepper. Sauté over high heat, stirring frequently, until the onion becomes a little transparent and brown around the edges. Remove the vegetables to a bowl. Immediately add the okra to the stockpot, and sauté until the okra begins to give up its liquid, which forms spider web-like threads between the pieces. Sauté just a little longer, then add the tomatoes and reduce the heat to low. Break up the tomatoes with a wooden spoon. Return the onions and green pepper to the pot. Add the water, cayenne, and juice concentrate. Stir, cover, and cook on low heat for 1 to 1 1/4 hours, until the okra is tender, stirring frequently. Place 2/3 cup cooked brown rice on each plate and spoon the okra and tomatoes over the rice.

FRESH MASHED POTATOES

This is for all of you who haven't eaten mashed potatoes since the invention of instant. I had forgotten how good fresh mashed potatoes are, until I made this recipe.

3 large potatoes
Skim milk
1/2 teaspoon dried basil

Peel the potatoes and cut in large pieces. Place in a large pot, cover with water, and bring to a boil. Boil for 10 to 15 minutes, until the potatoes are very tender. Drain off the water and mash with a potato masher. Add enough milk to make the potatoes fluffy and creamy. Add the basil and taste. You will be surprised at just how good plain potatoes and milk taste with nothing added but basil. (Unsalted potatoes really need that basil!)

VARIATION: CHEESY MASHED POTATOES

These are really yummy. Boil seven peeled and cut up medium potatoes in water to cover, until very tender, about 10 to 15 minutes.

While the potatoes are cooking, combine 6 tablespoons of nonfat cottage cheese or nonfat cream cheese with 6 tablespoons of skim milk in a blender or food processor, and blend until very smooth.

Drain the potatoes and mash. Add the cottage cheese-milk mixture and combine until the potatoes are fluffy and creamy. I serve them just as they are, but you can add 1/4 teaspoon cayenne pepper, 1 tablespoon dried parsley, and 1 teaspoon of dried basil. This makes 8 servings.

SCALLOPED POTATOES

Nutrition Facts

Amount Per Serving	
Calories 180	Calories from Fat 0

	% Daily Value*
Total Fat 0g	**0%**
Saturated Fat 0g	**0%**
Cholesterol 5mg	**2%**
Sodium 310mg	**13%**
Total Carbohydrate 29g	**10%**
Dietary Fiber 2g	**9%**
Sugars 9g	
Protein 16g	

Vitamin A 15%	•	Vitamin C 25%
Calcium 60%	•	Iron 6%

2 large potatoes or enough to equal 2 1/2 cups sliced
1/2 cup chopped scallions
2 cups skim milk
1 cup Alpine Lace grated nonfat cheddar cheese
3 tablespoons whole wheat flour
1 teaspoon dried basil
3 to 4 dashes of cayenne pepper
Paprika (optional)

Bake or boil the potatoes in their peels until tender. Cool and peel. Slice into a 1 1/2-quart baking dish. Mix in the chopped scallions.

In a blender, combine the milk, cheese, flour, pepper, and basil, and liquefy. Pour over the potatoes.

Microwave Directions: Bake uncovered, at 60 percent power for 20 minutes.

Oven Directions: Preheat the oven to 350 degrees F. Bake uncovered, for about 30 minutes until the sauce is thickened.

Stir the top a little to blend in the foam that will have formed on top. Sprinkle with a little paprika for color, if desired.

OVEN-FRIED POTATOES

YIELD: 1 SERVING

Nutrition Facts

Amount Per Serving	
Calories 150	Calories from Fat 0

	% Daily Value*
Total Fat 0g	**0**%
Saturated Fat 0g	**0**%
Cholesterol 0mg	**0**%
Sodium 10mg	**0**%
Total Carbohydrate 34g	**11**%
Dietary Fiber 2g	**9**%
Sugars 3g	
Protein 3g	

Vitamin A 0%	•	Vitamin C 35%
Calcium 0%	•	Iron 4%

These are a lot like French fries and have saved both me and my husband from breaking our diets on several occasions. Sometimes Ray has them for a snack, which is a pretty big snack, but at least he stays away from more fattening things. If I'm cooking oven-fried catfish, I arrange the raw potatoes on the same pan with the fish and cook them together.

1 large potato
Cayenne pepper

Preheat the oven to 400 degrees F.

Peel the potato, and cut it up as if you were making French fries. Spray a nonstick pan with butter-flavored or plain, nonstick spray and arrange the slices on it. Sprinkle lightly with cayenne pepper. Bake for 25 to 30 minutes, or until the potatoes are cooked through and light brown.

POTATO FRITTERS

Nutrition Facts

Amount Per Serving

Calories 70   Calories from Fat 0

	% Daily Value*
Total Fat 0g	**0%**
Saturated Fat 0g	**0%**
Cholesterol 0mg	**0%**
Sodium 25mg	**1%**
Total Carbohydrate 14g	**5%**
Dietary Fiber 1g	**5%**
Sugars 2g	
Protein 3g	

Vitamin A 0%	•	Vitamin C 25%
Calcium 2%	•	Iron 4%

8 medium potatoes, peeled
6 tablespoons nonfat cottage cheese
6 tablespoons skim milk
2 tablespoons dried minced onions
1/2 teaspoon dried parsley

Stove Top Directions: Place the potatoes in a stockpot with enough water to cover them, and bring to a boil. Continue to boil about 25 minutes, until the potatoes are soft when pierced with a sharp knife.

Microwave Directions: Place the potatoes in a microwave-proof container. Cover with water. Cook on high for about 25 minutes, or longer, until the potatoes are soft when pierced with a sharp knife.

While the potatoes are cooking, combine the cottage cheese and skim milk in a blender or food processor and blend on medium speed until the mixture is free of lumps.

Drain the potatoes in a colander and place them in a large bowl with the cottage cheese mixture. Mash the potatoes until they are smooth and fluffy. Add the onions and parsley. Place the potato mixture in the refrigerator for about 2 hours to blend the flavors and to plump the onions.

Form small, flat cakes from the potato mixture, about 2 1/2 inches in diameter and 3/4 inch thick. Spray a nonstick pan with butter-flavored nonstick spray. Place 6 or 7 cakes at a time in the pan and cook over high heat to start. When the bottoms of the cakes are brown, turn them over and reduce the heat to medium-low. Fry until the second side is brown. Remove to a hot plate and cook the rest of the cakes the same way. Serve hot. If you like, sprinkle with a little hot sauce or lemon juice.

To freeze extras, spray pieces of plastic wrap with a nonstick spray and wrap each fritter individually, spray side against the fritter. Place them in an airtight container and freeze. Reheat frozen fritters in a microwave oven on high or on a nonstick cookie sheet in the oven at 400 degrees F., until the centers are hot.

Variation: POTATO CORN FRITTERS

Prepare the recipe exactly as above, adding 1/2 cup of frozen whole kernel corn to the potato mixture just before shaping into cakes. Cook as above. Leftover corn fritters can be frozen and reheated as above.

Nutrition Facts

Amount Per Serving

Calories 70   Calories from Fat 0

	% Daily Value*
Total Fat 0g	**0%**
Saturated Fat 0g	**0%**
Cholesterol 0mg	**0%**
Sodium 25mg	**1%**
Total Carbohydrate 14g	**5%**
Dietary Fiber 1g	**5%**
Sugars 2g	
Protein 3g	

Vitamin A 0%	•	Vitamin C 25%
Calcium 2%	•	Iron 4%

STUFFED POTATO

YIELD: 1 SERVING

Nutrition Facts

Amount Per Serving

Calories 150	Calories from Fat 0

	% Daily Value*
Total Fat 0g	**0**%
Saturated Fat 0g	**0**%
Cholesterol 0mg	**0**%
Sodium 10mg	**0**%
Total Carbohydrate 35g	**12**%
Dietary Fiber 3g	**11**%
Sugars 3g	
Protein 3g	

Vitamin A 0%	•	Vitamin C 35%
Calcium 2%	•	Iron 4%

This recipe was originally developed before the coming of nonfat sour cream. If you substitute commercial nonfat sour cream, you will need to add 1/8 to 1/4 teaspoon hot sauce to taste and a teaspoon of finely chopped onion to the nonfat sour cream.

1 medium potato
1/2 cup Mock Sour Cream (page 338) or non-fat sour cream
1 scallion, sliced in rings (optional)
1/8 to 1/4 teaspoon hot sauce to taste
1 teaspoon finely chopped onion

Microwave Directions: Pierce the potato with a fork and microwave on high setting for 6 to 7 minutes. Split the cooked potato open with a knife and push the ends in to crumble the contents. Scoop out the potato and place the contents in a small bowl. Add the Mock Sour Cream and combine. Stuff the mixture back into the potato shell and return to the microwave for 2 minutes on high setting.

Oven Directions: Preheat the oven to 350 degrees F. Pierce the potato with a fork and bake for 45 to 60 minutes. Pierce with a sharp knife to see if it is done. Split open the cooked potato with a knife and push the ends in to crumble the contents. Scoop out the potato and place the contents in a small bowl. Add the sour cream and combine. Stuff the mixture back into the potato shell and bake in the oven for 15 to 20 minutes, until heated through. Sprinkle the top with chopped scallions and serve.

Nutrition Facts

Amount Per Serving	
Calories 150	Calories from Fat 0

	% Daily Value*
Total Fat 0g	**0%**
Saturated Fat 0g	**0%**
Cholesterol 0mg	**0%**
Sodium 15mg	**1%**
Total Carbohydrate 35g	**12%**
Dietary Fiber 2g	**10%**
Sugars 4g	
Protein 4g	

Vitamin A 0%	•	Vitamin C 35%
Calcium 2%	•	Iron 4%

Variation: BAKED POTATO SNACK

Pierce the potato with a fork and bake in a microwave or conventional oven, as above. Split open the potato with a knife and push the ends in to crumple potato insides. Sprinkle with 2 teaspoons finely chopped onion. Add 1 tablespoon of skim milk and combine in the potato. Place in a microwave oven for 2 minutes on high to heat, or wrap with aluminum foil and bake in a preheated 350 degree F.-oven for 20 minutes.

FRENCH POTATO LEEK SOUP

Nutrition Facts

Amount Per Serving

Calories 80	Calories from Fat 0

	% Daily Value
Total Fat 0g	**0**%
Saturated Fat 0g	**0**%
Cholesterol 0mg	**0**%
Sodium 45mg	**2**%
Total Carbohydrate 16g	**5**%
Dietary Fiber 2g	**7**%
Sugars 5g	
Protein 4g	

Vitamin A 70%	•	Vitamin C 25%
Calcium 10%	•	Iron 6%

1 1/2 cups chopped leeks including some of the green stalks
2 cups diced potatoes
1/4 teaspoon cayenne pepper
1 medium to large carrot, finely chopped
Water
1 1/2 cups skim milk
1/2 teaspoon dried basil

Microwave Directions: Place the leeks, potatoes, pepper, and carrot in a 2-quart container. Add enough water to cover the vegetables. Cover and cook on high setting for 10 minutes. Stir, cover, and cook on medium setting for 6 minutes. Stir and check to see if vegetables are tender. If not, cover and cook a few minutes more on medium setting until vegetables are tender. Add skim milk and basil and heat through before serving.

Stove Top Directions: Place the leeks, potatoes, pepper, and carrot in a 2-quart saucepan. Add enough water to cover the vegetables. Cover and cook over medium heat, stirring occasionally, until potatoes are very soft and leeks are tender, about 5 or 6 minutes after the water starts to boil. Stir occasionally. Add skim milk and basil and heat through before serving.

If you like, let the soup cool and process in a blender or food processor until the soup is very smooth. This tastes best if eaten the following day. Serve hot.

DEBUTANTE SOUP

Nutrition Facts

Amount Per Serving

Calories 70	Calories from Fat 5

	% Daily Value*
Total Fat 0.5g	**1**%
Saturated Fat 0g	**0**%
Cholesterol 0mg	**0**%
Sodium 85mg	**4**%
Total Carbohydrate 12g	**4**%
Dietary Fiber 2g	**9**%
Sugars 6g	
Protein 6g	

Vitamin A 6%	•	Vitamin C 50%
Calcium 15%	•	Iron 4%

It used to be that in New Orleans the mothers, aunts, or grandmothers of each season's debutantes used to give them what were called "pink teas." The flowers were pink, the mints were pink, and the petits fours (little iced cakes) were pink.

When I finished creating this soup it turned out such a pretty shade of pink and was so elegant it reminded me of the "pink teas" my mother used to tell me about.

This is really easy if you have leftover cauliflower and Cheesy Mashed Potatoes. If you don't, just cut down the recipe for Cheesy Mashed Potatoes, unless you want to have some for later.

2 cups cooked cauliflower
1/2 cup Cheesy Mashed Potatoes (page 229)
1 1/2 cups skim milk
1 tablespoon salt-free tomato paste
1/4 cup fresh sliced mushrooms (3 large mushrooms)
1/16 teaspoon cayenne pepper or more, to taste
1/8 teaspoon dried basil

Combine 1 cup of the cooked cauliflower, all of the potatoes, 1 cup of milk, and the tomato paste and combine in a blender or food processor to liquefy.

Microwave Directions: Pour the potato-cauliflower mixture into a quart-size container. Add the sliced mushrooms. Chop the remaining cauliflower by hand, leaving it rather chunky, and add it, the cayenne pepper, basil, and remaining 1/2 cup of skim milk. Combine thoroughly. Cook, uncovered, for 14 minutes on bake or 60 percent power. Stir once halfway through cooking. Serve hot.

Stove Top Directions: Pour the potato-cauliflower mixture into a 1 1/2-quart saucepan and add the sliced mushrooms. Chop the remaining cauliflower by hand, leaving it rather chunky, and add it, the cayenne pepper, basil, and remaining 1/2 cup of skim milk. Combine thoroughly. Cook, over medium-low heat, uncovered, for 20 to 25 minutes after it begins to simmer. Stir frequently and cook until the mushrooms are tender. Serve hot.

HALLOWEEN PUMPKIN DELIGHT

You could also serve this on Thanksgiving or any Fall holiday dinner. The miniature pumpkins are adorable and sweet. Be sure to get the ones with dull skins; the ones that are shiny are varnished and are just for decoration.

4 miniature pumpkins
1 banana, peeled and chopped
1/4 cup raisins
1 small apple, peeled and cut in small pieces
1/8 plus 1/16 teaspoon pumpkin pie spice or
   1/16 teaspoon ground mace
   1/16 teaspoon ground allspice
   1/16 teaspoon ground nutmeg
1 tablespoon apple juice concentrate
1 teaspoon I Can't Believe It's Not Butter!® Spray

Microwave Oven Directions: Pierce the tops of the pumpkins in a couple of places with a very sharp knife and microwave uncovered, on high setting for 15 minutes. They should be soft. Set aside to cool.

In a microwave bowl combine the bananas, raisins, apple, spices, juice concentrate, and I Can't Believe It's Not Butter!® Spray. Cover the bowl with plastic wrap and cook on high setting for 5 minutes. Mix and set aside.

Cut around the stems of the pumpkins and remove the tops as if you were going to make a jack-o-lantern. Scrape the pulp off of the tops into the bowl with the rest of the ingredients and set them aside. With a small spoon, remove the seeds from the pumpkins while leaving the pulp in the pumpkins. Then scrape the pulp out of the pumpkins into the bowl.

Mix all the ingredients in the bowl and then stuff the mixture back into the pumpkin shells. Put the little tops back on. Spray a microwave dish with nonstick butter-flavored spray, put the pumpkin on the dish, and cook uncovered, on high setting for 6 minutes to heat through. Serve immediately.

Oven Directions: These are easier to cook in the microwave. But you can fill a 2-quart pot with water, place the pumpkins whole in the water, bring to a boil and boil the pumpkins covered for about a half hour until tender. Pierce with a sharp knife to test. Follow the directions as above for stuffing. Place them in a covered baking dish, then place the baking dish in a pan of shallow water. Bake on the middle rack of the oven set at 350 degrees F. for 30 minutes. Serve immediately.

MUSHROOM SOUP

Nutrition Facts

Amount Per Serving

Calories 210	Calories from Fat 10

	% Daily Value*
Total Fat 1.5g	2%
Saturated Fat 0g	0%
Cholesterol 5mg	1%
Sodium 300mg	13%
Total Carbohydrate 41g	14%
Dietary Fiber 8g	31%
Sugars 19g	
Protein 13g	

Vitamin A 35%	•	Vitamin C 180%
Calcium 30%	•	Iron 20%

This mushroom soup is simply a good soup but it's not possible to use it as a thickener like the canned kind. Thickeners are built into the recipes in this book, usually flour or cornstarch mixed with a liquid and flavorings.

1/3 cup frozen or fresh green peas
4 large fresh mushrooms, sliced
2 tablespoons dried onion flakes
1 teaspoon dried celery flakes
1 teaspoon dried parsley
1/2 large green pepper, chopped
1/4 teaspoon red pepper flakes
Water
2/3 cup skim milk

Microwave Directions: Place the peas, mushrooms, onion flakes, celery flakes, parsley, chopped green pepper, and red pepper flakes in a quart-size container. Add water to just cover the vegetables. Cover and cook 5 minutes on high setting. Stir and check the onions and peas and if they are tender, remove from the microwave. If not, stir, cover, and cook for 3 minutes. Check again and cook until all vegetables are tender. Then add the skim milk, heat through, and serve.

Stove Top Directions: Place the peas, mushrooms, onion flakes, celery flakes, parsley, chopped green pepper, and red pepper flakes in a 1 1/2-quart saucepan. Cover the vegetables with water and cover with a lid. Bring to a boil, then lower the heat to medium, and cook about 7 to 10 minutes, or until vegetables are tender. Add the skim milk, heat through, and serve.

SPINACH CASSEROLE

Nutrition Facts

Amount Per Serving

Calories 100	Calories from Fat 5

	% Daily Value*
Total Fat 0.5g	**1%**
Saturated Fat 0g	**0%**
Cholesterol 5mg	**1%**
Sodium 320mg	**13%**
Total Carbohydrate 11g	**4%**
Dietary Fiber 3g	**12%**
Sugars 2g	
Protein 13g	

Vitamin A 90%	•	Vitamin C 15%
Calcium 30%	•	Iron 8%

1 package (10 ounces) chopped frozen spinach, defrosted enough to divide
1/2 cup nonfat cottage cheese
1/2 cup nonfat cheddar cheese
1 cup sliced mushrooms
3 jumbo egg whites
1/4 cup skim milk
1 teaspoon red hot sauce
1/4 teaspoon turmeric
2 slices Pritikin or commercial whole wheat bread
1 tablespoon grated sapsago cheese

Preheat the oven to 350 degrees F.

In a 1 1/2-quart casserole dish, layer half the spinach, the cottage cheese, cheddar cheese, the mushrooms, and finally the rest of the spinach.

In a bowl, lightly beat together the egg whites, milk, hot sauce, and turmeric. Pour the egg mixture over the casserole. Be sure that all the spinach is covered by the egg mixture. Cover the dish with aluminum foil, pressing it down so it is touching the top of the casserole. Place on the middle rack of the oven and bake for 25 minutes.

While the casserole is baking, break up the bread in chunks and combine with the sapsago cheese in a blender or food processor. Process to make bread crumbs.

After 25 minutes, remove the aluminum foil from the casserole and sprinkle with the crumb mixture. Pat it down a little, then spray with butter-flavored nonstick spray. Continue baking, uncovered, for 10 minutes. Reduce the oven temperature to 150 degrees F. and let the casserole sit in the oven for another 30 minutes, uncovered. Serve hot.

SPINACH FLORENTINE

Nutrition Facts

Amount Per Serving

Calories 190   Calories from Fat 15

	% Daily Value*
Total Fat 1.5g	3%
Saturated Fat 0g	0%
Cholesterol 0mg	0%
Sodium 560mg	23%
Total Carbohydrate 31g	10%
Dietary Fiber 11g	43%
Sugars 1g	
Protein 17g	

Vitamin A 450%	•	Vitamin C 60%
Calcium 45%	•	Iron 30%

When my husband and I were on Maui, some years ago, we went to an outdoor brunch at a swanky hotel complete with hula dancers, palm trees, and ocean waves. One of the dishes I particularly loved was Spinach Florentine. I couldn't wait to get home to adapt the recipe.

3 packages (10 ounces each) frozen chopped spinach (6 cups)
4 egg whites
1/2 teaspoon Tabasco® sauce
2 teaspoons low-sodium soy sauce
4 tablespoons grated sapsago cheese
3/4 cup bread crumbs (Pritikin or any other acceptable bread)
Cayenne pepper
Nutmeg

Microwave Directions: Place the frozen spinach in a 1-quart or 1 1/2-quart baking dish. Cover and cook on high setting for 8 minutes. Stir. Cook on high setting for 8 minutes more. Stir, remove from the oven and drain the liquid, but leave the spinach in the baking dish.

Stove Top Directions: Place the spinach in a saucepan with 1 cup water, cover, and cook over medium heat for about 3 to 4 minutes, after the water comes to a full boil. Drain and place in a 1-quart or 1 1/2-quart baking dish.

Add the egg whites, Tabasco® sauce, and soy sauce. Add half the cheese and combine. In a separate bowl, mix the other half of the cheese with the bread crumbs. Sprinkle over the top of the casserole. Set the oven temperature at 350 degrees F. and bake for 30 minutes. Sprinkle with cayenne pepper and nutmeg.

You can freeze the whole dish or individual portions. To reheat 1 serving, add 1 teaspoon of water to the bottom of the dish, cover, and heat. To reheat the whole casserole, add 4 teaspoons of water, cover, heat. Although this dish tends to dry out if you don't eat it right away, the water moistens it and brings it back to life.

NOODLES VILLA D'ESTE

Nutrition Facts

Amount Per Serving

Calories 220 Calories from Fat 15

	% Daily Value*
Total Fat 2g	3%
Saturated Fat 0g	0%
Cholesterol 5mg	2%
Sodium 1130mg	47%
Total Carbohydrate 39g	13%
Dietary Fiber 5g	20%
Sugars 2g	
Protein 14g	

Vitamin A 100%	•	Vitamin C 60%
Calcium 10%	•	Iron 20%

In about 100 A.D., the roman emperor Hadrian built a magnificent palace, the Villa d'Este, about 20 miles northwest of Rome, in Tivoli. Surrounded by exquisite gardens and five hundred spectacular fountains, the villa is built on the side of a mountain. My husband Ray and I sat in a little cafe overlooking the beautiful Italian countryside near the villa, and enjoyed something very similar to this.

1 1/2 cups uncooked, whole wheat elbow macaroni
1 batch of Italian Tomato Sauce (page 54)
1 1/2 cups nonfat cottage cheese
1 package (10 ounces) chopped, defrosted spinach
1 large zucchini, sliced
Grated sapsago cheese

Follow the directions on the package for cooking the macaroni.

Preheat oven to 350 degrees F.

In a 9-inch-by-13-inch baking dish, layer tomato sauce, half the macaroni, half the cottage cheese, and all of the spinach. (There is no need to squeeze the water out of the spinach.) Top with the remaining macaroni, more tomato sauce, the remaining cottage cheese, and the zucchini. Finish with tomato sauce. Place in the oven and bake for 40 minutes. Sprinkle with sapsago cheese before serving.

This can be refrigerated and reheated the next day, or cut into square about 4 inches wide, and frozen in sealed plastic bags.

ACORN SQUASH CHEESE BAKE

Nutrition Facts

Amount Per Serving

Calories 230	Calories from Fat 0

	% Daily Value*
Total Fat 0g	0%
Saturated Fat 0g	0%
Cholesterol 5mg	2%
Sodium 200mg	8%
Total Carbohydrate 50g	17%
Dietary Fiber 5g	20%
Sugars 30g	
Protein 11g	

Vitamin A 15%	•	Vitamin C 45%
Calcium 10%	•	Iron 10%

1 medium acorn squash
1/2 cup nonfat cottage cheese
1 tablespoon finely chopped onion
1/2 medium apple, peeled and chopped
1/4 cup raisins
1 tablespoon apple juice concentrate
1 tablespoon grated sapsago cheese

Microwave Directions for Cooking Squash: Pierce the squash with a fork and cook whole, on a plate, on high setting, for 8 minutes. Cool and cut in half lengthwise. Remove the seeds.

Stove Top Directions for Cooking Squash: Place the whole squash in saucepan with water to cover, for about 15 to 20 minutes after the water starts to boil, or until tender. Pierce with a knife to check. Cool and cut in half lengthwise. Remove the seeds.

Preheat the oven to 325 degrees F.

Combine the cottage cheese, onion, apple, and raisins in a bowl. Spoon about 1 1/2 teaspoons apple juice concentrate in the cavity of each squash and swirl it around to coat the insides of the squash. Then fill the cavities with the cottage cheese mixture. Set in the refrigerator, covered with plastic wrap, for 15 to 30 minutes or all day, if you like. This is to plump up the raisins and let the different tastes mingle. Sprinkle with sapsago cheese and bake for 15 minutes. Serve hot.

BAKED YELLOW SQUASH WITH CHEESE

YIELD: 5 SERVINGS

Nutrition Facts

Amount Per Serving

Calories 170   Calories from Fat 15

	% Daily Value*
Total Fat 1.5g	3%
Saturated Fat 0g	0%
Cholesterol 0mg	0%
Sodium 380mg	16%
Total Carbohydrate 26g	9%
Dietary Fiber 3g	11%
Sugars 4g	
Protein 12g	

Vitamin A 8%	•	Vitamin C 30%
Calcium 30%	•	Iron 10%

5 cups uncooked yellow squash, sliced
1/2 cup nonfat cheddar cheese
1 1/4 cups whole wheat bread crumbs
1/8 teaspoon cayenne pepper
4 jumbo egg whites
1/4 cup skim milk
2 tablespoons grated sapsago cheese

Preheat oven to 350 degrees F.

Spray a 1 1/2-quart casserole dish with butter-flavored nonstick spray. Layer half the squash in the dish, then sprinkle 1/4 cup of the cheddar cheese over the squash, then 1/2 cup of the bread crumbs, then the remaining squash, then the remaining cheddar, then 1/2 cup of the bread crumbs, and finally the cayenne pepper.

In a mixing bowl, beat the egg whites with the milk together lightly with a fork. Pour the milk mixture over the casserole, distributing it evenly. Sprinkle with the remaining bread crumbs. Cover the dish with foil and bake 30 minutes. Remove the cover, sprinkle the sapsago cheese over the casserole, and bake uncovered for another 30 minutes, approximately. Check as it bakes to see if the sides are getting too dark a brown. Pierce the squash with a knife and if it is soft, then the casserole is done.

YELLOW SQUASH AND TOMATOES OVER SPAGHETTI

Nutrition Facts

Amount Per Serving

Calories 470	Calories from Fat 20

	% Daily Value*
Total Fat 2g	3%
Saturated Fat 0g	0%
Cholesterol 0mg	0%
Sodium 35mg	2%
Total Carbohydrate 100g	33%
Dietary Fiber 18g	72%
Sugars 18g	
Protein 21g	

Vitamin A 30%	•	Vitamin C 80%
Calcium 15%	•	Iron 30%

1 can (14 1/2 ounces) salt-free tomatoes, chopped, and reserved juice
2 medium yellow squash, sliced
1 large onion, sliced in rings
1 tablespoon apple juice concentrate
1/8 teaspoon dried red pepper flakes
1/8 teaspoon dried basil
1/2 teaspoon dried parsley
4 cups cooked whole wheat or semolina spaghetti
2 tablespoons grated sapsago cheese

In a 2-quart saucepan, layer first the squash, then the onion, then the tomatoes. Add the juice from the tomatoes. Sprinkle the juice concentrate over the top, then the red pepper flakes, then the basil, then the parsley. *Do not stir.* Cover and cook over high heat for 8 to 10 minutes, or until the squash is soft. Check frequently to make sure that the bottom doesn't burn. Shake the pot back and forth a couple of times while cooking.

In a separate pot, cook the spaghetti in plenty of boiling water following the directions on the package, while the vegetables are cooking. Drain in a colander and transfer to a serving bowl. Stir the cooked vegetables, then spoon them and the pan juices over the spaghetti.

Sprinkle with sapsago cheese.

YELLOW SQUASH, TREE EARS, AND NOODLES

The first time I saw tree ears in a gourmet food store, I had to try them. The name really tickles me. They are a type of mushroom but with a very different texture and much more interesting flavor than that of a regular mushroom. They can be found in Asian markets as well as gourmet stores and they also go by the exotic names of: "cloud ears," "wood ears," "black fungus," "tree fungus," or "Szechwan mushrooms."

YIELD: 2 SERVINGS

Nutrition Facts

Amount Per Serving

Calories 290   Calories from Fat 20

	% Daily Value*
Total Fat 2.5g	**4%**
Saturated Fat 1g	**4%**
Cholesterol 10mg	**3%**
Sodium 470mg	**20%**
Total Carbohydrate 55g	**18%**
Dietary Fiber 14g	**56%**
Sugars 16g	
Protein 17g	

Vitamin A 210%	•	Vitamin C 120%
Calcium 10%	•	Iron 160%

1/4 cup dry tree ears (or 2 cups sliced fresh mushrooms)
1/2 cup hot water
3/4 cup fresh or frozen snow pea pods
1 large onion, coarsely chopped
1/2 large green pepper, coarsely chopped
1 large carrot, finely chopped
1 large yellow squash, finely chopped
1 teaspoon low-sodium tamari or soy sauce
1 tablespoon plus 1 teaspoon Red Rosé wine
1 can (6 1/2 ounces) sliced water chestnuts, drained and sliced
1/2 cup low-fat cottage cheese
1 cup cooked imitation egg noodles (or substitute cooked whole wheat spaghetti)
1/2 cup of roast beef gravy (page 48)

First, soak the tree ears in about 1/2 cup of hot water. By the time you are finished chopping the other vegetables in the recipe, they should be soft. They take about 20 minutes to open up into "flowers." When they are soft, drain the tree ears and feel them to see if they have any tough knots. If they do, cut them out and chop the rest as you would a regular mushroom.

Combine the snow pea pods, onion, green pepper, carrot, squash, and tamari or soy sauce in a nonstick frying pan. Add fresh mushrooms now if you are not using tree ears. Sauté over high heat until the onion looks transparent and a little brown. Add the wine and sauté for about 30 seconds. Add the tree ears, water chestnuts, cottage cheese, egg noodles, and gravy, and combine thoroughly. Taste to see if it is hot enough. If not, cover and heat through for about 1 minute. Serve with Chinese Mustard Sauce (page 53).

CRANBERRY BAKED SQUASH

Nutrition Facts

Amount Per Serving

Calories 180	Calories from Fat 0

	% Daily Value*
Total Fat 0g	**0%**
Saturated Fat 0g	**0%**
Cholesterol 0mg	**0%**
Sodium 15mg	**1%**
Total Carbohydrate 47g	**16%**
Dietary Fiber 5g	**22%**
Sugars 23g	
Protein 2g	

Vitamin A 15%	•	Vitamin C 50%
Calcium 8%	•	Iron 10%

1 medium acorn squash
1/4 cup water
1/4 cup apple juice concentrate
1 tablespoon cornstarch
1 cup cranberries

Microwave Directions: Pierce the squash with a small sharp knife in several places, and bake, uncovered, on high setting for 10 minutes. When completely cooked, cut in half lengthwise and remove the seeds.

Oven Directions: Pierce the squash with a small sharp knife in several places, and bake in a preheated, 350 degrees F.-oven for about 30 minutes. When completely cooked, cut in half lengthwise and remove the seeds.

In a saucepan, combine the water and juice concentrate. Add the cornstarch and blend with a wooden spoon until the lumps are gone. Cook over medium heat, stirring constantly, until the mixture thickens and is almost transparent. Add the cranberries and combine thoroughly. Divide the cranberry mixture between the two halves of the squash. Place on a nonstick baking pan and bake for 30 to 35 minutes, or until the cranberries are nice and soft.

Variation: BLUEBERRY BAKED SQUASH

Substitute 1 cup of blueberries for the cranberries. Bake at 350 degrees F. for about 10 minutes to heat through.

STUFFED SWEET POTATO

Nutrition Facts

Amount Per Serving	
Calories 300	Calories from Fat 5

	% Daily Value*
Total Fat 0.5g	**1%**
Saturated Fat 0g	**0%**
Cholesterol 0mg	**0%**
Sodium 30mg	**1%**
Total Carbohydrate 74g	**25%**
Dietary Fiber 6g	**23%**
Sugars 56g	
Protein 4g	

Vitamin A 500%	•	Vitamin C 50%
Calcium 8%	•	Iron 8%

Because sweet potatoes have so much vitamin E, I try to eat them at least once a week. I often just pierce them with a fork, bake them in their skins, and eat them plain, but if I want to be fancy I make this recipe.

1 medium sweet potato
1/4 medium apple, peeled and chopped
1 tablespoon apple juice concentrate
1 tablespoon skim milk
1/4 cup raisins (golden sultanas, if you can find them)

Microwave Directions: Pierce the potato with a fork and bake in the microwave on high setting for 6 to 7 minutes, depending on the size of the potato. Slice off one side of the potato and scoop out the contents and place in a small bowl. Add the other ingredients and combine. Stuff the mixture back into the potato shell and bake on high for 3 minutes.

Oven Directions: Preheat the oven to 350 degrees F. Pierce the potato with a fork and bake for about 1 hour. Pierce with a sharp knife after 45 minutes to check for doneness. When soft, slice off one side of the potato and scoop out the contents and place in a small bowl. Add the other ingredients and combine. Stuff the mixture back into the potato shell and bake in the oven until heated through, about 15 minutes.

SWEET POTATOES ST. HILAIRE

St. Hilaire is a very old name in my family and is pronounced "sant eelair." Sweet potatoes similar to these were a favorite on the old Louisiana plantations. They are so sweet and good, you could even eat them for dessert.

If you can't find the canned sweet potatoes, just boil 1 1/2 pounds of fresh sweet potatoes in lots of water with their skins on until they are soft, then remove the pulp and mash it.

2 jumbo egg whites
1 1/4 large over-ripe Baked Bananas (page 57)
1/4 cup apple juice concentrate
1/16 teaspoon cinnamon
1/16 teaspoon nutmeg
1 can (15 1/2 ounces) sugar-free, salt-free mashed yams or 1 1/2 pounds cooked fresh sweet potatoes
3/4 cup raisins
1 large apple (preferably Granny Smith)

Preheat oven to 375 degrees F.

Spray an 8-inch-square baking dish with nonstick spray.

Combine the egg whites, banana, juice concentrate, cinnamon, and nutmeg in a blender or food processor. Blend until foamy. Place the sweet potatoes in a bowl, add the contents of the blender, and combine. Add the raisins and combine again. Peel and core the apples, and slice as you would for apple pie in nice thick slices. Fold the apple slices into the potato mixture, then transfer to the baking dish. Bake on the middle rack of the oven for 25 minutes. The apple should still be crunchy when done. Serve immediately.

Variation: SWEET POTATOES ST. HILAIRE WITH BRANDY TOPPING

Two to three days before making the potatoes, combine 1/4 cup raisins, 1 tablespoon apple juice concentrate, and 1/2 tablespoon brandy in a small container and refrigerate. Follow the baking directions as above. When the sweet potatoes have baked 20 minutes, pour on the topping and bake for the last 5 minutes.

BAKED TOMATO

Nutrition Facts

Amount Per Serving

Calories 20	Calories from Fat 0

	% Daily Value*
Total Fat 0g	**0%**
Saturated Fat 0g	**0%**
Cholesterol 0mg	**0%**
Sodium 5mg	**0%**
Total Carbohydrate 4g	**1%**
Dietary Fiber less than 1 gram	**3%**
Sugars 2g	
Protein 2g	

Vitamin A 8%	•	Vitamin C 25%
Calcium 0%	•	Iron 2%

1 medium to large tomato
Lemon juice
Cayenne pepper
1 tablespoon grated sapsago cheese

Preheat the oven to 400 degrees F.

Cut tomato in half horizontally and remove stem. Place on a baking pan and squirt a little lemon juice over each half. Then sprinkle a little cayenne pepper and half the sapsago cheese over each tomato half. Place on the bottom shelf of the oven and bake for 15 minutes. Then place under the broiler for 3 minutes. Serve hot.

TURNIPS AND TURNIP GREENS

YIELD: 4 SERVINGS

Nutrition Facts

Amount Per Serving	
Calories 70	Calories from Fat 0

	% Daily Value*
Total Fat 0g	0%
Saturated Fat 0g	0%
Cholesterol 0mg	0%
Sodium 170mg	7%
Total Carbohydrate 16g	5%
Dietary Fiber 6g	22%
Sugars 7g	
Protein 3g	

Vitamin A 170%	• Vitamin C 140%
Calcium 25%	• Iron 8%

2 large purple turnips or 4-5 smaller ones, peeled and cubed
(2–2 1/2 cups)
1 large onion, coarsely chopped
1 teaspoon low-sodium soy sauce
Cayenne pepper
Water
8 cups young, tender turnip greens, destemmed and chopped

Place the turnips in a nonstick soup pot with the onions. Turn the heat on high, sprinkle the soy sauce and cayenne over the vegetables, and sauté until the onion and the turnips look brown around the edges, 4 1/2 minutes. Add about 1/2 inch of water to the pot. Add the greens and cover. Cook over medium heat for about 10 minutes, or until tender. Stir occasionally, and add more water if the greens begin to dry out.

MR. EVANS' TOMATO ASPIC

My college English teacher, Oliver Evans, loved this dish so much that my mother called it "Mr. Evans' Tomato Aspic." Mr. Evans knew Tennessee Williams. I asked him to ask Tennessee why he never wrote about nice people. Mr. Evans did, and the great playwright replied: "I didn't know there were any."

2 cans (16 ounces each) salt-free tomato sauce
1 celery rib, cut into large pieces
1 teaspoon crumbled thyme
1 bay leaf
1 teaspoon onion powder
1/4 teaspoon garlic powder
1/2 teaspoon dried basil
1 teaspoon medium red hot sauce
1 teaspoon dried parsley
1/16 teaspoon dried red pepper flakes
2 1/2 tablespoons apple juice concentrate
Juice of two lemons
2 envelopes unflavored gelatin

Microwave Directions: Combine the tomato sauce, celery, thyme, bay leaf, onion powder, garlic powder, basil, hot sauce, parsley, pepper flakes, and juice concentrate in a 2-quart microwave bowl, cover, and cook at 50 percent power for 35 minutes, stirring twice during cooking.

Stove Top Directions: Combine the tomato sauce, celery, thyme, bay leaf, onion powder, garlic powder, basil, hot sauce, parsley, pepper flakes, and juice concentrate in a 2-quart saucepan. Cover and cook over low heat for 30 minutes, stirring frequently. Remove from the heat.

Remove the celery and bay leaf. Add the lemon juice, then sprinkle the gelatin over the top and work it in a with a spoon, until dissolved. Pour into a 1-quart mold and chill until firm, 3 to 4 hours. To unmold, fill your kitchen sink with hot water. Dip the mold into the hot water for 5 or 6 seconds. Hold a plate over the mold and turn over. The salad should fall easily down onto the plate. If it doesn't release easily, repeat.

Variation: CRUNCHY TOMATO ASPIC

To either the microwave or stove top versions, add 2 chopped celery ribs after adding the gelatin. Follow the directions for molding the salad.

CHAPTER 8

Grain and Bean Side and Main Dishes

Beans are a real staple of the Pritikin diet, because they are a substitute for meat.

Beans can be awfully blah without salt, but you can spice them up with other things to make them taste better. Pinto beans taste the best without salt, followed by garbanzos, then black beans, then lima beans. If you absolutely can't stand them plain, it's all right to add a tablespoon of low-sodium soy or tamari sauce to the pot. But these sauces do contain some salt, so you might try to get used to doing without them. Now I like them, even without all the forbidden seasonings. I don't miss the way they used to taste at all. My husband, on the other hand, squirts hot sauce on his beans because he still misses that salty taste. Sometimes he puts chopped raw onions on his beans, for even more flavor.

Another trick to make beans taste better is to mix two or three kinds together. I don't usually cook the beans together, because different varieties often require different cooking times. I make up half-cup containers for the freezer and then take two or three different kinds out to defrost and mix together. Lentils are the least flavorful beans so I almost always mix them with other beans.

A little fresh lemon juice is good on beans and another great thing to cook with your beans is lemon grass, although I didn't include it in any of these recipes because it's only found in specialty Asian markets. It smells just like lemon but it has a sweet and slightly tangy taste and imparts a lovely aroma and flavor to any recipe. When I can get it I cut it up into 3-inch sections to freeze in sealed plastic bags. Three 3-inch sections are enough for a pot of beans.

Always start your beans with lots of water, usually nine or ten cups per pound. They don't do as well if you have to add water during cooking; they will often stay hard. I've found that there is really no need to soak beans first if you cook them in a slow cooker. Soaking them may help them cook a little faster, but in a slow cooker, who cares? Even if I cook them in a stockpot on top of the stove, I still don't soak them and they always come out fine. I've heard that while soaking, the beans can build up harmful bacteria, so that's another reason not to soak.

I usually start out cooking my beans in plain water in the slow cooker because if I add the seasonings in the beginning, they lose their taste. With the exception of bay leaf, which I recommend adding early, add seasonings in the slow cooker as well as on the stove during the last thirty or forty minutes of cooking time.

WHITE RICE

YIELD: 9 (1/3-CUP) SERVINGS

Nutrition Facts

Amount Per Serving

Calories 80	Calories from Fat 0

	% Daily Value*
Total Fat 0g	**0%**
Saturated Fat 0g	**0%**
Cholesterol 0mg	**0%**
Sodium 0mg	**0%**
Total Carbohydrate 16g	**5%**
Dietary Fiber 0g	**0%**
Sugars 0g	
Protein 1g	

Vitamin A 0%	•	Vitamin C 0%
Calcium 0%	•	Iron 4%

1 cup uncooked long grain white rice
2 cups water

Microwave Directions: Combine the water and rice in a 2-quart container (a 2-quart measuring cup is ideal). Cover and cook on high setting for 5 minutes. Reduce the temperature to simmer or low, and cook for 15 minutes. Remove from the heat and allow the rice to sit for about 10 to 15 minutes covered, after it is cooked. Fluff with a fork before serving.

Stove Top Directions: Combine the rice and water in a 2-quart saucepan. Bring to a boil, cover, and reduce the heat to low, and cook for 20 minutes. Remove from the heat. Let sit covered for 10 to 15 minutes. Fluff with a fork before serving.

WILD RICE

Mix about 1 part wild uncooked rice to 4 parts brown uncooked rice, and cook exactly as you would brown rice (see page 256).

Nutrition Facts

Amount Per Serving

Calories 70	Calories from Fat 5

	% Daily Value*
Total Fat 0.5g	**1%**
Saturated Fat 0g	**0%**
Cholesterol 0mg	**0%**
Sodium 0mg	**0%**
Total Carbohydrate 15g	**5%**
Dietary Fiber less than 1 gram	**3%**
Sugars 0g	
Protein 2g	

Vitamin A 0%	•	Vitamin C 0%
Calcium 0%	•	Iron 2%

BROWN RICE

Nutrition Facts

Amount Per Serving

Calories 80	Calories from Fat 5

	% Daily Value*
Total Fat 0.5g	**1%**
Saturated Fat 0g	**0%**
Cholesterol 0mg	**0%**
Sodium 0mg	**0%**
Total Carbohydrate 16g	**5%**
Dietary Fiber less than 1 gram	**3%**
Sugars 0g	
Protein 2g	

Vitamin A 0%	•	Vitamin C 0%
Calcium 0%	•	Iron 2%

1 cup uncooked brown rice (preferably long grain)
2 cups water

Microwave Directions: Combine the rice and water in a 2-quart container (a 2-quart measuring cup is ideal). Cover and cook on high setting for 5 minutes. Lower the temperature to simmer or low, and cook for 40 minutes. Remove from the oven and allow the rice to sit for about 10 to 15 minutes covered, after it is cooked. Fluff with a fork before serving.

Stove Top Directions: Combine the rice and water in a 2-quart saucepan. Bring to a boil, cover, reduce the heat to low, and cook for 40 minutes. Remove from the heat. Let sit covered for 10 to 15 minutes. Fluff with a fork before serving.

ORIENTAL "FRIED" RICE

YIELD: 2 SERVINGS

Nutrition Facts

Amount Per Serving

Calories 140	Calories from Fat 10

	% Daily Value*
Total Fat 1g	**1**%
Saturated Fat 0g	**0**%
Cholesterol 0mg	**0**%
Sodium 105mg	**4**%
Total Carbohydrate 26g	**9**%
Dietary Fiber 4g	**16**%
Sugars 8g	
Protein 8g	

Vitamin A 4%	•	Vitamin C 60%
Calcium 4%	•	Iron 8%

1 large onion, coarsely chopped
1 package (10 ounces) of frozen snow pea pods or 1 1/2 cups fresh snow pea pods
1/2 teaspoon low-sodium soy sauce
2 jumbo egg whites
2/3 cup cooked Brown Rice (page 256)
1/4 teaspoon cayenne pepper

Combine the onions, snow peas, and soy sauce in a nonstick frying pan. Set the heat on high and sauté. When the onions begin to look brown around the edges and appear fairly limp and transparent, add the egg whites and rice and stir. Reduce the heat to low and cover. Cook for 4 minutes, until the eggs are cooked and the snow peas are tender. Stir in the cayenne and serve hot. For variety you can add browned, drained, lean ground beef, cooked chicken, or even nonfat cottage cheese. If you want raw shrimp or raw chicken pieces, add them when you sauté the vegetables.

SPANISH RICE

YIELD: 6 SERVINGS

Nutrition Facts

Amount Per Serving

Calories 140 Calories from Fat 10

	% Daily Value*
Total Fat 1.5g	2%
Saturated Fat 0g	0%
Cholesterol 0mg	0%
Sodium 25mg	1%
Total Carbohydrate 30g	10%
Dietary Fiber 3g	12%
Sugars 3g	
Protein 3g	

Vitamin A 20%	•	Vitamin C 50%
Calcium 2%	•	Iron 6%

1 cup chopped onions
1 cup chopped green peppers
1 tablespoon chopped fresh parsley, firmly packed
2 cups water
1 small tomato, chopped
4 teaspoons chili powder
1/4 teaspoon red pepper flakes or less, to taste
1/2 teaspoon garlic powder
1 tablespoon salt-free tomato paste
1 cup uncooked Brown Rice and Wild Rice Mixed (page 255)

Combine onions, peppers, and parsley in a nonstick frying pan and sauté over high heat until the onions look brown around the edges and a little transparent. Add the water and stir. Add the tomato, chili powder, red pepper flakes, garlic powder, and tomato paste. Remove from the heat.

Pour the uncooked rice into a 1 1/2-quart casserole dish. Pour all the other ingredients into the dish with the rice. Combine and cover.

Microwave Directions: Cook on simmer or 50 percent power for 55 minutes. Remove from the oven and let stand covered, for 15 or 20 minutes. Fluff with a fork and serve.

Oven Directions: Preheat oven to 300 degrees F.

Bake casserole for 55 minutes. Remove from the oven and let stand for 15 or 20 minutes, covered. Fluff with a fork and serve.

For variety, instead of green pepper, add 1 4-ounce can of whole green chili peppers. Chop and combine with the other ingredients before cooking. (Don't get the ones that are already chopped. They don't have as much taste.)

HAWAIIAN RICE

YIELD: 8 SERVINGS

Nutrition Facts

Amount Per Serving	
Calories 190	Calories from Fat 10

	% Daily Value*
Total Fat 1g	**2**%
Saturated Fat 0g	**0**%
Cholesterol 0mg	**0**%
Sodium 150mg	**6**%
Total Carbohydrate 44g	**15**%
Dietary Fiber 4g	**14**%
Sugars 17g	
Protein 3g	

Vitamin A 0%	•	Vitamin C 20%
Calcium 2%	•	Iron 50%

Do try to get some wild rice because it really tastes much better than the brown rice alone. With its sweet, tropical, nut-like quality, this is wonderful served with Oven-Fried Chicken (page 131) and Cranberry Baked Squash (page 246).

1 1/4 cups uncooked brown rice and wild rice mixed
1/2 cup crushed unsweetened pineapple
1/2 cup raisins
1/2 large apple, peeled and cubed
1 small onion, coarsely chopped
1 can (8 ounces) water chestnuts, sliced
1 rib celery, chopped in medium-sized pieces
1/4 teaspoon red pepper flakes
1 tablespoon apple juice concentrate
1/4 teaspoon turmeric
Juice drained from pineapple plus enough water to equal 2 1/2 cups
2 tablespoons low-sodium soy sauce.

Combine all ingredients in a 1 1/2-quart casserole dish.

Microwave Directions: Cover the baking dish and cook on simmer or 50 percent power, for 55 minutes. Remove from the oven and let sit, covered, for 15 to 20 minutes, then fluff with a fork and serve.

Oven Directions: Preheat oven to 300 degrees F.

Bake covered on the middle rack of the oven for 55 minutes. Remove from the oven and let sit, covered, for 15 to 20 minutes, then fluff with a fork and serve.

SPAGHETTI ALFREDO

Nutrition Facts

Amount Per Serving

Calories 270	Calories from Fat 10

	% Daily Value*
Total Fat 1g	**2**%
Saturated Fat 0g	**0**%
Cholesterol 5mg	**1**%
Sodium 290mg	**12**%
Total Carbohydrate 47g	**16**%
Dietary Fiber 7g	**27**%
Sugars 7g	
Protein 20g	

Vitamin A 15%	•	Vitamin C 6%
Calcium 60%	•	Iron 10%

2 cups cooked semolina spaghetti (or whole wheat, if you prefer)
2/3 cup skim milk
1/4 teaspoon red pepper flakes
1/2 teaspoon parsley flakes or 1 tablespoon fresh chopped
1/2 teaspoon dried oregano
1/4 teaspoon garlic powder
1/2 teaspoon onion powder
1 tablespoon cornstarch
1/2 cup fat-free shredded mozzarella cheese
Grated sapsago cheese

Follow the cooking instructions on the package of spaghetti.

Pour the milk into a small saucepan. Add the seasonings and cornstarch and combine thoroughly. Place saucepan over a medium heat and stir until the mixture bubbles. Remove from heat, and add the mozzarella cheese, stirring until it melts. Add the hot, cooked spaghetti and combine with the sauce. Sprinkle a tablespoon of grated sapsago cheese over each serving.

RED OR KIDNEY BEANS

YIELD: 12 SERVINGS

Nutrition Facts

Amount Per Serving	
Calories 140	Calories from Fat 0

	% Daily Value*
Total Fat 0g	**0%**
Saturated Fat 0g	**0%**
Cholesterol 0mg	**0%**
Sodium 75mg	**3%**
Total Carbohydrate 26g	**9%**
Dietary Fiber 6g	**26%**
Sugars 3g	
Protein 9g	

Vitamin A 4%	•	Vitamin C 30%
Calcium 4%	•	Iron 15%

I knew a children's heart specialist from up north when she first began practicing in a New Orleans hospital. The first time she saw a young patient being served red beans and rice for dinner, she couldn't believe it. She marched down to the kitchen to bawl out the dietitian for giving the child two starches. The dietitian and the kitchen helpers looked at her like she was crazy. Everybody in New Orleans eats red beans and rice! It is probably on every menu in the city and if it isn't you could probably get it anyway especially on Mondays, because Monday is washday in New Orleans (most people stay home and wash and stir their red beans). Of course, now the doctor has come to love her red beans and rice, like any native of New Orleans. And even better—dietitians now know that eating beans and rice together makes a complete protein, so it's really one of the healthiest things you can eat.

2 2/3 cups (1 pound) dry, red kidney beans
2 bay leaves
9 1/2 cups water
1 rib of celery including leaves, chopped
1/2 cup chopped fresh parsley
1 medium to large onion, chopped
1 medium to large green pepper, chopped
2 teaspoons garlic powder or 4 fresh cloves, chopped
4 teaspoons low-sodium tamari or soy sauce
1/4 to 1/2 teaspoon red pepper flakes
1 teaspoon dried thyme, or 3 sprigs of fresh thyme

Slow Cooker Directions: Rinse the beans, then in a slow cooker combine the beans, bay leaves, and water. Cover and cook on high setting for 4 1/2 hours. Then add all other ingredients and cook for 30 to 40 minutes until the green pepper is tender.

Stove Top Directions: If you are going to cook the beans on top of the stove, be sure you are going to be home for 4 hours. Follow the directions above, but simmer covered, for about 3 hours, then add the seasonings and simmer for another 30 to 40 minutes. Stir every so often throughout the cooking time to keep the beans from burning. You shouldn't need any more water, but if the beans start to dry out, add more as needed.

SOPPIN' GOOD BEANS AND EGGPLANT BREAD

Nutrition Facts

Amount Per Serving

Calories 360   Calories from Fat 20

	% Daily Value*
Total Fat 2g	3%
Saturated Fat 0g	0%
Cholesterol 5mg	1%
Sodium 470mg	20%
Total Carbohydrate 69g	23%
Dietary Fiber 13g	52%
Sugars 19g	
Protein 21g	

Vitamin A 40%	•	Vitamin C 70%
Calcium 20%	•	Iron 30%

Once you get used to the idea of meatless meals, you will find that you really don't miss meat all that much. My husband used to be a confirmed carnivore, but even he has gotten used to a more vegetarian diet. He sops up all the beans and pot liquor with the eggplant bread and loves it!

The Red Beans
2 2/3 cups (1 pound) dried red or kidney beans
1 can (16 ounces) salt-free tomatoes
7 1/2 cups water
2 tablespoons salt-free chili powder
1 can (4 ounces) peeled, green, roasted chilies, drained and chopped
1 large onion, chopped
2 tablespoons apple juice concentrate
1/4 teaspoon cayenne pepper (optional)

The Eggplant Bread:
1 tablespoon water
1/2 cup plus 1 tablespoon apple juice concentrate
3 1/2 cups cubed, peeled raw eggplant (1 small or 1/2 large)
1/16 teaspoon cayenne pepper
1 1/2 cups yellow cornmeal
2 tablespoons salt-free chili powder
1 tablespoon low-sodium baking powder
1/4 teaspoon red pepper flakes
1/4 teaspoon garlic powder
1 can (16 ounces) salt-tree tomatoes
4 jumbo egg whites
1 large onion, chopped
1 large green pepper, chopped
1 cup frozen corn kernels
3/4 cup sliced fresh mushrooms
1/4 Baked Banana (page 57)
1 1/2 cups (12 ounces) nonfat cottage cheese
Paprika
1 large fresh tomato, sliced
2 tablespoons grated sapsago cheese
Extra red pepper flakes
1/2 cup chopped raw onion (optional)

Slow Cooker Directions for Beans: Rinse the beans. Combine with the tomatoes and water in a slow cooker. Cover and cook on high setting for 4 1/2 hours. Add the remaining ingredients, except the cayenne, and cook for another 30 to 40 minutes, until the onion is tender. Taste. If the chili powder you are using contains cayenne you probably won't need any more cayenne. Add the cayenne if the beans taste at all bland.

Stove Top Directions: Cooking beans on top of the stove is at least a half-day job, so be sure you will not have to leave the house once you start. Rinse the beans. Combine the beans and tomatoes in a 5-quart stockpot. Add the water, cover, and simmer for about 3 hours. Stir every so often to keep the beans from burning. Add the remaining ingredients, except for the cayenne, and simmer for another 30 to 40 minutes, until the onion is tender. You shouldn't need any more water, but if the beans start to dry out, add more, as needed. Taste. If the chili powder you are using contains cayenne you probably won't need any more cayenne. Add the cayenne if the beans taste at all bland.

When your red beans are almost cooked, preheat the oven to 400 degrees F. Spray a 9-inch-by-13-inch baking dish with nonstick spray. Pour 1 table-spoon of water and 1 tablespoon of juice concentrate into a nonstick frying pan. Add the eggplant. Sprinkle 1/16 teaspoon cayenne over the eggplant. Turn the heat to high and cook until the eggplant is sizzling and turning brown on the bottom; then turn it over. Let it sizzle a little longer, then stir constantly until the eggplant has changed to a darker color and is almost cooked through. Set aside.

In a large bowl, combine the cornmeal, chili powder, baking powder, 1/4 teaspoon red pepper flakes, and the garlic powder. Add the tomatoes by cutting them up right in the bowl. Combine thoroughly. Add the egg whites and the remaining 1/2 cup of juice concentrate and combine. Add the onion, green pepper, corn, mushrooms, the banana plus its baking juices, and cooked eggplant, mixing after each addition. Pour the mixture into the baking dish, spreading it evenly. Top with the cottage cheese and if a little red shows through here and there, it's all right. Sprinkle with a little paprika for color. Decorate the top with the tomato slices. Sprinkle with sapsago cheese and a few extra red pepper flakes for color and flavor. Cover the dish with aluminum foil and slit it with a knife to allow the steam to escape.

Place on the middle rack of the oven and bake for 25 minutes. Remove the aluminum foil and bake for another 30 to 40 minutes, or until the top has browned a bit, the tomatoes look cooked, and a toothpick inserted into the center comes out clean. Remove from the oven and let sit for 10 minutes before serving.

To serve, cut the bread in squares and serve with 1 cup of beans. Sprinkle with about 3/4 tablespoon chopped raw onions, if desired. My husband adds a little hot sauce. This bread freezes beautifully in sealed plastic bags for future meals, as do the beans in cup-size containers.

MEXICAN-STYLE RED BEANS

Nutrition Facts

Amount Per Serving	
Calories 250	Calories from Fat 15

	% Daily Value*
Total Fat 2g	3%
Saturated Fat 0g	0%
Cholesterol 0mg	0%
Sodium 45mg	2%
Total Carbohydrate 50g	17%
Dietary Fiber 9g	37%
Sugars 9g	
Protein 11g	

Vitamin A 20%	•	Vitamin C 60%
Calcium 4%	•	Iron 20%

Chilies Relleños (page 216) is the perfect accompaniment to this dish. Use only a slow cooker for cooking these beans because a pot on the stove needs to be watched.

2 2/3 cups (1 pound) dry red kidney beans
9 cups water
1/4 cup salt-free chili powder
1 cup chopped green pepper
2 tablespoons minced dried onion
1 tablespoon dried parsley
2 teaspoons dried celery flakes
1/4 teaspoon dried red pepper flakes
1/2 cup apple juice concentrate
1 1/2 cups frozen or 1 can (17 ounces) salt-free whole kernel corn, drained
1 cup yellow cornmeal
Chopped raw onions (optional)
Chopped raw jalapeño peppers (optional)
Apple cider vinegar (optional)
Medium red hot sauce (optional)

Combine the beans and water in a slow cooker. Cover and cook on high setting 4 1/2 hours. (Cook covered on low setting if you are going to be out of the house for more than 4 1/2 hours.) When the beans are soft, add the chili powder, green pepper, onion, parsley, celery flakes, pepper, and juice concentrate. Cover and continue cooking on high for 1 hour more. Add the corn and cornmeal. Stir to combine thoroughly, cover, and cook 40 minutes on high setting, stirring twice. Serve immediately. If you can't serve immediately, set the temperature on low, and stir occasionally.

At the table, pass raw chopped onions, chopped jalapeño peppers, vinegar, or red hot sauce.

Freeze leftovers in 1-cup or 2-cup portions. Reheat, covered, in the microwave, or on top of the stove in a double boiler. Add a little water if the mixture seems too thick.

PINTO BEANS

YIELD: 14 (1/2-CUP) SERVINGS

Nutrition Facts

Amount Per Serving

Calories 130	Calories from Fat 5

	% Daily Value*
Total Fat 1g	**1%**
Saturated Fat 0g	**0%**
Cholesterol 0mg	**0%**
Sodium 60mg	**2%**
Total Carbohydrate 26g	**9%**
Dietary Fiber 9g	**36%**
Sugars 4g	
Protein 7g	

Vitamin A 15%	•	Vitamin C 25%
Calcium 6%	•	Iron 15%

These are great served with heated corn or fat-free tortillas and a vegetable or a salad. Add a little Piquante Sauce. Add a small serving of broiled hamburger or steak, if you can afford the calories that day. This recipe is enough for two separate meals for most families.

2 2/3 cups (1 pound) dried pinto beans
9 cups water
1/4 cup dried celery flakes
1/4 cup dried onion flakes
1/4 cup chili powder
2 teaspoons garlic powder
2 teaspoons low-sodium soy sauce
1 large green pepper, diced
1/2 teaspoon red pepper flakes
3 tablespoons apple juice concentrate
2 tablespoons fresh lemon juice

Slow Cooker Directions: Rinse the beans and combine them in a 5-quart slow cooker with the water. Cover and cook on high setting for 4 1/2 hours. Add the remaining ingredients, except for the lemon juice, and cook for another 30 to 40 minutes. Stir in the lemon juice just before serving.

Stove Top Directions: Rinse the beans and combine them in a 5-quart stockpot with the water. Cover and simmer for 3 1/3 hours, stirring frequently. Add the remaining ingredients, except for the lemon juice, and simmer for another 30 to 40 minutes. Stir in the lemon juice just before serving.

QUICK AND EASY PINTO BEANS

These beans take just as long to cook as other bean recipes, but they are quick to prepare because you don't have to chop anything.

2 2/3 cups (1 pound) dried pinto beans
9 cups water
1/4 cup dried celery
1/4 cup dried chopped onion
1/4 cup salt-free chili powder
2 teaspoons garlic powder
1/4 cup dried green (sweet bell) pepper
1/4 to 1/2 teaspoon cayenne pepper
3 tablespoons apple juice concentrate
2 teaspoons low-sodium soy sauce
2 tablespoons fresh lemon juice

Slow Cooker Directions: Rinse the beans and combine with the water in a 5-quart slow cooker. Cover and cook on high setting for 4 1/2 hours. Add the remaining ingredients, except for the lemon juice, and cook for another 30 to 40 minutes. Stir in the lemon juice just before serving.

Stove Top Directions: Rinse the beans and combine them with the water in a 5-quart stockpot. Cover and simmer for 3 1/2 hours, stirring frequently. Add the remaining ingredients, except for the lemon juice, and simmer for another 30 to 40 minutes. Stir in the lemon juice just before serving.

Variation: PINTO BEANS AND PINEAPPLE

For a tropical touch and some really great flavor, cook the beans exactly as for Quick and Easy Pinto Beans, but instead of adding lemon juice, add one 20-ounce can of well-drained, unsweetened pineapple chunks.

PINTO BEANS AND MACARONI

YIELD: 14 SERVINGS

Nutrition Facts

Amount Per Serving	
Calories 200	Calories from Fat 5
	% Daily Value*
Total Fat 1g	**1%**
Saturated Fat 0g	**0%**
Cholesterol 0mg	**0%**
Sodium 15mg	**1%**
Total Carbohydrate 39g	**13%**
Dietary Fiber 9g	**37%**
Sugars 7g	
Protein 9g	
Vitamin A 35% • Vitamin C 30%	
Calcium 6% • Iron 15%	

2 2/3 cups (1 pound) dried pinto beans
9 cups water
1 large carrot, sliced
1 1/2 cups chopped onion
1 1/3 cups chopped green pepper
4 tablespoons salt-free tomato paste
6 tablespoons apple juice concentrate
1 1/2 teaspoons salt-free chili powder
1/4 teaspoon cayenne pepper
2 cups uncooked semolina or whole wheat elbow macaroni

Slow Cooker Directions: Rinse the beans and combine them with the water in a 5-quart slow cooker. Cover and cook on high setting for 4 1/2 hours. Add the remaining ingredients and cook for another 30 to 40 minutes, until the green pepper is tender. Remove 1 cup of the beans and purée in a blender, or mash with a fork. Return them to the pot to make the beans extra creamy.

Stove Top Directions: Rinse the beans and combine them with the water in a 5-quart stockpot. Cover and simmer for 3 1/3 hours, stirring frequently. Add the remaining ingredients and simmer for another 30 to 40 minutes, until the green pepper is tender. Remove 1 cup of beans and purée in a blender, or mash with a fork. Return them to the pot to make the beans extra creamy.

Boil 2 quarts of water in a 5-quart stockpot. Add 2 cups raw semolina or whole wheat macaroni to the fast boiling water. Stir. Cook about 10 minutes for semolina noodles and about 15 minutes for whole wheat noodles, stirring occasionally. Drain.

To serve, place the macaroni on individual serving plates and top with the beans. A little chopped, raw onion is good on top of the beans, or a little hot sauce.

BLACK BEANS

Nutrition Facts

Amount Per Serving

Calories 140	Calories from Fat 5

	% Daily Value*
Total Fat 0.5g	**1%**
Saturated Fat 0g	**0%**
Cholesterol 0mg	**0%**
Sodium 5mg	**0%**
Total Carbohydrate 26g	**9%**
Dietary Fiber 7g	**26%**
Sugars 7g	
Protein 9g	

Vitamin A 4%	•	Vitamin C 30%	
Calcium 6%	•	Iron 10%	

2 2/3 cups (1 pound) dried black beans
9 cups water
1 cup chopped onions (2 medium onions)
1 cup chopped green pepper (1 large pepper)
1 rib celery and leaves, chopped
1/2 cup chopped fresh parsley
1/4 teaspoon red pepper flakes
1/2 teaspoon garlic powder
1/2 teaspoon dried thyme

Slow Cooker Directions: Rinse the beans. Combine with the water in a 5-quart slow cooker. Cook on high setting for 4 1/2 hours. Add the remaining ingredients and cook for another 30 to 40 minutes.

Stove Top Directions: Rinse the beans. Combine them with the water in a 5-quart stockpot. Simmer for 2 1/2 hours until beans are tender. Add the remaining ingredients and simmer, covered, for another 30 to 40 minutes until vegetables are tender.

Just for fun, taste the beans before you add anything to them. I think you will be surprised how sweet and good they taste. You might like them just as they are.

Variation: BLACK BEAN SOUP

Just add water to cooked black beans to create a delightful soup. Serve with a crusty bread or warm tortillas.

BLACK BEAN POTATO SOUP

1 small potato, peeled and diced
1 medium onion, chopped
1/2 cup finely chopped carrots
2 cups chicken stock
1/2 cup cooked Black Beans (page 268)
Cayenne pepper (optional)

Microwave Directions: Combine potato, onion, carrots, and chicken stock in a 2-quart covered container, and cook 5 minutes on high setting. Then cook, covered, on medium setting for 5 minutes, or until the vegetables are tender. Add beans and a little water, if necessary, and heat through. Sprinkle with a little cayenne pepper if desired.

Stove Top Directions: Add the potato, onion, and carrots to the chicken stock in a 2-quart saucepan, and bring to a boil. Cover and cook over medium heat about 5 minutes, or until the vegetables are tender. Add beans and a little water, if necessary, and heat through. Sprinkle with a little cayenne pepper if desired.

CONFETTI BEANS

This is very good served with Spanish Rice (page 257)

1/2 cup cooked Black Beans (page 268)
1/2 cup frozen or fresh whole kernel corn
1/2 cup cooked lima beans
2 roasted green chili peppers, chopped or 1 can (4 ounces) of chopped green chili peppers

Microwave Directions: Combine all the ingredients in a quart-size container and cover. Microwave on high setting for 6 minutes, or until the corn is tender.

Stove Top Directions: Combine all the ingredients in a medium saucepan and cover. Cook over a medium heat for about 6 minutes, stirring frequently until the corn is tender.

BLACK-EYED PEAS

YIELD: 12 (1/2-CUP) SERVINGS

Nutrition Facts

Amount Per Serving

Calories 50	Calories from Fat 0

	% Daily Value²
Total Fat 0g	0%
Saturated Fat 0g	0%
Cholesterol 0mg	0%
Sodium 10mg	0%
Total Carbohydrate 11g	4%
Dietary Fiber 3g	10%
Sugars 3g	
Protein 2g	

Vitamin A 8%	•	Vitamin C 20%
Calcium 6%	•	Iron 4%

Black-eyed peas are delicious alone or as an ingredient in Jambalaya au Congri.

2 2/3 cups (1 pound) dried black-eyed peas
10 cups water
2 bay leaves
1 cup chopped celery with some leaves
2 medium onions, chopped
1 small green pepper, chopped
3/4 teaspoon cayenne pepper
1 1/2 teaspoon dried thyme
2 tablespoons orange juice concentrate

Slow Cooker Directions: Rinse the peas and combine them with the water and the bay leaves in a 5-quart slow cooker. Set on high setting and cook for 4 1/2 hours. Add the remaining ingredients and cook for another 30 to 40 minutes.

Stove Top Directions: Rinse the peas and combine them with the water and the bay leaves in a 5-quart stockpot. Cover and simmer for 1 hour. Add the remaining ingredients and simmer, covered, for another 30 to 40 minutes.

LIMA BEANS

Nutrition Facts

Amount Per Serving

Calories 50	Calories from Fat 0

	% Daily Value*
Total Fat 0g	**0%**
Saturated Fat 0g	**0%**
Cholesterol 0mg	**0%**
Sodium 5mg	**0%**
Total Carbohydrate 9g	**3%**
Dietary Fiber 2g	**9%**
Sugars 2g	
Protein 3g	

Vitamin A 35%	•	Vitamin C 25%
Calcium 2%	•	Iron 8%

These beans are really delicious by themselves, so taste them before you add the onions, green pepper, carrots, and cayenne. You might be surprised.

2 2/3 cups (1 pound) dried large or baby lima beans
9 cups water
3/4 cup chopped green pepper (1 small pepper)
1/2 cup chopped onion (1 medium onion)
1/4 cup chopped carrot (one small to medium carrot)
1/4 teaspoon cayenne pepper

Slow Cooker Directions: Rinse the beans. Combine with the water in a 5-quart slow cooker. Cover and cook on high setting for 4 1/2 hours. Add the remaining ingredients and cook for another 30 to 40 minutes, until the vegetables are tender.

Stove Top Directions: Rinse the beans. Combine with the water in a 5-quart stockpot. Cover and simmer for 3 hours, stirring frequently. Add the other ingredients and cook for another 30 to 40 minutes, until the vegetables are tender.

VARIATION: LIMA RED BEAN SOUP

Yield: 1 serving. Combine 1/2 cup cooked lima beans and 1/2 cup cooked Red Beans (page 261) in a microwave container or saucepan. Add about a half cup of water. Heat through in the microwave or on top of the stove. Add more water if mixture is not soupy enough.

LIMA BEAN SOUP

Nutrition Facts

Amount Per Serving

Calories 250	Calories from Fat 5

	% Daily Value*
Total Fat 1g	1%
Saturated Fat 0g	0%
Cholesterol 0mg	0%
Sodium 55mg	2%
Total Carbohydrate 46g	15%
Dietary Fiber 14g	58%
Sugars 9g	
Protein 16g	

Vitamin A 15%	•	Vitamin C 70%
Calcium 6%	•	Iron 25%

1/2 cup fresh or frozen green peas
1 cup cooked Lima Beans (page 271)

Microwave Directions: Combine peas in 1/2 cup water in a microwave-proof container. Cover and cook for 5 minutes on high setting, or a little longer, until peas are tender. Add the cooked lima beans, heat through, and stir. Add a little more water if necessary, and heat again before serving.

Stove Top Directions: Combine peas in 1/2 cup water in a covered saucepan, and cook over medium heat for 5 minutes, or until peas are tender. Add 1 cup of cooked lima beans, heat through, and stir. Add a little more water if necessary, and heat again before serving.

LIMA BEAN CORN SOUP

Nutrition Facts

Amount Per Serving

Calories 230	Calories from Fat 10

	% Daily Value*
Total Fat 1g	1%
Saturated Fat 0g	0%
Cholesterol 0mg	0%
Sodium 55mg	2%
Total Carbohydrate 45g	15%
Dietary Fiber 13g	50%
Sugars 8g	
Protein 13g	

Vitamin A 10%	•	Vitamin C 60%
Calcium 6%	•	Iron 20%

2 cups cooked Lima Beans (page 271)
1 cup frozen chuck wagon-style corn or equal parts corn kernels, green bell peppers, tomatoes, and onions of either fresh or frozen vegetables

Microwave Directions: Cook corn according to directions on the package, or for your own mixture, cook on high setting, covered in 1/2 cup water for 4 minutes, or until the vegetables are tender. Then add the beans and enough water to make a soup consistency. Heat through and serve.

Stove Top Directions: Cook corn according to directions on the package, or for your own mixture, add 3/4 cup of water and cook over a medium heat in a covered saucepan, 4 to 5 minutes after the water has begun to boil, or until the onions and corn are tender. Then add the beans and enough water to make a soup consistency. Heat through and serve.

NAVY BEANS

Nutrition Facts

Amount Per Serving	
Calories 170	Calories from Fat 5
	% Daily Value*
Total Fat 1g	**1%**
Saturated Fat 0g	**0%**
Cholesterol 0mg	**0%**
Sodium 55mg	**2%**
Total Carbohydrate 31g	**10%**
Dietary Fiber 12g	**48%**
Sugars 4g	
Protein 11g	
Vitamin A 35% • Vitamin C 15%	
Calcium 8% • Iron 20%	

2 2/3 cups (1 pound) dried navy beans
9 cups water
1 large carrot, finely chopped
1 small green pepper, chopped
1 small tomato, chopped
1 medium onion, chopped
1 tablespoon low-sodium tamari or soy sauce
1 tablespoon apple juice concentrate
1/4 teaspoon paprika
1/4 teaspoon cayenne pepper
1 teaspoon dry mustard

Slow Cooker Directions: Rinse the beans. Combine with the water and carrot in a 5-quart slow cooker. Cover and cook on high setting for 4 1/2 hours. Add the remaining ingredients and cook for another 30 to 40 minutes, until the vegetables are tender.

Stove Top Directions: Rinse the beans. Combine with the water and carrot in a 5-quart stockpot. Cover and simmer for 3 hours. Add the remaining ingredients and simmer for another 30 to 40 minutes, until the vegetables are tender.

Variation: GREAT NORTHERN BEANS

Substitute great northern beans for the navy beans and follow the directions.

NAVY BEANS IN A THERMOS

1 cup cooked Navy Beans (page 273)
1/4 cup chopped onions
1/2 jalapeño pepper, deseeded and chopped
1 sliced banana

Heat the navy beans and banana and pour into a thermos jug. Top with the raw onions and chopped pepper. Seal the thermos and take with you for a warm and hearty lunch.

NAVY BEAN PEPPER SOUP

1/2 cup Chicken Stock (page 44)
1 medium onion, sliced
1 teaspoon dried parsley or 1 tablespoon fresh chopped parsley
1/2 cup cooked navy beans
1/2 jalapeño pepper, deseeded and chopped

Microwave Directions: Combine the onion, parsley, and chicken stock in a quart-size container. Cover and cook on high setting for 5 minutes. Add the navy beans. Heat through. Add the raw peppers and serve.

Stove Top Directions: Combine the onion, parsley, and chicken stock in a medium saucepan. Bring to a boil, then lower the heat, cover, and cook over medium heat, until the onion is tender, about 5 minutes after the water starts to boil. Add the navy beans. Add water if necessary. Add the raw peppers and serve.

QUARTEE BEANS AND RICE

YIELD: 7 SERVINGS

Nutrition Facts

Amount Per Serving

Calories 330	Calories from Fat 20

	% Daily Value*
Total Fat 2g	3%
Saturated Fat 0g	0%
Cholesterol 0mg	0%
Sodium 25mg	1%
Total Carbohydrate 65g	22%
Dietary Fiber 10g	40%
Sugars 6g	
Protein 15g	

Vitamin A 10%	•	Vitamin C 50%
Calcium 6%	•	Iron 20%

My daddy used to tell the story about his grandfather John Peyronnin who ran away to join the Confederate Army when he was a young man. He was gravely injured during the Battle of Shiloh and was sent home to die, but he lived until age 95 with the bullet still in his head near his ear.

After the war, he opened a grocery store in New Orleans on Poydras Street near Baronne. Customers used to come in asking for a-half-a-nickel's worth of beans or a-half-a-nickel's worth of rice, but they would always pay with a nickel. Now how do you give a person 2 1/2 cents in change? Well, my great-grandfather solved the problem by minting his own coins with 2 1/2 cents printed on one side, and a "p" for "Peyronnin" on the other. People would come in and ask for a "quartee of beans" and a "quartee of rice," and it got to be a regular thing all over New Orleans to give "quartees" in change equal to half-a-nickel. I found this poem in a history of New Orleans:

> *"Gimme a quartee red beans,*
> *Quartee of rice,*
> *Little piece of salt meat to make it*
> *Taste nice.*
> *Lend me the paper, tell me the time,*
> *When papa passes by he will pay you a dime."*

1 1/3 cups (1/2 pound) dried red kidney beans
1 1/3 cups (1/2 pound) dried large lima beans
1 can (16 ounces) salt-free tomatoes
7 1/2 cups water
1 cup frozen whole kernel corn
1 onion, chopped
1 green pepper, sliced in strips
1/4 teaspoon cayenne pepper
7 cups cooked instant brown rice

Slow Cooker Directions: Rinse the beans and pour into a 5-quart slow cooker. Add the tomatoes and water. Break the tomatoes up with a wooden spoon. Cover, and cook on high setting for 4 1/2 hours. Add the remaining ingredients and cook for another 30 to 40 minutes, or until the green pepper is tender.

Stove Top Directions: Rinse the beans and pour them into a 5-quart stockpot. Add the tomatoes and water. Break the tomatoes up with a wooden spoon. Cover and simmer for about 3 hours. Add the remaining ingredients and simmer for another 30 to 40 minutes, or until the green pepper is tender.

LENTILS

YIELD: 12 (1/2-CUP) SERVINGS

Nutrition Facts

Amount Per Serving

Calories 150	Calories from Fat 0

	% Daily Value*
Total Fat 0g	**0**%
Saturated Fat 0g	**0**%
Cholesterol 0mg	**0**%
Sodium 55mg	**2**%
Total Carbohydrate 28g	**9**%
Dietary Fiber 12g	**49**%
Sugars 7g	
Protein 11g	

Vitamin A 30%	•	Vitamin C 15%
Calcium 2%	•	Iron 20%

Lentils are very bland by themselves, but they are nice to add to soups and other dishes. The mace and lemon juice in this recipe really wake this dish up.

2 2/3 cups (1 pound) dried lentils
9 cups water
1 cup chopped onions
1/2 cup chopped green pepper
1/2 cup chopped carrots
6 tablespoons apple juice concentrate
3/4 teaspoon cayenne pepper
1 tablespoon low-sodium tamari or soy sauce
1/2 teaspoon mace
4 teaspoons fresh lemon juice

Slow Cooker Directions: Rinse the lentils. Combine with the water in a 5-quart slow cooker. Cover and cook on high setting for 4 1/2 hours. Add the remaining ingredients, except for the lemon juice, and cook for another 30 to 40 minutes, until the vegetables are tender. Add the lemon juice, stir, and serve.

Stove Top Directions: Rinse the lentils. Combine with the water in a 5-quart stockpot. Cover and simmer for 2 hours, stirring occasionally. Add the remaining ingredients, except for the lemon juice, and simmer for another 30 to 40 minutes, until the vegetables are tender. Add the lemon juice, stir, and serve.

Variation: PINTO LENTIL SOUP

Mix 1/2 cup cooked Pinto Beans (page 265) and 1/2 cup cooked lentils. Add a little water to make a soup-like consistency. Heat. Taste. Add cayenne pepper if you think it needs some. Makes 1 serving.

LENTIL VEGGIE SOUP

1/2 cup cauliflower, carrots, and broccoli mixed in equal amounts (I find it mixed in a bag in the frozen food section of my grocery)
1/2 cup Cooked Lentils (page 276)
1 teaspoon dried onion flakes
Water
1/16 teaspoon cayenne pepper, or more to taste

Microwave Directions: Combine the cauliflower, carrots, broccoli, and onion flakes with 1/2 cup water in a 1 1/2-quart container. Cover and cook on high setting for 3 minutes. Add lentils and heat through. Add more water to thin, or cook it down a little to thicken, then stir in pepper. Serve hot.

Stove Top Directions: Combine the cauliflower, carrots, broccoli, and onion flakes with 1/2 cup water in a 1 1/2-quart saucepan. Cover and cook over high heat until the vegetables are tender, about for 3 minutes after the water starts to boil. Add lentils and heat through. Add more water if too thin, or cook it down a little to thicken. Stir in pepper last. Pour in a thermos for lunch.

LENTIL POTATO SOUP

1/2 cup uncooked, diced potato
3/4 cup Cooked Lentils (page 276)
Water

Microwave Directions: Combine the potato with 1/4 cup of water in a quart-size container. Cover and cook on high setting for 5 minutes. Add 3/4 cup Cooked Lentils, heat through, and serve.

Stove Top Directions: Combine the potato with 1/4 cup of water in a quart-size container. Bring to a boil, cover, and cook over low heat for 5 minutes, or until tender. Be careful not to burn them. Add a little more water, if needed. Add 3/4 cup cooked Lentils, and heat through. Pour in a thermos if you are taking it along with you for lunch.

SPLIT PEA SOUP

YIELD: 11 SERVINGS

Nutrition Facts

Amount Per Serving	
Calories 170	Calories from Fat 0

	% Daily Value*
Total Fat 0g	0%
Saturated Fat 0g	0%
Cholesterol 0mg	0%
Sodium 15mg	1%
Total Carbohydrate 31g	10%
Dietary Fiber less than 1 gram	3%
Sugars 3g	
Protein 11g	

Vitamin A 70%	•	Vitamin C	4%
Calcium 2%	•	Iron	10%

10 cups water
1 pound dried split peas (2 2/3 cups)
2 carrots, minced
3 ribs celery, minced
1 large onion, chopped to a 1/2-inch dice
3 bay leaves
1 teaspoon dried thyme, or 2 sprigs fresh thyme
Cayenne pepper

Slow Cooker Directions: Rinse peas and cover with water in a 5-quart slow cooker. Add the carrots, onion, and celery. Cook on the high setting for 4 to 5 hours, until the peas are soft. Before the last half hour of cooking, add the thyme and bay leaves.

Stove Top Directions: Rinse the peas. Combine the water, peas, carrots, celery, and onion in a 5-quart stockpot. Cover and simmer for 2 1/2 to 3 hours, stirring frequently, and adding water if it gets too thick. Before the last half hour of cooking add the bay leaves and thyme. Serve the soup in individual bowls and sprinkle with cayenne pepper. Freeze leftovers in individual airtight containers.

BEAUCOUP BEAN SOUP

YIELD: 14 SERVINGS

Nutrition Facts

Amount Per Serving	
Calories 160	Calories from Fat 5

	% Daily Value*
Total Fat 1g	1%
Saturated Fat 0g	0%
Cholesterol 0mg	0%
Sodium 160mg	7%
Total Carbohydrate 30g	10%
Dietary Fiber 8g	33%
Sugars 5g	
Protein 10g	

Vitamin A 10%	•	Vitamin C 40%
Calcium 6%	•	Iron 15%

This is an adaptation of an old Louisiana plantation recipe. Of course, originally it was seasoned with ham, but I promise, you won't miss the ham at all. You can, however, add shrimp or chicken chunks for a nice variation. "Beaucoup" (pronounced bo-koo) is the French word for "plenty," so the name literally means "lots of beans soup." If you can't find every type of bean, either leave some out, and make up for the difference with the beans you have, or add other kinds, such as split peas, another color lentil, or crowders.

1/3 cup uncooked large lima beans
1/3 cup uncooked red kidney beans
1/3 cup uncooked navy beans
1/3 cup uncooked lentils
1/3 cup uncooked black-eyed peas
1/3 cup uncooked black beans
1/3 cup uncooked baby lima beans
1/3 cup uncooked garbanzo beans (chick peas)
1/3 cup uncooked great northern beans
1/3 cup uncooked mung beans
1/3 cup uncooked pinto beans
13 cups water
1/3 cup Roast Beef Gravy, I or II (page 48 or page 50)
2 bay leaves
1/4 cup salt-free tomato paste
1 can (4 ounces) hot or mild whole green chilies
2 medium onions, coarsely chopped
1 very large green pepper, coarsely chopped
1 teaspoon garlic powder or 5 cloves, chopped
1/2 teaspoon red pepper flakes
1/2 teaspoon dried thyme
1 tablespoon low-sodium soy sauce
Juice of 1 large lemon

Slow Cooker Directions: Pour all the beans into a 5-quart slow cooker. Add the water and roast beef gravy, then add the bay leaves and tomato paste. Cook for 5 hours on a high setting. Thirty minutes before serving, rinse and chop the chilies and add them to the soup. Then add the remaining ingredients except the lemon juice. Cook for 30 minutes until the onions and green pepper are tender. Stir in the fresh lemon juice and serve. The lemon does something wonderful for this soup.

Stove Top Directions: Add the beans to a 5-quart stockpot. Add the water and roast beef gravy, then add bay leaves and tomato paste. Bring to a boil, then set the heat to low, cover, and simmer for about 3 1/2 hours, stirring occasionally, until the beans are tender. You will probably have to add a little more water as it cooks. Just simmer it slowly so you don't burn the beans. Thirty minutes before serving, rinse and chop the chilies and add them to the soup. Then add the remaining ingredients except the lemon juice. Cook for 30 minutes until the onions and green pepper are tender. Stir in the fresh lemon juice and serve.

This will keep very well in the refrigerator and tastes even better 1 or 2 days later. It freezes well, too.

BURRITO WRAP UPS

Nutrition Facts

Amount Per Serving

Calories 220	Calories from Fat 15

	% Daily Value*
Total Fat 2g	**3%**
Saturated Fat 0g	**0%**
Cholesterol 0mg	**0%**
Sodium 25mg	**1%**
Total Carbohydrate 42g	**14%**
Dietary Fiber 8g	**34%**
Sugars 3g	
Protein 10g	

Vitamin A 15%	•	Vitamin C 4%
Calcium 10%	•	Iron 15%

This is great for a quick lunch or dinner if you happen to have some cooked black beans on hand.

4 heated corn tortillas
1 cup cooked Black Beans (page 268)
1 1/2 teaspoons chili powder
Chopped onions (optional)

Microwave Directions: If your tortillas are frozen you can thaw and heat them at the same time. To do this in the microwave, place the tortillas in an open plastic bag and heat on high setting for 2 minutes. Check to see if they are hot enough and heat again if necessary.

Stove Top Directions: If your tortillas are frozen you can thaw and heat them at the same time. Place a large saucepan with about an inch of water in it on the stove. Set the heat on high. Place a colander over the water, place the frozen tortillas in the colander and cover. When the water starts to boil the tortillas will be ready to eat, in about 2 1/2 minutes.

If your tortillas are defrosted and refrigerated, reduce the heating times by half.

Mix chili powder with the beans and heat them in either a smaller container in the microwave or in a small saucepan on the stove top. To serve, pour beans over tortillas on the plates one at a time and fold each one over the beans. Pour extra beans over the folded tortillas. Sprinkle with raw onions, if desired.

Variation:

Use fat-free flour tortillas and follow the same directions as for using corn tortillas.

CHAPTER 9

Salads and Dressings

Salads are really an important part of your diet, and you can eat just about all you want of them.

I know that many of you think of salads in terms of lettuce, tomatoes, and maybe cucumbers, and some vinaigrette or a cream-based dressing. This chapter should convince you that almost any fruit or vegetable can be part of a salad and healthy dressings can be delicious.

I don't always specify a certain type of lettuce in the recipes because you can use any kind of lettuce you want. As far as the calorie count goes, lettuces are so low you don't have to worry if you add a leaf or two. The same goes for cucumbers, tomatoes, radishes, cabbage, asparagus, watercress, mushrooms, cauliflower, and parsley. Celery, broccoli, and artichokes have a little more sodium than other salad ingredients, but celery and artichokes are very low-cal. Do watch the calories with carrots, green peas, and broccoli, and when in doubt, refer to the charts in Chapter 1.

If you see some unusual things at the grocery that look like they might be good in a salad, go ahead and try them. Be creative and have fun.

Some of the dressings which last a long time in the refrigerator, such as Vinaigrette, Greek, and Italian Dressings, I make by the quart and use them over several nights. My husband likes to go in the kitchen *after* dinner to make himself snacks. To combat this behavior, I usually don't make salad for dinner except for the dressing. That way Ray can go wild after he eats his main meal, tearing up lettuce and chopping vegetables, taking up a lot of time, and not eating fattening things.

CHICKEN SALAD

Nutrition Facts

Amount Per Serving

Calories 160   Calories from Fat 35

	% Daily Value*
Total Fat 4g	**6%**
Saturated Fat 1g	**5%**
Cholesterol 40mg	**13%**
Sodium 170mg	**7%**
Total Carbohydrate 14g	**5%**
Dietary Fiber 3g	**12%**
Sugars 8g	
Protein 19g	

Vitamin A 30%	•	Vitamin C 90%
Calcium 6%	•	Iron 8%

This chicken salad is as delicious as any you will ever eat. Use nonfat cottage cheese if you want more calcium and don't mind the calories.

1 to 2 cooked, boned chicken breasts (approx. 6 ounces), diced
1 cup chopped celery
1/2 cup plus 1 teaspoon minced onion
1/2 cup nonfat cottage cheese or Kraft fat-free mayonnaise dressing
1 teaspoon apple juice concentrate
1/16 teaspoon cayenne pepper
1/16 teaspoon curry powder
1/2 teaspoon medium red hot sauce
Juice of 1/4 large lemon
4 medium tomatoes
8 lettuce leaves

In a large mixing bowl, combine the chicken, celery, and 1/2 cup of the chopped onion and set aside.

If Using Nonfat Cottage Cheese: In a blender, combine the remaining 1 teaspoon minced onion, cottage cheese, juice concentrate, pepper, curry powder, hot sauce, and lemon juice. Blend until very smooth, then combine with the chicken.

If Using Fat-Free Mayonnaise Dressing: In a large bowl, combine the fat-free mayonnaise dressing, onion, juice concentrate, pepper, curry powder, hot sauce, and lemon juice with the chicken.

Refrigerate for at least 20 minutes to mingle the flavors.

Crosscut the tomatoes at least 4 times, but do not cut all the way through. Open the tomatoes to look like a flower and set on beds of lettuce. Stuff each of the tomatoes with 2 to 3 tablespoons of the chicken salad.

CHICKEN SALAD WAIKIKI

Nutrition Facts

Amount Per Serving

Calories 130   Calories from Fat 20

	% Daily Value*
Total Fat 2g	3%
Saturated Fat 0.5g	3%
Cholesterol 20mg	7%
Sodium 80mg	3%
Total Carbohydrate 18g	6%
Dietary Fiber 1g	5%
Sugars 16g	
Protein 11g	

Vitamin A 2%	•	Vitamin C 20%
Calcium 4%	•	Iron 4%

This is a beautiful and delicious molded salad that has a clear, jelled top with the fruit showing through, and an opaque bottom which has to be made separately. Be sure to use canned pineapple and juice because fresh pineapple juice won't gel. Note: There are 4 cups of pineapple juice in all, so you will have to buy some canned pineapple juice other than what comes in the cans with the fruit.

For the Top:
1 can (20 ounces) unsweetened pineapple slices and juice
2 cups reserved juice from 1 (20 ounces) can unsweetened pineapple chunks
2 tablespoons apple juice concentrate
1 envelope unflavored gelatin
6 red seedless grapes

For the Bottom:
1 pound (16 ounces) cooked, white chicken meat, diced
1/2 cup finely chopped onion
1/2 cup chopped celery
1 cup diced red apple (do not peel)
2 cups canned pineapple juice (not reserved juice from above)
2 tablespoons apple juice concentrate
2 envelopes unflavored gelatin
1 1/2 cups (12 ounces) nonfat cottage cheese
1/4 teaspoon cayenne pepper
2 cups (one 20-ounce can) unsweetened pineapple chunks
1 banana, sliced
2 cups reserved pineapple rings, for garnish
More grapes, for garnish

For the top layer: Drain both cans of pineapple, set aside the fruit and reserve the juice. (You should have 2 cups of juice.) Add the apple juice concentrate to the 2 cups of reserved pineapple juice to make 4 cups of fruit juice in all. (If you don't have 4 cups, add more apple juice concentrate.) Pour 1/2 cup of the apple-pineapple juice mixture into a 2-cup container and mix in 1 envelope of gelatin to soften it. In a saucepan, bring the remaining juice mixture to a boil. Mix the hot juice with the gelatin mixture and stir until all the gelatin has dissolved.

Pour 1 1/4 cups of the gelatin-juice mixture into a 4-quart ring mold or bundt cake pan. Refrigerate for about 40 minutes, until almost solid.

Arrange 6 pineapple ring slices on top of the gelatin, and place a grape inside each ring. Reserve the leftover pineapple rings. Pour the rest of the gelatin mixture over the fruit carefully, so you don't disturb your design. Refrigerate for about 20 minutes, until almost solid. Meanwhile, prepare the bottom of the salad.

For the bottom layer: Combine the chicken, onion, celery, and apple in a large bowl and set aside. In a separate bowl, mix the 2 cups of reserved pineapple juice and the remaining 2 tablespoons of apple juice concentrate. Pour 1/2 cup of the juice mixture into a 2-cup container; sprinkle 2 envelopes of gelatin over and stir to soften. In a saucepan, bring the rest of the juice to a boil. Combine the hot juice with the gelatin mixture and stir until the gelatin completely dissolves.

In a blender, combine the cottage cheese, juice-gelatin mixture, and cayenne. Blend until smooth.

Combine the cottage cheese mixture with the chicken. Add the pineapple chunks and the banana. Let the mixture cool a little, then pour it over the gelled mixture in the ring mold. Cover and refrigerate for at least 4 hours, or overnight.

To unmold, fill your sink with hot water. Dip the mold for 5 or 6 seconds in the hot water. Hold a serving plate on top of the mold and turn it over. If the contents don't easily fall out, dip the mold in the hot water again, but only for a few seconds because you don't want a melted salad.

For garnish: Fill the center with red grapes, and pineapple pieces cut from the extra pineapple rings which you will have left over from the can of unsweetened pineapple rings. Place more red grapes and pineapple chunks around the salad on the plate. It will look spectacular. Cut with a serrated knife and serve with a pie server.

TUNA SALAD

YIELD: 3 SERVINGS

Nutrition Facts

Amount Per Serving

Calories 150   Calories from Fat 10

	% Daily Value*
Total Fat 1g	2%
Saturated Fat 0g	0%
Cholesterol 20mg	7%
Sodium 350mg	14%
Total Carbohydrate 14g	5%
Dietary Fiber 3g	13%
Sugars 9g	
Protein 21g	

Vitamin A 25%	•	Vitamin C 60%
Calcium 6%	•	Iron 10%

1 cup chopped onion
2 celery ribs, coarsely chopped
1/2 cup nonfat cottage cheese or Kraft fat-free mayonnaise dressing
1/2 teaspoon apple juice concentrate
1/16 teaspoon cayenne pepper
1/8 teaspoon Tabasco® sauce
1/8 teaspoon curry powder (optional)
1 can (6.5 ounces) water-packed tuna, drained
1 teaspoon dried parsley or 3 tablespoons chopped fresh parsley
3 fresh tomatoes
3/16 teaspoons paprika
12 lettuce leaves
3 lemon wedges

Combine the onions and celery in a bowl and set aside.

If using nonfat cottage cheese: Combine the cottage cheese, juice concentrate, cayenne, Tabasco® sauce, and curry powder in a blender. Purée until very smooth and pour into a bowl. Mix in the onions, celery, tuna, and parsley.

If using fat-free mayonnaise dressing: Thoroughly combine the dressing with the juice concentrate, cayenne, Tabasco® sauce, and curry powder in a bowl. Mix in the onions, celery, tuna, and parsley.

To serve, cut 3 tomatoes crisscrossed almost all the way through 4 times, and open the tomatoes to form "stars"; there is no need to dig out the seeds. Arrange the lettuce leaves on salad plates with a tomato on each plate. Mound the tuna salad in each tomato and sprinkle with a little paprika. Serve with lemon wedges on the side.

TUNA APPLE SALAD

1/4 cup finely chopped white onion
1 large Red Delicious apple, cored and cubed (do not peel)
1 banana, sliced
1/2 lemon
1 can (6.5 ounces) water-packed tuna, drained
1/2 cup coarsely chopped celery stalks (no leaves)
8 iceberg lettuce leaves
Apple Dressing (below)

Place the onion, apple, and banana in a salad bowl. Drizzle with the lemon juice and toss. Add the tuna and celery and toss to combine. Serve on beds of lettuce in individual salad bowls and pass the Apple Dressing at the table.

APPLE DRESSING

1 tablespoon cornstarch
1/4 cup water
1/4 cup apple juice concentrate
1/4 cup apple cider vinegar
1/2 large Red Delicious apple, peeled, cored, and quartered
Lemon juice
1/16 teaspoon dry mustard
1/16 teaspoon curry powder
1/16 teaspoon celery seed
1/8 teaspoon cayenne pepper, or to taste

Combine the cornstarch, water, juice concentrate, and vinegar in a saucepan, mixing until the cornstarch is dissolved. Place the saucepan over high heat and stir constantly. Continue stirring until the mixture begins to thicken and turn almost transparent. When it begins to bubble, cook for about 1 minute more, stirring constantly, then remove from the heat, and set aside to cool for about 10 minutes.

Rub the apple pieces with lemon juice. Combine the apple pieces in a blender with the mustard, curry powder, celery seed, and cayenne. Add the cornstarch mixture. Blend on medium speed until the mixture has liquefied. Serve immediately over Tuna Apple Salad or any fruit salad. Leftovers do not keep well.

SALADE DE LA MER

Nutrition Facts

Amount Per Serving

Calories 50	Calories from Fat 5

	% Daily Value*
Total Fat 0.5g	**1%**
Saturated Fat 0g	**0%**
Cholesterol 5mg	**2%**
Sodium 35mg	**2%**
Total Carbohydrate 8g	**3%**
Dietary Fiber 2g	**9%**
Sugars 5g	
Protein 4g	

Vitamin A 15%	•	Vitamin C 45%
Calcium 2%	•	Iron 4%

In New Orleans we eat a fish called Sheepshead. It is a large fish caught along the Atlantic coast that tastes like crabmeat when used in a salad, although you could make this with any fish that has flaky white meat, like talapia or flounder.

Start with a whole, poached fish (be sure you leave the head attached, but have your fishmonger scale and gut your fish for you), and if you are making the Molded Salade de La Mer, reserve all the cooking liquid.

1–2 1/2 pound whole fish
1 small onion, finely chopped
1 celery rib, diced
2 cooked celery ribs from the poaching liquid, diced
1/4 cup cooked onion from the poaching liquid, finely chopped
1/4 teaspoon Tabasco® sauce
1/2 cup Creamy Onion Dressing (next page)
12 lettuce leaves, torn
3 tomatoes, sliced

Poach the fish in water with 1/2 a carrot, 1/2 a large onion, and 1 rib of celery. After the fish has cooled, remove it to a platter. Discard the poaching liquid. Pick the meat off the bones and place it in a salad bowl. Don't forget to pick the meat out of the head—it has the most flavor. Discard the bones and head. You should have 11 to 12 ounces of meat. Add the onions and celery. Mix the Tabasco® sauce with the Creamy Onion Dressing and combine it with the fish mixture. Cover and refrigerate for at least 3 hours, preferably overnight.

Serve on individual salad plates arranged on beds of lettuce and sliced tomatoes.

Nutrition Facts

Amount Per Serving

Calories 100   Calories from Fat 15

	% Daily Value*
Total Fat 2g	3%
Saturated Fat 0g	0%
Cholesterol 30mg	9%
Sodium 75mg	3%
Total Carbohydrate 8g	3%
Dietary Fiber 2g	9%
Sugars 5g	
Protein 15g	

Vitamin A 15%	•	Vitamin C 45%
Calcium 4%	•	Iron 6%

Variation: MOLDED SALADE DE LA MER

Prepare Salade de la Mer as on previous page, and refrigerate (save the poaching liquid). Strain the poaching liquid through a colander (not a strainer) to remove bones and scales. Pour 1 cup of the cooled poaching liquid into a small container and add 2 envelopes of unflavored gelatin. Soften the gelatin for 10 minutes. In a saucepan, bring the remaining poaching liquid to a boil, then remove from the heat, add the gelatin mixture, and stir to dissolve.

Pour about 1/2 inch of the heated liquid into 6 cup-size containers. Refrigerate until gelled, about 4 hours. Also refrigerate the remaining liquid to keep it fresh. Into each cup, add some of the Salad de la Mer, leaving room around the sides. Reheat the remaining poaching liquid until it is just soft enough to pour, but not so hot that it will melt the gelled part at the bottom of the cups. Pour the liquid around the sides of the cups and cover the Salade with about 1/2 inch of liquid. Refrigerate until gelled, about 4 hours. Unmold by running warm water over the outsides of the cups. Gently turn the molded salads out onto beds of lettuce and tomato slices. Garnish with lemon slices and wedges.

CREAMY ONION DRESSING

Nutrition Facts

Amount Per Serving

Calories 10   Calories from Fat 0

	% Daily Value*
Total Fat 0g	0%
Saturated Fat 0g	0%
Cholesterol 0mg	0%
Sodium 45mg	2%
Total Carbohydrate 1g	0%
Dietary Fiber 0g	0%
Sugars 1g	
Protein 2g	

Vitamin A 0%	•	Vitamin C 0%
Calcium 0%	•	Iron 0%

1/2 cup nonfat cottage cheese
1 teaspoon minced onion
1 teaspoon apple juice concentrate

Combine all the ingredients in a blender or food processor and blend until smooth. Store any unused dressing in an airtight container in the refrigerator.

PETER RABBIT SALAD

YIELD: 2 SERVINGS

Nutrition Facts

Amount Per Serving

Calories 410	Calories from Fat 35

	% Daily Value*
Total Fat 4g	6%
Saturated Fat 1g	4%
Cholesterol 5mg	2%
Sodium 690mg	29%
Total Carbohydrate 72g	24%
Dietary Fiber 13g	54%
Sugars 34g	
Protein 28g	

Vitamin A 480%	•	Vitamin C 230%
Calcium 45%	•	Iron 35%

22 fresh or thawed frozen snow pea pods
1 medium onion sliced into very thin rings
5 radishes sliced into very thin rings
1 medium carrot, grated
1 small turnip, grated
1/4 cup chopped green pepper
1 cup coarsely chopped fresh parsley
3 scallions, sliced
1 rib celery, sliced
1 large tomato, diced
4 slices Pritikin or commercial whole wheat bread
7 or 8 romaine lettuce leaves (more if needed) torn into bite-size
    pieces
1/2 cup nonfat cottage cheese (use 1 cup if serving 4 salads)
1 carrot, for garnish
1 cup Plantation Dressing (page 310)

If using fresh snow peas, break off the ends, wash the pods, and toss into a salad bowl. Thawed frozen snow peas are ready to use. Add the onion and radishes to the salad bowl, then add the grated carrot, turnip, green pepper, parsley, green onions, celery, and tomato. Toss all the vegetables together in the salad bowl.

Preheat oven to 400 degrees F.

Remove the crusts from the bread and cut the bread into cubes. Spread them on a cookie sheet. Bake for 3 to 4 minutes, until they are brown and toasted, but not burned. Set aside.

Arrange lettuce leaves on either 2 dinner plates or 4 salad plates. Just before serving, toss the croutons with the vegetables and divide the salad among the plates. Top each salad with 1/4 cup cottage cheese. Peel the remaining carrot and slice a section about 2 1/2 inches long. Then cut it into 4 pieces lengthwise. Lay a carrot slice on top of the cottage cheese on each salad, the inside of the carrot facing up. It will look like a whole small carrot. Dress and serve.

FULL MEAL SALAD

YIELD: 2 SERVINGS

Nutrition Facts

Amount Per Serving

Calories 200	Calories from Fat 10

	% Daily Value*
Total Fat 1g	2%
Saturated Fat 0g	0%
Cholesterol 5mg	2%
Sodium 250mg	10%
Total Carbohydrate 36g	12%
Dietary Fiber 9g	34%
Sugars 12g	
Protein 15g	

Vitamin A 190%	•	Vitamin C 120%
Calcium 10%	•	Iron 15%

1/2 cup fresh or thawed frozen green peas
1/2 head iceberg lettuce, torn in bite-size pieces
10 tomato slices
1/2 cup cucumber slices
2 radishes, sliced
1 cup cubed boiled potatoes
1/2 cup alfalfa sprouts
1/2 cup sliced mushrooms
1/2 cup sliced celery
1/2 medium green pepper, chopped
1/2 cup nonfat cottage cheese
1/2 cup grated carrot
1 cup B & B Dressing (below)

If you use fresh peas, steam for 3 or 4 minutes in a little water, drain, cool, and set aside.

Divide the lettuce between 2 dinner plates. Arrange tomato slices over the lettuce, then the cucumber slices, then the radishes, and finally the cubed potatoes. Place the alfalfa sprouts in the middle of each salad with the mushrooms, celery, and green pepper arranged on top of each salad. Then place a 1/4-cup mound of nonfat cottage in the center of each salad. Arrange the grated carrot around each cottage cheese mound like a nest and sprinkle with the peas. Dress with B & B Dressing just before serving.

B & B DRESSING

YIELD: 1 CUP

Nutrition Facts

Amount Per Serving

Calories 15	Calories from Fat 0

	% Daily Value*
Total Fat 0g	0%
Saturated Fat 0g	0%
Cholesterol 0mg	0%
Sodium 0mg	0%
Total Carbohydrate 3g	1%
Dietary Fiber 0g	0%
Sugars 2g	
Protein 0g	

Vitamin A 0%	•	Vitamin C 8%
Calcium 0%	•	Iron 2%

The first "B" stands for beans and the second one, believe it or not, stands for bananas. The puréed bananas add richness and sweetness, and the curry blends all the flavors together beautifully. It's delicious—trust me. One of my friends serves this with tacos and she says it tastes like guacamole.

1/2 cup Cooked Lima Beans (page 271)
1/4 cup cider vinegar
1 teaspoon grapefruit juice concentrate
2 tablespoons orange juice concentrate
1/2 cup sliced banana, firmly packed
1/16 teaspoon curry powder
1/8 teaspoon cayenne pepper

In a blender or food processor blend all the ingredients together until very smooth. Use immediately. This dressing does not keep well overnight, but you can use any extra dressing twice in the same day—just mix again before using.

ANTIPASTO SALAD

YIELD: 4 SERVINGS

Nutrition Facts

Amount Per Serving	
Calories 100	Calories from Fat 10

	% Daily Value*
Total Fat 1g	2%
Saturated Fat 0g	0%
Cholesterol 5mg	2%
Sodium 510mg	21%
Total Carbohydrate 13g	4%
Dietary Fiber 4g	17%
Sugars 6g	
Protein 11g	

Vitamin A 90%	•	Vitamin C 120%
Calcium 6%	•	Iron 15%

1 can (14.5 ounces) cut asparagus, drained and rinsed
1 jar (4 ounces) pimento pieces and juice
1/2 medium onion, sliced into paper-thin rings
1 celery rib, diced
1/2 large carrot, finely chopped in a food processor
1 cauliflower floret about an inch in diameter, finely chopped in a food processor
3/4 cup Antipasto Dressing (below)
12 lettuce leaves
1 cup nonfat cottage cheese
2 tomatoes, cut into wedges

Place the asparagus in a 1 1/2-quart bowl. Add the pimento juice. Roughly chop the pimentos and add them along with the onion, celery, carrot, and cauliflower. Add the dressing and combine thoroughly. Cover and marinate the salad for one hour or longer in the refrigerator.

To serve, arrange the lettuce on salad plates. Mound 1/4 cup low-fat cottage cheese on each plate with the tomato wedges alongside. Spoon the Antipasto Salad over the tomatoes and then a little more dressing over the lettuce.

ANTIPASTO DRESSING

YIELD: 1 1/3 CUPS

Nutrition Facts

Amount Per Serving	
Calories 5	Calories from Fat 0

	% Daily Value*
Total Fat 0g	0%
Saturated Fat 0g	0%
Cholesterol 0mg	0%
Sodium 0mg	0%
Total Carbohydrate 1g	0%
Dietary Fiber 0g	0%
Sugars 1g	
Protein 0g	

Vitamin A 0%	•	Vitamin C 0%
Calcium 0%	•	Iron 0%

1/2 cup apple cider vinegar
2 tablespoons apple juice concentrate
3/4 cup water
1/16 teaspoon cayenne pepper
1/2 teaspoon garlic powder
1/8 teaspoon dried basil
1/4 teaspoon dried oregano
1/16 teaspoon cumin
1/2 teaspoon onion powder
1/2 teaspoon coriander seeds

Combine all the ingredients in a blender and set on high to liquefy, including the coriander seeds. Pour over salad immediately. Leftover dressing will keep well for several days in an airtight container in the refrigerator.

CHRISTMAS SALAD

YIELD: 6 SERVINGS

Nutrition Facts

Amount Per Serving	
Calories 50	Calories from Fat 0
	% Daily Value*
Total Fat 0g	**0%**
Saturated Fat 0g	**0%**
Cholesterol 0mg	**0%**
Sodium 65mg	**3%**
Total Carbohydrate 10g	**3%**
Dietary Fiber 3g	**10%**
Sugars 4g	
Protein 2g	
Vitamin A 20% • Vitamin C 60%	
Calcium 2% • Iron 6%	

This is a pretty, layered salad that can be made as much as 4 hours ahead. To make this for a large crowd or for a bring-a-dish affair, just double the ingredients and use a 9 x 13-inch casserole dish.

1/4 head iceberg lettuce, shredded and chopped
1 medium tomato, chopped
1/2 medium onion, sliced into rings
2/3 cup frozen, uncooked green peas
2/3 cup frozen whole kernel corn, cooked and cooled
1 1/3 cups Creamy Dill Dressing (below)
1 green pepper, sliced
1 jar (4 ounces) pimentos, chopped or sliced

On the bottom of an 8-inch square baking dish or similar container, layer first the lettuce, then the tomatoes, then the onion rings. Sprinkle with the peas and then the corn. Pour the dressing over the salad and spread it evenly. Arrange the green pepper and pimentos decoratively on top. Cover and refrigerate before serving, but do not leave this salad in the refrigerator overnight because the dressing will liquefy and saturate the salad.

CREAMY DILL DRESSING

YIELD: 1 1/3 CUPS

Nutrition Facts

Amount Per Serving	
Calories 10	Calories from Fat 0
	% Daily Value*
Total Fat 0g	**0%**
Saturated Fat 0g	**0%**
Cholesterol 0mg	**0%**
Sodium 30mg	**1%**
Total Carbohydrate 1g	**0%**
Dietary Fiber 0g	**0%**
Sugars 1g	
Protein 1g	
Vitamin A 0% • Vitamin C 0%	
Calcium 0% • Iron 0%	

2 tablespoons skim milk
1 cup nonfat cottage cheese
2 tablespoons apple juice concentrate
2 tablespoons finely chopped onion
1/16 teaspoon cayenne pepper
1/4 teaspoon dillweed

Combine all the ingredients in a blender or food processor and blend on medium speed until smooth. Leftovers will keep for about a day in the refrigerator.

OLD-FASHIONED SALAD

1 medium cucumber, sliced
1/3 cup sliced scallions
1/8 cup very thinly sliced white onion
Vinaigrette Dressing (below)
1 medium tomato, diced
5 romaine lettuce leaves, torn into bite-size pieces

In a mixing bowl, toss the cucumbers, green onions, and white onion rings with the dressing. Cover and marinate in the refrigerator for at least 2 hours.

When you are ready to serve, drain the vegetables and reserve the dressing. Add the diced tomatoes to the cucumber and onions. Arrange lettuce leaves on 2 salad plates. Place the mixed vegetables on the lettuce and drizzle desired amount of dressing. Store leftover dressing in an airtight container in the refrigerator.

VINAIGRETTE DRESSING

1/2 cup wine vinegar
2 tablespoons apple juice concentrate
3/4 cup water
1/16 teaspoon cayenne pepper

In a jar or salad dressing bottle, combine all the ingredients. Store in an airtight container in the refrigerator.

SOCRATES SALAD

2 cups firmly packed fresh spinach leaves
1/2 cup alfalfa sprouts (optional)
1/2 medium cucumber, sliced
6 radishes, sliced
1 cup sliced button mushrooms
1/2 cup sliced red or green bell peppers
3 small scallions or green onions including green parts, sliced
Greek Dressing (below)

Arrange the spinach leaves on dinner or salad plates. Layer with the alfalfa sprouts, then the cucumber slices, radish slices, mushroom slices, bell pepper slices, and finally, the green onions. Dress and serve.

GREEK DRESSING

The grape juice and coriander give this dressing its uniquely Greek flavor and beautiful red color.

1/2 cup apple cider vinegar
1/2 cup water
2 tablespoons grape juice concentrate
4 coriander seeds
1/16 teaspoon ground ginger
1/16 teaspoon curry powder
1/16 teaspoon cayenne pepper

Combine all the ingredients in a blender and blend until the coriander seeds have disappeared. This dressing will keep for several days in an airtight container in the refrigerator.

CREAMY MIXED SALAD

Nutrition Facts

Amount Per Serving

Calories 180   Calories from Fat 15

	% Daily Value*
Total Fat 1.5g	**2%**
Saturated Fat 0g	**0%**
Cholesterol 0mg	**0%**
Sodium 370mg	**15%**
Total Carbohydrate 34g	**11%**
Dietary Fiber 7g	**30%**
Sugars 7g	
Protein 9g	

Vitamin A 80%	•	Vitamin C 15%
Calcium 8%	•	Iron 15%

This is great for a crowd and easy to make.

1 cup chopped onion
1 cup chopped celery
2 cups sliced mushrooms
1 can (15.25 ounces) salt-free, sugar-free whole kernel corn, drained
1 can (14.5 ounces) sliced, salt-free carrots, drained
1 cup thawed frozen green peas
1 can (15 ounces) garbanzo beans (chick peas), drained
1 can (15 ounces) lima beans, drained
1 cup commercial nonfat sour cream
1/2 teaspoon garlic powder
1/2 teaspoon red hot sauce
Fancy lettuce leaves

Line a large salad bowl with the lettuce leaves and set aside.

In a separate bowl, combine all the ingredients, then add to the bowl with the lettuce. Cover and refrigerator for 1 hour before serving.

SORT OF CAESAR SALAD

YIELD: 4 SERVINGS

Nutrition Facts

Amount Per Serving	
Calories 60	Calories from Fat 10

	% Daily Value*
Total Fat 1g	1%
Saturated Fat 0g	0%
Cholesterol 0mg	0%
Sodium 85mg	4%
Total Carbohydrate 13g	4%
Dietary Fiber 3g	11%
Sugars 4g	
Protein 3g	

Vitamin A 25%	•	Vitamin C 50%
Calcium 2%	•	Iron 6%

8 to 12 Romaine lettuce leaves
2 medium tomatoes, sliced
1/2 medium onion, sliced into very thin rings
2 slices Pritikin or commercial whole wheat bread
Garlic Green Pepper Dressing (below)

Arrange the lettuce leaves on 4 salad plates. Slice the tomatoes and arrange over the lettuce. Place the onion rings over the tomatoes. Cut the bread into small squares for untoasted croutons; sprinkle over the salads. Pass the Garlic Green Pepper Dressing at the table.

GARLIC GREEN PEPPER DRESSING

YIELD: 1 3/4 CUPS

Nutrition Facts

Amount Per Serving	
Calories 10	Calories from Fat 0

	% Daily Value*
Total Fat 0g	0%
Saturated Fat 0g	0%
Cholesterol 15mg	5%
Sodium 10mg	0%
Total Carbohydrate 1g	0%
Dietary Fiber 0g	0%
Sugars 1g	
Protein 1g	

Vitamin A 0%	•	Vitamin C 2%
Calcium 0%	•	Iron 0%

I like to use the frozen, chopped green peppers in this recipe because they are soft when they defrost, which is just the right consistency for this dressing.

1 garlic clove
2 tablespoons nonfat cottage cheese
1 cup apple cider vinegar
1/4 cup water
1/4 cup apple juice concentrate
1/4 cup thawed frozen, chopped green pepper
1/8 teaspoon cayenne pepper
2 jumbo eggs

Combine the garlic, cottage, cheese, vinegar, water, juice concentrate, green peppers, and cayenne in a blender or food processor and blend briefly at slow speed so you don't chop up the green pepper pieces too much.

Drop the eggs into a saucepan of rapidly boiling water, and cook for 3 minutes. Remove and let cool. Crack the eggs and carefully remove the yolks. Scrape the whites into the blender with the rest of the dressing. Blend on low speed for 1 second. (I just touch the blender button and stop it immediately.) You want to be able to see pieces of egg white. Use immediately. Leftovers will keep in an airtight container in the refrigerator for about 4 days.

MARDI GRAS SALAD

Nutrition Facts

Amount Per Serving

Calories 45	Calories from Fat 0

	% Daily Value*
Total Fat 0g	0%
Saturated Fat 0g	0%
Cholesterol 0mg	0%
Sodium 40mg	2%
Total Carbohydrate 10g	3%
Dietary Fiber 3g	12%
Sugars 6g	
Protein 2g	

Vitamin A 60%	•	Vitamin C 50%
Calcium 4%	•	Iron 6%

In New Orleans, the colors of Mardi Gras are purple, green, and gold, which is where this salad got its name. Making this salad is a good way to clean out the vegetable bin in your refrigerator. If you have a few green peas or something else, go ahead and add them.

1 large tomato, diced
3/4 cup sliced yellow squash
1 cup shredded red cabbage
1 cup unpeeled, sliced purple turnip
1/2 cup sliced radishes
1/4 cup sliced carrots
1 medium onion, sliced very thinly
3/4 cup sliced cucumber
1/4 cup coarsely chopped fresh parsley
Red leaf lettuce
Vinaigrette Dressing (page 296)

In a large salad bowl, toss together everything except the lettuce and dressing. Arrange beds of lettuce on plates with the salad on top, and dress.

SCHEHERAZADE PASTA SALAD

Nutrition Facts

Amount Per Serving

Calories 360	Calories from Fat 15

	% Daily Value*
Total Fat 1.5g	2%
Saturated Fat 0g	0%
Cholesterol 0mg	0%
Sodium 160mg	7%
Total Carbohydrate 75g	25%
Dietary Fiber 8g	33%
Sugars 30g	
Protein 15g	

Vitamin A 210%	•	Vitamin C 60%
Calcium 30%	•	Iron 25%

The dates in this salad give it an exotic, almost Oriental flavor. It reminds me of Scheherazade spinning her tales of the Arabian nights.

1 cup raw rotini twist macaroni, whole wheat or semolina
1/4 cup frozen or fresh green peas
1/2 cup diced carrot
1/2 cup diced, uncooked yellow squash
1 medium cucumber, sliced
1/4 cup sliced scallions
1/4 cup chopped celery
1/4 cup chopped parsley
1/3 cup chopped unsweetened dates
Lettuce
1 recipe Cayman Islands Dressing (page 312)
1/4 cup fat-free cheddar cheese

In a saucepan, bring a quart of water to a boil and add the macaroni. Boil for 9 minutes if semolina or about 15 minutes if whole wheat. Drain in a colander, rinse with cold water, and set aside. If the peas are fresh, place in a saucepan with about 1/2 inch of water and bring to a boil. Cover and continue to boil for 2 minutes. Drain and cool. Use frozen peas right out of the package.

In a salad bowl, combine the macaroni, peas, carrot, squash, cucumber, scallions, celery, parsley, and dates. Arrange lettuce on salad plates with the pasta-vegetable mixture mounded on top. Drizzle with the dressing, sprinkle on the cheese and serve.

ARTICHOKE SALAD

Nutrition Facts

Amount Per Serving	
Calories 100	Calories from Fat 0
	% Daily Value*
Total Fat 0g	**0**%
Saturated Fat 0g	**0**%
Cholesterol 0mg	**0**%
Sodium 370mg	**15**%
Total Carbohydrate 18g	**6**%
Dietary Fiber 5g	**19**%
Sugars 5g	
Protein 6g	

Vitamin A 20%	•	Vitamin C 50%
Calcium 4%	•	Iron 15%

Lettuce leaves
5 to 6 canned water-packed artichoke hearts
3/4 cup fresh or frozen peas
Sour Cream Dressing (below)

Arrange the lettuce on 2 plates. Cut the artichoke hearts in half and distribute over lettuce. Frozen peas can be used right out of the package. You might want to cook fresh ones for just a minute or two in a little water in a covered sauce pan. Spoon the peas over the artichokes. Top with the Sour Cream Dressing.

Nutrition Facts

Amount Per Serving	
Calories 80	Calories from Fat 0
	% Daily Value*
Total Fat 0g	**0**%
Saturated Fat 0g	**0**%
Cholesterol 5mg	**2**%
Sodium 55mg	**2**%
Total Carbohydrate 14g	**5**%
Dietary Fiber 0g	**0**%
Sugars 5g	
Protein 4g	

Vitamin A 8%	•	Vitamin C 2%
Calcium 8%	•	Iron 0%

SOUR CREAM DRESSING

This all-purpose dressing tastes great on any fresh green salad or tomatoes.

1/2 cup no-fat sour cream
1/4 teaspoon Tabasco® sauce
1/2 small onion, minced

Combine the ingredients and pour over salads.

SENORITA SALAD

YIELD: 2 SALADS

Nutrition Facts

Amount Per Serving

Calories 310   Calories from Fat 40

	% Daily Value*
Total Fat 4.5g	**7%**
Saturated Fat 0.5g	**3%**
Cholesterol 0mg	**0%**
Sodium 30mg	**1%**
Total Carbohydrate 52g	**17%**
Dietary Fiber 15g	**59%**
Sugars 6g	
Protein 17g	

Vitamin A 40%	•	Vitamin C 80%
Calcium 15%	•	Iron 40%

1/2 cup thinly sliced white onions
1 cup sliced cucumbers
1 cup diced tomatoes
2 cups cooked or canned garbanzo beans (chick peas)
  (one 15-ounce can)
1 cup coarsely chopped parsley, loosely packed
Lettuce
Fresh Tomato Dressing (double the recipe below)

Place onions, cucumbers, and tomatoes in a bowl. Drain and rinse the garbanzo beans, then add them to the bowl and toss with the other vegetables. Serve over beds of lettuce and top with the dressing.

FRESH TOMATO DRESSING

YIELD: 2 SERVINGS

Nutrition Facts

Amount Per Serving

Calories 30   Calories from Fat 0

	% Daily Value*
Total Fat 0g	**0%**
Saturated Fat 0g	**0%**
Cholesterol 0mg	**0%**
Sodium 860mg	**36%**
Total Carbohydrate 7g	**2%**
Dietary Fiber 2g	**7%**
Sugars 4g	
Protein 1g	

Vitamin A 15%	•	Vitamin C 100%
Calcium 2%	•	Iron 4%

1 medium ripe tomato
1/8 cup apple cider vinegar
2 whole, canned, green chili peppers
1 teaspoon dry onion flakes

Place all the ingredients in a blender or food processor and purée.

FRESH BEET SALAD

Nutrition Facts	
Amount Per Serving	
Calories 50	Calories from Fat 0
	% Daily Value*
Total Fat 0g	**0**%
Saturated Fat 0g	**0**%
Cholesterol 0mg	**0**%
Sodium 65mg	**3**%
Total Carbohydrate 12g	**4**%
Dietary Fiber 3g	**11**%
Sugars 8g	
Protein 2g	
Vitamin A 4% • Vitamin C 10%	
Calcium 2% • Iron 6%	

Canned, unsalted beets may be used in this salad, but fresh beets are really special.

2 cups torn iceberg lettuce
3 fresh cooked beets, sliced
1 small white onion, sliced paper thin
Dill Dressing (below)

Arrange the lettuce on 2 salad plates. Layer the beets over the lettuce. Top with the onion, then pass the Dill Dressing at the table.

DILL DRESSING

Nutrition Facts	
Amount Per Serving	
Calories 5	Calories from Fat 0
	% Daily Value*
Total Fat 0g	**0**%
Saturated Fat 0g	**0**%
Cholesterol 0mg	**0**%
Sodium 0mg	**0**%
Total Carbohydrate 1g	**0**%
Dietary Fiber 0g	**0**%
Sugars 1g	
Protein 0g	
Vitamin A 0% • Vitamin C 0%	
Calcium 0% • Iron 0%	

1/2 cup apple cider vinegar
1/2 cup water
1/2 teaspoon dried dillweed
1/2 teaspoon garlic powder
1/16 teaspoon cayenne pepper
1/2 teaspoon dried onion flakes
2 tablespoons apple juice concentrate

Combine all the ingredients into a jar or salad dressing bottle, shake, and let sit in the refrigerator for at least one hour. Shake well before serving. Leftovers keep well in an airtight container in the refrigerator for several days.

CARROT SALAD SUPREME

YIELD: 4 SERVINGS

Nutrition Facts

Amount Per Serving	
Calories 90	Calories from Fat 0

	% Daily Value*
Total Fat 0g	0%
Saturated Fat 0g	0%
Cholesterol 0mg	0%
Sodium 25mg	1%
Total Carbohydrate 22g	7%
Dietary Fiber 2g	9%
Sugars 20g	
Protein 1g	

Vitamin A 230%	•	Vitamin C 10%
Calcium 2%	•	Iron 4%

I have quadrupled this recipe for larger groups. Everyone loves it and no one believes it doesn't have mayonnaise in it.

1 1/2 cups grated carrots lightly packed (3 large carrots)
1 rib celery, diced
1/2 cup raisins
Imitation Mayonnaise (below)
2 teaspoons apple juice concentrate
1/16 teaspoon cayenne pepper
1/16 teaspoon curry powder
Lettuce

In a salad bowl, combine the carrots with the celery and the raisins. Set aside.

Prepare the Imitation Mayonnaise in a blender or food processor. Add the juice concentrate, cayenne pepper, and curry powder and blend thoroughly. Mix with the carrots, raisins, and celery. Serve on beds of lettuce arranged on salad plates.

IMITATION MAYONNAISE

YIELD: 1/2 CUP

Nutrition Facts

Amount Per Serving	
Calories 10	Calories from Fat 0

	% Daily Value*
Total Fat 0g	0%
Saturated Fat 0g	0%
Cholesterol 0mg	0%
Sodium 45mg	2%
Total Carbohydrate 1g	0%
Dietary Fiber 0g	0%
Sugars 1g	
Protein 2g	

Vitamin A 0%	•	Vitamin C 0%
Calcium 0%	•	Iron 0%

Of course, this does not taste exactly like mayonnaise, but it does have the tanginess and sweetness that mayonnaise has. It doesn't keep very long, so don't make more than you need for one meal.

1/2 cup nonfat cottage cheese
1 teaspoon finely chopped onion
1 teaspoon apple juice concentrate

Combine all the ingredients in a blender or food processor and blend until smooth. If you need larger amounts, this recipe can be successfully doubled, tripled, or even quadrupled.

HOMINY SALAD

YIELD: 4 SERVINGS

Nutrition Facts

Amount Per Serving

Calories 120   Calories from Fat 15

	% Daily Value*
Total Fat 1.5g	2%
Saturated Fat 0g	0%
Cholesterol 0mg	0%
Sodium 260mg	11%
Total Carbohydrate 24g	8%
Dietary Fiber 5g	20%
Sugars 6g	
Protein 3g	

Vitamin A 15%	•	Vitamin C 45%
Calcium 4%	•	Iron 8%

Hominy (grits before being ground) are really large kernels, but with a very different texture from ordinary canned corn—it is something like chick peas.

8 lettuce leaves (Boston lettuce, preferably)
2 medium tomatoes, sliced
2 celery stalks, coarsely chopped
1 can (15.5 ounces) white hominy (1 1/2 cups), rinsed
1 medium white onion, sliced in thin rings
3/4 cup Kiwi Dressing (below)

Rinse the hominy of excess salt by draining off the liquid in the can, then filling the can with water and draining again, then repeating the process. Set aside.

In 4 individual salad bowls, layer first the lettuce, then the sliced tomatoes, then the celery, then 3/8 cup of hominy in each bowl. Top with the onion rings. Pass the Kiwi Dressing at the table.

KIWI DRESSING

YIELD: 3/4 CUP

Nutrition Facts

Amount Per Serving

Calories 15   Calories from Fat 0

	% Daily Value*
Total Fat 0g	0%
Saturated Fat 0g	0%
Cholesterol 0mg	0%
Sodium 0mg	0%
Total Carbohydrate 4g	1%
Dietary Fiber 0g	0%
Sugars 3g	
Protein 0g	

Vitamin A 0%	•	Vitamin C 10%
Calcium 0%	•	Iron 0%

This dressing is delicious on banana slices, mixed fruit salad, or any type of tomato salad.

1 tablespoon cornstarch
1/4 cup water
1/4 cup apple juice concentrate
1/4 cup apple cider vinegar
1 kiwi

In a small saucepan, mix the cornstarch, water, juice concentrate, and vinegar until there are no more lumps in the cornstarch. Set over high heat and stir until the mixture thickens and looks almost transparent. Continue to cook, stirring constantly, for about 25 seconds more to make sure the cornstarch is fully cooked. Remove from the heat to cool for about 10 minutes.

In the meantime, cut the kiwi in half and scoop the pulp out into a blender. Add the cornstarch mixture and blend until smooth. Use immediately. Leftovers don't refrigerate very well.

SNOW PEA SALAD

Nutrition Facts

Amount Per Serving

Calories 50	Calories from Fat 5

	% Daily Value*
Total Fat 0.5g	**1%**
Saturated Fat 0g	**0%**
Cholesterol 0mg	**0%**
Sodium 35mg	**2%**
Total Carbohydrate 11g	**4%**
Dietary Fiber 4g	**15%**
Sugars 6g	
Protein 3g	

Vitamin A 40%	•	Vitamin C 80%
Calcium 6%	•	Iron 10%

3 ounces or about 28 fresh or frozen snow pea pods
1/8 cup very thinly sliced white cooking onion
2 radishes, very thinly sliced
1 small yellow squash, very thinly sliced
1 celery rib, sliced 1/8-inch thick
Vinaigrette Dressing (page 296)
1/4 cup curly parsley, destemmed
4 to 5 romaine lettuce leaves
1 large tomato, cut into wedges

If you are using fresh snow peas, cut off ends and ragged tips. In a salad bowl, toss together the snow peas, onions, radishes, yellow squash, and celery. Add the dressing and set aside to marinate for 2 hours.

When ready to serve, drain and reserve dressing. Toss the parsley with the marinated vegetables. Tear up the lettuce leaves and arrange on salad plates. Layer the tomato wedges over the lettuce, and then the marinated vegetables over the tomatoes. Dress with the reserved dressing and serve.

POTATO SALAD

Nutrition Facts

Amount Per Serving

Calories 180	Calories from Fat 0

	% Daily Value*
Total Fat 0g	**0%**
Saturated Fat 0g	**0%**
Cholesterol 0mg	**0%**
Sodium 380mg	**16%**
Total Carbohydrate 38g	**13%**
Dietary Fiber 3g	**10%**
Sugars 9g	
Protein 4g	

Vitamin A 2%	•	Vitamin C 30%
Calcium 2%	•	Iron 4%

8 medium potatoes
1 1/2 large onions, coarsely chopped
4 ribs celery, coarsely chopped
Pickled cucumbers, chopped
4 jumbo egg whites, hard-boiled and chopped
1 3/4 cup fat-free mayonnaise dressing
2 cloves garlic, finely chopped
1 teaspoon Tabasco® sauce

In a stockpot, cover the potatoes with water and boil for 15 to 20 minutes, or until they are soft. Drain off water, uncover, and set aside to cool. Peel and dice potatoes and place them in a large bowl. Add the chopped onions, celery, cucumbers, and egg whites. In a separate bowl, combine the mayonnaise, garlic, and Tabasco® sauce, then add the mayonnaise-mixture to the potatoes, and combine. Serve cold.

HOT GERMAN POTATO SALAD

YIELD: 8 SERVINGS

Nutrition Facts

Amount Per Serving

Calories 120	Calories from Fat 30

	% Daily Value¹
Total Fat 3.5g	**5%**
Saturated Fat 1.5g	**7%**
Cholesterol 15mg	**4%**
Sodium 230mg	**10%**
Total Carbohydrate 15g	**5%**
Dietary Fiber 3g	**11%**
Sugars 1g	
Protein 9g	

Vitamin A 8%	•	Vitamin C 30%
Calcium 2%	•	Iron 10%

A friend of mine whose parents originally came from Germany introduced me to Hot German Potato Salad. In Wisconsin where he lives, they add hot bacon grease to the vinegar, but the almost fat-free Hot and Sour Dressing is excellent and totally in keeping with how this salad is supposed to taste. Serve as a main meal with plain cabbage on the side and a little dressing over the hot cabbage.

1 1/2 cups Hot and Sour Dressing (below)
1 medium onion, sliced into thin rings
2 celery ribs, coarsely chopped
1 jar (4 ounces) pimento pieces and juice
10 ounces trimmed ground beef round, or an equally lean cut
2 cups water
1 quart potatoes (4 to 5 potatoes), peeled and diced (1-inch pieces)

Pour the dressing into a bowl. Add the onion, celery, and liquid from the pimentos. In a separate bowl, cut up the pimentos and then add them to the dressing mixture. Set aside to marinate.

Brown the ground beef in a large nonstick frying pan. Remove and drain the beef on paper towels, then pat the meat with more paper towels. Wipe any grease out of the pan.

Pour the water into the frying pan. Add the potatoes. Cover and cook over high heat for about 20 minutes, until just tender. Drain the potatoes, saving the cooking water to make soup. Add the dressing mixture to the pan, and combine with the potatoes. Set aside to marinate for about 1 hour, stirring occasionally.

Serve at room temperature or cold if you have any leftovers.

HOT AND SOUR DRESSING

YIELD: 1 1/2 CUPS

Nutrition Facts

Amount Per Serving

Calories 5	Calories from Fat 0

	% Daily Value¹
Total Fat 0g	**0%**
Saturated Fat 0g	**0%**
Cholesterol 0mg	**0%**
Sodium 0mg	**0%**
Total Carbohydrate 1g	**0%**
Dietary Fiber 0g	**0%**
Sugars 1g	
Protein 0g	

Vitamin A 0%	•	Vitamin C 0%
Calcium 0%	•	Iron 0%

1 cup apple cider vinegar
1/4 cup water
1/4 cup apple juice concentrate
2 teaspoons medium red hot sauce

Thoroughly combine all the ingredients in a pint jar. Use immediately. Leftovers will keep in an airtight container in the refrigerator for several days.

ITALIAN SALAD DRESSING

YIELD: 1 1/2 CUPS

Nutrition Facts

Amount Per Serving	
Calories 5	Calories from Fat 0
	% Daily Value*
Total Fat 0g	**0%**
Saturated Fat 0g	**0%**
Cholesterol 0mg	**0%**
Sodium 0mg	**0%**
Total Carbohydrate 2g	**1%**
Dietary Fiber 0g	**0%**
Sugars 1g	
Protein 0g	
Vitamin A 0% • Vitamin C 0%	
Calcium 0% • Iron 0%	

This all-purpose dressing tastes great on any fresh green salad or tomatoes.

1 cup apple cider or wine vinegar
1/2 small onion
1/4 cup water
1/4 cup apple juice concentrate
1/2 teaspoon garlic powder or 4 crushed garlic cloves
1/2 teaspoon onion powder
1/2 teaspoon dried basil
1/2 teaspoon dried oregano
1/8 teaspoon cayenne pepper
1/4 teaspoon cumin

Combine all ingredients in a blender or food processor and liquefy. Store in an airtight container in the refrigerator.

PLANTATION DRESSING

YIELD: 1 CUP

Nutrition Facts

Amount Per Serving	
Calories 10	Calories from Fat 0
	% Daily Value*
Total Fat 0g	**0%**
Saturated Fat 0g	**0%**
Cholesterol 0mg	**0%**
Sodium 10mg	**0%**
Total Carbohydrate 2g	**1%**
Dietary Fiber 0g	**0%**
Sugars 2g	
Protein 1g	
Vitamin A 0% • Vitamin C 0%	
Calcium 4% • Iron 0%	

1 cup commercial nonfat yogurt or Skim Milk Yogurt (page 56)
1/8 teaspoon cayenne pepper
15 coriander seeds
1/16 teaspoon allspice
1/2 medium banana
2 teaspoons grated sapsago cheese

Combine all the ingredients in a blender or food processor and blend until the coriander seeds are pulverized. Don't make any more than you plan to use immediately because this dressing really doesn't keep well.

MUSTARD SEED DRESSING

1 cup apple cider vinegar
1/4 cup water
1/4 cup apple juice concentrate
1/4 cup nonfat cottage cheese
1/8 teaspoon cayenne pepper
3 teaspoons mustard seeds

Combine the vinegar, water, juice concentrate, cottage cheese, cayenne, and 2 teaspoons of the mustard seeds in a blender or food processor. Blend on high speed until smooth. Pour into a 2-cup dressing bottle and add the remaining 1 teaspoon of mustard seeds. Shake well before using. Leftovers keep well in an airtight container in the refrigerator for several days.

CHIVE DRESSING

1/2 cup apple cider vinegar
1/2 cup water
2 tablespoons apple juice concentrate
1/4 teaspoon garlic powder
1/16 teaspoon cayenne pepper
1 tablespoon dried chives

Combine all the ingredients in a jar or salad dressing bottle. Shake well and set aside for several hours in the refrigerator before serving. Be sure to shake before using. Leftovers will keep well in an airtight container in the refrigerator for several days.

COLE SLAW À LA TROPIQUE

This is perfect to serve at a luau, or on a winter day when you wish you could be snorkeling in warm, crystal clear, blue-green water off a tropical island.

2 1/2 cups shredded cabbage
1/2 cup finely chopped carrot
1/2 cup raisins
1/3 cup chopped red bell pepper
1/4 cup finely chopped onion
1 medium banana, sliced
1 cup grated nonfat cheddar cheese
1 recipe Cayman Islands Dressing (below)

In a salad bowl, toss together all ingredients, dress, and serve. If you want to stretch this recipe, you can add a little more cabbage.

CAYMAN ISLANDS DRESSING

1/2 plus 1/3 cup commercial nonfat yogurt or Skim Milk Yogurt (page 56)
1 medium banana, broken up
1/2 cup cubed apple
1 tablespoon fresh lime juice
1 penny-size piece of lime rind
1/8 teaspoon cayenne pepper

Combine all the ingredients in a blender or food processor. Blend until smooth.

SUMMER FRUIT SALAD

Nowadays so many wonderful summer fruits are available throughout the year, you can enjoy this refreshing salad almost any time.

1 cup diced watermelon
1 cup diced cantaloupe
1/2 cup seedless grapes
1/2 cup sliced peaches
1/2 cup sliced bananas
1/2 cup sliced strawberries
1/2 cup sliced kiwi fruit (optional)
Cayman Islands Dressing (page 312)
Lettuce (optional)

Toss all the fruits together in a bowl. The measurements are just to give you an idea of how much to use, but feel free to add more of your favorite fruits.

To serve, arrange lettuce leaves on salad plates and spoon the fruit on top. Dress with Cayman Islands Dressing.

STRAWBERRY MOUNTAIN

1/2 cup fresh or frozen chopped peaches
1 cup nonfat cottage cheese
2 tablespoons apple juice concentrate, divided
2 cups bite-size pieces iceberg lettuce
1/2 cup fresh or frozen sliced peaches
1 cup whole fresh or frozen strawberries
1/4 cup water

Arrange the lettuce on salad plates.

In a bowl, combine the peaches with the cottage cheese and 1 tablespoon of the juice concentrate, then mound the cottage cheese mixture in the center of each plate on top of the lettuce. Surround with the peach slices and place a whole strawberry on top of each mound. Arrange the rest of the strawberries around the peaches. In a separate small bowl, combine the remaining 1 tablespoon of juice concentrate with the water and dress the salads, making sure to get some on the lettuce leaves.

MOLDED FRUIT SALAD

This makes a lovely fruit salad for a buffet dinner. I serve this to a crowd every New Year's Day along with cabbage for money, black-eyed peas for good luck, and corned beef.

3 cups orange juice
1 can (20 ounces) of unsweetened pineapple chunks and juice
1 can (16 ounces) of unsweetened grapefruit sections and juice
1 can apple juice or cider
1/2 cup apple juice concentrate
3 envelopes unflavored gelatin
1 3/4 cups (12 ounces) nonfat cottage cheese

Pour the orange juice, the pineapple chunks and juice, and grapefruit sections and juice into a large 3-quart ring mold and set aside.

In a saucepan, bring the apple juice and apple juice concentrate to a boil. Remove from the heat, add the gelatin, and stir to dissolve. Add to the mold and mix with the other ingredients. Refrigerate about 4 hours until solid, or overnight.

To unmold the salad, immerse in a sink full of hot water for several seconds. Place a large serving plate on top of the mold. Turn the whole thing over. The salad should fall right out on to the plate. If it doesn't, run a knife around the edges of the mold and place in the hot water again. Repeat if necessary.

Fill the center of the molded salad with cottage cheese. Garnish around the sides and top with kumquats and fancy lettuce leaves or use curly parsley and halved orange slices.

The taste is rather tart so if you prefer it sweet, replace the grapefruit juice with the same amount of apple juice concentrate.

RAISIN-APPLE SALAD

YIELD: 2 SERVINGS

Nutrition Facts

Amount Per Serving

Calories 150	Calories from Fat 0

	% Daily Value*
Total Fat 0g	**0%**
Saturated Fat 0g	**0%**
Cholesterol 5mg	**2%**
Sodium 310mg	**13%**
Total Carbohydrate 24g	**8%**
Dietary Fiber 2g	**6%**
Sugars 21g	
Protein 13g	

Vitamin A 8%	•	Vitamin C 4%
Calcium 25%	•	Iron 2%

1/2 cup nonfat cottage cheese
1/4 cup nonfat shredded cheddar cheese
1/4 cup raisins
1 tablespoon finely chopped onion
1/2 medium apple, peeled and chopped
Lettuce

In a bowl, combine the cottage cheese, cheddar cheese, raisins, onion, and apple. Cover and refrigerate for 1 hour. Serve on beds of lettuce.

CHAPTER 10

Snacks, Dips, and Tidbits

For many of us, snacks keep us going between meals and sometimes even instead of a meal when we just get too busy or distracted. I always take some popcorn and fruit with me in my car when I leave the house, along with a thermos of hot or iced herb tea, so I won't be tempted to stop for a hamburger or a soft drink.

When you give or go to a party, you really need to supply something a little bit special to snack on that won't break your diet. On a daily basis keep some Mock Sour Cream or some Creole Cream Cheese or some no-fat cream cheese or no-fat sour cream or yogurt on hand in the refrigerator with some fresh vegetables for dipping or spreading on bread. Count the dairy products as your milk servings for that day. Serve some to your guests—they'll never know they are eating something really healthy. And you don't have to give up popcorn either. It's so easy to make without oil. Grapefruit sweetened with a little apple juice concentrate makes a very refreshing snack as well as a fruit serving, and a microwave Baked Banana is delicious and satisfying.

Use your imagination. It's your best friend when you are trying to eat a really healthy diet. Many of the recipes in this book can be used as snack food in small portions.

PARTY MEAT BALLS

YIELD: ABOUT 65 MEAT BALLS

Nutrition Facts

Amount Per Serving	
Calories 80	Calories from Fat 30

	% Daily Value*
Total Fat 3g	5%
Saturated Fat 1g	6%
Cholesterol 10mg	3%
Sodium 390mg	16%
Total Carbohydrate 7g	2%
Dietary Fiber 1g	5%
Sugars 0g	
Protein 7g	

Vitamin A 10%	•	Vitamin C 15%
Calcium 2%	•	Iron 6%

You can make these meat balls ahead of time and store them in a sealed plastic bag in your freeze. When you need them, remove from the freezer to defrost while you make the Italian Tomato Sauce. Place the meat balls in the sauce and keep them warm in either a slow cooker set on low or a large food warmer. Serve with toothpicks but not over your good pastel Oriental rug, as I did the first time I served them. Now I serve them in the kitchen where it's safer.

If you would like these for dinner, they weigh about 1 ounce each, so 3 to 4 meat balls with some gravy over spaghetti would be considered a serving.

4 pounds very lean ground beef
4 jumbo egg whites
4 slices commercial whole wheat bread or Pritikin bread
2 tablespoons onion powder
1 teaspoon cayenne pepper or more, to taste
4 teaspoons garlic powder
Italian Tomato Sauce (page 54) (multiply the recipe by 4)

If you have an extra large food processor, you can do this in one batch; otherwise process 1/2 at a time.

Put the ground beef in a food processor. Add the egg whites and the spices. Hold the bread under the faucet to wet it. Squeeze the water out, then tear the bread up and add to the food processor. Process the ingredients until it forms a ball. You can mix up all the ingredients by hand in a large bowl, however, the cutting blade on the processor grinds the meat very finely, and the meat balls hold together much better.

Preheat the oven to 450 degrees F.

Roll walnut-size balls between the palms of your hands. The preparation goes faster this way than if you try to pat them together. Set the balls on a nonstick broiler rack or on a nonstick pan. Bake until they become brown on one side, then turn over. When they brown on both sides, remove and drain on paper towels 4 sheets-thick. There should be very little grease, but the paper towels will absorb any traces. In a large saucepan, heat the meat balls in Italian Tomato Sauce and serve hot.

CATFISH NUGGETS

Nutrition Facts

Amount Per Serving	
Calories 25	Calories from Fat 10

	% Daily Value*
Total Fat 1g	2%
Saturated Fat 0g	0%
Cholesterol 5mg	2%
Sodium 10mg	0%
Total Carbohydrate 1g	0%
Dietary Fiber 0g	0%
Sugars 0g	
Protein 3g	

Vitamin A 0%	•	Vitamin C 0%
Calcium 0%	•	Iron 0%

These are great for parties. Serve with toothpicks and Piquante Sauce, Horseradish Sauce, or ketchup if you want to cheat a little.

1/2 cup yellow cornmeal
1/16 teaspoon cayenne pepper
1/2 teaspoon dried thyme
1/2 teaspoon ground sage
6 catfish fillets measuring about 6 inches by 3 inches
Water

Preheat the oven to 400 degrees F.

Spray a nonstick cookie sheet with nonstick spray.

In a plastic or paper bag, combine the cornmeal, cayenne, thyme, and sage. Shake well to mix.

Cut the catfish fillets into bite-size pieces. Place the fish in a colander, rinse, and drain but do not dry them. Place a few pieces at a time in the bag with the cornmeal. Shake to coat. Arrange pieces so that they are not touching each other on the cookie sheet. Bake on the top rack of the oven for 20 to 25 minutes, until lightly brown. Turn once if they look like they won't stick when you run a spatula under the pieces. If they appear to be sticking, leave them alone. Don't worry, they'll be fine. Serve the fish brown-side up, on a platter around a container of dipping sauce. Each serving will contain less than 1/2 ounce of fish.

SHRIMP TIDBITS

YIELD: 40 TIDBITS

Nutrition Facts

Amount Per Serving

Calories 20	Calories from Fat 5

	% Daily Value*
Total Fat 0.5g	**1%**
Saturated Fat 0g	**0%**
Cholesterol 10mg	**3%**
Sodium 15mg	**1%**
Total Carbohydrate 3g	**1%**
Dietary Fiber 0g	**0%**
Sugars 0g	
Protein 1g	

Vitamin A 0%	•	Vitamin C 0%
Calcium 0%	•	Iron 0%

1 pound of large, fresh, peeled shrimp (2 pounds if weighed unpeeled)
1 cup yellow cornmeal
1/4 teaspoon dried marjoram
1/4 teaspoon dried thyme
1/4 teaspoon cayenne pepper
1/4 teaspoon dried sage

Preheat the oven to 400 degrees F.

Wash the shrimp, then peel and devein them. Do not wash after they are peeled.

In a plastic or paper bag, combine the cornmeal, marjoram, thyme, cayenne, and sage. Shake well to mix.

Spray a nonstick pan with butter-flavored nonstick spray. Add a few shrimp at a time into the bag with the seasoned cornmeal and shake to coat. Place the shrimp so that they are not touching each other on the pan. Place on the middle rack of the oven and bake for 15 minutes, but spray with butter-flavored Pam after 10 minutes to crisp. Serve immediately with toothpicks and Horseradish Sauce (page 60) or Piquante Sauce (page 55). Each shrimp will weigh less than 1/4 ounce.

ARTICHOKE BALLS

Nutrition Facts

Amount Per Serving

Calories 25	Calories from Fat 0

	% Daily Value*
Total Fat 0g	**0**%
Saturated Fat 0g	**0**%
Cholesterol 0mg	**0**%
Sodium 45mg	**2**%
Total Carbohydrate 5g	**2**%
Dietary Fiber less than 1 gram	**4**%
Sugars 1g	
Protein 2g	

Vitamin A 4%	•	Vitamin C 2%
Calcium 0%	•	Iron 8%

1 can (14 ounces) artichoke hearts, rinsed
3 ounces very lean ground top round beef steak
2 cups Grape-Nuts®
1/4 teaspoon dried oregano
1/4 teaspoon garlic powder
1/16 teaspoon ground cumin
1/8 teaspoon dried basil
1/2 teaspoon dried parsley flakes
1/8 teaspoon cayenne pepper
3 tablespoons sapsago cheese
4 jumbo egg whites, lightly beaten
3 tablespoons dry vermouth
1 teaspoon medium red hot sauce
1/4 Baked Banana (page 57)

Preheat the oven to 400 degrees F.

Spray two 9 x 13-inch baking dishes with nonstick spray.

Drain the artichoke hearts and set aside.

Sauté the meat in a nonstick frying pan, turning constantly until brown. Drain on paper towels and pat with more paper towels to absorb all the grease.

While the meat is browning, pour the Grape-Nuts into a blender or food processor and process until they are very fine crumbs. Then in a large mixing bowl, combine the Grape-Nuts crumbs, oregano, garlic, cumin, basil, parsley, cayenne, and sapsago cheese and set aside.

Place the artichoke hearts in the blender or food processor and pulse 6 or 7 times—being careful not to grind them to mush. Combine the chopped artichoke with the sautéed meat, and the crumb-mixture.

In a separate bowl, combine the eggs, vermouth, hot sauce, and banana and baking liquid and beat lightly with a fork or whisk. Add to the artichoke-meat-crumb mixture and combine thoroughly.

Form bite-size balls and arrange them so that they are not touching each other in the baking dishes. Cover the baking dishes with aluminum foil and place on the middle and top racks of the oven to bake for 15 minutes. Eat hot or let cool, covered, to serve at room temperature, or refrigerate and serve cold. Each ball will contain 0.07 ounces of meat.

MOCK STUFFED EGGS

YIELD: 18 SERVINGS

Nutrition Facts

Amount Per Serving	
Calories 80	Calories from Fat 35

	% Daily Value*
Total Fat 3.5g	6%
Saturated Fat 1g	5%
Cholesterol 140mg	46%
Sodium 45mg	2%
Total Carbohydrate 6g	2%
Dietary Fiber 1g	6%
Sugars 1g	
Protein 6g	

Vitamin A 6%	•	Vitamin C 2%
Calcium 2%	•	Iron 6%

The first time I made these, my husband was so suspicious that these were real stuffed eggs that he was leery of eating them. To convince him I had to show him the garbanzo bean can and the egg yolks I had set aside, and I suspect that he still isn't totally convinced that they don't contain mayonnaise and real egg yolks.

9 jumbo eggs
1/2 medium cucumber
Apple cider vinegar
1 1/2 teaspoons onion powder
1/2 teaspoon garlic powder
2 cups cooked garbanzo beans (chick peas) (one 15-ounce can)
1/8 teaspoon curry powder
1/2 teaspoon red hot sauce
Paprika, or garnish

Place the eggs in a large saucepan and cover with cold water. Bring the water to a boil, then lower the heat to medium and continue to boil for 10 minutes. Remove from the heat and cool in cold water.

While the eggs are boiling, peel and finely dice the cucumber. In a small bowl, combine the cucumber with 1 teaspoon of the onion powder, 1/4 teaspoon of the garlic powder, and enough apple cider vinegar to cover. Stir to combine, then set aside to marinate until you are ready to mix with the garbanzo beans—5 or 6 minutes is enough, but if you wish, you can fix them a day ahead and let them marinate overnight in the refrigerator. They taste about the same either way.

Drain and rinse the garbanzo beans to remove as much salt as possible, and put them in a blender or food processor. Add the curry powder, the remaining garlic and onion powder, hot sauce, and 1 teaspoon of vinegar. Process until very creamy.

When the eggs are cooled, peel and slice them in half lengthwise. Remove the yolks and discard or give them to your dog or cat.

Drain the diced cucumber and mix with the garbanzos. Stuff the mixture into the egg halves. Sprinkle with a little fresh paprika for garnish.

EGG ROLLS

Nutrition Facts

Amount Per Serving	
Calories 550	Calories from Fat 25

	% Daily Value*
Total Fat 3g	5%
Saturated Fat 0.5g	3%
Cholesterol 70mg	23%
Sodium 1120mg	47%
Total Carbohydrate 103g	34%
Dietary Fiber 5g	22%
Sugars 6g	
Protein 26g	

Vitamin A 10%	•	Vitamin C 130%
Calcium 10%	•	Iron 40%

My kids are crazy for these. Instead of the usual egg roll wrappers, this recipe calls for lumpia wrappers, which are sometimes called pastry wrappers and are available in Asian markets. The ingredients listed should include just flour, water, and salt, so be sure to check them. If you can't find lumpia wrappers, try using round rice papers.

The rice papers must be dipped in water before you fill them. Use 2 rice papers together. The lumpia or pastry wrappers are easier to work with, are more flaky, and are more successful.

1 large white or yellow onion, coarsely chopped
1 large green pepper, coarsely chopped
1 teaspoon low-sodium soy sauce
2 jumbo egg whites
3 1/2 ounces peeled fresh shrimp (about 10 large unpeeled shrimp)
10 sheets large lumpia wrappers (or 4 round rice papers)

Preheat oven to 350 degrees F.

Combine onion and green pepper in a nonstick frying pan. Set the heat on high and sauté them, stirring constantly. When the onions begin to look transparent, add the soy sauce, and continue stirring until the onions start to look a little brown. Lower the heat to medium. Continue to stir until the onions are almost cooked. Add the egg white and stir until cooked and white. Then add the shrimp whole and remove from the heat; they don't need to cook.

Pile 5 lumpia wrappers on top of each other on a large nonstick cookie sheet. Place half of your shrimp mixture in the center. Roll lumpia wrappers around the mixture and place them seam-side down, on a cake rack on top of a cookie sheet. There is no need to seal the seam in any way. The rolls will stay together after they are cooked. Cut the roll in half and move the halves about an inch apart. Do the same thing again with the rest of the mixture. Bake uncovered for about 15 minutes until nice and lightly browned like bread crust. Check every 5 minutes as they bake. You can set the rolls on a nonstick pan instead of on the cake racks, but the racks make them extra crispy. When the rolls are brown, serve immediately with Sweet and Sour Sauce (page 55) and Chinese Mustard (page 53). This recipe makes 4 nice, fat, crisp egg rolls. One per person may be enough, but they are so good you had better double this recipe for 4 people if you are serving them as your main course. Each egg roll contains less than 1 ounce of shrimp.

ZUCCHINI SQUARES

This frittata makes lovely hors d'oeuvres or can be served as an interesting addition to almost any dinner plate. They can be prepared ahead and frozen, then reheated for a party.

5 jumbo egg whites
1/4 cup skim milk
1 tablespoon low-sodium baking powder
1/2 cup oat bran cereal
1/2 cup whole wheat flour
1 1/2 cups nonfat cheddar cheese
2 tablespoons grated sapsago cheese
1/4 teaspoon cayenne pepper
1/2 teaspoon dried oregano
1 teaspoon dried parsley
1/4 teaspoon dried basil
1/4 teaspoon garlic powder
1 cup diced zucchini squash
1/3 cup finely chopped onion

Preheat oven to 400 degrees F.

Mix all the ingredients in a large bowl, then pour into an 8-inch-square nonstick cake pan. Place on the middle rack of the oven and bake for 35 to 40 minutes, until the top is almost fully brown and a toothpick comes out clean.

Cool in the pan for 10 minutes, then turn out onto a cutting board. Cut into squares with an electric knife or a good serrated knife. Serve at once.

I like to put the squares on a cookie sheet and bake at 400 degrees F. for another 10 minutes to crisp the sides of the squares. These can be reheated, uncovered, one at a time in the microwave for 20 seconds on a high setting. Use more time for more squares. Reheat, uncovered, in a conventional oven on a cookie sheet for about 10 minutes at 300 degrees F.

PICKLED SHRIMP

Nutrition Facts

Amount Per Serving

Calories 40	Calories from Fat 0

	% Daily Value*
Total Fat 0g	**0%**
Saturated Fat 0g	**0%**
Cholesterol 25mg	**9%**
Sodium 40mg	**2%**
Total Carbohydrate 6g	**2%**
Dietary Fiber 0g	**0%**
Sugars 5g	
Protein 3g	

Vitamin A 2%	•	Vitamin C 6%
Calcium 2%	•	Iron 4%

This hors d'oeuvre is lovely to serve and easy to make. The first time I made them, my husband Ray ate the whole platter, onions and all. I only got to taste one shrimp. (No, you're not supposed to eat the platter.)

Shrimp:
6 cups water
1 medium onion, quartered (do not peel)
1 teaspoon salt-free chili powder
2 tablespoons apple cider vinegar
1 lemon, halved
6 medium garlic cloves (do not peel)
1/4 teaspoon red pepper flakes
1/3 bag commercial crab boil or 1/3 recipe for Homemade Crab Boil (page 170)
1 pound unpeeled large shrimp, heads left on (about 20 shrimp)

Pickling Juice:
7/8 cup apple cider vinegar
1 cup water
3/4 cup apple juice concentrate
1/2 teaspoon red pepper flakes
1 medium red onion, sliced into rings

For the Shrimp: Combine the water, onion, chili powder, vinegar, lemon, garlic, and pepper in a 3-quart stockpot. If you use commercial crab boil, make a bag for it out of cheesecloth as you would for Homemade Crab Boil. Drop the bag in the pot. Cover and over high heat, bring to a rolling boil. Continue to boil for about 10 minutes, or until the onion is tender. Add the unpeeled shrimp. Cover and return to a boil. Remove the pot from the heat and let it sit for 10 to 12 minutes. Remove the shrimp to a colander, but reserve 1/2 cup of the cooking liquid. Discard the rest. Set the shrimp aside to cool.

For the Pickling Juice: Combine the vinegar, water, juice concentrate, pepper, and onion in a mixing bowl, and set aside.

After the shrimp have cooled, peel and devein them, but leave the little red tails on. Drop them into the pickling juice. Add 1/2 cup of the reserved cooking liquid. Cover and refrigerate for at least 2 hours.

Drain the shrimp and serve on a small platter with the onion rings, and, if you like, a container of Horseradish Sauce (page 60) for dipping. Each shrimp will weigh less than 1/4 ounce.

One pound of unpeeled shrimp will yield 1/2 pound of peeled shrimp.

PICKLED OKRA

Nutrition Facts

Amount Per Serving	
Calories 5	Calories from Fat 0
	% Daily Value*
Total Fat 0g	**0%**
Saturated Fat 0g	**0%**
Cholesterol 0mg	**0%**
Sodium 0mg	**0%**
Total Carbohydrate 1g	**0%**
Dietary Fiber less than 1 gram	**2%**
Sugars 0g	
Protein 0g	
Vitamin A 2% • Vitamin C 6%	
Calcium 2% • Iron 2%	

This is a New Orleans favorite where so many people have okra growing in abundance in their yards. It makes a very nice snack, or you can place a couple of okra on top of a salad for a spicy touch, or serve it alongside roast beef. Always choose the youngest, smallest, freshest okra you can find.

For the Okra:
2 quarts water
1 pound fresh okra (about 4 cups)

For the Pickling Juice:
1 cup water
7/8 cup apple cider vinegar
1 whole clove garlic, peeled
1/4 teaspoon red pepper flakes
1 cinnamon stick
1/2 teaspoon mustard seeds
1 bay leaf, broken in several pieces
1 teaspoon coriander seeds
17 whole allspice berries
4 cloves

Bring 2 quarts of water to a rapid boil in a 5-quart stockpot. Add the okra, cover, and boil for 5 minutes. Pour the okra immediately into a colander to drain. While the okra is cooking, make the pickling juice.

Microwave Directions: Pour the water and vinegar into a 1-quart container. Add the garlic, pepper, cinnamon, mustard seeds, bay leaf, coriander seeds, allspice, and cloves. Microwave uncovered, on high setting for 4 minutes, then simmer at 50 percent power for 8 minutes. Let cool.

Stove Top Directions: Pour the water and vinegar into a 1 1/2- or 2-quart saucepan. Add the garlic, pepper, cinnamon, mustard seeds, bay leaf, coriander seeds, allspice, and cloves. Cover, bring to a boil, then simmer for 8 minutes. Set aside to cool.

Using tongs, transfer the cooked okra, one at a time, into a 1-quart jar. If you don't have tongs, use a fork, but be careful not to break the okra. Pour the cooled pickling juice into the jar over the okra. If you have a little more juice than will fit, strain out all the spices and put them in the jar with the okra. Reserve the extra juice to use for salad dressing. Cover the jar and refrigerate. The okra is better if you let it sit for at least a day, but if you can't wait, it is certainly spicy enough as soon as it is cold. Be sure to lift it out of the jar with tongs or a fork so you don't contaminate the liquid with your fingers.

GARLIC CHEESE BREAD

YIELD: 4 SERVINGS

Nutrition Facts

Amount Per Serving

Calories 45	Calories from Fat 5

	% Daily Value*
Total Fat 0.5g	**1%**
Saturated Fat 0g	**0%**
Cholesterol 0mg	**0%**
Sodium 105mg	**4%**
Total Carbohydrate 8g	**3%**
Dietary Fiber 1g	**4%**
Sugars 1g	
Protein 3g	

Vitamin A 2%	•	Vitamin C 0%
Calcium 6%	•	Iron 4%

Butter-flavored nonstick spray
2 slices commercial whole wheat bread or oat bran bread
2 tablespoons grated fat-free mozzarella cheese
1 tablespoon chopped garlic
1/16 teaspoon cayenne pepper
1/8 teaspoon anise seeds (optional)

Preheat the oven to 450 degrees F.

Spray a 12-inch-square of aluminum foil on one side with butter-flavored nonstick spray. Spray one piece of bread on both sides with butter-flavored spray. Place the bread on the sprayed side of the aluminum foil. Sprinkle the cheese over the bread, then the garlic and the anise if you like an Italian flavor. Spray the remaining slice of bread with butter-flavored spray on both sides. Place on top of the first piece of bread making a "sandwich." Wrap the foil over the "sandwich" and place on the middle rack of the oven. (If you want more of these, make several "sandwiches.") Bake for 10 minutes, then turn the sandwich over and bake for about 5 minutes. Depending on how hot your oven is, it might cook faster, so open the sandwich and check after the first 10 minutes. When the bread appears lightly toasted it is done. Slice the "sandwich" into 4 pieces with a bread knife and serve immediately.

FUNNY PIZZA

YIELD: 1 SERVING

Nutrition Facts

Amount Per Serving

Calories 160	Calories from Fat 15

	% Daily Value*
Total Fat 1.5g	**2%**
Saturated Fat 0g	**0%**
Cholesterol 5mg	**1%**
Sodium 400mg	**17%**
Total Carbohydrate 23g	**8%**
Dietary Fiber 4g	**15%**
Sugars 5g	
Protein 15g	

Vitamin A 20%	•	Vitamin C 20%
Calcium 50%	•	Iron 10%

I call this funny pizza rather than phony pizza because it sounds better. If you are having this for supper and you can have more complex carbohydrates or bread exchanges, use two pieces of bread. You could either double everything, or split your milk exchange mozzarella between the two pieces of bread, or just top with a second piece of toast for a sandwich.

1 slice Pritikin or commercial whole wheat bread
1/4 cup nonfat grated mozzarella cheese
1/4 cup Italian Tomato Sauce (page 54), or more, to taste
1 large mushroom, sliced
1/4 cup minced onion
1 tablespoon grated sapsago cheese

Preheat the oven to 350 degrees F.

Lay the bread on a nonstick pan, and sprinkle with the mozzarella cheese, then spread with tomato sauce. Arrange the mushroom slices over the sauce, then the minced onion. Bake for about 10 minutes, or until mushrooms are limp and the bread begins to look toasted. Sprinkle the sapsago cheese and serve.

Variation:

Use zucchini slices and green pepper slices as well as the mushrooms and onions.

CUCUMBER SANDWICHES

YIELD: 4 FINGER SANDWICHES

Nutrition Facts

Amount Per Serving	
Calories 40	Calories from Fat 5

	% Daily Value*
Total Fat 0.5g	1%
Saturated Fat 0g	0%
Cholesterol 0mg	0%
Sodium 125mg	5%
Total Carbohydrate 7g	2%
Dietary Fiber 0g	0%
Sugars 2g	
Protein 2g	

Vitamin A 4%	•	Vitamin C 2%
Calcium 2%	•	Iron 2%

I usually make this for my husband and myself for lunch to go with some soup. We each get two, but you could make a whole tray of them for a party by multiplying the amounts given here.

2 tablespoons Kraft fat-free mayonnaise dressing
1 tablespoon finely chopped onion
1/4 teaspoon medium red hot sauce
1/2 teaspoon chili powder
1 tablespoon fresh, chopped parsley
1/4 cup thinly sliced cucumber
2 slices Pritikin or commercial whole wheat bread

In a bowl, thoroughly combine the fat-free mayonnaise dressing, onion, hot sauce, chili powder, and parsley. Spread the mixture on both slices of the bread. Top one slice with the cucumbers. Cover with the other slice of bread. This makes one big sandwich, or cut off the crusts and cut into 4 party-size sandwiches.

ASPARAGUS SANDWICHES

YIELD: 18
SANDWICHES

Nutrition Facts

Amount Per Serving

Calories 230	Calories from Fat 0

	% Daily Value*
Total Fat 0g	0%
Saturated Fat 0g	0%
Cholesterol 5mg	2%
Sodium 200mg	8%
Total Carbohydrate 50g	17%
Dietary Fiber 5g	20%
Sugars 30g	
Protein 11g	

Vitamin A 15%	•	Vitamin C 45%
Calcium 10%	•	Iron 10%

These rolled sandwiches are delicious and different to take to a pot-luck luncheon.

9 slices whole wheat bread, crusts removed
1/2 cup Dill Dip (below)
1 can (14.5 ounces) cut asparagus spears, drained
Fresh parsley, for garnish
Cherry tomatoes, for garnish

Place a slice of bread on a cutting board and flatten it with a rolling pin. Spread with 1 tablespoon Dill Dip. Place 3 or 4 asparagus pieces in a line on one end of the slice of bread. Roll that end over the asparagus. Place more asparagus where the roll ends, then place a sprig of parsley at each end allowing the parsley to stick out a little. Roll the sandwich all the way up. Cut the roll in half to make 2 sandwiches. Place the sandwiches, seam-side-down, on a serving platter. Continue with the remaining slices of bread. Garnish the platter with cherry tomatoes and more parsley.

DILL DIP

YIELD: 1/2 CUP

Nutrition Facts

Amount Per Serving

Calories 10	Calories from Fat 0

	% Daily Value*
Total Fat 0g	0%
Saturated Fat 0g	0%
Cholesterol 0mg	0%
Sodium 45mg	2%
Total Carbohydrate 1g	0%
Dietary Fiber 0g	0%
Sugars 1g	
Protein 2g	

Vitamin A 0%	•	Vitamin C 0%
Calcium 0%	•	Iron 0%

This dip is wonderful with cut fresh vegetables and is the perfect spread for Asparagus Sandwiches (above).

1/2 cup nonfat cottage cheese
1 teaspoon finely chopped onion
1 teaspoon apple juice concentrate
1/8 teaspoon dried dillweed
1/8 teaspoon red hot sauce

Combine all the ingredients in a blender or food processor. Process until smooth and creamy. Don't make more than you need because it doesn't keep well for long periods in the refrigerator.

BLACK BEAN SALAD SANDWICH

Nutrition Facts

Amount Per Serving

Calories 300 Calories from Fat 20

	% Daily Value*
Total Fat 2g	**3%**
Saturated Fat 0g	**0%**
Cholesterol 0mg	**0%**
Sodium 360mg	**15%**
Total Carbohydrate 59g	**20%**
Dietary Fiber 13g	**53%**
Sugars 5g	
Protein 15g	

Vitamin A 2%	•	Vitamin C 8%
Calcium 4%	•	Iron 20%

1 cup cooked Black Beans (page 268)
1 celery rib, chopped
Italian Salad Dressing (page 310)
2 whole wheat pita bread pockets
1/2 cucumber, peeled and sliced
1/2 onion, thinly sliced

In a bowl, combine the black beans, celery, and enough Italian Salad Dressing to coat the celery and beans. Set aside to marinate before serving if you have time. Stuff pita bread pockets with the bean and celery mixture. Add 3 or 4 cucumber slices and some onion slices. Save extra salad dressing for later use.

ARTICHOKE DIP

YIELD: ABOUT 1 1/2
CUPS

Nutrition Facts

Amount Per Serving	
Calories 25	Calories from Fat 0
	% Daily Value*
Total Fat 0g	0%
Saturated Fat 0g	0%
Cholesterol 0mg	0%
Sodium 140mg	6%
Total Carbohydrate 2g	1%
Dietary Fiber 0g	0%
Sugars 0g	
Protein 3g	
Vitamin A 4% • Vitamin C 0%	
Calcium 4% • Iron 0%	

For a spectacular party presentation serve this dip in a hollowed out cabbage bowl with the large, outer cabbage leaves arranged around it. Surround with fresh vegetables for dipping and wait for the compliments.

4 water-packed canned artichoke hearts
2 cups (8 ounces each) fat-free cream cheese
1/4 cup fat-free mayonnaise dressing
1/4 teaspoon medium red hot sauce

Drain and rinse canned artichokes.

Put the cream cheese and fat-free mayonnaise dressing in the bottom of your blender and place the artichokes on top. Begin to blend on a slow speed, occasionally scraping down the sides. When everything is pretty well blended, add the red hot sauce, and switch to high speed for about a minute. Or you can do this in a food processor fitted with a cutting blade. Add all the ingredients and process until smooth.

ROUILLE SAUCE

YIELD: 3 SERVINGS

Nutrition Facts

Amount Per Serving	
Calories 10	Calories from Fat 0
	% Daily Value*
Total Fat 0g	0%
Saturated Fat 0g	0%
Cholesterol 0mg	0%
Sodium 105mg	4%
Total Carbohydrate 2g	1%
Dietary Fiber 0g	0%
Sugars 1g	
Protein 0g	
Vitamin A 0% • Vitamin C 0%	
Calcium 0% • Iron 0%	

My husband Ray and I first had Rouille Sauce in St. Raphael on the French Riviera. It was served on top of a crouton on Bouillabaisse and it was absolutely delicious. I have always wanted to make a diet version and with the advent of fat-free mayonnaise, voilà!

3 tablespoons Kraft fat-free mayonnaise dressing
1/8 teaspoon saffron
1 medium clove fresh garlic, crushed

In a small bowl, mix the mayonnaise dressing with the saffron and garlic and let it sit for at least an hour. Refrigerate and stir occasionally. The mixture should turn yellow and absorb the flavors of the saffron and garlic.

Serve on top of a soup crouton, or with an artichoke, or anything that would be enhanced by a flavored mayonnaise. This recipe can be made successfully in any quantity.

SALSA CHEESE DIP

YIELD: 1 CUP

Nutrition Facts

Amount Per Serving

Calories 10	Calories from Fat 0

	% Daily Value*
Total Fat 0g	**0%**
Saturated Fat 0g	**0%**
Cholesterol 0mg	**0%**
Sodium 80mg	**3%**
Total Carbohydrate 1g	**0%**
Dietary Fiber 0g	**0%**
Sugars 1g	
Protein 1g	

Vitamin A 2%	•	Vitamin C 8%
Calcium 6%	•	Iron 0%

1/2 cup shredded, fat-free cheddar cheese
1/2 cup Piquante Sauce (page 55)

Microwave Oven Directions: Pour the cheese into a microwave-safe bowl, then pour the Piquante Sauce over it. Cover the bowl with plastic wrap and cook on high setting for 2 minutes. Remove the cover and stir to combine.

Conventional Oven or Stove Top Directions: In a small glass bowl set over a small saucepan of boiling water, melt the cheddar cheese and Piquante Sauce, stirring constantly until combined.

Serve with baked tostidos or corn chips, over baked potatoes, steamed vegetables, or Huevos con Papas (page 72), cooked macaroni, baked chicken, fish, or anything that would benefit from a cheesy Mexican flavor.

BEAN DIP

YIELD: 2 CUPS

Nutrition Facts

Amount Per Serving

Calories 30	Calories from Fat 5

	% Daily Value*
Total Fat 0.5g	**1%**
Saturated Fat 0g	**0%**
Cholesterol 0mg	**0%**
Sodium 10mg	**0%**
Total Carbohydrate 6g	**2%**
Dietary Fiber 1g	**5%**
Sugars 2g	
Protein 1g	

Vitamin A 2%	•	Vitamin C 6%
Calcium 0%	•	Iron 2%

2 cups cold, cooked, Quick and Easy Pinto Beans (page 266)
2 very small onions or 1/2 large onion, quartered
1 fresh jalapeño pepper
2 teaspoons medium red hot sauce
1 tablespoon apple cider vinegar
1 teaspoon garlic powder
1/4 cup raisins
1 teaspoon paprika
Juice of 1 lemon

Place all the ingredients in a blender or food processor and blend until smooth. Serve with Piquante Sauce (page 55), Toasted Tortilla Chips (below), or commercial baked tortilla chips which have equal or less sodium than corn tortillas.

TOASTED TORTILLA CHIPS

YIELD: 48 CHIPS

Nutrition Facts

Amount Per Serving

Calories 10	Calories from Fat 0

	% Daily Value*
Total Fat 0g	**0%**
Saturated Fat --g	--%
Cholesterol --mg	--%
Sodium 0mg	**0%**
Total Carbohydrate 2g	**1%**
Dietary Fiber 0g	**0%**
Sugars --g	
Protein 0g	

Vitamin A --%	•	Vitamin C --%
Calcium 2%	•	Iron 0%

I have found that some commercial, baked, corn tortilla chips containing salt are lower in sodium than corn tortillas. But if you can't find them, you can make your own using this recipe.

Preheat oven to 350 degrees F.

Place 12 fresh or frozen soft corn tortillas on the racks of the oven and bake for 3 to 5 minutes. Keep your eye on the tortillas on the bottom rack because they will be done more quickly than the others. Tortillas are rather temperamental, so in order not to burn them, I set my oven timer for 2 minutes, check them, then set the timer for each minute after that if they aren't done. When the tortillas are crisp, remove them from the oven and break each one into 4 chips.

BEAN TOSTADOS

YIELD: 8 TOSTADOS

Nutrition Facts

Amount Per Serving

Calories 150   Calories from Fat 10

	% Daily Value*
Total Fat 1g	**1%**
Saturated Fat 0g	**0%**
Cholesterol 5mg	**1%**
Sodium 340mg	**14%**
Total Carbohydrate 21g	**7%**
Dietary Fiber 2g	**8%**
Sugars 8g	
Protein 15g	

Vitamin A 15%	•	Vitamin C 15%
Calcium 60%	•	Iron 4%

8 frozen or refrigerated corn tortillas
2 cups Bean Dip (page 335)
1 cup Piquante Sauce (page 55)
1/2 cup chopped onions
2 cups shredded lettuce
2 cups nonfat yogurt
2 cups shredded nonfat cheddar cheese
2 tomatoes, chopped

Preheat oven to 350 degrees F.

Place the tortillas on the racks of the oven and bake for 3 to 5 minutes. Check the tortillas on the bottom rack frequently. I set my oven timer for 2 minutes, look at them, then set the timer for each minute after that if they aren't done. When the tortillas are crisp, remove them from the oven and spread each toasted tortilla with 1/4 cup Bean Dip, then layer with 2 tablespoons of Piquante Sauce, 1 tablespoon chopped onions, 1/4 cup shredded lettuce, 1/4 cup nonfat yogurt, 1/4 cup nonfat cheddar cheese, and finish with chopped tomato on top.

TACO SALAD

YIELD: 6 SERVINGS

Nutrition Facts

Amount Per Serving

Calories 670   Calories from Fat 150

	% Daily Value*
Total Fat 17g	26%
Saturated Fat 5g	26%
Cholesterol 55mg	18%
Sodium 570mg	24%
Total Carbohydrate 92g	31%
Dietary Fiber 7g	30%
Sugars 27g	
Protein 38g	

Vitamin A 50%	•	Vitamin C 90%
Calcium 50%	•	Iron 30%

This is a good recipe to make if you have some leftover cooked lima beans to use in the B & B Dressing. This recipe is really a variation of the recipe for Tacos (page 112). It's just a different way to put it together. You could leave off one of the cheeses if both are too much sodium or calories for your present diet. The baked tortilla chips have a little salt, but the sodium is usually less than in the regular plain corn tortillas.

54 toasted tortilla chips (page 335)
Meat and seasoning for Tacos (page 112)
Vegetable and cheese filling for Tacos (page 112)
Taco Sauce (page 112) or Piquante Sauce (page 55)
2 sliced banana peppers or jalapeño peppers
A double recipe for B & B Dressing (page 293)
3/4 cups nonfat shredded cheddar cheese

Place 1 ounce of the tortilla chips (about 9) on each plate; spread 1/6 of the meat and seasoning over the chips; then the vegetables and the cottage cheese, then the Taco Sauce or Piquante Sauce; then the sliced peppers; then the B & B Dressing; and finally 1/8 cup of cheddar cheese sprinkled over each salad. Each salad will contain about 3 1/2 ounces of meat.

MOCK SOUR CREAM OR ONION DIP

Nutrition Facts

Amount Per Serving	
Calories 10	Calories from Fat 0

	% Daily Value*
Total Fat 0g	**0%**
Saturated Fat 0g	**0%**
Cholesterol 0mg	**0%**
Sodium 35mg	**1%**
Total Carbohydrate 1g	**0%**
Dietary Fiber 0g	**0%**
Sugars 0g	
Protein 1g	

Vitamin A 0%	•	Vitamin C 0%
Calcium 0%	•	Iron 0%

This mixture is so versatile it can be used as a dip, instead of mayonnaise, and as a topping for many of the dishes in this book.

1 3/4 cups (12 ounces) nonfat cottage cheese
1 small onion
1 teaspoon red hot sauce
1 tablespoon skim milk

Place all the ingredients in a blender or food processor and blend until the cottage cheese is free of lumps. This mixture doesn't blend easily, so if it looks as if it is just sitting there, stop the blender and scrape down the sides with a spoon or rubber spatula to move it around and help get it going.

GRAPEFRUIT SNACK

It may seem a little odd to create a recipe for just a half a grapefruit, but I eat more grapefruit since I discovered this, and I think you will too.

Over a half of a grapefruit, spread 1/4 teaspoon of apple juice concentrate or more to taste.

CREAMY FRUIT DIP

Serve this dip with sliced cantaloupe, strawberries, apples, pineapples, and other fruits and even vegetables, arranged on a decorative tray for a party. (Be sure to coat apple slices with lemon juice so they won't turn brown.)

2 packages (8 ounces each) fat-free cream cheese
3/4 cup drained, unsweetened, canned crushed pineapple or chopped fresh
1 1/2 teaspoon vanilla extract
1/2 teaspoon cinnamon
1/4 banana
1/8 teaspoon cayenne pepper (optional)
1 tablespoon toasted sesame seeds

Place all ingredients, except the seeds, in a blender or food processor and blend on a low speed until smooth and creamy. Stir in the seeds and serve.

POPCORN

YIELD: 1 SERVING

Nutrition Facts

Amount Per Serving

Calories 25   Calories from Fat 0

% Daily Value*

Total Fat 0g	**0%**
Saturated Fat 0g	**0%**
Cholesterol 0mg	**0%**
Sodium 0mg	**0%**
Total Carbohydrate 5g	**2%**
Dietary Fiber less than 1 gram	**4%**
Sugars 0g	
Protein 1g	

Vitamin A 0%	•	Vitamin C 0%	
Calcium 0%	•	Iron 0%	

Microwave Directions: 1/3 cup raw popcorn kernels

Place the popcorn kernels in a lunch-size brown paper bag. Twist the top of the bag lightly to let steam escape leaving lots of room for the corn to pop. Place in the microwave set on high setting, and cook for 3 minutes 30 seconds. Some microwaves are quicker so experiment on timing. Serve immediately,

Stove Top Directions: 1/4 cup raw popcorn kernels

Place the popcorn kernels in a small, nonstick pot with a handle and cover. Place on the burner over high heat. As it begins to heat up, shake the pot, and after a minute or two, when you hear the kernels starting to pop, shake the pot constantly until you don't hear any more popping. Transfer to a bowl, and if you let the popcorn cool a little, it will become light and fluffy. Spray with nonstick butter-flavored spray. Some people like to sprinkle it with onion or garlic powder, but sometimes I cheat and use a little salt. Mix and spray again with the butter-flavored spray.

ANDREA'S VERMONT-STYLE POPCORN

YIELD: 1 SERVING

Nutrition Facts

Amount Per Serving

Calories 90   Calories from Fat 5

% Daily Value*

Total Fat 1g	**1%**
Saturated Fat 0g	**0%**
Cholesterol 0mg	**0%**
Sodium 10mg	**0%**
Total Carbohydrate 17g	**6%**
Dietary Fiber 5g	**20%**
Sugars 2g	
Protein 5g	

Vitamin A 2%	•	Vitamin C 15%	
Calcium 2%	•	Iron 10%	

Andrea, the editor of my first cookbook, lives in Vermont and says that up there they shake soy sauce and Brewer's yeast on their popcorn. I tried it and then I came up with 1 tablespoon of orange juice over 2 cups of popcorn, sprinkled with 1 tablespoon of the Brewer's yeast. It tastes pretty good if you don't mind the calories!

CHAPTER 11

Desserts

Believe it or not, you can make absolutely wonderful desserts without sugar or butter or margarine or chocolate.

But a word of warning: If you eat these desserts in addition to the regular meals you have planned, don't think you are eating no calories or very few calories. A slice of blueberry pie is about 230 calories, which is almost the same as a slice of traditional apple pie. The difference is you are eating stuff that is really good for you instead of things that aren't. So if you are going to eat a dessert, incorporate it into your servings for different foods during the day.

These desserts are nice, too, for bringing along to potluck dinners. Then you have something you can eat, and no one will suspect it is diet food. The funny thing is my desserts always disappear faster than other desserts. Don't tell anyone they're eating a healthy cake or pie, just relax and enjoy the compliments.

In a couple of recipes I use a little fructose, which is made from fruit, not sugar cane. It is not sucrose, which is the kind of sugar that gives people the most trouble. Fructose is okay to use in small amounts on a sugar-free diet. But, for the most part, I have stuck to using whole fruits or fruit juices, since they are better for you than fructose.

SPONGE CAKE BASE

I never dreamed I could make a sponge cake without sugar or oil, but after some trial and error, I'm thrilled with this recipe—it's so light, sweet, and delicious.

I use a nonstick flan pan to make this cake. A flan pan is fluted around the edges and has a depression in the center. Be sure the pan measures 10 1/2 inches at the widest point. The cake part of the pan should hold 4 cups, and the center, which will hold the fruit filling, should hold 2 cups.

1 cup unbleached white flour
1 teaspoon low-sodium baking powder
4 jumbo egg whites
1 cup apple juice concentrate
1/2 teaspoon lemon extract

Preheat the oven to 325 degrees F.

Spray a nonstick flan pan with nonstick spray.

Sift together in a bowl the flour and baking powder.

In another deep mixing bowl, beat the egg whites with an electric mixer on high speed until they form stiff peaks.

In still another deep mixing bowl, combine the juice concentrate and the lemon extract. Gradually beat the flour into the juice-extract mixture. Then carefully fold the eggs into the batter, gently mixing until all streaks disappear. Pour the batter into the flan pan. Place the pan on the middle rack of the oven and bake for about 30 minutes, or until the cake is golden brown and a toothpick inserted in the center comes out clean. Remove the cake to a cake rack and let it cool in the pan 10 minutes. Turn the cake out of the pan and let it continue to cool on the cake rack.

PEACHES AND CREAM CAKE

Nutrition Facts

Amount Per Serving

Calories 160	Calories from Fat 0

	% Daily Value*
Total Fat 0g	0%
Saturated Fat 0g	0%
Cholesterol 5mg	1%
Sodium 75mg	3%
Total Carbohydrate 31g	10%
Dietary Fiber 1g	5%
Sugars 21g	
Protein 6g	

Vitamin A 4%	•	Vitamin C 4%
Calcium 2%	•	Iron 6%

1 Sponge Cake Base (page 343)
Creamy Pie Topping (page 359)
2 cans (16 ounces each) sliced yellow cling peaches packed in unsweetened pear juice

Prepare the Sponge Cake Base according to the recipe directions and cool. Then prepare the Whipped Topping.

Place the cooled sponge cake on a plate and pour about 1/4-inch of the juice from the peaches into the cavity. Pierce the cake all over with a toothpick so the juice will absorb into the cake. Pour some more juice on the plate around the cake and on the high sides of the cake. As the juice is absorbed into the sides of the cake, add more juice. Try to get as much juice into the cake as possible. Fill the cavity of the cake with as many peach slices as will fit.

Spread the Creamy Pie Topping over the cake and arrange the rest of the peaches on top, using as many as you can.

Chill the cake for about an hour. You can also pour more juice around the sides of the cake, sort of basting it with juice, while it is chilling. The juicier, the better.

HAWAIIAN MOONLIGHT

YIELD: 10 SERVINGS

Nutrition Facts

Amount Per Serving	
Calories 340	Calories from Fat 5

	% Daily Value*
Total Fat 0.5g	1%
Saturated Fat 0g	0%
Cholesterol 5mg	1%
Sodium 100mg	4%
Total Carbohydrate 73g	24%
Dietary Fiber 3g	13%
Sugars 58g	
Protein 10g	

Vitamin A 2%	•	Vitamin C 40%
Calcium 6%	•	Iron 15%

I just loved eating by moonlight in the romantic, torchlit, terrace restaurants in Hawaii. With all the pineapple and bananas, and creamy whipped topping, this cake is just like Hawaiian moonlight.

1 Sponge Cake Base (page 343)
Creamy Pie Topping (page 359)
1 can (20 ounces) unsweetened crushed pineapple
1 can (20 ounces) unsweetened sliced pineapple
3 1/2 cups canned unsweetened pineapple juice
2 tablespoons apple juice concentrate
2 bananas, sliced
1 envelope of unflavored gelatin

Drain the crushed pineapple and the sliced pineapple and reserve the juice. Pour the juice concentrate into a 2-cup measuring cup and add some of the reserved pineapple juice to equal 2 cups.

Pierce the sponge cake all over with a fork and place the crushed pineapple in the cavity of the Sponge Cake Base. Arrange the banana slices over the pineapple so that the slices touch each other.

Pour 1/2 cup of reserved pineapple juice into another container and add 1 envelope of unflavored gelatin to soften it. Heat the remaining reserved pineapple juice to the boiling point and add it to the gelatin mixture. Mix well. Pour the gelatin mixture over the bananas and the cake, letting it seep in, as much as the cake can absorb. Make sure you pour some juice on all the banana slices to coat them, and on the sides of the cake. Place the cake in the refrigerator to gel. Also place the remaining juice-gelatin mixture in the refrigerator.

After about an hour, whip the Creamy Pie Topping and spread it on top of the cake. (You don't want to whip it sooner because it won't spread as well.)

Dip one slice of pineapple into the juice-gelatin mixture, which should be syrupy by now. Place a pineapple slice on the middle of the cake. Cut another slice of pineapple in equal pieces, dip them one by one into the gelatin mixture, and arrange the pieces geometrically around the pineapple ring in the center. Dip the banana slices one by one into the juice-gelatin mixture. Put the first slice inside the pineapple ring and place the others between the cut pieces of the pineapple. Refrigerate the cake for at least 2 hours. If you aren't going to use the cake right away, after it has gelled, it will keep for up to 2 days if covered with plastic wrap that has been sprayed with nonstick spray, spray-side down.

The leftover pineapple juice-gelatin mixture is what we in Louisiana call "langiappe"—pronounced "*lan-yap*," which means a little something extra for free. Add some more banana slices and leftover pineapple to the rest of the juice-gelatin mixture, refrigerate, and you have pineapple gelatin.

Variation: CAROB FRUITY CHIFFON CAKE

Make the cake exactly as you would Hawaiian Moonlight, but instead of using the white cream topping, make some Carob Banana Mint Pudding (page 367) omitting the bananas and pineapple in the pudding. The resulting pudding makes a wonderful creamy, chocolate-like top.

BLUEBERRY MAGIC

Nutrition Facts

Amount Per Serving

Calories 290	Calories from Fat 5

	% Daily Value*
Total Fat 0.5g	**1**%
Saturated Fat 0g	**0**%
Cholesterol 5mg	**1**%
Sodium 100mg	**4**%
Total Carbohydrate 62g	**21**%
Dietary Fiber 3g	**12**%
Sugars 46g	
Protein 9g	

Vitamin A 2%	•	Vitamin C 30%
Calcium 4%	•	Iron 10%

1 Sponge Cake Base (page 343)
Creamy Pie Topping (page 359)
1 1/2 cups unsweetened pineapple juice
1/2 cup apple juice concentrate
1 1/2 cups Blueberry Jelly (page 63)
Fresh blueberries

Prepare the sponge cake according to the recipe directions and cool. When cool, pierce the Sponge Cake Base all over with a fork, cover and refrigerate. Prepare the Creamy Pie Topping.

Mix the pineapple juice and juice concentrate and pour over the cake to moisten it. Fill the cavity in the cake with Blueberry Jelly. Spread the topping on the cake. Decorate with more blueberries and serve.

KING'S CAKE

YIELD: 20 SERVINGS

Nutrition Facts

Amount Per Serving

Calories 190   Calories from Fat 0

	% Daily Value*
Total Fat 0g	**0**%
Saturated Fat 0g	**0**%
Cholesterol 0mg	**0**%
Sodium 50mg	**2**%
Total Carbohydrate 41g	**14**%
Dietary Fiber 1g	**6**%
Sugars 17g	
Protein 5g	

Vitamin A 2%	•	Vitamin C 0%
Calcium 8%	•	Iron 15%

The twelfth day of Christmas, January 6th, is yet another day of celebration in New Orleans. Known as the Feast of the Epiphany, or Le Petit Noel, it is traditionally the day that the Three Kings found the baby Jesus in Bethlehem, and in New Orleans it's an excuse to have a party and begin the Mardi Gras season with a King's Cake party.

Originally these were elegant balls given in people's homes where a large King's Cake in the shape of a ring was served. There is still one formal ball called the Twelfth Night Revelers that officially starts the Carnival or Mardi Gras season.

A little doll is hidden inside the cake and whoever discovers it is king or queen for a week. If it is a gentleman who becomes king, he chooses a queen, and if it is a lady who becomes queen, she chooses a king and the queen must give a party at her house the following week and serve another King's Cake. The king must pay for the party, and this goes on for weeks until the first day of Lent, Ash Wednesday. It is perfectly proper and traditional for the king to give a present to the queen, and even if she is a single girl, her parents allow her to keep it.

The Spanish settlers began this custom and the French, being avid party givers, adopted it as their own, and so it continues to this day.

When I was a child, the cakes contained tiny hand-painted porcelain dolls. Now, they are plastic, but we all endure, and we love our delicious King's Cakes and our King's Cake parties.

This cake is a little more sugary than some of my desserts, so go a little easy when you serve it.

1/2 cup warm water
1 teaspoon fructose
1 tablespoon yeast
1 1/3 cups skim milk, scalded
1/4 cup fructose
2 jumbo egg whites
5 cups unbleached white all purpose flour

Combine the water, 1 teaspoon fructose, and yeast in a cup or small bowl and sit it in a warm place for about 10 minutes or until it is foamy.

To scald the milk, either heat in the microwave until it just boils, or heat in a saucepan on the stove until tiny bubbles form around the edges of the pan and the temperature of the milk is 180 degrees F. Let the milk cool to lukewarm. Note: You could kill the yeast with milk that is too hot.

Combine the yeast mixture, the milk, the 1/4 cup of fructose, and the egg whites in your largest mixing bowl or a very big salad bowl. Beat well to combine thoroughly. Add the flour and mix again, then let the batter rest, uncovered, for 10 minutes.

Spray your hands with butter-flavored nonstick spray and knead the dough lightly in the bowl, pulling it from the edge to the center, and pressing down lightly. Spray your hands again if the dough starts to stick to your fingers. You don't want to knead the dough too much or the cake will be tough. Stop kneading when the dough begins to resist you, which means if you poke it with your finger, it will spring back slowly.

Spray plastic wrap with butter-flavored nonstick spray and cover the bowl, spray-side down. Set the bowl in the refrigerator to let the dough rise for up to 6 hours. It is ready when it doubles in bulk.

You can make one big cake, but I make two because they are easier to handle.

Spray 1 piece of aluminum foil with butter-flavored nonstick spray, and have 2 baking trays ready. Punch the dough down and divide into 2 portions. Place the aluminum foil spray-side up on the counter and place one portion of dough on it. Leave the other portion on the bowl. Make the Cream Cheese Fruit Filling.

4 ounces fat-free cream cheese
1/4 cup fructose
1/2 teaspoon vanilla
1 jumbo egg white
1 jar (10 ounces) your favorite all-fruit preserves

To make the filling place all the ingredients in a bowl and combine thoroughly with a fork.

Spray your hands with butter-flavored nonstick spray and spread the portion of the dough on the foil out as thin as you can into a long rectangle. Spread with half of the filling, covering the dough except for one long edge. Roll the dough up jelly-roll style, from the long edge that has the filling on it. Continue rolling until you reach the edge without filling. Pinch the plain edge to the rest of the roll. Form into a ring, pinching the ends together. Lift the cake by the foil beneath it and set it on a baking tray. Spray plastic wrap with butter-flavored nonstick spray and cover the cake, spray-side down. Set it in a warm place to rise until doubled. Repeat this process with the remaining dough and filling.

Preheat oven to 400 degrees F.

When both cakes have doubled, bake uncovered, for about 20 minutes, or until golden. The cake on the bottom rack will probably cook first. I like to use two ovens and bake each cake on the middle rack, or you could bake them one at a time, on the middle rack to avoid burning them.

Remove the cakes and cook on wire racks. Place the cakes on cake plates. Press a dried kidney bean or a very small plastic or porcelain doll, or a ring into the cake from underneath, so that you can't see it from the top. Make the Colored Fructose.

Colored Fructose:
1/4 cup fructose
4 drops yellow food coloring
1/4 cup fructose
4 drops blue food coloring

Put 1/4 cup fructose in a cup and add 4 drops yellow food coloring. Rub together with your fingers. Let dry for about 10 minutes. In another cup, put 1/4 cup fructose, add 4 drops of blue food coloring, and rub together with your fingers. Let dry for 10 minutes.

Make the Cake Icing (page 358). Spread Cake Icing over the tops of the cakes, letting it drizzle over the sides. Sprinkle the cake with alternate spots of colored fructose, overlapping the colors a little. If you don't want to use food color, you could mix the fructose with a little cinnamon instead.

Tell your guests who are new to this that the bean or doll, etc., is in the cake so they don't break their teeth, and tell them they will become the queen or king if they find it, and they will have the pleasure of giving a party the following week.

SHIRLEY'S CARROT CAKE

This is a delicious, moist, as-good-as, or better-than your regular recipe carrot cake that I adapted from my friend Shirley's recipe. For an extra treat, spread the top with a sugar-free all-fruit spread, Blueberry Jelly (page 63), or Icing (page 358).

2 cups whole wheat flour
1 teaspoon low-sodium baking powder
2 teaspoons baking soda
1 teaspoon cinnamon
8 jumbo egg whites
1 1/2 cups apple juice concentrate
1 teaspoon vanilla extract
1 cup raisins
2 cups finely grated carrots

Preheat the oven to 350 degrees F.

Spray two 8-inch-square nonstick cake pans with a nonstick spray.

Sift into a large mixing bowl, the flour, baking powder, baking soda, and cinnamon.

In a separate bowl, beat the egg whites until frothy. Add the egg whites, juice concentrate, and vanilla extract to the flour. Stir with a spoon until all the ingredients are wet, then beat with an electric mixer for 3 minutes. With a spoon, add the raisins and carrots. Pour the batter into the cake pans. Bake on the middle rack of the oven for 40 to 50 minutes. The cakes are done when a toothpick inserted into the centers comes out clean.

Let the cakes cook in the pans for 20 minutes. Loosen the cakes with a nonstick spatula, sliding the spatula underneath, if necessary. Turn the cakes over onto a clean cloth which is resting on a solid surface. They might just fall out, but if they don't, bang the pan down on the cloth. Try the cloth first because it's hard to bang a cake down on a wire rack. Move the cake to a wire rack to finish cooling. On a chopping board cut the cake into squares with a serrated or electric knife.

Freeze extras in a plastic bag for a long-lasting supply of healthy, sweet snacks. Defrost by placing individual squares in a microwave oven on high setting for 30 seconds, or let the cake defrost to room temperature.

FLOATING PINEAPPLE UPSIDE-DOWN CAKE

I never meant for this cake to float, but it just did. I was trying to add a gelatin-fruit juice mixture to the cooked cake to add moisture, and lo and behold, the cake floated. Some surprises are absolutely delightful. Be sure to use only canned fruit and juices because fresh pineapple and juice won't gel.

4 canned unsweetened sliced pineapple rings
1/2 cup raisins
1 1/3 cups crushed unsweetened pineapple or 1 can (20 ounces), drained and juice reserved
1 cup whole wheat flour
1 1/2 teaspoons low-sodium baking powder
1 cup apple juice concentrate
2 jumbo egg whites
1/2 teaspoon vanilla extract
Apple juice concentrate
1 envelope unflavored gelatin

Preheat the oven to 350 degrees F.

Arrange the 4 pineapple rings in an 8-inch-square nonstick cake pan. Sprinkle the raisins over the pineapple rings, then spread the drained, crushed pineapple over the raisins and set aside.

Sift the flour into a large bowl and mix in the baking powder. Add 1 cup of apple juice concentrate, the egg whites, and the vanilla. Beat with an electric mixer for 2 minutes, until smooth. Pour the batter over the fruit in the cake pan.

Place on the middle rack of the oven and bake for 30 to 40 minutes, until a toothpick inserted into the center comes out clean. Let cool on a wire rack in the pan for 10 minutes.

Pierce the cake all over with a fork and loosen the sides with a spatula. In a measuring cup, pour the reserved pineapple juice and enough additional apple juice concentrate to equal 2 cups of liquid. Pour 1/4 cup of the liquid into another container and add the gelatin. Mix together and let sit to soften the gelatin. In a saucepan, bring the rest of the fruit juice to a boil. Add the hot juice to the gelatin mixture and completely dissolve the gelatin. Pour the gelatin-fruit juice mixture over the cake in the pan. Wait about 5 minutes. The cake will float up. If it doesn't, poke more holes in the cake and loosen the sides of the cake again with a spatula. I guarantee, the cake will float.

Chill the cake for about 4 hours in the refrigerator, then fill a sink with hot water, and place the cake pan in the water for just a second or two. Hold a cake plate over the pan and turn the cake over. The cake will fall out onto the plate with the gelatin-side up. If the cake doesn't readily fall out of the pan, repeat the process with the hot water, but don't leave the pan in the hot water for too long. You don't want to have runny gelatin. Garnish with fresh strawberries, or slice 1/4-inch slivers out of a watermelon and cut out stars or flowers with decorative cutters available at gourmet supply stores. One way or another you will need something red on this cake. If you want to cheat, use Maraschino cherries. But don't eat them! Take them off as if they were birthday candles.

CHEESECAKE

YIELD: 10 SERVINGS

Nutrition Facts

Amount Per Serving

Calories 180	Calories from Fat 0

	% Daily Value*
Total Fat 0g	**0%**
Saturated Fat 0g	**0%**
Cholesterol 5mg	**1%**
Sodium 270mg	**11%**
Total Carbohydrate 35g	**12%**
Dietary Fiber 2g	**9%**
Sugars 21g	
Protein 10g	

Vitamin A 25%	•	Vitamin C 6%
Calcium 20%	•	Iron 30%

Topping:
1 can (12 ounces) evaporated skim milk
1 envelope unflavored gelatin
1/2 Baked Banana (page 57)
1 teaspoon vanilla extract

Cake:
2 cups (8 ounces) fat-free cream cheese
3/4 cup canned crushed unsweetened pineapple, drained
1/2 Baked Banana (page 57)
1 1/2 teaspoons vanilla extract
1/2 teaspoon cinnamon
3/4 cup apple juice concentrate
2 envelopes unflavored gelatin
Basic Dessert Pie Crust (page 355)

To make the topping, pour about 1/2 cup of the milk into a cup and add the gelatin and banana and let it sit until the gelatin softens. In a saucepan, heat the remaining milk. When the gelatin is soft, add the heated milk and dissolve. Add the vanilla. Pour the mixture in a blender or food processor and blend until very smooth. Place in a mixing bowl. Cover with plastic wrap and have the wrap touching the milk so a skin does not form. Place in the refrigerator for about 4 hours, or until gelled.

When it has gelled, beat with an electric mixer, starting on a low speed and building up to the highest speed. Mix until smooth and fluffy.

Spray a 9-inch round cake pan or baking dish with a nonstick spray, plain or butter-flavored; a round fluted baking dish is prettiest. Or you can use an 8 x 8-inch cake pan or dish.

Spread the topping over the bottom of your baking dish or pan.

To make the cake, combine the cream cheese, pineapple, banana, vanilla, and cinnamon in a blender or food processor and blend on medium speed and building to the highest, until liquefied.

Mix the juice concentrate in a saucepan with the gelatin and let sit for 3 minutes. Bring to a boil, remove from the heat, and stir to dissolve the gelatin. Let cool, then add to the cheese mixture and blend in the blender or food processor. Pour the mixture over the topping. Refrigerate until gelled, about 4 hours.

Prepare the pie crust according to the recipe directions. Spread the crust over the cake.

Turn the cake upside-down by removing the cake from the pan onto a flat cake plate to accomplish this, loosen the cake by sitting the cake pan in hot water for a few seconds, then sliding a knife carefully around the edge. Place a cake plate by placing a cake plate upside-down on top of the cake. Turn the cake and plate over together and the cake should fall onto the cake plate. If it doesn't, sit the cake pan in the hot water for a couple of seconds more and repeat.

I decorate this cake by emptying a jar of all-fruit preserves over the top. Blueberry with the whole blueberries looks and tastes really scrumptious. Refrigerate for about 2 hours before serving.

BASIC DESSERT PIE CRUST

YIELD: 10 SERVINGS

1 1/2 cups Grape-Nuts® cereal
1/4 cup apple juice concentrate

Pour the Grape-Nuts® into a nonstick 9-inch pie pan. Add the juice and stir until the Grape-Nuts® are moist. Press into the pan until they take the shape of the pan. Set aside while you make the filling.

Nutrition Facts

Amount Per Serving

Calories 70	Calories from Fat 0

	% Daily Value*
Total Fat 0g	**0**%
Saturated Fat 0g	**0**%
Cholesterol 0mg	**0**%
Sodium 115mg	**5**%
Total Carbohydrate 16g	**5**%
Dietary Fiber 2g	**7**%
Sugars 4g	
Protein 2g	

Vitamin A 15%	•	Vitamin C 0%
Calcium 0%	•	Iron 25%

HOLIDAY FRUIT CAKE

YIELD: 256 BITE-SIZED SERVINGS

Nutrition Facts

Amount Per Serving	
Calories 15	Calories from Fat 0

	% Daily Value*
Total Fat 0g	0%
Saturated Fat 0g	0%
Cholesterol 0mg	0%
Sodium 0mg	0%
Total Carbohydrate 3g	1%
Dietary Fiber 0g	0%
Sugars 2g	
Protein 0g	

Vitamin A 0%	•	Vitamin C 0%
Calcium 0%	•	Iron 0%

At Christmas time, I just can't do without my fruit cake. Make sure the dried fruit contains no honey or sugar. If you can't find one of the fruits, substitute an equal amount of raisins. All the dried fruits you can find at your local super-market, but look for the pineapple at a health food store. I chop the lemon rind and mandarin rind in a food processor, but the remaining fruit has to be chopped by hand. In the interest of saving calories and limiting fruit servings, I always cut the cake up into approximately 1-inch cubes, to enjoy as a nice little "bon bite" every now and then, like candy.

2 tablespoons chopped lemon rind
2 tablespoons chopped mandarin or orange rind
1/2 cup brandy
3/4 cup plus 1 tablespoon apple juice concentrate
1 1/2 cups dried pineapple
1 1/4 cups raisins
1/2 cups pitted dates
1/4 cup dried pears
1/2 cup pitted prunes
3/4 cup dried figs
4 jumbo egg whites
1 1/2 teaspoon vanilla extract
1/8 teaspoon baking soda
1 1/4 cups whole wheat flour

Combine the lemon and mandarin rinds in a mixture of 1/4 cup brandy and 1/4 cup juice concentrate. Cover and marinate this mixture in the refrigerator for a few days before you start the cake. You can chop up all your dried fruit at this time, too, and put it in a plastic bag or a covered container. No need to refrigerate.

When you want to assemble your cake, first preheat the oven to 275 degrees F. Then combine the egg whites, the remaining 1/2 cup plus 1 tablespoon juice concentrate, the reserved brandy-rind-juice concentrate mixture, the vanilla, and baking soda in a large bowl. Sift the flour over the mixture, add the kernels left in the sifter of the whole wheat flour, and combine until smooth. Then add the chopped fruit and mix everything together.

Spray an 8-inch-by-5-inch loaf pan with a nonstick spray and pack the mixture into it. Set the cake on the middle rack of the oven and bake for 2 1/2 hours, until a toothpick inserted in the center comes out clean. Remove from the oven and turn it out onto a cake rack to cool. You might have to loosen it with a knife. If some of it sticks to the bottom of the pan, just scrape it off and pat it back firmly onto the bottom of the cake.

When the cake is cooled, turn right-side-up onto a cake plate. Pierce holes all over the top of the cake with a fork. In a metal measuring cup or a very small saucepan, pour in the remaining 1/4 cup brandy. Hold the cup or pan over a candle until the brandy feels warm, but not hot to the touch. Strike a match and hold over the top of the brandy and it will flame immediately. If it doesn't, heat it a little longer. Let it flame until it goes out. Dribble the brandy over the cake by the teaspoon and let it soak in. Cover with aluminum foil and let it sit for 48 hours before serving.

CAKE ICING

Nutrition Facts

Amount Per Serving	
Calories 40	Calories from Fat 0
	% Daily Value*
Total Fat 0g	**0%**
Saturated Fat 0g	**0%**
Cholesterol 0mg	**0%**
Sodium 55mg	**2%**
Total Carbohydrate 9g	**3%**
Dietary Fiber 0g	**0%**
Sugars 8g	
Protein 2g	
Vitamin A 4% • Vitamin C 0%	
Calcium 4% • Iron 0%	

This is particularly good on top of Shirley's Carrot Cake, but you could dip strawberries in it or eat it on top of a fresh fruit bowl, or on top of a fruit cake or bread pudding.

1 tablespoon apple juice concentrate
1 cup (8 ounces) fat-free cream cheese
3/4 cup fructose

Combine all the ingredients in a blender or food processor fitted with a cutting blade. Process until smooth. Spread on cake and refrigerate. The texture is best the first day.

CREAMY PIE TOPPING

YIELD: 10 SERVINGS OR 1 WHOLE PIE

Nutrition Facts

Amount Per Serving	
Calories 35	Calories from Fat 0
	% Daily Value*
Total Fat 0g	**0%**
Saturated Fat 0g	**0%**
Cholesterol 0mg	**0%**
Sodium 45mg	**2%**
Total Carbohydrate 6g	**2%**
Dietary Fiber 0g	**0%**
Sugars 5g	
Protein 3g	

Vitamin A 2%	•	Vitamin C 2%
Calcium 10%	•	Iron 0%

You won't believe how creamy and good this topping turns out. This alone may keep you on your diet. It takes the place of whipped cream.

1 can (13 ounces) evaporated skimmed milk
1/2 Baked Banana and juice (page 57)
1 packet unflavored gelatin
1/2 teaspoon lemon extract (optional)

Pour about 2 inches of milk into a cup, add the banana, and sprinkle with the gelatin to soften. Combine thoroughly.

Scald the rest of the milk in a quart-size container and microwave on high setting for 3 minutes, or until it just comes to a boil. Or, scald the rest of the milk in a quart-size saucepan and bring to the point when tiny bubbles form around the edge of the pan. Remove from the heat.

Remove any skin that forms on top of the milk. Add the rest of the milk mixed with the gelatin and banana to the scalded milk. Pour the mixture into a blender or food processor and blend on high speed until very smooth. Pour into a mixing bowl and cover with plastic wrap. Let the wrap touch the top of the milk to keep the gelatin from forming a hard skin on top. Refrigerate 3 to 4 hours until gelled.

When it has gelled, beat with an electric mixer. Start slowly, building up to the fastest speed, until the mixture is fluffy and creamy. Spread on top of the cooked pie, or on other recipes that need whipped topping.

BLUEBERRY CREAM PIE

Nutrition Facts

Amount Per Serving

Calories 180	Calories from Fat 0

	% Daily Value*
Total Fat 0g	**0%**
Saturated Fat 0g	**0%**
Cholesterol 0mg	**0%**
Sodium 170mg	**7%**
Total Carbohydrate 40g	**13%**
Dietary Fiber 3g	**11%**
Sugars 24g	
Protein 6g	

Vitamin A 20%	•	Vitamin C 10%
Calcium 15%	•	Iron 30%

If you double this recipe, it fits very nicely into a 9 x 13-inch baking dish for serving a crowd.

Creamy Pie Topping (page 359)
1 Basic Dessert Pie Crust (page 355)
1 cup apple juice concentrate
1/4 cup water
3 tablespoons cornstarch
2 cups fresh or frozen blueberries, plus a few extra for the top of the pie

Prepare the Creamy Pie Topping according to the recipe directions and refrigerate for 3 to 4 hours, or overnight. Don't whip it until you are ready to spread it on the pie.

Prepare the Basic Dessert Pie Crust according to the recipe directions, and set aside.

Combine the juice concentrate and water in a saucepan. Add the cornstarch and stir until smooth. Cook over medium heat, stirring constantly, until it starts to thicken. Continue to stir rapidly. When it begins to look transparent, remove from heat. Fold in the blueberries and then pour into the pie shell and set aside. When the pie is cool, whip the Creamy Pie Topping and spread it over the top. Decorate with the extra blueberries. Chill for about 1 hour before serving.

UPSIDE-DOWN CALYPSO CREAM PIE

Nutrition Facts

Amount Per Serving

Calories 270   Calories from Fat 10

	% Daily Value*
Total Fat 1g	**1%**
Saturated Fat 0g	**0%**
Cholesterol 0mg	**0%**
Sodium 180mg	**7%**
Total Carbohydrate 61g	**20%**
Dietary Fiber 4g	**15%**
Sugars 45g	
Protein 8g	

Vitamin A 25%	•	Vitamin C 15%
Calcium 15%	•	Iron 30%

Use a round, 10 1/2-inch nonstick, fluted flan pan that will hold 4 cups of liquid that has an indentation in the center that will hold 2 cups of liquid.

1 recipe for Creamy Pie Topping (page 358)
1 recipe for Nectarine Creamy (page 371)
40 seedless green grapes
2 nectarines, sliced (do not peel)
1 1/2 cups Grape-Nuts® cereal
1 1/4 cup apple juice concentrate
1 banana, sliced
1/2 envelope unflavored gelatin

Spray the flan pan with a nonstick spray. Spread the Creamy Pie Topping in the pan. Chill in the refrigerator until set, about 2 hours.

Prepare the Nectarine Creamy but do not refrigerate. Layer the Nectarine Creamy over the Whipped Topping, leaving about 1/4-inch of pan still above the Nectarine Creamy. (If there is a little Nectarine Creamy left over, put it in a custard cup and chill it for an extra snack.) Arrange 20 grapes and the slices of 1 nectarine over the Nectarine Creamy. Chill in the refrigerator for about 3 hours.

In a bowl, mix the Grape-Nuts® with 1/4 cup juice concentrate, then sprinkle and spread over the Nectarine Creamy. Chill in the refrigerator for 3 hours.

If your flan pan has a little hole in the side for hanging, stop it up with some aluminum foil. Fill the sink with a little hot water and set the pan in the water for just a few seconds. Hold a serving plate on top the pan and turn the pie over. It should fall out onto the plate. If it doesn't, return the flan pan in the hot water for a few more seconds. Unmold the pie on top of the plate. Refrigerate while you prepare the fruit topping.

Put the remaining grapes in a bowl. Add the remaining nectarine slices and the banana slices. Pour 1/4 cup of the remaining juice concentrate into a cup. Add the gelatin to soften it. In a saucepan, bring the remaining 3/4 cup of the juice concentrate to a boil. Pour the hot juice into the gelatin mixture. Mix until the gelatin is dissolved. Let cool. Pour the juice mixture over the fruit in the bowl and combine. Distribute the fruit around the center of the pie. Pour the juice-gelatin mixture over the fruit and fill the cavity of the flan pan. Pour leftover juice around the sides of the pie, and let it drizzle under it. If it won't go underneath the pie, don't worry about it, just pour it over the leftover Nectarine Creamy in the custard cup (if you haven't already eaten it), and chill the pie again for 3 to 4 hours before serving.

PEACH PIE

Nutrition Facts

Amount Per Serving

Calories 140	Calories from Fat 0

	% Daily Value*
Total Fat 0g	**0%**
Saturated Fat 0g	**0%**
Cholesterol 0mg	**0%**
Sodium 120mg	**5%**
Total Carbohydrate 33g	**11%**
Dietary Fiber 3g	**11%**
Sugars 17g	
Protein 2g	

Vitamin A 20%	•	Vitamin C 6%
Calcium 0%	•	Iron 30%

Basic Dessert Pie Crust (page 355)
2 1/2 cups sliced fresh, frozen, or canned unsweetened peaches
3 tablespoons cornstarch
1/2 cup plus 1/3 cup water
1/2 cup plus 1/3 cup apple juice concentrate
1/2 teaspoon vanilla extract

Prepare the pie crust according to the recipe directions. Arrange the peaches in the pie shell and set aside.

Spoon the cornstarch into a saucepan. Slowly add the water, stirring constantly until the mixture is free of lumps. Add juice concentrate and vanilla extract. Stir. Cook over medium heat, stirring constantly until the mixture thickens and turns almost transparent. Pour the sauce over the peach slices. Serve when cooled to room temperature or chill in the refrigerator.

BLACKBERRY PIE

Nutrition Facts

Amount Per Serving

Calories 160	Calories from Fat 0

	% Daily Value*
Total Fat 0g	**0%**
Saturated Fat 0g	**0%**
Cholesterol 0mg	**0%**
Sodium 125mg	**5%**
Total Carbohydrate 37g	**12%**
Dietary Fiber 5g	**19%**
Sugars 20g	
Protein 3g	

Vitamin A 15%	•	Vitamin C 20%
Calcium 2%	•	Iron 30%

Basic Dessert Pie Crust (page 355)
4 cups fresh or frozen sugar-free blackberries
1 cup apple juice concentrate
3 tablespoons cornstarch

Prepare the pie crust according to the recipe directions and set aside.

In a saucepan, simmer the blackberries in the apple juice until they are soft. Drain the berry liquid into a separate saucepan and combine with the cornstarch, stirring slowly and constantly. When the mixture is smooth, cook over a medium heat until it thickens, stirring constantly. Add the blackberries. Stir, then pour into the pie shell. Cool and serve.

LEMON CREAM PIE

Nutrition Facts

Amount Per Serving

Calories 310	Calories from Fat 10

	% Daily Value*
Total Fat 1g	**1%**
Saturated Fat 0g	**0%**
Cholesterol 0mg	**0%**
Sodium 170mg	**7%**
Total Carbohydrate 74g	**25%**
Dietary Fiber 5g	**22%**
Sugars 48g	
Protein 8g	

Vitamin A 20%	•	Vitamin C 70%
Calcium 15%	•	Iron 30%

Creamy Pie Topping (page 359)
Basic Dessert Pie Crust (page 355)
Juice of 4 1/2 lemons
3/4 cup apple juice concentrate
3/4 cup water
4 1/2 tablespoons cornstarch

Prepare the Creamy Pie Topping according to the recipe directions, and refrigerate for 3 to 4 hours, or overnight. Don't whip it until you are ready to spread it on the pie.

Prepare the pie crust according to the recipe directions and set aside.

Squeeze the lemons and pour the juice into a saucepan. Add the juice concentrate, the water, and the cornstarch. Stir until the mixture is smooth. Cook over medium heat, stirring constantly, until the mixture thickens and looks transparent. Pour into the pie shell. Chill in the refrigerator for about a half hour.

When the pie has cooled, whip the Creamy Pie Topping according to the recipe directions. Spread it on top of the pie and refrigerate for at least 2 hours before serving. A lemon slice on top makes a nice garnish.

PUMPKIN PIE

Nutrition Facts

Amount Per Serving

Calories 140	Calories from Fat 0

	% Daily Value*
Total Fat 0g	**0%**
Saturated Fat 0g	**0%**
Cholesterol 0mg	**0%**
Sodium 150mg	**6%**
Total Carbohydrate 30g	**10%**
Dietary Fiber 4g	**15%**
Sugars 15g	
Protein 5g	

Vitamin A 230%	•	Vitamin C 6%
Calcium 2%	•	Iron 30%

Basic Dessert Pie Crust (page 355)
1 can of cooked, sugar-free pumpkin
1 medium ripe banana + 1/4 ripe banana
1/4 cup apple juice concentrate
1/4 cup raisins (golden if you can find them)
1/4 teaspoon nutmeg
1/4 teaspoon ginger
1/4 teaspoon cinnamon
1/4 teaspoon mace
1/2 teaspoon allspice
1 teaspoon vanilla extract
6 jumbo egg whites
Cake Icing (page 358) (optional)

Prepare the crust in a 9-inch nonstick pie pan, and set aside.

Put the pumpkin in the blender or food processor. Add the banana, apple juice concentrate, raisins, nutmeg, ginger, cinnamon, mace, allspice, vanilla, and egg whites. Blend until all trace of the raisins disappears. Pour into the crust, set the oven temperature at 375 degrees F. and bake until a toothpick comes out clean, about 30 minutes or a little longer. Don't let the top of the pie get dark. Let it cool before serving. It tastes exactly like regular pumpkin pie.

To prevent the crust from burning around the edges, place an aluminum foil circle over the crust edge while baking. If it won't lay down, use aluminum pellets or weights (available at gourmet kitchen shops) to weigh it down.

Depending on the size eggs you use and how fresh they are, you will come out with a bit more or less pie filling. Sometimes the eggs froth up so much you will have almost enough to fill 2 pies, so make a second crust and make 2 pies. With the 6 egg whites, you will always have enough to fill 1 crust. When cooled, spread with Cake Icing if you like.

BANANA CUSTARD

Nutrition Facts

Amount Per Serving

Calories 60	Calories from Fat 0

% Daily Value*

Total Fat 0g	**0%**
Saturated Fat 0g	**0%**
Cholesterol 0mg	**0%**
Sodium 60mg	**3%**
Total Carbohydrate 9g	**3%**
Dietary Fiber less than 1 gram	**3%**
Sugars 8g	
Protein 4g	

Vitamin A 2%	•	Vitamin C 6%
Calcium 4%	•	Iron 0%

3/4 cups skim milk
2 Baked Bananas (page 57)
8 teaspoons water
6 jumbo egg whites
1/2 teaspoon vanilla

Combine the milk, baked bananas, and baking liquid in a blender or food processor. Blend until smooth. Pour into a mixing bowl and add the eggs and vanilla. Beat with a rotary mixer for about 1 minute. Pour the mixture into seven 4-ounce custard cups.

Into a wide roasting pan, pour 1/2 inch of water. Set the filled cups in the water and place the pan on the center rack of the oven, set the oven temperature at 300 degrees F. and bake uncovered, for 50 to 60 minutes until a knife comes out clean. Sprinkle with a little nutmeg if you like.

To reheat 1 serving in a microwave oven, cover the cup with plastic wrap and heat for 1 1/2 minutes on high setting, or less if your microwave is very fast. Or cover with foil and sit the dish in a pan of water in a conventional oven and reheat at 300 degrees F. for 15 to 20 minutes. (I like to eat this ice cold.)

BREAD PUDDING

YIELD: 12 SERVINGS

Nutrition Facts

Amount Per Serving

Calories 160	Calories from Fat 10

	% Daily Value*
Total Fat 1g	1%
Saturated Fat 0g	0%
Cholesterol 0mg	0%
Sodium 150mg	6%
Total Carbohydrate 28g	9%
Dietary Fiber 2g	10%
Sugars 19g	
Protein 6g	

Vitamin A 2%	•	Vitamin C 6%
Calcium 8%	•	Iron 6%

This is a lovely dessert enjoyed by old Creole families and is also served in the best French restaurants in New Orleans. This bread pudding is as good or better, than any I've ever tasted. Use fresh bread, though, because if you use stale whole wheat bread, it doesn't soften very well. This not only makes a great dessert, you can have it for breakfast, too. Serve on its own, or with Blueberry Jelly (page 63), or Cherry Preserves (page 64).

4 cups fresh Pritikin or commercial whole wheat bread, diced (about 7 slices)
1 cup raisins
2 cups skim milk
1/2 cup brandy
8 jumbo egg whites
1 teaspoon vanilla extract
2 Baked Bananas (page 57)
1 ripe medium banana
Zest of 1/2 of a medium orange
1/16 teaspoon nutmeg
1/16 teaspoon cinnamon

Combine the diced bread and the raisins in a 2 quart round baking dish and set aside.

Combine the milk, brandy, egg whites, vanilla extract, baked bananas and baking liquid, uncooked banana, orange zest, nutmeg, and cinnamon in a blender or food processor. Mix with a spoon first to get the spices wet, then blend on slow speed for a few seconds, then switch to high and blend for about 3 minutes, until you no longer see the orange rind. Pour the mixture over the bread and raisins and push down any bread that floats to the surface. Refrigerate for 1 hour.

Push any floating bread down gently, but don't stir. Spray a piece of aluminum foil with a nonstick spray. Cover the pudding with it spray-side down so that it touches the top of the pudding. Crimp the foil around the edges of the dish. Set the dish in the oven, set the temperature at 350 degrees F., and bake for 45 minutes. Remove the foil carefully and bake for 15 minutes more. Recover the pudding with foil and let it sit out of the oven for 20 minutes before serving.

Serve bottom-side up, because it's the moistest. This pudding will keep for 4 days, covered, in the refrigerator. You can warm covered portions in the microwave on high setting for 1 1/2 minutes, or wrap portions in foil and place in a 300-degree oven for about 10 minutes, to rewarm. Extra portions can be frozen.

CAROB BANANA MINT PUDDING

Nutrition Facts

Amount Per Serving	
Calories 180	Calories from Fat 5

	% Daily Value*
Total Fat 0.5g	1%
Saturated Fat 0g	0%
Cholesterol 5mg	1%
Sodium 135mg	6%
Total Carbohydrate 35g	12%
Dietary Fiber 3g	14%
Sugars 28g	
Protein 12g	

Vitamin A 10%	•	Vitamin C 15%
Calcium 35%	•	Iron 4%

This recipe tastes just like chocolate pudding. Carob tastes like chocolate except carob has none of the caffeine, sugar, fat, emulsifiers, artificial flavor, or other additives that chocolate has. (Look at a label on a chocolate bar sometime.) Carob is naturally sweet, but check the label to see if any sugar has been added. You can find carob powder at the health food store.

You can also use this pudding without the sliced banana or pineapple, as a topping for Carob Fruity Chiffon Cake (page 346).

1 can (12 ounces) evaporated skim milk
1 envelope unflavored gelatin
1/2 Baked Banana (page 57)
2 tablespoons carob powder
1/16 tablespoon peppermint extract
1 sliced banana
1/2 cup unsweetened canned pineapple chunks, drained
1 teaspoon fructose

Pour about 1/3 of the milk into a cup, sprinkle the gelatin over it to soften and stir to combine.

Meanwhile, scald the rest of the milk in a microwave oven on high setting for 2 1/2 to 3 minutes or on top of the stove by heating to almost a boil: to 180 degrees F. or to the point of bubbles forming around the edges of the pan. Remove any skin that forms on top of the milk. Add the gelatin mixture to the scalded milk and stir. Let it cool a little and then pour into a blender or food processor. Add the baked banana and baking liquid, carob powder, peppermint extract, and fructose. Blend on high setting until very smooth. Pour into a mixing bowl and cover with plastic wrap. Let the wrap touch the top of the pudding to keep the gelatin from forming a hard skin. Refrigerate for 3 to 4 hours, until gelled.

When it has gelled, beat with an electric mixer. Start slowly, building up to the fastest speed. Beat until the mixture is fluffy and creamy. Fold in the banana slices and pineapple. Serve immediately, or put into individual pudding cups and refrigerate to serve later.

PEAR SLUSHY

Nutrition Facts

Amount Per Serving

Calories 90	Calories from Fat 0

	% Daily Value*
Total Fat 0g	**0**%
Saturated Fat 0g	**0**%
Cholesterol 0mg	**0**%
Sodium 5mg	**0**%
Total Carbohydrate 23g	**8**%
Dietary Fiber 2g	**8**%
Sugars 19g	
Protein 0g	

Vitamin A 0%	•	Vitamin C 6%
Calcium 2%	•	Iron 2%

Fruit slushies are a delicious and refreshing way to eat your fruit servings. You can make them out of almost any kind of fruit.

1 Bartlett pear (do not peel)
10 ice cubes
1 cup sparkling sodium-free bottled water
3 tablespoons apple juice concentrate
1/16 teaspoon peppermint extract (optional)

Core and cut up the pear, then place all the ingredients in a blender or food processor. If you use the peppermint extract, just pour it out of the spoon—don't dunk the spoon in the mixture or the slushy will be too minty. Blend on high speed until no more pear is visible.

Serve over more ice to serve immediately or freeze for an hour or so, stir, and serve.

KIWI SLUSHY

Nutrition Facts

Amount Per Serving

Calories 120	Calories from Fat 0

	% Daily Value*
Total Fat 0g	**0**%
Saturated Fat 0g	**0**%
Cholesterol 0mg	**0**%
Sodium 15mg	**1**%
Total Carbohydrate 29g	**10**%
Dietary Fiber 3g	**11**%
Sugars 26g	
Protein 1g	

Vitamin A 2%	•	Vitamin C 130%
Calcium 2%	•	Iron 4%

2 kiwis, cut in half
10 ice cubes
5 tablespoons apple juice concentrate
1 cup water

Scoop out the flesh from the kiwi halves, and place in a blender or food processor. Add the ice cubes, juice concentrate, and water. Blend on high until the ice is finely chopped.

Serve over more ice cubes, or freeze for about an hour, stir, and serve.

NECTARINE SLUSHY

Nutrition Facts

Amount Per Serving

Calories 80	Calories from Fat 0

	% Daily Value*
Total Fat 0g	**0**%
Saturated Fat 0g	**0**%
Cholesterol 0mg	**0**%
Sodium 5mg	**0**%
Total Carbohydrate 19g	**6**%
Dietary Fiber 1g	**5**%
Sugars 17g	
Protein 1g	

Vitamin A 10%	•	Vitamin C 8%
Calcium 0%	•	Iron 2%

1 nectarine, sliced (do not peel)
10 ice cubes
1 cup water
3 tablespoons apple juice concentrate
1/8 teaspoon vanilla extract

Place all the ingredients in a blender or food processor, and blend on high speed until the ice disappears. Add more apple juice concentrate if you want it sweeter.

Freeze for an hour or serve immediately over more ice.

LEMONADE SLUSHY

Nutrition Facts

Amount Per Serving

Calories 100	Calories from Fat 0

	% Daily Value*
Total Fat 0g	**0**%
Saturated Fat 0g	**0**%
Cholesterol 0mg	**0**%
Sodium 15mg	**1**%
Total Carbohydrate 27g	**9**%
Dietary Fiber 0g	**0**%
Sugars 23g	
Protein 1g	

Vitamin A 0%	•	Vitamin C 50%
Calcium 2%	•	Iron 2%

Juice of 1 medium lemon
1 cup water
6 tablespoons apple juice concentrate
10 ice cubes

Combine the lemon juice, water, apple juice concentrate, and 10 ice cubes in a blender or food processor. Blend on high until the ice is pulverized. Taste. Add more apple juice concentrate if it's not sweet enough and blend again.

Serve over more ice cubes, or freeze for an hour or so until the mixture is almost like a snowball in texture. Stir and serve.

PARIS-STYLE PEACH ICE CREAM

YIELD: 4 SERVINGS

Nutrition Facts

Amount Per Serving

Calories 90	Calories from Fat 0

	% Daily Value*
Total Fat 0g	**0%**
Saturated Fat 0g	**0%**
Cholesterol 0mg	**0%**
Sodium 35mg	**1%**
Total Carbohydrate 22g	**7%**
Dietary Fiber 2g	**7%**
Sugars 19g	
Protein 2g	

Vitamin A 6%	•	Vitamin C 10%
Calcium 2%	•	Iron 2%

During our first trip to Paris, Ray and I found ourselves at the foot of the Eiffel Tower and we came upon a man with a rolling cart full of pastel green, pink, peach, and orange, fruit-flavored ice creams. His peach ice cream was so refreshing on a hot day because it had tiny crystals of ice in it. Later I learned that most French ice cream is somewhere between American ice cream and sherbet. The secret of making a similar ice cream is to get everything measured ahead except for the ice cubes. I use ice cubes that measure 2-inches-by-1-inch.

10 ice cubes
6 frozen peach slices
1 very ripe banana
1 1/2 tablespoons nonfat cream cheese
4 tablespoons apple juice concentrate
1 tablespoon fructose (optional)

Place the ice cubes in a blender or food processor and process until pulverized. Add the peaches, banana, cream cheese, and juice concentrate. Process until the ingredients are finely ground. Taste. If the ice cream is not sweet enough, add the fructose and process for 1 or 2 seconds more. Serve immediately.

NECTARINE CREAMY

Nutrition Facts

Amount Per Serving

Calories 100	Calories from Fat 0

	% Daily Value*
Total Fat 0g	**0**%
Saturated Fat 0g	**0**%
Cholesterol 0mg	**0**%
Sodium 10mg	**0**%
Total Carbohydrate 23g	**8**%
Dietary Fiber 1g	**5**%
Sugars 21g	
Protein 1g	

Vitamin A 6%	•	Vitamin C 8%
Calcium 2%	•	Iron 2%

Do you ever dream you're in the tropics? Squeeze a little fresh lime juice over Nectarine Creamy and you'll swear you're on a beach in Jamaica, Hawaii. You can add chunks of fruit if you like—it's delicious no matter how you make it.

2 very ripe nectarines (do not peel)
1 1/4 large ripe bananas
1 envelope unflavored gelatin
1 cup apple juice concentrate

Cut up the nectarines and banana directly into a blender or food processor. Add the gelatin, and using a spoon, mix it with the fruit to soften it. Set aside in the blender or processor.

Heat the apple juice in a microwave or in a saucepan on top of the stove until it comes to a boil. Pour the juice concentrate over the fruit. Blend at a high speed for about 1 1/2 minutes, or until you don't see any signs of fruit peel. Pour mixture into a 1 1/2-quart bowl or into individual pudding or custard dishes. Refrigerate for 3 to 4 hours, until set. Enjoy as it, or squeeze some fresh lime juice over them.

Variation: NECTARINE CREAMY WITH FRUIT

After you have poured the Nectarine Creamy into a 1 1/2-quart bowl, add 20 seedless grapes and 2 chopped nectarines. Refrigerate for 3 to 4 hours, until set.

STRAWBERRY CREAM DESSERT

Nutrition Facts

Amount Per Serving

Calories 100	Calories from Fat 0

	% Daily Value*
Total Fat 0g	**0%**
Saturated Fat 0g	**0%**
Cholesterol 5mg	**1%**
Sodium 65mg	**3%**
Total Carbohydrate 19g	**6%**
Dietary Fiber 1g	**6%**
Sugars 16g	
Protein 4g	

Vitamin A 2%	•	Vitamin C 40%
Calcium 2%	•	Iron 6%

Creamy Pie Topping (page 359)
Basic Dessert Pie Crust (page 355)
1 envelope unflavored gelatin
1/2 cup water
1/2 cup apple juice concentrate
3 cups sliced fresh or frozen strawberries

Prepare the Creamy Pie Topping according to the recipe directions and refrigerate 3 to 4 hours, or overnight. Don't whip it until you are ready to spread it on top of the pie.

Prepare the pie crust according to the recipe directions, and set aside.

Soften the gelatin in 1/4 cup of the water. Combine the remaining 1/4 cup water and juice concentrate in a saucepan and bring to a boil. Remove from the heat, and add the gelatin and water. Mix until the gelatin dissolves. Set aside to cool.

Add the strawberries (reserving a few for garnish) to the cooled gelatin mixture. Place the strawberry mixture in the refrigerator and chill until lightly gelled. Pour into the crust and chill until firm, about 2 hours.

Whip the Creamy Pie Topping according to the recipe directions and spread on top of the pie. Garnish with a few whole strawberries. Chill for 1 hour before serving.

FRESH FRUIT FIRENZE

**YIELD: AS MANY AS YOU LIKE
1 CUP = 1 SERVING**

Nutrition Facts

Amount Per Serving	
Calories 70	Calories from Fat 5

	% Daily Value*
Total Fat 0.5g	1%
Saturated Fat 0g	0%
Cholesterol 0mg	0%
Sodium 5mg	0%
Total Carbohydrate 17g	6%
Dietary Fiber 2g	7%
Sugars 15g	
Protein 1g	

Vitamin A 35%	•	Vitamin C 45%
Calcium 2%	•	Iron 2%

Desserts don't have to be elaborate to be good. A simple dessert of fresh fruit can be elegant and delicious.

When Ray and I were in Florence, Italy, some years back, and after a day of sightseeing, we were hot, tired, and thirsty. So we stopped at a little cafe where we had the most refreshing fruit dessert I have ever tasted. They mixed the fruit together, then covered them with watermelon juice. It was very well chilled and for a few extra lira they put a scoop of ice cream on top. Paris Style Peach Ice Cream would be lovely (page 371).

This is my version of that unexpected treat.

Equal parts:
Watermelon
Cantaloupe
Seedless grapes
Peach chunks
Watermelon juice
Apple juice concentrate (optional)

Use equal parts of each fruit cut into bite size pieces. Use the seedless part of the watermelon for the dessert. Then cut up the pieces of watermelon that have the most seeds and put them in a colander. Set the colander over a bowl and with a potato masher, mash the watermelon to extract the juice. After mashing some, with very clean hands squeeze the juice from the watermelon. Pour into the bowl with the fruit to almost cover. If you don't have enough, add some water and apple juice concentrate. You should choose very ripe fruit so this will be sweet but you can add more apple juice concentrate if you need it.

Chill for at least 1 hour before serving.

PINEAPPLE-BANANA POPS

YIELD: 8 POPS

Nutrition Facts

Amount Per Serving

Calories 35	Calories from Fat 0

	% Daily Value*
Total Fat 0g	**0**%
Saturated Fat 0g	**0**%
Cholesterol 0mg	**0**%
Sodium 0mg	**0**%
Total Carbohydrate 8g	**3**%
Dietary Fiber 0g	**0**%
Sugars 7g	
Protein 0g	

Vitamin A 0%	•	Vitamin C 8%
Calcium 0%	•	Iron 0%

You can buy the forms to make frozen fruit pops in your grocery. I use a form that has 8 sections with plastic tops and sticks attached, which holds a total of about 2 cups of liquid.

1 cup pineapple juice
1 large banana, cut into chunks
1/4 teaspoon vanilla extract

In a blender or food processor, combine the pineapple juice and the banana chunks. If necessary, add enough pineapple juice to bring the liquid up to the 2-cup mark. Add the vanilla and blend until smooth. Pour into the pop molds almost to the tops, and attach the plastic tops. Freeze for about 5 hours.

Unmold by running cool water over the mold. Pull the pops out gently. Note: If these pops are not sweet enough for you, substitute a little apple juice concentrate, to taste, for some of the pineapple juice.

BRANDY BON-BITES

YIELD: 32 TREATS

Nutrition Facts

Amount Per Serving

Calories 50	Calories from Fat 0

% Daily Value*

Total Fat 0g	**0%**
Saturated Fat 0g	**0%**
Cholesterol 0mg	**0%**
Sodium 50mg	**2%**
Total Carbohydrate 10g	**3%**
Dietary Fiber less than 1 gram	**3%**
Sugars 4g	
Protein 1g	

Vitamin A 6%	•	Vitamin C 0%
Calcium 0%	•	Iron 10%

My mother called a "bon-bite" something that was good in the mouth—half French, half English. Brandy Bon-Bites certainly live up to that description.

12 tablespoons brandy
2 cups Grape-Nuts®
1/2 tablespoon carob powder
4 tablespoons fructose
1/2 cup raisins
1 jumbo egg white
1/2 Baked Banana (page 57)
1/4 teaspoon orange extract
1/4 teaspoon lemon extract
Apple juice concentrate (optional)

Pour the brandy into a small saucepan. Warm over high heat, then turn the heat off. Leave the pot on the stove and be sure nothing is around, above, or nearby that will catch on fire. With a long match, standing well away from the pot, light the fumes coming up from the pan. The alcohol will flame up and the flames will leap a foot or more into the air over the pan. Let the alcohol in the brandy burn itself out. Don't leave the pot unattended while it is flaming.

Process the Grape-Nuts® in a blender or food processor until they are fine crumbs. Place the crumbs in a bowl, add the carob powder and 1 tablespoon of fructose, and mix. Then add the raisins and mix. In a separate bowl, combine the egg, brandy, banana and baking liquid, orange extract, and lemon extract. Add to the crumbs and combine thoroughly. If the mixture isn't wet enough to hold together, add a tablespoon or so of apple juice concentrate.

Form bite-size balls and roll them in the remaining fructose. Store in a tightly covered container in the refrigerator. They will keep for a week.

RAISIN CHEWIES

Nutrition Facts

Amount Per Serving

Calories 10	Calories from Fat 0

	% Daily Value*
Total Fat 0g	**0%**
Saturated Fat 0g	**0%**
Cholesterol 0mg	**0%**
Sodium 0mg	**0%**
Total Carbohydrate 2g	**1%**
Dietary Fiber 0g	**0%**
Sugars 2g	
Protein 0g	

Vitamin A 0%	•	Vitamin C 0%
Calcium 0%	•	Iron 0%

2 jumbo egg whites
1 tablespoon fructose
1 teaspoon vanilla
1/2 cup raisins

Preheat oven to 350 degrees F.

Spray a nonstick cookie sheet with a nonstick spray.

In a mixing bowl, beat the egg whites until they form stiff peaks. Beat in the fructose and vanilla extract, then fold in the raisins. With a teaspoon, spoon the mixture out in bite-size clumps onto the pan, not touching each other. Place in the oven and leave the oven on for 1 minute—no longer. Turn the oven off and leave the door closed. Let the candies sit until the oven is totally cool, about 3 hours. They will be ready to eat.

You can refrigerate these chewies or freeze them in a plastic bag and they won't stick together.

Variation: RAISIN RUM CHEWIES

Make as you would Raisin Chewies, but when you add the vanilla, also add 1 teaspoon rum extract.

LISTING OF RECIPES

COOKBOOKS FROM THE CROSSING PRESS

The Balanced Diet Cookbook
Easy Menus and Recipes for Combining Carbohydrates, Proteins, and Fats

By Bill Taylor

Based on Barry Sears' bestselling Zone Diet plan, which emphasizes a 40-30-30 ratio of carbohydrates, proteins, and fats, *The Balanced Diet Cookbook* provides simple recipes, complete menu plans, and food charts for followers of the Zone plan and others interested in balanced eating for better health. Each recipe fulfills the balance ratio for food blocks, making breakfast, lunch, dinner, and snacktime easy for those following the balanced eating lifestyle.

6 x 9 • 240pp • $16.95 • Paper • ISBN 0-89594-874-5

Good Food
The Complete Guide to Eating Well

By Margaret M. Wittenberg

This indispensable guide and nutritional resource is perfect for both the adventurous cook and the inquisitive novice.

"*Good Food* makes good sense for anyone interested in shopping smart for eating well."

—Dr. Bob Arnot,
author of *Turning Back the Clock*

8¾ x 9¾ • 380pp • $18.95 • Paper • ISBN 0-89594-746-3

The Great Turkey Cookbook
385 Turkey Recipes for Every Day and Holidays

By Virginia and Robert Hoffman

Each recipe includes a nutritional analysis and is indexed by name and turkey part.

$16.95 • Paper • ISBN 0-89594-792-7

The Great Chicken Cookbook
More than 400 Chicken Recipes for Every Day

By Virginia and Robert Hoffman

The Great Chicken Cookbook provides new ideas and includes clever time-saving tips and low-budget suggestions for leftovers.

$16.95 • Paper • ISBN 0-89594-828-1

International Vegetarian Cooking

By Judy Ridgway

International Vegetarian Cooking presents more than 400 new vegetarian dishes adapted from the world's most popular cuisines, outlines dietary guidelines, and offers tips for successful menu planning.

The recipes include delicious soups, casseroles, and pies in the Northern European tradition, emphasizing the healthy Mediterranean diet with its use of olive oil, garlic, fresh vegetables, beans, and pasta.

6 X 9 • 192pp • $14.95 • Paper • ISBN 0-89594-854-0

Japanese Vegetarian Cooking
From Simple Soups to Sushi

By Patricia Richfield

Japanese Vegetarian Cooking includes more than 100 vegetarian recipes, with easy-to-follow directions and information on techniques, as well as a glossary of Japanese ingredients and utensils. The recipes range from flavorful soups, to rice, tofu and soybean dishes, to vegetables, salads, pickles, and drinks, to elegant vegetarian sushi. This is a cookbook for anyone who loves Japanese food and wants to prepare it at home. Vegans and vegetarians will also welcome it as an opportunity to expand their menus.

6 X 9 • 176pp • $14.95 • Paper • ISBN 0-89594-805-2

Low-Fat Vegetarian Cooking
Classic Slim Cuisine

By Sue Kreitzman

Adapting popular vegetarian dishes from the cuisines of the world, Master chef Sue Kreitzman has created more than 100 new low-fat or non-fat dishes for vegetarians and anyone wanting to reduce the fat in their diets. With this collection, eating a healthful diet does not mean skimping on flavor.

Sue Kreitzman's easy-to-follow recipes and clever low-fat cooking techniques are sure to produce meals that satisfy the appetite and the palate.

6 X 9 • 208pp • $14.95 • Paper • ISBN 0-89594-834-6

COOKBOOKS FROM THE CROSSING PRESS

Marinades
Dry Rubs, Pastes & Marinades for Poultry, Meat, Seafood, Cheese & Vegetables

By Jim Tarantino

The most comprehensive book available! Tarantino recreates marinades and flavoring pastes from all over the world, and provides instructions for preparing seafood, poultry, meat, vegetables, and cheese—indoors and out.

8 X 9 • 240pp • $16.95 • Paper • ISBN 0-89594-531-2

Mother Nature's Garden
Healthy Vegan Cooking

By Florence and Mickey Bienenfeld

In addition to eliminating animal products, including eggs and dairy, these 400 vegan recipes are low in fat and salt, cholesterol-free and sugar-free. Includes breakfast and brunch specialties, soups, appetizers, entrees, and festive holiday dishes.

"If you want to eat healthier, but still want that homey old world taste, this book could make you happy."
—*Vegetarian Times*

8⅛ x 9 • 234pp • $14.95 • Paper • ISBN 0-89594-702-1

Homestyle Mexican Cooking

By Lourdes Nichols

This tantalizing collection of over 180 authentic recipes from Mexican cuisine includes dozens of succulent meat and poultry dishes and mouth-watering recipes for rice dishes, vegetables, salads, desserts, and drinks.

8 X 10 • 208pp • $16.95 • Paper • ISBN 0-89594-861-3

Homestyle Middle Eastern Cooking

By Pat Chapman

This is a landmark collection of truly unique, authentic recipes, many available here for the first time. These spicy, regional dishes were selected from hundreds of recipes the author collected while traveling throughout the Middle East.

8 X 10 • 192pp • $16.95 • Paper • ISBN 0-89594-860-5

Homestyle Thai and Indonesian Cooking

By Sri Owen

This delightful book introduces the marvelous flavors, exotic ingredients, and culinary techniques of Indonesian and Thai cuisine. Sri Owen offers authentic recipes for savory satés, exotic curries, fragrant rice dishes, spicy vegetables, and scrumptious snacks and sweets. She includes adaptations using available Western ingredients.

8 X 10 • 192pp • $16.95 • Paper • ISBN 0-89594-859-1

Homestyle Italian Cooking

By Lori Carangelo

This is an outstanding selection of more than 180 recipes collected by the author while traveling through the Italian countryside. These wonderful dishes use fresh ingredients, carefully prepared to bring out the special flavors of the best Italian cooking. From "Zuppa alla Contadina" to "Fiche al Cioccolato", these recipes will delight both family and friends.

8 x 10 • 192pp • $16.95 • Paper • ISBN 0-89594-867-2

To place an order or receive a current catalog from The Crossing Press, please call toll-free, 800-777-1048.
Visit our Website on the Internet at: www.crossingpress.com